The Postsecular Imagination

The Postsecular Imagination presents a rich, interdisciplinary study of postsecularism as an affirmational political possibility emerging through the potentials and limits of both secular and religious thought. While secularism and religion can foster inspiration and creativity, they also can be linked with violence, civil war, partition, majoritarianism, and communalism, especially within the framework of the nation-state. Through close readings of novels that engage with animism, Buddhism, Christianity, Hinduism, Islam, and Sikhism, Manav Ratti examines how questions of ethics and the need for faith, awe, wonder, and enchantment can find expression and significance in the wake of such crises.

While focusing on Michael Ondaatje and Salman Rushdie, Ratti addresses the work of several other writers as well, including Shauna Singh Baldwin, Mahasweta Devi, Amitav Ghosh, and Allan Sealy. Ratti shows the extent of courage and risk involved in the radical imagination of these postsecular works, examining how writers experiment with and gesture toward the compelling paradoxes of a non-secular secularism and a non-religious religion.

Drawing on South Asian Anglophone literatures and postcolonial theory, and situating itself within the most provocative contemporary debates in secularism and religion, *The Postsecular Imagination* will be important for readers interested in the relations among culture, literature, theory, and politics.

Manav Ratti completed his doctorate at Oxford University and is Assistant Professor of English at Salisbury University in Maryland, USA. A recent faculty Fulbright Scholar at New York University, he is Fellow Designate at the Institute of Advanced Study at Jawaharlal Nehru University in New Delhi, India.

ROUTLEDGE RESEARCH IN POSTCOLONIAL LITERATURES

Edited in collaboration with the Centre for Colonial and Postcolonial Studies, University of Kent at Canterbury, this series presents a wide range of research into postcolonial literatures by specialists in the field. Volumes will concentrate on writers and writing originating in previously (or presently) colonized areas, and will include material from non-anglophone as well as anglophone colonies and literatures. Series editors: Donna Landry and Caroline Rooney.

Related Titles:

The Postsecular Imagination

Postcolonialism, Religion, and Literature

Manav Ratti

Routledge
Taylor & Francis Group
NEW YORK AND LONDON

First published 2013
by Routledge
711 Third Avenue, New York, NY 10017

Simultaneously published in the UK
by Routledge
2 Park Square, Milton Park, Abingdon, Oxfordshire OX14 4RN

First issued in paperback 2014

Routledge is an imprint of the Taylor & Francis Group, an informa business

Library of Congress Cataloging-in-Publication Data

Ratti, Manav.
    The postsecular imagination : postcolonialism, religion, and literature / by Manav Ratti.
        p. cm. — (Routledge research in postcolonial literatures)
    Includes bibliographical references and index.
    1. Commonwealth fiction (English)—History and criticism.   2. English fiction–
20th century–History and criticism.   3. Secularism in literature.   4. Religion in
literature.   5. Postcolonialism in literature.   6. Postsecularism.   7. Religion and literature–
Commonwealth countries–History–20th century.   I. Title.
    PR9080.5.R38 2012
    823'.91409–dc23
    2012029539

ISBN 13: 978-0-415-48097-0 (hbk)
ISBN 13: 978-1-138-82237-5 (pbk)

Typeset in Baskerville
by IBT Global.

for my parents and my brother

Contents

Permissions

Parts of an earlier version of Chapter 4 of this book originally appeared as "Michael Ondaatje's *Anil's Ghost* and the Aestheticization of Human Rights," *ARIEL: A Review of International English Literature* 35.1–2 (2004): 121–141. Reprinted by permission of *ARIEL*.

Figures

All photographs © Manav Ratti

"Believe what I say as one believes in a miracle."

Jacques Derrida (2002: 98)

"Break a vase, and the love that reassembles the fragments is stronger than that love which took its symmetry for granted when it was whole."

Derek Walcott (1992)

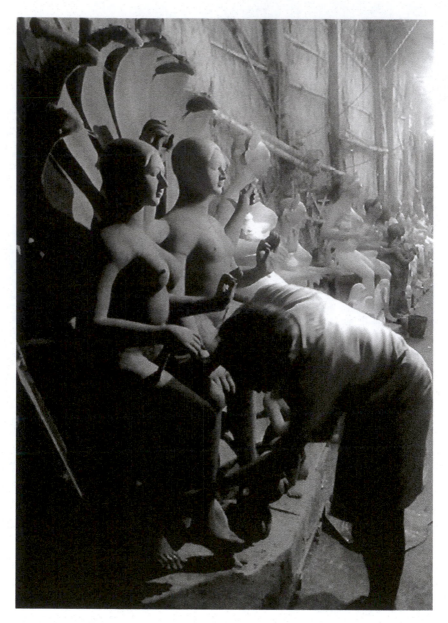

Figure 1   Preparations for Durga Puja, Kolkata, India. Photograph by the author.

Preface

The Literary and The Postsecular

Cold—the New Delhi night air clings with unrelenting cruelty. It is late November 2008, and a light fog has descended upon the city, muting it into a fantastical nightscape whose contours are illuminated by the occasional orange-yellow glow of street lamps. I am waiting for an autorickshaw. I have come to India from the UK for a research visit, my winter coat warmly enveloping me. The streets are virtually empty until a driver expertly veers toward me. As he approaches, I notice he is in his mid-twenties. He stops the vehicle, and we proceed in Hindi to negotiate the destination and cost. Before we begin the journey, he tells me that I must be prepared for security checks. It is a day after the Mumbai attacks, security checkpoints around the city, alerts issued by various foreign embassies. *Theek hai, chalo.* That's fine, let's go. Clearing several checkpoints, we continue into the darkness. And then, materializing before us in the left margin of our world—almost invisible, almost unbelievable—is a large elephant, shadows among shadows, each of its steps slow, majestic, measured. I ask the driver to slow down. Can the ancient elephant of India be seen through the modern eye of terrorism's needle?

There is yet another animation in the air. The world's largest democracy is on the brink of elections. Will Sheila Dixit, Chief Minister of New Delhi and member of the Congress Party, be voted into an historic third term? I arrive at my destination and through the darkness, smoke, and music, I see the face of Sheila Dixit—on tv, speaking of her dedication to the city. My driver had decided I would be his last passenger for the night. During our journey, he had enthusiastically discussed his views on the election; right before we parted, he reaffirmed his support for Dixit, stating that she truly cares about his city. Everyone is following the elections closely—autorickshaw drivers, the night guards outside my accommodation, academics and journalists across the city—the colour and noise of this momentous event flickering across radios, newspapers, televisions, and shops alike. Heads are literally turned toward tvs, everyone has something to say, everyone waits anxiously for the results. And so do I, my gaze fixed on the tv as I reflect on the amazing diversity of peoples throughout the city, hoping for the best possible outcome for them all.

I offer the above opening experience because what fascinates me is that on one hand there are powerful modes of living together in spite of the divides of religion and nation: indigenous, personal modes that can be marked by fellowship, community, open-mindedness, and an acceptance and embracing of others. On the other hand, political systems, concepts, and forms of organization—such as state concepts like multiculturalism and secularism—fall short of recognizing and organizing "the people." What can we make of this difference between individual practices of good will toward others and state-sanctioned, political ideas about how we should relate to one another?

Secularism: it is a political concept in India asking the state to respect and recognize citizens of all religions, guided by values of freedom and equality, with allied consideration for ethnicity, language, and caste. The word has tremendous resonance in India—used and overused in media, politics, academia—polarizing and unifying people alike, reaching across the domains of religion, public policy, and ethics. But is this resonance simply the sound of one hand clapping? Is it disconnected from other parts of the nation's body, whose sound can only be heard by those privileged with the modern gifts of elite citizenship? What a privilege to be in the thickness of location, each of us holding on to a different part of the elephant: the tail, the tusk, the ear, the hide, the foot. But this is no ancient elephant. Can it be constructed to fit through the needle of everyday life, the political demands of the vanishing present, the real struggles of real people? Can we believe in it? In India, my secular has to be *your* secular: *our* secular is the secular of the nation-state, extending to the promise of freedom, equality, and democracy. How could we not want this?

After my visit to India, I return to the UK and witness David Cameron proclaim in February 2011 that state multiculturalism has failed the UK, given extremist ideologies that lead young people to violence, instead of their being drawn to a cohesive concept of "Britishness" (Cameron 2011). Angela Merkel, a few months before Cameron, had made a similar pronouncement, on the failure of "multikulti" in Germany. History then produces a figure like Anders Breivik, the Norwegian who on July 22, 2011 bombed government buildings in Oslo, killing eight, and then shot sixty-nine youth at a camp on a Norwegian island near Oslo, making sure to shoot teenagers lying on the beach who were hoping to survive by feigning death. Breivik was enraged by immigration to Norway, viewing immigration and Islam as the enemies of the pure nation, a position he elaborates in a manifesto over a thousand pages in length. At Breivik's trial, a Norwegian hurled a shoe at Breivik, avenging the honour of his murdered brother. The attack echoed the shoe hurled at George Bush in 2008 by an Iraqi journalist at a press conference in Baghdad. With European leaders exasperated by the uncontrollable violence inside their borders, and with South Asian intellectuals and politicians struggling to create a viable secular state, what are the large questions about religion, secularism, and nation raised by our small world—and how can we tackle them?

We can go back even further in time. In a provocative September 2006 speech, Pope Benedict XVI expressed his worry about the increasing secularization of the west, by which he meant that western science and philosophy have divorced themselves from faith (John Paul II 2006). He argued that such secularization makes it impossible for the west to communicate with those cultures that have worldviews to which faith is fundamental. Such a polarization of secularism (as reason) and faith (as religion), along the lines of the "secular west" and the "non-secular non-west," has become especially problematic after 9/11. The negative reaction by Muslims to the Pope's speech is a sign that much work still remains to address such differences and divides. For an effective dialogue of cultures to occur in such a global climate, the solution might lie in a discourse which offers the ethical, imaginative, and generative intensities of religious thought within a viable and robust framework of political secularism.

Political science, cultural studies, sociology, religious studies, history, anthropology: these are just some of the disciplines that have been compelled to address the issues I present above. This book joins this collective effort by pursuing how literature can provide insights into thinking through the limits of secularism and religion. Such a focus seems especially necessary in a world where political and clerical leaders, religious groups, ordinary people, and concerned citizens must face realities they perhaps never had to face before. In a globalized world where Twitter, texting, Facebook, and BlackBerry® smartphones can catalyze a movement like the Arab Spring and where cell phone photographs taken by soldiers and aid workers in the battlefields of rural Sri Lanka can catalyze international awareness of a civil war, it compels us to ask how we should live with one another, when the other is no longer distant, and perhaps even emerging within us—and now that the stakes are high everywhere.

Literary criticism will be at the heart of this study, inviting readers to consider how questions raised by close readings of literary texts can resonate with questions of religion, culture, and politics. I discuss Anglophone novels that reflect the multireligious nature of India and Sri Lanka, including animism, Buddhism, Christianity, Hinduism, Islam, and Sikhism. I focus on the work of Michael Ondaatje and Salman Rushdie, as well as that of Shauna Singh Baldwin, Amitav Ghosh, and Allan Sealy. I choose this set of writers because they allow me to explore the range of religions I list above. All the writers also embody a diasporic position, giving them access to the lived experience of at least two different national and cultural worldviews. I also consider the work of Mahasweta Devi, although she is neither an Anglophone writer nor situated as part of a diaspora. Her work interests me for its ability to move between the worldviews of majoritarian Hindu India and that of the tribals, as I elaborate in the Introduction.

I argue that this set of writers struggles toward seeking some values that might emerge by working within and against the ideologies of nationalism, secularism, and religion. Their questioning is very much a process: a risky, open-ended, individualistic path they hew and which treads the borders of received pieties and orthodoxies of nationalism, secularism, and religion. In their exploration of the dilemmas of faith and the dilemmas of ethics—*what should we believe, how should we live?*—these writers seek possibilities that avoid the ideologies of politicized religion, and in doing so are avowedly secular in their politics. Ondaatje and Rushdie, for example, cannot be viewed as anything but secular, Rushdie insistently so.

Yet secularism has been unsatisfactory, particularly as a state policy in India, as evidenced, for example, by the continuing eruption of violence motivated by the real and imagined affiliations of religion. Nationalism also has had its failures in the postcolonial world, marked especially by violence, civil war, partition, majoritarianism, and communalism. In India and Sri Lanka, the "god" of religion has often been linked with the "god" of nationalism. The combination continues to be explosive, with religion and nationalism either in alliance or in conflict, in spite of the nation-building aspirations of secularism, seen as religion's antidote and nation's succour. I examine these potentials and perils of secularism in India and Sri Lanka in depth in the Introduction.

In western societies, what began as the Enlightenment separation of church and state is now manifest, however real or imagined, as a "secular west," ideologically contrasted with the "non-secular non-west." In Max Weber's well-known diagnosis, industrialization and the emphasis on scientific-rationalist worldviews that western societies have developed have resulted in disenchantment (Weber 1946: 155). Although Weber's notion of disenchantment resulted in part from the Protestant Reformation of Catholicism and the latter's associated practices and perceived valuing of magic (Pecora 2006: 11), the idea of disenchantment becomes reinforced by the increasing mechanization of societies and their privileging of technologies. Alongside disenchantment, Charles Taylor adds a lack of "fullness" or richness, where life could be "fuller, richer, deeper, more worth while, more admirable, more what it should be. This [fullness] is perhaps a place of power: we often experience this as deeply moving, as inspiring" (Taylor 2007: 5). Apart from its function as a state policy in India, secularism's western inflection as an existential outlook has produced its dissatisfactions.

In the wake of such crises, how can the need for faith, awe, wonder, and transcendence find expression and significance without the political and ideological constraints of nationalism, secularism, and religion? Writers understandably seek some form of belief, however tenuous such a space of belief might be. The task then is to explore secular alternatives to secularism: ones that can gesture to the inspiring features of religious thought, without the violence that can attach itself to religion. The paradox thus becomes to find a non-secular secularism, a non-religious religion. It is this broad sense that

I denote by the term "postsecular." I elaborate upon this relation in greater detail in the Introduction.

Literature is powerfully poised to demonstrate the undoing of the ideological oppositions between secularism and religion, for in its ability to represent a multiplicity of voices and in its acceptance and juxtaposition of contradictory and conflicting perspectives, it can represent, imagine, and pursue a rich array of possibilities. The postsecular possibilities that writers can gesture toward through literature are not anti-secular, nor are they abandoning secularism or turning to religion. The postsecular neither proselytizes secularism nor sentimentalizes religion. It can recognize that enchantment is not the provision of religion alone, and can tackle the hard questions of the political while acknowledging the dimensions of religion.

I explore how literature can form a valuable contribution to the emerging terrain of scholarly work in the social sciences, political theory, and religious studies that is interrogating the limits of the secular (Asad 1993, 2003; Connolly 1999; Derrida 2002; Mahmood 2005; Taylor 2007; Viswanathan 1998). I focus on India and Sri Lanka, for they are both democracies, republics, and places of great religious, ethnic, and linguistic diversity. They contain exemplary coexistence—yet also strife—between religious communities, historically and into the present. The world's largest democracy, and the largest country to emerge from European colonial rule following World War II, India remains a secular state. Sri Lanka offers a point of comparison, for its constitution privileges Buddhism. Also importantly, there has been significant Anglophone writing within India and Sri Lanka and from their diasporas, and this study limits itself to this Anglophone writing. There is a vast amount of literature in the other Indian languages, and in Sinhala and Tamil in Sri Lanka, which is beyond the scope of this study.

I do not focus on Bangladesh and Pakistan, for I do not wish to make "religion" a defining national feature for a comparison between different South Asian nation-states. Both Bangladesh and Pakistan are of course grappling with questions of how practices of religion and secularism can shape the nation-state. In Bangladesh, Taslima Nasreen's novel *Lajja*, first published in 1993 and critical of majoritarian Muslim violence against Hindus, was famously banned by the Bangladeshi government and provoked a *fatwa* against Nasreen. And now in contemporary Bangladesh, practices such as women's *taleem* or Qur'anic discussion circles—which do not affiliate with any political party or religious group—are blurring the divide between secularism and religion and their associated public and private spheres (Huq 2012). In 1973, Pakistan integrated the phrase "Islamic Republic" into its constitution, and debates have flourished on whether, and to what degree, Pakistan can and should become a secular state. What interests me is the diversity of religions and ethnicities within nation-states, and how writers will represent and think through such differences. What models for personal, interpersonal, and intercultural understanding can the examples, national and diasporic, from India and Sri Lanka offer?

Most of the novels I discuss were published between approximately the late 1980s and the late 1990s, in addition to the Rushdie and Ghosh texts published between 2005 and 2007; most of the theoretical work I draw upon stretches from approximately the late 1990s to the present. A series of crises of state secularism mark the decade of the 1990s in India, which I elaborate upon in the Introduction, to say nothing of the ongoing war at the time in Sri Lanka. The liberalization of the Indian economy in the 1990s—its opening onto the global stage—might at the same time have provoked majoritarian Hindu sentiments trying to assert nationalist pride and recapture a sense of "nation." From the Ayatollah Khomeini's death sentence against Rushdie in 1989, to the rise of religiously-inflected terrorism in the west beginning with 9/11, to the economic crisis in Euro-America that has called into question the nature and vibrancy of capitalism, the world has become a smaller place. Contemporary theoretical work is arising from these and other crises of the late 1980s onward. The intellectual response to the Rushdie controversy, including the articles by Talal Asad (1990) and Charles Taylor (1989), has sparked enormous scholarly work about secularism. The literature of the 1990s could perhaps be part of the historical force shaping contemporary paradigms about nation, secularism, and religion. The question could not be more compelling: how do we understand and live with one another, across differences of nation, religion, and ideology?

Saba Mahmood has argued that

> we can no longer presume that secular reason and morality exhaust the forms of valuable human flourishings. In other words, a particular openness to exploring nonliberal traditions is intrinsic to a politically responsible scholarly practice, a practice that departs not from a position of certainty but one of risk, critical engagement, and a willingness to reevaluate one's own views in light of the Other's.
>
> (Mahmood 2001: 225)

Postsecularism emerges in that precarious space of risk. The postsecular is caught in a double bind between religion and secularism. It cannot be captured through dichotomies like "neither religion nor secularism" or "either religion or secularism." If it emerged in such stark and easy dichotomies, then the intricacies and subtleties of postsecularism's arguments, potentials, cautiousness, and debates would devolve to become something like "religionists versus secularists," with a series of banal phrases clustering around it, such as "identity politics," "reactionary polemics," and "self-loathing colonials." To justify or attack any pole among the dichotomies, arguments or assertions could feature an insecure, absolute turn to the prestige and tradition of "great western institutions" or "great Asian traditions" in order to appear rational while consciously or unconsciously perpetuating pride and prejudice. Exploring the postsecular within literature and also within everyday life—for example, as individual practice, the indigenous secularism with which I began this Preface—requires a self-vigilance. It requires an awareness that posting the secular can be productive as long as it is not polarizing, so that it is not simply, for example, European secularism as "rationality" versus the Subaltern School as "fundamentalists."

The postsecular affirmative values that emerge for the writers I analyze include love, friendship, community, art, literature, music, nature, the migrant's eye-view, hybridity, and "newness." These in themselves might not seem particularly novel or "new." What interests me is *how* these affirmative values emerge, how they subsume and demonstrate the edge of the postcolonial, the national, the diasporic, the minority position. I am interested in how writers write *through* religion by invoking its great signifiers and great ethics, and then translate and secularize them within the contingency—and urgency—of material and historical circumstance. The postsecular moments in the literature that I analyze contain decisions made out of human choices and human risks, without the fixity of the nation-state. Such moments will not result in immediate juridico-legal change, but they can gesture to an epistemic change, which is unpredictable, and the trajectories of which are unknown. The process of pursuing such possibilities will take an immense imaginative manoeuvre, and an immense form of "belief" as well. This is where I am interested in how writers and individuals can radically *imagine* postsecularism.

This book seeks to offer a new conception of the secular, one that links it intimately with literature, diaspora, and postcolonialism. I endorse the insights of Jürgen Habermas in his recognition that there must now be a respectful and mature engagement with the full diversity of religions, secularisms, beliefs, and practices within nation-states (Habermas 2008). Habermas focuses on Europe and the west, but I extend this focus to include not only western nation-states like the US, Canada, and the UK, but also India and Sri Lanka. Studies of secularism have often been confined to the single nation-state. Can and should India be secular? What does it mean for Sri Lanka to strive toward secularism? How is the Christian right in the US challenging the secular foundations of the country? How can Israel become secular? What has secularism meant for modernization in Turkey? How can France preserve the secularism of its public spaces? These are important and necessary questions. What *postcolonial postsecularism* can bring to these discussions is a consideration of how the interactions and collisions between at least two different worldviews, variously philosophical and political, can provoke the imagining and re-imagining of some of the greatest ideas of our times: what it means to be secular, religious, a citizen, a minority, a majority—and, by implication, an intellectual, a writer, an artist, each committed to making a difference in the world, whether it be by exploring what constitutes religious thought, or by trying one's best to represent with dignity and seriousness the violence and injustices of war.

In that act of imagination and reimagination, literature can contribute to the workings of civil society, as a critique of the state. Postsecularism does not mean the wholesale abandonment of the principles of political secularism as an alternative organization of the state. It does not advocate classical anarchism by turning to the affirmation of humanitarian feelings as a complete rejection of the "political." In discussions of secularism, such as in the work of John Rawls (1993) and Achille Mbembe (1992a, 1992b, 2001), the concept is often tied to the relations between civil society and the state as well as the norms that govern civil society. My focus will be mainly on features of intercultural and interreligious relations within and between nation-states rather than a detailed investigation of civil society as such.

In India, civil society organizations are important for keeping watch over how well the state can deliver its constitutional guarantees, such as secularism and minority rights (Aiyar and Malik 2004). At the same time, civil society should not reproduce the hegemonies and elitism of the state itself, so as to prevent its component parts—social movements, non-governmental organizations—from representing the full spectrum of a group, including the socioeconomically disadvantaged (Chandhoke 1993). In Sri Lanka, civil society organizations such as the International Centre for Ethnic Studies (ICES) are crucial for challenging and re-thinking questions of democracy, minority rights, and human rights. The ICES was founded in 1982, precipitously before one of the strongest periods of violence during the civil war, July 1983, marked by an anti-Tamil pogrom in Colombo. Certainly the engagement of scholars there with a novel like *Anil's Ghost* demonstrates the ability of literature to enable civil society organizations to be thoughtful about their own work—about the *fullness* of their representation, across culture, religion, and socioeconomics. Such organizations might also see how literary imaginings can inspire ethical commitments, including across nation-states.

The call for expanding the discourses and imaginaries of civil society is echoed in the work of the US-based scholar Nancy Glazener, who argues that "the cosmopolitan sampling of world beliefs risks putting in jeopardy the heart of belief: its power to constitute a meaningful version of reality that presses on unbelievers as well, requiring some form of response. In order to engage belief, we need to avoid dismissing it as superstition, reducing it to personal preference, or reifying it as tradition or custom" (Glazener 2008: 227). Interrogating the secularist biases of civil society, Glazener draws upon an example offered by the US statesman Benjamin Franklin, who had affirmed civic virtue, republicanism, and religious pluralism (Isaacson 2003: 93). A Swedish missionary has just told a group of Native American chiefs the story of the Garden of Eden. In turn, an orator among the chiefs narrates the story of the sacrifice of venison to a magical woman, for which staple plants are received in return. The Swede is not impressed:

> The good Missionary, disgusted with this idle Tale, said, what I delivered to you were sacred Truths; but what you tell me is mere Fable,

Fiction & Falsehood. The Indian offended, reply'd, my Brother, it seems your Friends have not done you Justice in your Education; they have not well instructed you in the Rules of common Civility. You saw that we who understand and practise those Rules, believed all your Stories; why do you refuse to believe ours?

(quoted in Glazener 2008: 227)

Glazener begins her article by quoting the work of Sunil Khilnani, who argues that civil society requires a self that is flexible, one that is open to debate and deliberation and a revision of one's views (Glazener 2008: 203). This is precisely the openness to revising one's beliefs and values that writers can represent in their novels—and which we will see in the pages that follow.

Writers are doing this work of the postsecular. In the very act of their writing, in the very search for affirmative values, they are creatively on the borderlines of received ideas of the secular and the religious. Philosophers and theorists within the west have also been taking these imaginative and intellectual risks on borderlines, undertaking the difficult work of imagining the boundaries of the secular, the religious, and even the aesthetic—and here I think of the work of Jacques Derrida, Emanuel Levinas, Maurice Blanchot, and Mieke Bal. In the chapters that follow, I engage with these thinkers to explore how literary fiction and theoretical work—emerging from Europe, India, North America, and Sri Lanka—can together constitute the imaginative inroads into the "newness" of postsecularism. Could Blanchot's writings on disaster and his search for some "outside" to the limits of representing disaster find their arc in the fiction of a writer like Michael Ondaatje, born and raised in Sri Lanka, now living in Canada, and striving to represent the civil war in Sri Lanka? Could European theoretical production find its arc in South Asian diasporic literary production? These are some of the questions raised by the transnationalism of the postsecular, and the chapters that follow will elaborate these questions, through close readings of the literature.

Imagining the postsecular is provoked by the real historical embeddedness in which we find ourselves. By "we" I mean not just those of us writing about secularism, but all of us "in this world" (certainly not all as "citizens," and this is also not to suggest that "we" all constitute a form of "world history"). Can this effort at "speaking for" secularism, for thinking *through* it, be connected in any way to the individual's real, on-the-ground struggle for protection, for basic rights? If this book is a small step toward achieving genuine national and transnational social justice, the evidence that that dream is coming to fruition has to be manifest "on the ground."

Although scholarship in theological studies is marking a turn to "postsecular" Christianity, I see this usage of the postsecular as reinforcing Christianity, and as Christianity rediscovering itself. The postsecularism that I pursue is a different concept, informed intimately by the historical and ongoing struggles of postcolonialism's and literature's role within such struggles.

The 2011 volume *Rethinking Secularism*, even while interrogating the limits, contradictions, and complexities of secularism, reinforces secularism. The articles in this collection are not debates about issues of faith, doctrine, and the good life. The debates are not about religious matters. Even while essays in this volume might be against Islamophobia, they are not *for* Islamic teachings, wisdom, and doctrines. I recognize that my work joins this trajectory of scholarship. This book is scholarship: it is not a manifesto, it is not a religious tract. But the issues it explores raise the question of *raising* the question of how writers pursue and work through the intertwined dilemmas of secularism and religion, both inside and outside South Asia and the west. This final caveat marks my own immersion, as indeed it marks anyone's, within the hegemonies of the secular, the religious, the postcolonial, and diaspora. Yes, it is a risk. But it is one worth taking. This risk is inspired by everyday life: ordinary people around the world peacefully live their lives because of their faith in secularism and religion, in spite of the pressures of nation, colonialism, and other forms of control. And with that openness and humbleness toward knowledge that I admire in the unsung heroes who have achieved dignity and self-respect in spite of inherited and ongoing inequality and oppression, I invite you to join me in the following pages.

Acknowledgments

This book is the culmination of many intellectual and geographical journeys, and I am grateful to all of my colleagues in Bangladesh, Canada, India, Pakistan, Sri Lanka, the UK, and the US for providing critical insights from a wide range of scholarly and cultural perspectives. I began this research in the Faculty of English at Oxford University, and would like to thank Rajeswari Sunder Rajan for the generosity and brilliance of her guidance, from the work's initial conceptions to its present form. I would also like to thank Robert J. C. Young for reading the manuscript and providing key suggestions with wisdom and warmth. For reading drafts of chapters, I am grateful to Robert Adolph, Talal Asad, Upendra Baxi, Vijay Mishra, Ankhi Mukherjee, Anjali Pandey, Benita Parry, Ato Quayson, Roseann Runte, Neluka Silva, and Asha Varadharajan.

For recurring conversations on points ranging from the general arguments of the project to the specifics of national literatures, cultures, histories, and politics, I am grateful to Meena Alexander, Asantha Attanayake, Sweety Bandopadhaya, Susan Bassnett, Rajeev Bhargava, Arpana Caur, Ajeet Cour, Neloufer de Mel, David Dabydeen, Nabanita Deb, Ashminder Kaur, Leela Gandhi, V. G. Hegde, Chelva Kanaganayakam, Sucheta Kapoor, S. I. Keethaponcalan, Dean Kotlowski, Neil Lazarus, Sachidananda Mohanty, Ashis Nandy, Makarand Paranjape, Prabhjot Parmar, G. J. V. Prasad, Vijaya Ramaswamy, Dylan Ratti, Jaiden Ratti, John Thompson, Harish Trivedi, and Rose Wolfe. For talking with me about the theoretical aspects of this work, I am grateful to Gil Anidjar, Emily Apter, Faisal Devji, Gayatri Spivak, and Gauri Viswanathan; and for a discussion about Sri Lankan politics after the war, I am grateful to Malathi de Alwis and Pradeep Jeganathan. I would like to thank members of the Graduate Seminar in Postcolonial Literatures in the Faculty of English at Cambridge University for their feedback, and Priya Gopal for providing the forum. I am also grateful to Linda Hutcheon for supervising my undergraduate senior thesis on Michael Ondaatje, thus laying one of the foundations for this study. The errors that remain are of course mine.

For support of this research, I am grateful to the Academy of Fine Arts and Literature in New Delhi; the British Council; the Canadian Centennial

Scholarship Fund; the Centre for the Study of Developing Societies in New Delhi; the Centre for South Asian Studies and the Department of English at the University of Toronto; the Centre for Translation and Comparative Cultural Studies and the Department of English and Comparative Literary Studies at Warwick University; the Department of English and the Fulton School of Liberal Arts at Salisbury University; the Faculty of English and Linacre College at Oxford University; Fulbright Canada for a faculty fellowship at the Department of English at New York University; the International Centre for Ethnic Studies in Colombo; Jawaharlal Nehru University; the School of English at Queen's University Belfast; the Shastri Indo-Canadian Institute; the Social Sciences and Humanities Research Council of Canada; the University of Toronto Moss Scholarship; and Victoria College in the University of Toronto.

For their inspiring enthusiasm in engaging with many of the ideas and texts I pursue here, I thank my students. For giving shape to this book, I would like to thank members of this project's editorial and production process: Liz Levine, John Rogers, Michael Watters, Andrew Weckenmann, and Erica Wetter. Last but not least, I thank my family and friends for their love and support. I dedicate this book to my parents and my brother.

Figure 2 Closing Ceremony, Commonwealth Games, Jawaharlal Nehru Stadium, New Delhi, India. Photograph by the author.

Introduction
Situating Postsecularism

Back to India—packing my Kindle again, and en route to Heathrow for the Closing Ceremony of the Commonwealth Games in New Delhi. A couple of days later I am using the shiny, air-conditioned New Delhi metro, heading for the Jawaharlal Nehru Stadium. The entrance security screenings are seamless and well-coordinated. The youth volunteers have veritable libraries between their ears of directions and trivia, all communicated with warmth and enthusiasm. I walk around the oval stadium, looking for my gate, and there it is. At the top of the gate's stairs is an opening giving glimpses of the enormous open space of the stadium and the wide sky beyond. The stadium fills to capacity as the New Delhi sky silently transforms from a golden azure into a bejewelled midnight indigo. The light shows are stunning and spectacular, almost other-worldly in their precision, speed, and colour. The groups of athletes steadily streaming onto the grounds are energized. Suresh Kalmadi, the chief organizer who would later be imprisoned for embezzlement, makes his welcome remarks, with heckles crescendoing throughout the stadium. The opposite occurs during the final live musical performances. The crowds are on their feet, waving flags of India. The energy is astounding. And then come the cheers, emerging one after another like a thousand aural fireworks arching everywhere: *Jai Hind!* Victory to India, the national slogan.

How can writers capture such a range of phenomena: nationalism, a world event, a booming economy that can lavishly build the latest infrastructure, and an officially democratic state that permits public criticism of its officials? Sri Lankan President Mahinda Rajapaksa was among the dignitaries at the event. I wondered whether he felt it was a strange juxtaposition: his country having just emerged from a decades-long civil war, and now a technicolour national celebration with the world watching. How can literature represent both crisis and affirmation?

In this Introduction, I situate debates about secularism and religion within national and international contexts by outlining the emergence of secularism as an ideology in the west, secularism as a state policy in India, and the possibilities of a secular state in Sri Lanka. I also discuss the work of Michael

Ondaatje and Salman Rushdie, who are the main focus of this study, in relation to their national and diasporic contexts.

I have chosen to focus on the work of Michael Ondaatje (born 1943) and
Salman Rushdie (born 1947), for they are almost exact contemporaries, are
situated in a similar historical moment—variously termed postmodern, postcolonial—and are also located diasporically. Ondaatje was born in Sri Lanka
and moved to England in 1954, where he attended Dulwich College before
moving to Canada in 1962. He has since remained resident in Canada, having completed a bachelor's degree in English at the University of Toronto and
a master's degree at Queen's University. Rushdie was born in India, and in
1964 moved to England, where he read for his bachelor's degree in History
at King's College, Cambridge. In 1968 he worked briefly in Pakistan, and
then returned to England, where he remained until he moved to New York
City in 2000.

Among Ondaatje's fiction, I dedicate a chapter in this book to *The English Patient* (1992), and another chapter to *Anil's Ghost* (2000). From Rushdie's work, I examine *The Satanic Verses* (1988), and how the death sentence
or *fatwa* influenced Rushdie's subsequent fiction. Specifically, I investigate
Rushdie's work right after the *fatwa—Haroun and the Sea of Stories* (1990) and
The Moor's Last Sigh (1995)—and his most recent works, *Shalimar the Clown*
(2005) and *The Enchantress of Florence* (2008), with reference as well to *Luka
and the Fire of Life* (2010). In terms of style, Ondaatje's fiction, which shares
significant stylistic similarities with his poetry, is marked by its reverential
and admirational overtones. Rushdie's fiction, in contrast, is marked famously
by its irreverence and ironic challenge, even mockery, of the expected, the
accepted, and the assumed. Such an outwardly unlikely pairing of writers
will allow me to offer readings of their texts that demonstrate how writers
can search for affirmative values through diverse trajectories.

Ondaatje is entrenched in Canada's literary scene and national culture
as a major writer, although there are a variety of critical approaches in Canada that variously construct Ondaatje as a Sri Lankan, Canadian, diasporic,
or transnational writer, showing the challenge of recognizing the fullness
and complexity of his multivocal work (Halpé 2010a). A special issue of
the *University of Toronto Quarterly* on the ethical turn in Canadian literature
includes articles on Ondaatje; consider the following acceptance of how
postcolonial concerns can contribute to questions of ethics within Canada:
"negotiation of diversity, and the sustained challenge to the monocultural,
colonial view of Canadian society and Canadian literature it has entailed,
is certainly one of the principal ways in which contemporary Canadian
literature and literary criticism can be viewed as ethically engaged" (Wyile
2007: 831). Ondaatje can be seen as "the good immigrant," writing pieces
that represent Sri Lanka, both to himself and to Canada, in ways that
are aesthetically pleasing. Moreover, he undertakes few direct criticisms of
dominant Canadian culture in his work, perhaps reinforcing the national

imaginary that enjoys viewing Canada as a global peacekeeper. To be sure, there are depictions of violence in his major novels *The English Patient* and *Anil's Ghost*, but there are also many elements of lyricism and beauty. In the chapters on these novels, I discuss criticism of these novels regarding their privileging of beauty at the cost of political and historical insensitivity toward "other" places and people.

Rushdie's writing continues to be polarizing in India. In a sense, he can be viewed as "the bad migrant," producing literature that has offended South Asian and diasporic Muslims, who believed that they did not need another misrepresentation of their religion. The good/bad distinction I present here is not meant in absolute terms. For example, on one hand, Rushdie in *The Satanic Verses* could be seen as favourable toward British interests that might seek to preserve stigmatizing and scapegoating representations of Islam— even though at the same time Rushdie depicts the xenophobia possible in London, thereby highlighting the failures of the secular discourse of British multiculturalism. Both Ondaatje and Rushdie are situated in the setting of the *multicultural metropolis*: Ondaatje in Toronto, Rushdie now in New York City, after living in London. For them, literature has been a way of establishing their presence in their multicultural settings, gaining credibility and stature within the dominant culture through the prestige of "high art." The act of writing thus serves as a means not just for survival, but also for recognition, perhaps even a measure of acceptance.

Alongside the chapters on Ondaatje and Rushdie, I devote shorter chapters to Allan Sealy's *The Everest Hotel* (1998) and Shauna Singh Baldwin's *What the Body Remembers* (1999), exploring how Sealy's novel resonates with *The English Patient*, and how Baldwin's novel resonates with *Anil's Ghost*. There is also a short chapter on Mahasweta Devi's "Pterodactyl, Puran Sahay, and Pirtha" (1995) and Amitav Ghosh's *The Hungry Tide* (2005).

The works of Sealy, Baldwin, and Devi are of interest to me, for they represent and/or write from the "minority" position in India: Anglo-Indians, Sikhs, and tribals, respectively. The constant exhortation from the secular nationalist position in India is to subsume particularistic identity in favour of the nation. These writers pursue the challenge of representing minority identity without necessarily being anti-nationalist. Whereas Sealy secularizes Christianity, Baldwin secularizes Sikhism. By "secularize," I mean that they preserve the great ethical elements of these religions, but then translate them into thoroughly worldly, contingent situations, ones that emerge from a minority position like that of the Anglo-Indians or the real challenges and struggles of women's experiences.

Devi's text is the only one I examine in this book that is not originally written in English. In her preface to the collection of Devi's stories, *Imaginary Maps*, Devi's translator, Gayatri Spivak, raises some of the problems of translating Devi. By translating Devi into English, Spivak recognizes that Devi and her work can constitute a sort of "museum" of so-called "Third

World experience" for a western readership. But such asymmetries are of course also reproduced within the nation—India. The tribals about whom Devi has so often written can themselves be seen *as* ethnographic objects by majoritarian India. Consider the January 2012 incident when members of the Jarawa tribe in the Andaman and Nicobar islands off the coast of mainland India danced for tourists, with the video clip going viral, causing even India's Home Minister to weigh in on the controversy. Devi herself has thematized such misunderstandings of tribals in her work, exposing the hypocrisies and contradictions of Hindu India, particularly within the upper castes. In the concluding body chapter, I discuss how Devi, in her riveting novella "Pterodactyl, Puran Sahay, and Pirtha," imagines majoritarian India's understanding of the tribals across a religious and ethnic divide that might be definitionally inaccessible.

From *The Satanic Verses* (1988) to *Anil's Ghost* (2000), the novels I examine emerge from a moment in South Asian history, roughly a decade long, marked by political, ethnic, and religious turmoil that collectively signaled crises of secularism. As a consequence, fiction here becomes an experimental space, one where writers do not simply represent the turbulence and dilemmas of historical events, but actually structure them, or are informed by them, demonstrating the ethical potentials of imaginative fictional space. Amitav Ghosh's *The Hungry Tide* (2005) and Rushdie's *Shalimar the Clown* (2005) and *The Enchantress of Florence* (2008) are of course written after 9/11. I choose these works because they thematize the challenge of how the "west" can understand the "east." I argue that there is a similarity between *The Hungry Tide* and *Anil's Ghost*. Like the latter, *The Hungry Tide* engages the ethical questions of knowability and unknowability, especially across the divides of secularism and animism and their associated knowledges.

As I stated in the Preface, the writers I have chosen allow me to examine the relations between secularism and a range of religions and belief systems, namely, animism, Buddhism, Christianity, Hinduism, Islam, and Sikhism. There is no text in this study whose focus is a critique of Hinduism. This could be attributed to the fact that Hinduism exercises majoritarian hegemony in India and therefore could occupy a certain invisibility. The focus of my study, then, is the minority perspective and how it can critique majoritarianism. In Sri Lanka, Ondaatje's voice is in some ways a minority voice, which I elaborate upon in my chapter on *Anil's Ghost*. His writing has the potential to stand outside both Buddhism and Hinduism, as I suggest through the closing image of the eye-painting ceremony of the Buddha statue in *Anil's Ghost*. Anglophone writing in India tends to be secular and minoritarian in its ethos. Yet, even with this concern for minority perspectives, the use of the English language reinforces the ideology of secularism as the only means to exercise and express rationality (Dhareshwar 1993: 117).

1.0   Secularism and Religion: The Debates

In this section I outline some of the debates and tensions arising from secularism and religion within the west, India, and Sri Lanka. I do so in order to provide a framework for the wider cultural, national, and transnational contexts within which and *into* which writers' work can provoke questions of civility, interreligious relations, and intercultural understanding.

Secularism in the West

The term *secular* has spatial and temporal dimensions, both with Christian inflections. It is derived from the Latin noun *saeculum*, which, according to the Oxford English Dictionary, can denote "age" or "generation," and, in Christian Latin, "the world." Each of these is the age, generation, or world to which humanity belongs, in opposition to the timelessness and world of God. "Secular" also referred to clergymen who lived outside the monastery, and therefore in the "world." *Secular* thus can designate the observable here-and-now, the visible world, a category distinct from religion, given the latter's ideas of the transcendental.[1] *Secularization* in western societies is the name for the various processes that separated institutionalized religion (for example, "the church") from the state, pushing religion into the private sphere; the term's oldest meaning is the state's expropriation of church property (Pecora 2006: 13). Secularization can be a specifically political term denoting the relation between the political and the religious as a model for the organization of the state, and its ultimate relation with the nation. The secularization thesis or theory is that as societies become more modern—from agrarian to industrial to post-industrial—they become more secular, relying less and less on the narratives of religion for a sense of security, increasingly pushing the presence and power of religion into the private sphere. According to Vincent Pecora, "the practical link between modernization and secularization remains alive and well, and that the role of 'science' as an antidote to 'superstition' remains a significant part of what major Western social institutions—from the academies to the courts of law—consider the social good" (Pecora 2006: 17). *Secularism* is the name for the *ideologies* that emerge alongside or as a result of secularization, such as the ideology that people should confine their beliefs to what they can observe in the material world, or that to have a secular outlook, including the belief that state and religion should be separate, is to be modern, progressive, and rational. The word "secularism" was coined in 1851 by the British theologian George Holyoake to denote this confining of belief to the observable, material world.

European nation-states have undergone secularization for centuries, so that the sense of being "secular" now goes hand-in-hand with being "modern." Jürgen Habermas has produced some of the most perceptive theorizations on the pressures being felt by European nation-states as their sense of "secularism" faces great challenges. In his article "Notes on a Post-Secular Society," Habermas refers in particular to the pressures in Germany as its dominant majority, white Christians, must face and even accept an increasingly diverse nation, most prominently in the form of individuals identifying as Turk and Muslim. An ethics of tolerance in this instance would state, "let them have the right to believe as they wish, as we too have that right." But the situation is more complex. How does the presence of those who are religiously, linguistically, ethnically, and racially different influence people's image of themselves and their nation? This is not a simple consideration. Habermas uses the term *postsecular* to designate the challenge faced by secularized societies in contemporary nation-states in which "religion maintains a public influence and relevance" while "the secularistic certainty that religion will disappear worldwide in the course of modernisation is losing ground" (Habermas 2008: 21). This persistence of religion leads Habermas to the question, "How should we see ourselves as members of a post-secular society and what must we reciprocally expect from one another in order to ensure that in firmly entrenched nation states, social relations remain civil despite the growth of a plurality of cultures and religious world views?" (Habermas 2008: 21).

What are some of the historical forces leading to the cultural and religious diversity within Europe and North America? Imagine the year 1945. A man is in prison, and within a couple of years he would become the prime minister of a newly decolonized and independent nation. Over a six-month period in prison he writes what would become one of his greatest works. The conditions in the jail are terrible—cold, damp, uncomfortable. But he keeps going, his spirit encouraged and inspired by the warm company of his fellow inmates. This is Jawaharlal Nehru and the book he is writing is *The Discovery of India*. Throughout the book he uses the idea of *karma*—the law of cause and effect, of every action having an opposite and equal reaction—to assert that the British colonization of India is producing *destinies* for both nations. As Nehru seeks to frame India's inevitable march toward freedom, he invokes a phrase by Rabindranath Tagore: political independence is a "tryst with destiny." Interestingly, this phrase is similar to the words of another consequential political leader, Franklin D. Roosevelt. Seeking to inspire the generation of Americans struggling to survive the Great Depression, and who would go on to defeat the Axis powers in World War II, FDR in 1936 predicted that Americans had a "rendezvous with destiny." Nehru's and Roosevelt's invocations of destiny signal watershed moments in the lives of both their nations—and, as it turned out, across nations—moments full of potential and hope for the future.

What are some of the destinies now? The formerly national and colonial other—perhaps imagined as oppressed, exploited, disempowered, dispossessed—has arrived in Europe and North America, born there, growing up there, studying there, working there. For some, on both sides of the equation, this might be difficult to accept. For others, it can be a welcome development, an opportunity for mutual flourishing and prosperity. In both cases, the *fact* of "presence" remains, on both sides of the equation. Various names have emerged to mark what the relation and ethics should or might be between the "majorities" and "minorities": integration, multiculturalism, racism, privilege, disprivilege, stigmatization, fear, love, acceptance, and now postsecularism. Among this group of people, there will be writers, individuals who might have originally been born or raised in countries such as India or Sri Lanka, and have grown up, studied, or lived significant portions of their lives within countries such as Canada, the UK, and the US. How would these at least double cultural and national influences shape these writers' imagination of the secular and the religious? How can writers retain the best features of state secularism while also preserving the inspiring, generative, imaginative features of religious thought and practice, such as faith, awe, wonder, transcendence? At the same time, these writers undertake the work of *writing* that literature within a nation-state context, say the UK or the US, where *ideologies* of secularism, whether real or imagined, can characterize religious belief and practice as irrational and intolerant, including when those religions are embodied by the ethnic minority. If postsecularism is one of the destinies of postcolonialism, then literature stands as a forum where new conceptions of secularism and religion can emerge, gesturing to ethics that grow from individual and cultural memories of secular, religious, and national violence, combined with the hope of a better future for all.

There have been different models of secularization within Canada, the UK, and the US, but *secularism* and its legacies have exerted, and indeed continue to exert, enormous power over these nation-states to *imagine* themselves as secular and therefore as modern and progressive. In the UK, the church and state are constitutionally identified with one another, although in practice the formal influence of the church over the state is minimal. France stands as an exemplar of the separation of church and state, replacing the authority of God with the republican conception of equal citizenship. With religion thus relegated by the state to the private sphere, what has emerged in its place is the overarching value of equality (*égalité*).

My interest is in the *ideologies* of secularism. They are ideologies because they have been intimately linked with ideas of modernity, progress, civilization, and the othering of religions different from Christianity. As José Casanova has observed, although a majority of Europeans might in practice be religious, it would also be compelling for them to *imagine* themselves as secular (Casanova 2011: 67–72). Why? Because here "secular" denotes being tolerant, modern, and progressive; each of the former three terms is relationally-defined, dependent on an "other." The "other" in this case is "religion," understood as premodern Christianity and/or non-Christian religions, all of which are seen as "irrational" and "intolerant"—now, especially Islam. In Casanova's words, a negative view of religion is "a secular construct that has the function of positively differentiating modern secular Europeans from 'the religious other,' either from premodern religious Europeans or from contemporary non-European religious people, particularly Muslims" (Casanova 2011: 69). Secularism thus contradicts itself, for in its ideological circulation as rationality, tolerance, modernity, and progressiveness, it is liable to misunderstanding religion and the ethnic other as irrational, intolerant, unmodern, and unprogressive. In describing the enormous pressure that secularism exerts on western societies, Charles Taylor argues that this leads to the hegemony of what he terms the "immanent frame," that is, the observable, material world, and the power of that world to act as the delineator and regulator of what *is* real, true, and knowable, acting itself as the limit of the real, true, and knowable, devoid of any reference to or concept of a transcendent frame (Taylor 2007: 542).

In Canada, the Canadian Charter of Rights and Freedoms sends a mixed message. It includes the following Preamble: "Whereas Canada is founded on principles that recognize the supremacy of God and the rule of Law" (*Canadian Charter of Rights and Freedoms* 1982). But the Charter also includes—and this has actual juridico-legal power—Section 2 (a), which recognizes freedom of conscience and religion as fundamental freedoms. This section has been crucial for recognizing diversities of religions and their related cultures and ethnicities. The US presents another interesting example: it is among the world's most developed and modernized countries, one of the earliest to separate church and state based on a model of mutual exclusion, and also contains a high percentage of practising Christians. In the case of the US, with religion thus relegated by the state to the private sphere, what has emerged in its place is the overarching value of individual liberty. This is where the ideologies of secularism that I mentioned above can assert themselves, through beliefs, for example, that freedom *is* secularism—and that secularism *is* freedom, perhaps perniciously so, in the case of justifying military intervention.

A final caveat. If a state is definitionally secular, then it would be intolerant if it prohibited the formation of religiously-informed parties, such as the Christian Democratic Union in Germany. In the words of Habermas, "a constitutional democracy, which explicitly *authorizes* citizens to lead a religious life, may not at the same time discriminate against these citizens in their role as democratic co-legislators" (Mendieta 2010: 12; italics original). A key word in Habermas's argument is "democratic," and that is an interesting feature of secular democratic liberalism, for although it might envision a pluralistic ethos of tolerance for all perspectives, it must also include "all" "others" within its political concept of democracy. In the US context, John Rawls has proposed a model for political engagement based on "overlapping consensus," that groups with different modes of belief—religious, secular— *can* and should converse with one another, based on common, unbiased principles of reason, and guided by specific ideals, such as justice (Rawls 1993: 144). As a parallel to Habermas's and Rawls's ideas of inclusion (or exclusion), consider the following quotation from Rushdie's short story "At the Auction of the Ruby Slippers": "What price tolerance if the intolerant are not tolerated also?" (Rushdie 1995a: 92). This is where contemporary debates in Europe, Canada, and the US have provoked questions pertaining to multiculturalism and ethno-religious pluralism: to what extent should the state tolerate differing religiously-justified practices, such as wearing the veil or carrying a ceremonial Sikh dagger?

Secularism in India

Having given some background to secularism in western societies, I will focus now on some of the historical issues of secularism in India, both those that writers represent in their novels and those that are likely to have informed their consciousness. The constitutions of France, the US, and also Turkey were avowedly secular in their origins, and the Indian constitution reflected this model. The actual word "secularism" was integrated into the Indian constitution in 1976. Perhaps the most fitting place to begin a discussion of Indian secularism is through its relation with nationalism, given the writers' interest in interrogating "nation," and given also that secularism and nationalism have had such intertwined fates, especially after India's Independence from Britain in 1947.

Secularism has deep political resonances in India, and has become virtually synonymous with nationalism, with Nehru and Gandhi playing key roles as architects of the "new" nation. Embedded in the idea of nationalism in India are the notions of liberalism and democracy, namely, that of protecting individual rights while also fairly recognizing the rights of religious groups, the largest of which are the Hindus, with Muslims constituting the largest religious minority. Democracy thus involves non- discrimination against any particular group while recognizing the rights of individuals to practise their faiths. The fascinating factor here is that although religion is on one hand a private matter, exercised and believed in at the level of the individual, it can also have social and collective expressions. Such a public manifestation of religious identity was of course used by the British to develop a divisive mentality ("us versus them") between Hindus and Muslims, thus legitimizing the "stability" of colonial rule. Such divisiveness would ultimately inform the partition of British India into India and Pakistan, on the premise that "different" religious groups require physically separate national spaces, a "Two-Nation" theory I elaborate in Chapter 4 on Shauna Singh Baldwin's *What the Body Remembers*.

In part to resist such unjust colonial control and violence, Indian leaders recognized the need for fostering an "Indian" identity that was greater than particular religious identities. Hindu identity was translated as an "Indian" identity in an effort to build anti-colonial resistance. In the years leading up to and after Independence, secularism came to do the work of nationalism in fostering a pan-Indian identity. To ensure a robust and inclusive concept of Indianness, this secularism also had to uphold *equality*—across caste, ethnicity, language, and gender—in order to mobilize as many members of the "nation" as possible. Among Gandhi's most well-known statements is that "nationalism is greater than sectarianism [. . .]. In that sense we are Indians first and Hindus, Mussalmans, Parsis, Christians after" (quoted in Pandey 1990: 238). But sectarianism, and the violence that often results from it, have been real threats to any unifying nationalism and peaceful interreligious coexistence. Secularism was essential for national unification, especially after Partition in 1947, marked as it was by violence fuelled by the oppositions of religious identity (such as Hindus vs. Muslims; Sikhs vs. Muslims; Hindus vs. Christians).

Aamir Mufti has argued that Partition should be read not as a *culmination* of separatism, but as part of the *process* of constructing nationhood, the latter consisting of the "turning of two-thirds of the Muslims of India into non-Indians in order for the remaining one-third to be successfully cast in the role of national minority" (Mufti 1995: 87). This division of peoples might seem categorically elegant given the aspiration toward *successfully* casting a group as a "national minority." The actual story of postcolonial India has been a different one. Violence has continued to erupt, particularly between Hindus and Muslims. But in the same sense that "nation" emerges as an *aspiration* toward a unifying peaceful coexistence, so too we can view secularism as aspirational, emerging not out of the divisions and antagonisms of religion (bad religion, then good secularism), but as part of a discourse that seeks to accommodate religious difference for the sake of national unity and peace.

Nehru and the Indian National Congress party adopted secularism as the official state ideology of independent India in order to promote not an irreligious or anti-religious state, but a state that was non-sectarian. In *The Discovery of India*, Nehru emphasizes India as historically a place of religious and cultural tolerance. Gyan Prakash argues that Nehru's project sought to modernize India by promoting the nation as a "secular entity, not a Hindu nation, that had cradled a variety of religions and sects through centuries, and had acquired a degree of unity while surviving conquests and conflicts" (1990: 389). For Nehru, it was this unity that nationalism could set free. In 1945, he insisted that "the future government of India must be secular in the sense that government will not associate itself with any religious faith but will give freedom to all religious functions" (quoted in Tambiah 1998: 422).

Like Nehru, Gandhi also believed in the new nation's responsibility toward recognizing religious differences. In 1910 he affirmed that "India cannot cease to be one nation because people belonging to different religions live in it" (Gandhi 1997: 52). But where Nehru believed in the ideology of modernization, Gandhi was antimodernist, turning to indigenous cultural and religious traditions through which to inspire and lead the peoples of India. Prasenjit Duara has compellingly argued for reading Gandhi and Nehru as having different approaches to the idea of history, with Nehru turning to Enlightenment models based on progress and emancipation (Duara 1995: 213), and Gandhi turning to a religio-moral vision: "Having no anchor in History, or even in history (which has no permanent anchor), the nation would have to embody the transcendent Truth" (Duara 1995: 216). I highlight this argument to show how a productive difference in attitudes toward history combined to animate the emergence of state secularism.

It was important to Gandhi that the nation must respect peoples of all castes and classes, such as the peasant classes, in whose worldview religion plays a central role. Gandhi had insisted that caste discrimination, along with discrimination against the so-called "untouchables," should be eradicated, in order to build India as a nation (Pandey 1990: 237). As we can see from Gandhi's insistence on the caste and class inclusiveness of secularism, secularism was never only about the relation between "politics" and "religion," but also about representativeness *within* religions. Nevertheless, the idea of secularism, like nationalist thought itself, was largely conceptualized by Hindu men privileged by caste and class, so that "secularism"–like the idea of what is "India"–could easily become a cover for preserving patriarchal and Hindu majoritarian interests (Tejani 2011: 14–15). Although the Indian constitution was based in part on the American and French models, religion in India, unlike that in western nation-states, is not pushed into the private sphere. Rajeev Bhargava has argued that a "principled distance" from all religions is what marks the distinctiveness of Indian secularism (Bhargava 2007). The state *can* intervene in different religious communities through law and policy, but although that treatment of people and communities might be differential–allowing religion to enter the public sphere–the state must be guided by non-sectarian values of freedom and equality.

Despite this state commitment to a nuanced and subtle secularism, and the almost intuitive value of secularism as a state policy, even termed *Nehruvian secularism* for Nehru's commitment to a state respectful of religion, secularism in India has been marked by several crises since Independence. Perhaps one of the bleakest moments is the period of Emergency between 1975 and 1977, when Prime Minister Indira Gandhi effectively led a dictatorship, imprisoning any opponents, curtailing civil liberties, and censoring the press. She deployed the concept of the "nation" by claiming to institute economic reforms, but in fact eroded the people's faith in democracy, the very system of government that was central to the idea and ethos of state secularism: representation of and equal treatment of all peoples. In 1984, following the assassination of Indira Gandhi by her Sikh bodyguards, there were massacres of Sikhs in New Delhi and other parts of India, with evidence suggesting involvement of politicians from the ruling Congress party (Tambiah 1996: 128–131). Shah Bano, an elderly Muslim woman, successfully petitioned the Supreme Court for alimony in 1985. The judgment outraged some conservative Muslims, who believed the state should not be meddling in personal divorce laws already established by and for religious communities. The Prime Minister at the time, Rajeev Gandhi, reversed the Supreme Court decision. This decision was widely perceived as pandering to Muslim voters. It was also condemned as not just privileging a particular religious community, but doing so at the cost of women's rights.

Another sign of secularism's failure occurred a few years later, in 1989. The Mandal Commission had recommended a significant increase in quotas in governmental jobs and educational institutions for members of tribes and lower castes. The decision was heavily criticized by upper-caste Hindus, and remains a contentious issue in India. Also in 1989, an armed insurgency began in Kashmir, India's only Muslim-majority state, with insurgents seeking independence for Kashmir. Although the Indian state could have employed diplomacy, its response in the 1990s was instead brutal, effectively converting Kashmir into a conflict zone under the pretence of "protecting" secular nationalism. Human rights violations have proliferated in the state, marked by custodial disappearances, civilian killings, and sexual violence against women.

One of the greatest failures of secularism is the continuing violence between religious communities. Christian communities—including nuns, missionaries, churches, schools—have been targeted by extremist Hindus. Perhaps the most internationally visible and provocative example of secularism's failure to address religious violence occurred on December 6, 1992, when hundreds of thousands of cadres of Hindu nationalists destroyed the Babri mosque in Ayodhya, claiming it had been built on top of the birthplace of the Hindu god Ram. The structure fell to the ground within hours. As part of the Indian intellectual response to this violence, Anand Patwardhan has produced the excellent documentaries *Ram Ke Naam* (*In the Name of Ram*, 1992) and *Pitr, Putr, aur Dharmayuddha* (*Father, Son, and the Holy War*, 1995). As a threat to secularism, the early 1990s onward have seen the rise of the Hindu nationalist party, the Bharatiya Janata Party (BJP), with its militant ideology of Hindutva ("Hinduness"); the BJP held national power from 1998 to 2004. In 2002, a mob of Muslims burned a train in Gujarat containing Hindu pilgrims returning from Ayodhya. Later that year, and in the wake of a BJP government in Gujarat led by Chief Minister Narendra Modi, Hindu mobs killed thousands of Muslims, and made even more homeless.

Emerging from these provocations to secularism in the public sphere in the mid to late nineties, 1998 saw the publication of *Secularism and its Critics*, one of the first major academic volumes in India to investigate the limits and crises of secularism. Among critics of secularism in India, the Subaltern Studies historians have pointed to the class biases of secularism, especially as the latter has been imagined by political-intellectual elites. Ranajit Guha argues that Indian nationalist elites are "unable to grasp religiosity as the central modality of peasant consciousness in colonial India," and that they fail "to conceptualize insurgent mentality except in terms of an unadulterated secularism" (Guha 1988: 81). If secularism is part of a rationalist scientific worldview, then Dipesh Chakrabarty identifies the difficulties in understanding and representing the otherness of religious belief and faith. According to Chakrabarty, a religiously-informed lifeworld is radically different from the scientific language of history or sociology:

[A]lthough the sciences signify some kind of sameness in our understanding of the world across cultures, the gods signify difference [...]. Writing about the presence of gods and spirits in the secular language of history or sociology would therefore be like translating into a universal language that which belongs to a field of differences.

(Chakrabarty 2008: 76)

The larger problem is that of conceptualizing such difference. The modernizing, nationalizing apparatus of secularism faces the challenge of addressing that which is so resistant to conventional, rational understanding in the first place: ghosts, spirits.

Ashis Nandy's well-known criticisms of Indian secularism include his argument that an official policy of Enlightenment-inspired secularism overlooks the long traditions and histories of interreligious tolerance in India, particularly among the peasant classes. According to Nandy, secularism comes to "hegemonize the idea of tolerance, so that anyone who is not secular becomes definitionally intolerant" (Nandy 2002: 60). Nandy's critique demonstrates state secularism's rigid conception of tolerance: tolerance is worthwhile, and secularism is the only route toward tolerance.

Consider the parallel of multiculturalism in western nations: *because* the state is officially multicultural (e.g., Australia, Canada, the UK), it is definitionally tolerant, and therefore the work of accommodating cultural, ethnic, linguistic, and racial differences need go no further. Because western countries are predominantly white European, whiteness can become the silent core reference point of any multicultural agenda. That majoritarianism makes such agendas vulnerable to orientalism and stereotyping in general, whether positive or negative. Also operating within multiculturalism can be the orientalist construct of "non-white" cultures as the sole bearers of "culture," with a supposedly neutral or unbiased whiteness as the benevolent, rational manager of those other "cultures."

Similarly, political "secularism" in India reinforces the idea of unbiased, rational state benevolence toward (irrational) citizens. Nandy also asserts that a state policy of secularism minimizes the importance of religious belief in India. Making a distinction between religion-as-ideology (as a public identity, one that the state can identify and categorize) and religion-as-faith (as personal belief), Nandy argues that although secularism absorbs the concept of religion-as-ideology, it also interferes with religion-as-faith: "[secularism] is hardly appealing to the faithful, to whom religion is an overall theory of life, including public life, and life does not seem worth living without a theory, however imperfect, of transcendence" (Nandy 1998: 333).

The problem with religious ideas containing a theory of public life is that they can be manipulated by cadres such as those of right-wing Hindutva ("Hinduness") politics in order to attack the secular state as "pseudosecular" while arguing that their Hinduism is the "true" secularism. I elaborate this ideology in Chapter 6, in my discussion of Rushdie's *The Moor's Last Sigh*. Nandy also valorizes aesthetic creativity as an example of interreligious tolerance because such creativity often arises from the translation of cultural traditions. He refers to examples from Indian architecture and music which are the result of encounters between Hinduism and Islam. I will extend this view of creativity by demonstrating how literature too can constitute a site for translations across the different modes of the secular and the religious.

Secularism in Sri Lanka

What is the scene of Sri Lankan politics and history onto which *Anil's Ghost* arrives? How does Michael Ondaatje's novel address and incorporate some of the majority-minority tensions that fueled the civil war in Sri Lanka for over twenty-five years? In this section I present some of the challenges faced by secularism in Sri Lanka. In Chapter 3, on Ondaatje's *Anil's Ghost*, I provide a context for understanding facets of Sri Lanka's civil war, particularly as the end of the war has now raised questions of human rights.

Given the ongoing challenges of accommodating ethnic difference and civil rights, Sri Lanka is in urgent need of state secularism, for the reasons that informed the need to ensure secularism in post-Independence India: the protection of minorities, and as part of an exercise in democratic nation-building. The Sinhalese, who are mostly Buddhist, constitute the majority ethnic group in Sri Lanka. The Tamils, who are mostly Hindu, form the largest ethnic minority in the country. One of the most salient differences between current Indian and Sri Lankan state policies is that whereas India remains officially secular, Sri Lanka privileges Buddhism, encoding such privilege in its national constitution. This informed the civil war which devastated the country for over two decades. Article 9 of the present Sri Lankan constitution (last significantly modified in 1978) states: "The Republic of Sri Lanka shall give to Buddhism the foremost place and accordingly it shall be the duty of the State to protect and foster the Buddha Sasana, while assuring to all religions the rights granted by Articles 10 and 14(1)(e)" (*Constitution of Sri Lanka* 1978). The wording of Article 10 is as follows: "Every person is entitled to freedom of thought, conscience and religion, including the freedom to have or to adopt a religion or belief of his choice" (*Constitution of Sri Lanka* 1978). And Article 14(1)(e) states: "(1) Every citizen is entitled to: (e) the freedom, either by himself or in association with others, and either in public or in private, to manifest his religion or belief in worship, observance, practice or teaching" (*Constitution of Sri Lanka* 1978).

As part of the historical forces shaping the rise of Buddhist nationalism in Sri Lanka, there have been three major periods of European colonization of Sri Lanka, beginning with the arrival of the Portuguese in 1505. The Dutch gained control over the island in approximately the mid-seventeenth century, and then ceded control to the British at the beginning of the nineteenth century. Buddhist nationalism grew in the nineteenth century as a reaction against Christian missions in the country and the Christianity of the British (Tambiah 1996: 38–43). In pre-independence Sri Lanka, Anagarika Dharmapala (1864–1933) was instrumental to invigorating the Buddhist nationalist movement, which was similar to the self-modernizing, reformist Hinduism and its associated nationalism inspired in India by the religious leader Swami Vivekananda (1863–1902). An almost exact contemporary of Vivekananda, Dharmapala was originally a layman, born as David Hewavitarana. Dharmapala denounced the corruptness of Buddhism in Sri Lanka, seeking instead to modernize and reform the religion, and to give it a political role. Buddhism thus became for him a key form of anti-colonial nationalism, and he himself became an icon of Sinhalese Buddhist nationalism, praising the virtues of Buddhism against other religious traditions (Christianity, Islam, Brahminical Hinduism) and the British.

Beyond specific individuals, texts such as the *Mahavamsa*, a Pali verse written by Buddhist monks from the sixth century onward, can also have their intersections with nationalism, manipulated by politicians and the like to serve as the "national chronicle" of Sri Lanka. The *Mahavamsa* is thought to extend to about a thousand years previous to the sixth century, chronicling the Buddha's three sojourns in Sri Lanka. Given the importance of this document for Sinhalese identity, in 1977 the President of Sri Lanka, J. R. Jayewardene, extended the chronicle to include the beginning of *his* administration. He stated that the history of Buddhism in Sri Lanka has emphasized that the "connection between past and present must be unbroken, whether between a sacred place and the historical events that created its importance or between a group of monks and the historical origins that guarantee the authenticity of their teachings" (quoted in Kemper 1991: 33). The *Mahavamsa* came to serve as a marker of Buddhist "national" unity, which, in Steven Kemper's words, warranted the beliefs that "the island and its government have traditionally been Sinhala and Buddhist, and that a person cannot be Buddhist without being Sinhala" (Kemper 1991: 2). The *Mahavamsa* thus becomes a source for the reinforcement of the exclusivity of "ethnic" identity, regulating what it means to be Sinhalese, Buddhist, and, by implication, Sri Lankan. As an example of how the regulation of ethnic identity can find its expression in politics, in 1956 Prime Minister Bandaranaike instituted the "Sinhala Language Act," making Sinhala the official national language. Article 7 of the constitution thus stated: "The Official Language of Sri Lanka shall be Sinhala as provided by the Official language Act, No. 33 of 1956" (*Constitution of Sri Lanka* 1978). In an amendment in 1987 to Article 18 of the constitution, the government added Tamil as an official national language, and English as a link language.

In order to give representation to Tamil concerns in Sri Lanka, the All Ceylon Tamil Congress (ACTC) was founded in 1944. The Pan Sinhala Executive Committee had been similarly founded in 1936. The first Governor General of independent Ceylon was Lord Soulbury. He had headed the Commission appointed by the British Government in 1944 to examine and discuss proposals for the constitutional reform of the newly emerging nation-state. The Commission quickly recognized that stable relations between the majorities and the minorities, particularly the Sinhalese and the Tamils, were essential to the well-being of the island. When Lord Soulbury wrote about Sri Lanka in 1963, his earlier concerns had become only too true. He expressed regret that the Commission "did not also recommend the entrenchment in the constitution of guarantees of fundamental rights, on the lines enacted in the constitutions of India, Pakistan, Malaya, Nigeria and elsewhere" (quoted in Farmer 1963: xiii). He concluded: "the reconciliation of Tamils and Sinha-lese will depend not on constitutional guarantees but on the goodwill, com-mon sense and humanity of the Government in power and the people who elect it" (quoted in Farmer 1963: xiii).

Contemporary instances of the Buddhist majority's discrimination toward religious minorities are an echo of the nineteenth-century anti-Christian sen-timents of Buddhist nationalism. They include two bills that would prohibit religious conversions. On July 21, 2004, the leading Buddhist cleric in Sri Lanka, who is a member of the nationalist Buddhist party—the Jathika Hela Urumaya (JHU) party—proposed an anti-conversion bill, called the Prohibi-tion of Forcible Conversion of Religions Bill, to the Sri Lankan Parliament. The bill states: "No person shall convert or attempt to convert, either directly or otherwise, any person from one religion to another by the use of force or by allurement or by any fraudulent means nor shall any person aid or abet any such conversions" ("Prohibition of Forcible Conversion of Religions Bill" 2004). This bill would force anyone who underwent conversion to inform local authorities within a prescribed period. Depending on who is converted, those who convert others and fail to follow the above stipulations can be imprisoned up to seven years, or fined up to five hundred thousand rupees. Similarly, there is the Freedom of Religion Bill, proposed by the Minister of Buddhist Sasana in 2005. This bill stipulates that no person shall "unethi-cally convert or attempt to unethically convert, any other person espousing one religion, or holding or belonging to, one religious belief, religious per-suasion or faith, to another religion, religious belief, religious persuasion or faith which such person does not espouse, hold or belong to. No person shall abet any such unethical conversion" ("Freedom of Religion Bill" 2005). As with the bill against forced religious conversions, the maximum imprison-ment sentence for infractions against this bill is seven years. The fine can also be up to five hundred thousand rupees. These two measures have worried Christians in Sri Lanka, especially evangelists, who fear it impinges on their right to proselytize. It also highlights that there are other religious minori-ties in Sri Lanka other than the Hindus. The National Christian Evangelical Alliance of Sri Lanka (NCEASL) has stated that the bill would "enforce limi-tations on religious freedom, legitimize violence and harassment of minor-ity religious groups and further de-fragment our already divided society" ("Statement" 2005).

The war in Sri Lanka also had a class dimension, particularly in the nation's capital, Colombo. Although some upper-class Tamil and Sinhalese families might have believed that the war was happening to "others"—the lower classes—an incident in 1990 challenged this seeming certitude. A well-known journalist, Richard de Zoysa, was abducted from his home by a group of armed Sinhalese men, some of them police officers, in the darkness of the early morning of February 18, 1990. It is believed the men took his body and dumped it from a helicopter into the sea, far off the coast of Colombo. The perpetrators assumed the body would sink to the bottom of the sea. De Zoysa's body, however, surfaced onto a beach just south of Colombo. The war was no longer "elsewhere" or happening to ordinary, anonymous people (Pathirana 2011).

De Zoysa had published what would become his last article only a week before his abduction. He urged that Sri Lanka should be a secular state. It is perhaps best to end this section on Sri Lanka with the words of Richard de Zoysa. He called for Sri Lanka to be "a secular state—truly secular, with no icons except the institutions of the state itself, and guided by the principles of sound management within an ideological framework which does not carry within itself the seeds of either extremism of Jathika Chintanaya ["National Ideology" group, which eulogizes ancient Sinhalese culture] or the potential anarchy of cultural populism" (de Zoysa 1990).

2.0 Postsecularism and Enchantment

With such deeply entrenched ideas, legacies, and worldviews surrounding debates about secularism and religion, I want to focus on the notion of enchantment, because disenchantment is the condition so often perceived as a feature of modernized, secularized societies. This disenchantment is something authors can write through and/or against, but without rejecting the stability of politically secular societies. Akeel Bilgrami argues that the historically dehumanizing worldviews of western colonial powers—worldviews centered in scientific rationality, which perceived and reinforced perceptions of colonized peoples as subhuman, thus justifying colonial conquest and violence—have resulted in a disenchanted west (Bilgrami 2000: 407). According to Bilgrami, this is, for example, an America where ordinary people are left with searches for re-enchantment, a quest not for mere entertainment or recreation, but for *values* (Bilgrami 2000: 411). This resonates with the questions pursued by the writers in this book. How should we live our lives? What choices should we make? How should we think of our responsibility to others? Given the threat of right-wing religious extremism, particularly in its expressions in Red-State America, Bilgrami wonders what forms of secular enchantment there might be.

Faith, awe, wonder, and transcendence. Are these not the irresistible dimensions of the human experience, infusing everyday life with richness, imagination, and inspiration? Literature written under the conditions of post-colonialism and diaspora can be the site for enchantment and re-enchantment, and it is thus postsecular within the framework of *secularism as ideology*. It is a brave new imagination of the religious and the secular, informed by the violence of colonialism and the ongoing traumas and individual and cultural memories resulting from that violence. It is a brave new imagination because writers must contend with the weight of orientalizing characterizations and mischaracterizations of religion, secularism, race, majority, minority, and nation. It is a brave new imagination because the imagining of the postsecular is a risky journey into the unknown, where writers challenge received ideologies—of religion, secularism, race, majoritarianism, minoritarianism, and nation. At the same time, these writers must explore forms for aesthetically *representing* that challenge.

I thus also use postsecularism in relation to literary form, as a marker of impossibility and possibility in capturing that which might be resistant to representation—such as a kind of "postsecular belief" for which there might not be an easy creative or critical vocabulary mediating between the secular and the religious. That representational challenge for writers is not merely reactive. It involves moving beyond such statements that "religion is empowering" or "secularism is limiting" or "colonialism is violent." There is a certain commitment that these writers have, which might be called "faith" or "belief." I use both terms ironically, given the ongoing legacies of religious and colonial violence that have misused the ethical, affective power of "faith" and "belief." But even irony is ultimately and inextricably a relation to that which it ironizes. That commitment to faith and belief is, in my conception, a marker of postsecularism, in which the "post" signals a form of commitment that risks moving beyond the "secular," defined in this context as "unbelieving," without falling prey to the ideology of the secular that defines such belief as irrational, intolerant, and unmodern. Making visible the various kinds of faith will require its own faith, which I view as belief in oneself, belief in the process one uses, and belief in the literary craft at one's disposal.

Given the constitutive complexity of the postsecular, existing between religion and secularism and having its own ethical commitments, what sort of conceptual language could express and imagine a critique of secularism and religion? A special "space" for the articulation and praxis of belief is envisioned by Jacques Derrida in his concept of a "messianicity without messianism" (Derrida 2002: 56). Derrida imagines a space he calls the desert, an abstract location where he can reflect on the religious without the historical phenomena of religions. This special space gives rise to a kind of messianicity which, for Derrida, is a "faith without dogma which makes its way through the risks of absolute night" (Derrida 2002: 57). This faith "cannot be contained in any traditional opposition, for example that between reason and mysticism" (Derrida 2002: 57). It is thus, for Derrida, a faith that is open-ended and deconstructive. It is a faith that resists any predictable goal or end, and is similar to Derrida's idea of messianicity, which is an "opening to the future [. . .] but without horizon of expectation and without prophetic prefiguration" (Derrida 2002: 56). When Derrida speaks of a faith without dogma, he captures the struggle of writers for a kind of "faith" that avoids the ideologies of organized religion. And when he writes about the "risks of absolute night," this too is reflected in writers' postsecular search, underscoring that their search is very much a process, and not fixed on any goal, but an openness to the future without any "prophetic prefiguration." Nor are the writers' explorations merely or simply a reactive oscillation between "reason" and "mysticism."

If a reimagined desert, faith, and messianicity are Derrida's forms of enchantment and *re*-enchantment, then so too has William Collony turned to examining the disenchantments of secularism. Beginning with what he views as secularism's failures in the west at the level of existential life, and building on Max Weber's notion of disenchantment as a product of capitalist western modernity, Connolly argues that modern secularism fails to provide for individual needs for ethics and reverence. I want to focus in particular on what Connolly terms the "visceral register." Connolly identifies the "visceral register" as a fundamental part of the self which religion can successfully access. It can also animate and sustain a public sphere otherwise relying on reason, morality, and tolerance alone:

> The visceral level of subjectivity and intersubjectivity [. . .] is at once part of thinking, indispensable to more conceptually refined thinking, a periodic spur to creative thinking, and a potential impediment to rethinking. The visceral register, moreover, can be drawn upon to thicken an intersubjective ethos of generous engagement between diverse constituencies or to harden strife between partisans. [. . .] [M]odern secularism [. . .] either ignores this register or disparages it. It does so in the name of a public sphere in which reason, morality, and tolerance flourish. By doing so it forfeits some of the very resources needed to foster a generous pluralism.
>
> (Connolly 1999: 3)

By accessing this visceral subjectivity, religion can inspire followers whose commitment is informed by a deep and multi-dimensional engagement of the self: affective, conceptual—and also literally visceral. The ethics and sense of partisanship—"belonging to a community"—that emerge from this deep engagement of the self are thus almost literally binding. This belonging provides for what Connolly calls an ethical sensibility. This would also be consonant with Ashis Nandy's arguments that secularism in the Indian context is an alienating concept because there are already rich traditions that organize and inform people, both individually (religion as faith) and relationally ("tolerance," according to Nandy), because they operate at the

visceral level. (The flipside of this is that the same visceral, "total" register can fuel religiously-motivated violence.) In Connolly's view, secularism's
insistence on a public sphere governed by reason, morality, and tolerance
fails to acknowledge and incorporate the visceral register which is so essential to an intersubjective ethos, a failure that perpetuates disenchantment
and alienation.

Connolly's first essay in his book *Why I Am Not a Secularist* begins sensationally with his recounting a childhood example of clashing religious beliefs
and how such vivid experiences become literally "burned into [the] brain"
(Connolly 1999: 3). This is the "real," that irreducible register of experience
that then "writes" through the domain of the public and political in order to
produce an intersubjective ethos. It also writes into the domain of literature,
and indeed this is the *real*, the material worldliness that is reflected in the
fiction I discuss, and of course in *this* book itself. This core—that is informed,
for instance, by the "religious"—is certainly present, but it comes to be negotiated, even translated within the space of literature. Connolly similarly hopes
for a "non-theistic faith," one which can provide the need for enchantment,
awe, and wonder, without the politicizing constraints of theistic and religious
faith. He argues:

> Secularism is represented by some of its religious detractors to be a set
> of procedures that eventually drives virtue, morality, and faith out of cul-
> ture. What if that charge is onto something, even in its false reduction of
> secularism to proceduralism, while the authoritative conceptions of vir-
> tue, morality, and faith prominent antisecularists often endorse are too
> stingy, exclusionary, and self-sanctifying? If that were so, the last thing
> needed would be the introduction of another perspective asserting its
> obligation to occupy the authoritative center. *We need, rather, to renegotiate
> relations between interdependent partisans in a world in which no constituency's
> claim to* embody *the authoritative source of public reason is sanctified.*
>
> (Connolly 1999: 7; italics mine)

It is in this sense of avoiding the status of an "authoritative center" that the
postsecular differs from the religious. It is also in this sense that writers'
literary searches and experimentations can dislodge the self-rationalizing
authority created by religion (e.g., "Buddhism," "Christianity," "Hinduism," "Islam," "Judaism," "Sikhism") or national-cultural assemblages (e.g.,
"America," "Canada," "India," "Pakistan," "South Asia," "Sri Lanka," "the
UK," the "west"). And this too in an increasingly interconnected world.

3.0　What Does the "Post" in Postsecularism Mean?

To suggest a term like "postsecular" may connote an unmaking of or attack
upon progressive or Enlightenment thought. But the postsecular is neither a

rejection of nor a substitute for the secular. It does not signal a teleological end of secularism. Rather, it is an intimately *negotiated* term. Crucially, the postsecular does not represent a return to religion, especially not in postcolonial nation-states where the combination of religion and nationalism continues to be explosive and often violent. The postsecular can be a critique of secularism and religion, but it cannot lead us back to the religious, and certainly not to the violence undertaken in the name of religion or secularism. Postsecularism advocates neither a religious, sectarian nation-state nor the espousal of religious belief at the personal level. Even my efforts at clarifying that the postsecular is not a return to the religious is a sign of at least the depth of Enlightenment imagination that valorizes secularism as the sole bearer of rational progress. Peter van der Veer has argued that "the very distinction between religious and secular is a product of the Enlightenment that was used in orientalism to draw a sharp opposition between irrational, religious behaviour of the Oriental and rational secularism, which enabled the westerner to rule the Oriental" (Breckenridge and van der Veer 1993: 39). Given such a framework, the "postsecular" could be read catachrestically—a productive misuse that might connote "return to the religious" but in fact denotes its negotiated relation with the secular.

In addition to the well-known temporal sense of "post" as in "coming after," Robert Young has focused on the term's overlooked spatial dimensions by examining the relation between structuralism and poststructuralism. For Young, given the suggestive visual metaphor of the concept of a structure, "the prefix 'post' now means 'behind', as in 'post-jacent', 'post-scenium', or 'post-oral'. [. . .] So 'post-structuralism' suggests that structuralism itself can only exist as always already inhabited by post-structuralism, which comes both behind and after" (Young 1982: 4). The "behind" inhabitant of the secular can be viewed as the religious, but the "after" of secularism is not simply a return to its "behind." Rather, it is a cumulative, not cyclical, relation. If the spectre of religion always haunts the secular, then the "space" which the secular comes to occupy will always already beg the question of its alternatives.

I would like to flesh out this complex relation between secularism and its post by turning to an example from Indian politics. Specifically, I want to consider the metaphors that appeal to Aamir Mufti in his argument for the links between secularism and religion for the task of nation-building in India. Mufti argues:

> [I]t is the unequivocally religious symbolism and density of Gandhism that allows the simultaneous representation of Indian modernity as the emergence of a "secular" polity, while the securing of a leadership role for the "secular" national elite makes possible the gesture of inclusion towards the culture and morality of rural subaltern life.
>
> (Mufti 1995: 84)

A number of interesting oppositions operate here. The first is between Gandhi and Jawaharlal Nehru, and the respective conceptions of "religion" and "secularism" in their worldviews. Gandhi's thought is anchored in the symbolism of "the spinning of yarn, passive resistance, the *Gita* and *Ramarajya*" (Mufti 1995: 83; italics original). Nehru's thought is driven by the imperative to construct a modern national identity that can unify the "elite"—who will engineer the secular socioeconomic transformation of the postcolonial nation—and the rural subaltern masses, to whose worldview religion is foundational. The opposition here between the secular and the religious can also contain the opposition between the traditional and the modern.

Mufti builds upon Partha Chatterjee's work on the emergence of nationalism as it is negotiated between Nehruvian political rationality and Gandhi's intervention in mass politics. Chatterjee argues that the consequences of Gandhi's intervention, filled with religious symbolism, were "capable of being appropriated" for the nation-building project (Chatterjee 1993: 153). Using this relation of "appropriation," Mufti turns to Fredric Jameson's argument that the central concept-metaphor of cultural studies is derived from Althusser's notion of "articulation." This articulation, in Jameson's words, is

> a kind of turning structure, an ion-exchange between various entities, in which the ideological drives associated with one pass over and interfuse the other—but only provisionally, for a "historically specific moment," before entering into new combinations, being systematically worked over into something else, decaying over time in interminable half-life, or being blasted apart by the convulsions of a new social crisis.
>
> (quoted in Mufti 1995: 83)

Mufti uses this metaphor to illuminate the relation between the religious and the secular. I want to extend this metaphor to the relation between the secular and its post. It is in the senses of "new combinations," "social crisis," and "[interfusing] the other" that the relation between secularism and its post is a *negotiated* one. It is through the closeness and interwovenness of these relations that the postsecular is caught in a double bind between religion and secularism.

In the sense that religious symbolism and secularism can be closely linked for the historically specific task of nation-building, that is an example of their circulation in the postcolonial age as not merely "the other" of each other. Anuradha Needham and Rajeswari Sunder Rajan argue that

> religious debates and conflicts are no longer waged over matters of belief, the true god, salvation, or other substantive issues of faith . . . it is instead religion as the basis of *identity* and identitarian cultural practices—with co-religionists constituting a community, nation, or "civilization"—that comes to be the ground of difference and hence conflict. Secularism is

therefore interrogated for its usefulness in addressing other issues, without reference to religion.

(Needham and Sunder Rajan 2007: 2; italics original)

Needham and Sunder Rajan state that the issues secularism must address in India include those of national unity (the co-existence of different people) and democracy (the protection of minorities). Given that secularism in the postcolonial world has been so central to nation-building, they argue that secularism is "a more comprehensive and diffuse package of ideas, ideals, politics and strategies than its representation solely as religion's 'other'" (Needham and Sunder Rajan 2007: 3). Postsecularism can subsume this deconstruction of the received opposition between the secular and the religious.

4.0　Ondaatje and Rushdie in Context

The literature of Michael Ondaatje and Salman Rushdie forms the major literary focus of this study. Accordingly, in this section I provide some cultural and political context for understanding these writers' literary production. A feature of Ondaatje's and Rushdie's questioning of secularism and religion is their diasporic location. That Ondaatje and Rushdie have both inherited aspects of the various histories, cultures, and religions of South Asia is highly probable. Through an historical and cultural context, they negotiate a sense of their particular understanding of phenomena, developed and exhibited in their fiction through critiques of aspects of their "original" cultural location. That both writers also occupy positions in what broadly might be termed the "west" is well-known. This diasporic location has given them exposure, either directly or indirectly, to Enlightenment values, and to postmodern, avant garde, European deconstructive models and forms of understanding. How might such a double cultural context influence and inform their fiction?

Ondaatje and Rushdie are writing about *real* places—India, Sri Lanka—which are fraught with political and historical difficulties. The politics are not just nationalist, secular, and religious, but also global. The question of geography is thus crucial. These writers embark on processes of affirmational exploration, but they are not always aware of the consequences of such an open-ended questioning, namely, the reception of their work. Although their diasporic location can enable a quest for an understanding of an "other" place, it can also result in political insensitivity to those "other" locations. I identify these conflictual, controversial aspects of their fiction in my analysis of the postsecularism of these novelists.

Ondaatje and Rushdie use their location to make *sense* of other places. Theorizing why Ondaatje's works are set outside Canada, Sam Solecki states that Ondaatje's "imagination needs stories and landscapes that on some deep level mimic his sense of estrangement and displacement in a

way that Canada, with which he is now familiar, can't" (Solecki 2003: 162). Rushdie and Ondaatje must construct these terrains in order to put *themselves* in relation to the other. *The English Patient* is set in Europe at the end of World War II. Ondaatje invokes a time past and a different space in his exploration of nationalism and patriotism during the war, with nationalism emerging as a kind of religion. The novel's characters are transgressive—betrayers, deserters, spies—and thus represent a kind of blasphemy against the religion of nationalism. In *Anil's Ghost*, Ondaatje seeks to represent the civil war in Sri Lanka and questions the pieties of human rights. In *The Satanic Verses*, Rushdie famously questions the ideology of religion itself. Rushdie constructs an other space, which he frames through a dreamscape, the mythic city of Jahilia, named after the term *jahilia* as the period of ignorance preceding Islam.

Ondaatje's fiction prior to *The English Patient* includes *Coming Through Slaughter* (1976), about the life of a jazz musician; *Running in the Family* (1982), about his own family; and *In the Skin of a Lion* (1987), a story of immigrant labourers in Toronto. Each of these works is about the "local," situated mostly in a single location. Similarly, Rushdie's novels before *The Satanic Verses—Midnight's Children* (1981) and *Shame* (1983)—are about the native region, the nation. *Midnight's Children* and *Shame* deal, respectively, with India and Pakistan. It is with *The English Patient* and *The Satanic Verses* that Ondaatje's and Rushdie's explorations become most ambitious, reflected in the transnational scope of these novels.

Having spent their youth in Sri Lanka and India respectively, Ondaatje and Rushdie likely will have carried with them at least some sense of secularism's aspirations in the South Asian context. This is not to suggest that Ondaatje and Rushdie are entirely attuned to the complex debates surrounding secularism in South Asia; because they are situated diasporically, they cannot access the day-to-day life of secularism's reifications, contestations, hegemonies, and circulations in the region. In a 2005 article entitled "The Trouble With Religion," Rushdie states:

> I never thought of myself as a writer about religion until a religion came after me. Religion was a part of my subject, of course—for a novelist from the Indian subcontinent, how could it not have been? [. . .] [W]hen the attack came, I had to confront what was confronting me, and to decide what I wanted to stand up for in the face of what so vociferously, repressively and violently stood against me. [. . .] [R]eligions continue to insist that they provide special access to ethical truths, and consequently deserve special treatment and protection. And they continue to emerge from the world of private life—where they belong [. . .]—and to bid for power. The emergence of radical Islam needs no redescription here, but the resurgence of faith is a larger subject than that.
>
> (Rushdie 2005)

Thus, for Rushdie the secular comes to be "internationalized," a concept and a politics that is doubly informed by its inflections in South Asia (religion's importance and massive reach in India) and the west (religion as part of the private sphere).

The space that Ondaatje and Rushdie diasporically, constitutively inhabit is one that is not just "secular." Their fiction can be seen to challenge notions of a "secular" west by venturing into those borderline areas that question received orthodoxies. And their diasporic location allows them to challenge the binary oppositions of majority-minority and religious-secular, and the complicities between the two binaries. Ondaatje and Rushdie, interestingly, occupy both the majority and the minority in the west; they are ethnically visible minorities but, in the forces of globalization, also inhabit the majoritarian western "secularism." How can Ondaatje and Rushdie be expected to respond to this global influence? In the postcolonial age, migration and movement have become the defining features of a globalized world. Gauri Viswanathan has argued that conversion of religious identity involves a migration not unlike that of border-crossing (Viswanathan 1998: 244). The value of such an understanding for a postcolonial context is immense. It draws attention to the potential of a religious inflection of the already heavily-theorized process of migration. This is not to suggest, however, that any act of migration will have a religious dimension. Rather, the reverse: the embracing of a religious identity can critically involve a movement not unlike that of border-crossing migration.

This notion of movement invites compelling ideas on the role of diasporic situatedness in postsecular affirmations. Viswanathan has also argued that blasphemy might be punished by the blasphemer's transgressing infinitely through consignment to permanent exile. In this sense, the diasporic citizen, in the permanence and fixity of his or her location, also represents, paradoxically, an infinity of motion (Viswanathan 1998: 244). I am extending Viswanathan's metaphoric figuration of transgression—infinity of one action parallels permanence of one location—in order to suggest that diaspora can constitute a form of removal from the home country. This does not necessarily assume that "country" can be located in a fixed geographical place. What it suggests is that the motion and the distancing will produce a specularity of otherness, "seeing" Sri Lanka, "seeing" India from a distance. Thus Sri Lanka becomes other, and India too becomes other. Such a removal can become a condition of possibility for affirming the "home" nation, for affirmational insights *into* it. As Jean-Luc Nancy states, "I suspect that one would need to move away, to find a place at some remove in order to say of the gods that they are the gods" (quoted in Viswanathan 1998: 244). Diaspora, of course, can produce the positive of nostalgia and the negative of insensitivity. Both processes assume one motion: specular otherness, a re-cognition.

Ondaatje's and Rushdie's texts are suffused with such movement: Almásy into the asceticism of the desert; Palipana into the asceticism of his forest grove; Saladin and Gibreel toward England, and Mahound into the desert. Almásy discovers his own form of God in the desert, as I shall demonstrate in Chapter 1 on *The English Patient*. In *Anil's Ghost*, the young girl Lakma's faith in people is restored in the special space that is Palipana's "grove of ascetics." In *The Satanic Verses*, migrating to England and a fantastic journey through the demonic allows Saladin to re-embrace Islam, his father, and India. That Islam is uniquely Saladin's. It is a postcolonial Islam, similar to a mystical Sufism or the Hindu *Bhakti* movement, emphasizing the devotional, personal elements of faith rather than conventional rituals or uncritical acceptance of religion's self-rationalizations.

In addition to such spatial negotiation, we can also *historicize* Ondaatje and Rushdie by considering their fiction as it is appears on the international scene of the 1980s and 1990s: globalization, increased western attention toward Islam (which Rushdie inadvertently catalyzes), postmodernism, and postcolonialism. *The Satanic Verses* (1988) and *The English Patient* (1992) enter onto the "global scene" in the same late capitalistic conjuncture as Fredric Jameson's article "Postmodernism, or the Cultural Logic of Late Capitalism," published in 1984. Jameson theorizes how the new historical subjects of transnational capitalism could imagine the large moment of cultural globality and new internationalism that they inhabit (as they are produced by the decentering of global capital). This leads Jameson to postulate that in order to perceive the global unrepresentable requires us "to grow new organs, to expand our sensorium and our body to some new, as yet unimaginable, perhaps ultimately impossible, dimensions" (Jameson 1984: 80).

Homi Bhabha, as much as Jameson, works this conjuncture theoretically, as the postcolonial theorist appearing alongside the postmodernist. Bhabha challenges Jameson's "dialectical" reading by proposing a "third space": "The non-synchronous temporality of global and national cultures opens up a cultural space—a third space—where the negotiation of incommensurable differences creates a tension peculiar to borderline existences" (Bhabha 1994: 218). In addition to postulating a "third space," Bhabha introduces a temporal dimension, as a critique of Jameson's spatially-driven analytic. Bhabha elaborates the notion of a "borderline" existence by speaking of the disintegrations, splittings, and displacements that occur at such a location:

> What must be mapped as a new international space of discontinuous historical realities is [. . .] the problem of signifying the interstitial passages and processes of cultural difference that are inscribed in the "in-between", in the temporal break-up that weaves the "global" text. It is, ironically, the disintegrative moment, even movement, of enunciation— that sudden disjunction of the present—that makes possible the rendering of culture's global reach. And, paradoxically, it is only through a structure of splitting and displacement [. . .] that the [. . .] new historical subject emerges at the limits of representation itself.
>
> (Bhabha 1994: 217)

The "limits of representation" of which Bhabha writes are ones with which Rushdie and Ondaatje experiment in their novels. Crises—violence, war, disaster—make Rushdie and Ondaatje acutely aware of the limits of their capacity to represent that which remains so resistant to representation. The shape-shiftings of Gibreel and Saladin, and the shape-shifting of literary form, constitute the splitting and displacement in *The Satanic Verses*, activities and movements that paradoxically allow for a "new" postsecular "faith" to emerge at the limits of Islam, the political, ideological Islam of which Rushdie is so critical. The "third space" in Bhabha's formulation stands as that unrepresentable and uncontainable presence—a sort of sublime—that can at best be gestured toward, but which in its creativity allows for the emergence of new forms. This becomes similar to Rushdie's postsecular "faith," that which allows for the emergence of "magically real" forms, ones that I examine in Chapter 5 on *The Satanic Verses*, showing how such forms might gesture toward a *postsecular magical realism*. For Ondaatje, it is postsecular "faith" that allows both Almásy and Ondaatje to attend "religiously" to describing the desert: Almásy with an awareness of the desert as his lover, Ondaatje with an awareness of writing as his craft, devoting seven continuous paragraphs to describing the desert.

It is within the disjunctures and schizophrenia of identity that the "global" text can be woven. This global text can include and reflect not just cultural dislocation, but also religious dislocation. Islam, for example, is for Rushdie always already an issue of culture, and he wishes to show the religion's *range* of cultural expressions, a commitment which in itself can be blasphemous. The problem of faith is that it resists representation, as much as it resists categorization within rational, conventional terms; in this it is like violence, terror, the desert. Ondaatje in *The English Patient* thematizes such disjunctures of representation through the novel's structure, constructed by Ondaatje as a series of flashbacks. The villa in Italy is itself ruined, destroyed. The interstitiality of the entire moment and set-up allows Ondaatje to affirm the "global" reach of the aesthetic and of affect (friendship, love, community). "Global" here is that which stretches across nation and ethnicity. It is this disjuncture that, ironically, becomes the condition of the possibility of the postnational. The postnational thus stands as that newness resulting from the splitting and displacement of the national self.

Rushdie's binaries are blatant: postmodernist, schizophrenic Gibreel and modernist, home-returning Saladin. The text bursts with "representational visibility," and it relentlessly, irrepressibly pursues the unrepresentable. What is an idea? What is newness? What is faith? *How do they each emerge?* By pursuing such important questions, the text disrupts the easy binary of one and the other—history vs. future, self vs. other, faith vs. disbelief, angelic vs. demonic, native vs. foreigner—and instead situates itself in the in-between. Homi Bhabha rightly observes that

The Satanic Verses has been mainly represented in spatial terms and binary geopolitical polarities—Islamic fundamentalism vs. Western literary modernists, the quarrel of the ancient (ascriptive) migrants and modern (ironic) metropolitans. This obscures the anxiety of the irresolvable, borderline culture of hybridity that articulates its problems of identification and its diasporic aesthetic in an uncanny, disjunctive temporality that is, at once, the *time* of cultural displacement, and the *space* of the "untranslatable."

(Bhabha 1994: 225; italics original)

Bhabha's theorization of the "untranslatable" and the "uncanny" interestingly gestures to a non-discursive space—or, following Bhabha's rhetorical terms, let us call it "spacetime"—where there might reside, if we push this theorization to its logical limit, the generative presence of the postsecular. Bhabha's spacetime of the uncanny can be the engine producing the newness which so fascinates Rushdie. Maurice Blanchot, in *The Writing of the Disaster*, states, "[t]he new, because it cannot take place in history, is also that which is most ancient: an unhistorical occurrence to which we are called upon to answer as if it were the impossible, the invisible—that which has always long since disappeared beneath *ruins*" (Blanchot 1986: 37). Blanchot's "new"—like Bhabha's untranslatable and in-between—is outside of spacetime, that generative engine which can produce a newness from a kind of negativity: in sum, disaster.

If for Dipesh Chakrabarty ghosts and spirits are signs of a religious faith, and thus raise challenges to their representation by historians, then we can say that Ondaatje and Rushdie face a similar challenge of representation in their struggle with finding forms of belief that are in part *other* to secularism. The interesting case for Ondaatje and Rushdie is that they must simultaneously try to understand such a "secular belief" and also endeavour at *representing* such belief. Such a process, of course, also occurs in a public forum, the international arena of literary production, so that any subsequent statements by Rushdie that people did not actually read *The Satanic Verses* or understand its subtleties could be seen as naive. Rushdie's explorations might be highly individualistic processes, but the objective novel that results from them is *other* to him, circulating in the public domain and therefore outside his control.

In his essay "Is Nothing Sacred?," stemming from a lecture he prepared in 1990, a year after the Ayatollah Khomeini issued the death sentence, Rushdie clarifies that *The Satanic Verses* is not anti-religious. He states that "the idea of god is at once a repository for our awestruck wonderment at life and an answer to the great questions of existence, and a rule book, too. The soul needs all these explanations—not simply rational explanations, but explanations of the heart" (Rushdie 1991: 421).[2] In an essay from the same year, "In Good Faith," seen as Rushdie's extended apology following the *fatwa*, Rushdie echoes William Connolly's notion of a non-theistic faith: "I believe in no god [. . .]. I have spiritual needs, and my work has, I hope, a moral and spiritual dimension, but I am content to try and satisfy those needs without recourse to any idea of a Prime Mover or ultimate arbiter" (Rushdie 1991: 405). He is keen to highlight in the same essay that believing in secularism requires just as great a courage and rigor as a life lived with religious faith, calling upon religious believers to show respect, not contempt, for secularism. He ends the essay on a note of humility: "Our lives teach us who we are" (Rushdie 1991: 414).

As demonstrated by Rushdie's 2005 article "The Trouble With Religion" ("I never thought of myself as a writer about religion until a religion came after me"), after the *fatwa*, Rushdie's secularism becomes hardened. He resists religion's claims to be an authoritative centre ("special truths," "bid for power") and is particularly anxious about religion's fundamentalist manifestations ("radical Islam"). So where Rushdie previously spoke of a kind of "faith," he now speaks of "religion." Rushdie clearly seeks some sort of faith or enchantment, particularly when he states above that he hopes his work has a moral and spiritual dimension, but without the political and epistemological constraints of conventional religious thought and practice. This is where we can read him through the conceptual lens of postsecularism, that which captures his negotiated position between the political secularism he inherited from his Indian background and the ideology of secularism that surrounds him in the UK and the US. Arthur Bradley and Andrew Tate argue that Rushdie's novels from *The Satanic Verses* onward demonstrate his "faith in fiction as a free imaginative space" (Bradley and Tate 2010: 14). For Bradley and Tate, such faith in fiction is in contrast to Rushdie's resistance to religion, as evidenced in part by his support of the work of the atheist Christopher Hitchens, leading Bradley and Tate to categorize Rushdie as "new atheist." Although I would agree that Rushdie is skeptical of religion, "postsecular" encompasses not only a form of "faith," but also includes Rushdie's working through the dissatisfactions of Indian secularism, in addition to western secularism as exemplified by Hitchens.

Where Rushdie is skeptical about "religion," Ondaatje wishes to avoid the hegemonies and metanarratives of such encompassing terms as the "political." Instead, his too is a process of individual discovery and exploration, a working toward some values. In a 2000 interview about *Anil's Ghost*, Ondaatje's comments demonstrate the force of personal exploration that drives his work. Writing is a vocation for him, a commitment to discovering values: "it has to be somehow connected with the story, but everything you know about passion or politics or love or truth—all those things—somehow must go in that book" (Welch 2000). The values that Ondaatje explores are not just personal, but are also reflected in the form of his writing, in his experimentation with new techniques. He has stated that although *Anil's Ghost* might share certain similarities with *The English Patient*, the novel feels new to him, with a new vocabulary and pace reflecting his dedication to writing the novel in an innovative way, to challenge himself, to debate with himself (Welch 2000). This innovation and questioning are in part enabled for Ondaatje by the characters that he creates, such as when they explore and debate the many faces of truth, whether political, historical, moral, or otherwise (Welch 2000).

As another example of interrogating religion and its symbols from a diasporic situatedness, we can consider Derek Walcott's insights into an open-air staging in Trinidad of the *Ramleela*, the dramatization of the Hindu epic the *Ramayana*. Whereas I have argued that a diasporic situation can lead to sentimentalization, Walcott's views on the diasporic appropriation of religious symbols offer another perspective. Looking at the colourful costumes and large-scale props, Walcott had first understood the enactment in terms "of elegy, of loss, even of degenerative mimicry, [a] desperate resignation with preserving a culture" (Walcott 1992). But he was also able, eventually, to see within the spectacular assemblage the intense faith informing the actors, who saw themselves as believers (not "amateur actors"), ones who believed in the sacredness of the text, so that their artistic performance was a way of affirming their belief, in both the text and their vocation. In sum, theirs was "a delight in conviction, not loss" (Walcott 1992).[3] That conviction was purely in reference to itself, and not defined in relation to or yearning for the "home" nation (India), or in the stereotypical terms through which the Caribbean is imagined: "illegitimate, rootless, mongrelized" (Walcott 1992). Walcott concludes: "We make too much of that groan ["the sigh of History"] which underlines the past" (Walcott 1992).

For Walcott, the aesthetic celebration he notices and is keen to affirm can be an affirmation of faith and conviction not necessarily tied to the history of the home nation and its struggles. Although such affirmation can also devolve into sentimentality, Walcott emphasizes the self-referential religious faith behind such aesthetics. One way of imagining this dual view of the performance—is it reactive and tragic mimicry, or is it creative conviction?—is as a palimpsest: the past is present, but so is the present. I will pursue this idea of the palimpsest in Chapter 3 in my reading of Ondaatje's reconstruction of the Buddha statue in the closing scene of *Anil's Ghost*. The statue can be seen through the layer of religious and ethnic majoritarianism, but it can also be seen to contain the layer of emergent positives: peace, hope, regeneration. Walcott's observation raises interesting possibilities. Can *religious* faith in the "diasporic postcolony" be affirmed, however aesthetically, in ways that do not depend on the original national expression of that religion, and which do not reproduce the political ideologies of such nationalism?

5.0   The Work of Secularism

This book joins a number of studies that have approached the issue of secularism in South Asia from various angles, including its literary representations.[4] By way of redressing the secular-religious divide, Rajeev Bhargava has called for a "spiritualized, humanist" secularism (Bhargava 1995: 341). Rajeswari Sunder Rajan and Anuradha Needham, in their introduction to *The Crises of Indian Secularism*, point to the existence of indigenous traditions other to secularism as a state doctrine, traditions which can provide both a form of tolerance and an inspiring ethics. They term this an "indigenous secularism," examples of which include "traditions of popular tolerance, rationalism, secular humanism, and attitudes skeptical and ironic about religion, which are not reducible to the forms of elite or cosmopolitan secularism that are routinely attributed to the influence of Nehru and/or a deracinated modernity" (Needham and Sunder Rajan 2007: 21). They offer the following examples of secular people and practices: Buddhism, Kabir, Akbar's Din-ilahi, Dara Sikoh, Ram Mohan Roy and Brahmo Samaj (reformist Hinduism), Ambedkar and Periyar (Needham and Sunder Rajan 2007: 21). In Chapter 6, focusing on Rushdie's novels after *The Satanic Verses*, I discuss the secularism of Akbar's Din-ilahi as an instance of Indian, and not western, secularism. Needham and Sunder Rajan refer above to Buddhism as broadly "secular" in spirit. Ondaatje's location in Canada could help him perceive those more "secular" elements of Buddhism, but the political manifestation of Buddhism within Sri Lanka is another matter: it is in this dangerous tension between the secular and the political that Ondaatje can imagine a postsecular Buddhism. In Chapter 4, I examine how exactly he pursues this postsecularism.

Arguing that it is not only subaltern sentimentalism that can imagine a "counter-religious strain," Needham and Sunder Rajan refer to the poet Arun Kolatkar, whose work "signals the resonance of a skepticism that is marked with compassion and even what we might call, paradoxically, faith" (Needham and Sunder Rajan 2007: 22). Sunder Rajan and Needham state the case succinctly, by indicating the need to link a secularism that emerges indigenously from Indian intellectual traditions with an official secularism that must operate at the level of political ideology. In this "work of the secular," in the sense of *making* it work (secularism as object), and also the work that it must *undertake* (as subject), the space of literature can be an imaginative space in which these different workings can unfold. The secular can be experimented with, interrogated, and equally triumphed or lamented.

The dual, even multiple, senses of the secular—political and philosophical, across South Asia and the west—will thus inform my engagement with the literary fiction in the pages that follow. Given their awareness of the violence, inequalities, and injustices pursued in the name of religion, nation, and secularism, the postsecularism that these writers pursue is deconstructive, self-conscious of its tenuous status. As Sam Solecki has argued with respect to Ondaatje's fiction, "Life in [Ondaatje's] world is tentative, anxious, and always menaced by the possibility of disaster. Even moments of stability, order, and happiness are presented with reminders of their opposites and are therefore marked by ambiguity and ambivalence" (Solecki 2003: 136). It is this sense of the fragility of life that also marks the fragility of the postsecular search.

Figure 3 Cathedral of Santa Maria Assunta, Siena, Italy. Photograph by the author.

1 Postsecularism and Nation
Michael Ondaatje's *The English Patient*

Is it possible to think beyond the nation? For a category that has been so central to colonialism and postcolonialism, and so consequential over countless lives—and deaths—around the world, what would a *literary* exploration of the limits of nation look like? *The English Patient* is set at the end of World War II in 1945, in Italy. A destroyed villa could exist anywhere, but this is no isolated precipice or free-floating transit camp. Ondaatje situates the villa at the *end* of the war, to see what comes in the wake of the collapse of nationalism. He is skeptical of nation and nationalism, and uses the extreme nationalism of Nazism as a metonym for nationalism. It is not that *nation* in and of itself is necessarily problematic—but *nationalism* can be. At the end of the novel, India has a certain attractiveness for Kip, giving him a sense of home, nostalgia, and belonging. But even this sense of the nation emerges contrastively in the novel, as a succour to the war that culminates in the bombing of Hiroshima and Nagasaki. The problem with Nazism was the hate and violence spread by its virulent nationalism. In this novel, Nazism is not simply a synonym for German nationalism; instead, it represents *an* extreme nationalism. And that extreme nationalism is manifest in Nazism to such a degree that it can mimic a virulent religious fundamentalism. Nation is supposed to be a secular construct, not a doctrine or expression of religious thought. Yet, if the nation can produce an extreme nationalism, how is that not unlike the fundamentalism and pieties of a religion—commanding absolute, undoubting assent? Is *postsecular* then the name for that which comes after the nation and nationalism? Is the postsecular a form of the postnational? Does the European Union represent the collapse of nationalism? What about the collapse of the USSR, which occurred around the time when Ondaatje was writing and researching *The English Patient* in the late 1980s and early 1990s?

Even as critics of *The English Patient* have celebrated Ondaatje's postnational vision, postnationalism itself demonstrates how deeply buried the idea of nation remains within the novel.[1] This chapter departs from such criticism by reading the postnational through the questions of the postsecular, and on the premise that even the concept of "postnation" as a method of thinking beyond the nation (and the nationalism to which it can lead) is inadequate, for it simply reproduces the logic of nation. This is similar to Qadri Ismail's argument, building upon the work of Partha Chatterjee and Dipesh Chakrabarty, that anti-colonial nationalism in *The English Patient*—symbolized by the Indian nationalism of Kip's brother—occurs reactively within the Eurocentric logic of the "nation" (Ismail 1999: 428). Any true difference would have to be manifest at least at the epistemological level. This is where the postnational can link with the postsecular.

Where organized religion has failed, virulent nationalism can emerge in its wake, demanding, not unlike religious-based fundamentalism, a devotedness, following, dedication, and loyalty to its organizing principles. So if nation is the new secular religion—an overarching ideology in which people have faith in the nation as a source, as the case might be, of identity, relevance, power, meaning, strength, superiority, or significance—then the postsecular negotiation with religion will also be a questioning of nation. Stathis Gourgouris has argued:

> If indeed secularization takes at one point a normative track (whereby the law of God becomes automatically reconfigured to Law as such—Law *as* God, one might say) and therefore secularism emerges as a new metaphysics, the response is surely not to subscribe to an allegedly liberational space of "native-religious" sentiment suppressed by colonial or imperial power but, rather, to unpeel the layers of normativity from secularist assumptions and reconceptualize the domain of the secular.
>
> (Gourgouris 2008: 440; italics original)

Gourgouris's call for detranscendentalizing the secular can be translated in this chapter and *through* this novel as detranscendentalizing the nation. In the case of virulent nationalism, the law *does* act as God, commanding absolute belief from its followers.

I argue that Ondaatje uses *The English Patient* to imagine forms of identity and belonging that might exist as alternatives to the nation, especially when nation can lead to violent nationalism. But Ondaatje's imagination does not simply replace nation with something else. Instead, *The English Patient* is *experimental* in ways. It is the oscillation between nation and its others that explores the *possibility* of those others. Here is where Ondaatje's diasporic situatedness becomes significant, given his distance from both Sri Lanka and the majority communities in Canada, realities which allow him to experiment with nation. The liberal space of Canadian multiculturalism and Ondaatje's situatedness as a minority there also informs his imagining of difference from nation and nationalism. In a sense, with this novel Ondaatje has preceded contemporary debates about secularism, given the challenges to the *secular* nation-state, across South Asia and the west. I want to use *The English Patient* as a foil for other novels in this book, particularly because this is the only novel I examine which is not set, either directly or diasporically, within South Asia. For example, both Ondaatje in *The English Patient* and Mahasweta Devi in "Pterodactyl, Puran Sahay, and Pirtha" depict the setting of a cave. I pursue the implications of this usage in Chapter 7.

How does the secular operate in *The English Patient*? Almásy is "secular" in Edward Said's sense of the term. For Said, secular criticism meant a resistance to the supposed authority of disinterested truth, a commitment to unpacking the ideological agendas behind such apparently neutral positions. Said was resistant to the ideology of the group, including the tribalistic solidarity of "pure" communities that are homogenously, ethnically, and geographically defined. Secular criticism also resists, in Said's words, "quasi-religious quietism; nationalism; any grounding of intellectual mission and activity" (Said 1984: 11). Instead, it positions itself as a critique of "the entire matrix of meanings we associate with 'home,' belonging and community" (Said 1984: 11). Bruce Robbins has argued that Said's notion of secular criticism stands in opposition not so much to religion as to nationalism, quoting Said's skepticism toward nation: "The dense fabric of secular life [. . .] can't be herded under the rubric of national identity or can't be made entirely to respond to this phony idea of a paranoid frontier separating 'us' from 'them'" (quoted in Robbins 1994: 27).

In this Saidian sense, *The English Patient* is insistently secular, by not being attached to any one nation, taking within its purview Italy, Canada, India, and the countries of northern Africa, a cosmopolitanism informed no doubt by Ondaatje's diasporic situatedness. The postsecular space that emerges for both Almásy and Ondaatje is one that is not "post" to Said's sense of secular. But it is post to the sense of nation as religion, to the *religion of nationalism*. Nationalism allows for an affiliative relation among peoples, expressed in the deceptively ordinary phrase "national affiliation." I view the phrase as "deceptive" because I am thinking here of Said's idea of affiliation as "the transition from a failed idea or possibility of filiation to a kind of compensatory order that, whether it is a party, an institution, a culture, a set of beliefs, or even a world-vision, provides men and women with a new form of relationship [. . .] a new system" (Said 1984: 19). Such compensatory affiliative relations can produce orthodoxies of their own kind, demonstrating the potential for virulence contained within nationalism. Said asks: "What does it mean to have a critical consciousness if [. . .] the intellectual's situation is a worldly one and yet, by virtue of that worldliness itself, the intellectual's social identity should involve something more than strengthening those aspects of culture that require mere affirmation and orthodox compliancy from its members?" (Said 1984: 24).

In place of nationalism's orthodoxies, the heterodoxy that emerges in *The English Patient* includes the postsecular values of love, friendship, and community—and of *dharma*, exemplified in the novel by the characters' commitment to their respective vocations. If Ondaatje's gaze in *The English Patient*, as compared to his previous novels, has become transnational, this move "beyond nation" is reflected in his choice of setting, the North African desert. Through the trope and setting of the desert, Ondaatje is able to reflect on the nature of nation, in the process gesturing to that which might stand outside its domain.

Ondaatje uses the idioms of affect and love to allow for intercultural friendship, even romance, that can move beyond nation. He invokes the space of the aesthetic in order to affirm such forms of affective community. In the process, what Ondaatje also affirms is the aesthetic *itself*, as a framing device and as a cognitive device, one that gives insight and perspective into a relation. The domain of affect is highlighted through friendships and the various fractured identities that transcend nationalities; the aesthetic field for its part is reflected in the aestheticized descriptions of landscape, the desert, and the interior of buildings. The aestheticized descriptions act as important forces of cognition that are not just event-oriented but also processual, giving insight based on secular, lived experience. The visual expansiveness of the desert is the visual expansiveness of the Christian tableaus: that *filling* of the field of vision *is* enchantment.

Extending the concept of community, what is important is that the relations among the characters in the novel are made possible in spite of their national differences. Each of the four central characters—Almásy, Caravaggio, Hana, Kip—is dislocated, and the desert becomes the agent of their dislocation. When at the beginning of the novel Almásy is blindfolded and forced to identify military weapons for the desert tribe that has rescued him, he recalls his childhood card games, a world in which he was not blindfolded, a "fully named world" (Ondaatje 1992: 21).[2] The desert represents the dissolution of names, the blindfold a metaphor for the collapse of identities and constructs—nation among them—secured through a named and categorized world. Following his time in the desert, Almásy urges for the erasure of family names, nations, and the clothing of countries (139). Almásy's initial unrecognizability—nameless, his body burned—parallels the absence of a nationality; Almásy becomes labeled by the German officers as "English" based on his accent.

Ondaatje understands well such nationalizing construction, given his diasporic location in Canada, as demonstrated in this statement in a 1996 interview: "I don't think we're in an age now where the influences on us have simply to do with the country we're born in or grew up in. Certainly the mongrel influences from other parts of the world and other art forms have influenced me" (Presson 1996: 90). Two years earlier, Ondaatje had stated that he is "a great believer in the mongrel" (Bush 1994: 254). In another interview in the same year, he stated: "The characters in *The English Patient*, especially the Patient and Kirpal Singh, are displaced or, as one of them says, 'international bastards.' [. . .] Those migrants don't belong here but want to belong here and find a new home" (Wachtel 1994: 255). Although Ondaatje acknowledges the cosmopolitan influences on his art and on the displacement of the characters in *The English Patient*, he states that his characters' quest is for a sense of belonging and a new home. This might be informed by Ondaatje's own diasporic situatedness. It is also the thread of faith and hope that runs throughout the novel, and that manifests, tenuously, in the form of the friendship and community that establishes itself in the villa. What is significant is the effort at *gesturing* toward some belonging, however temporary, in place of a merely reactionary disavowal of nationalism. Though each of the characters will at the end of the novel part ways (including through death), the villa functions for them as a "non-home home," a special marked space, a temporary moment.

This chapter has five sections. In the opening section, "The Desert," I explore how the desert represents a tabula rasa, a utopic place of possibility, however precarious; the body without organs represents a possibly new beginning, away from the historical ideologies of skin colour and race. In the section "The Politics of Friendship and the Problem of Nation," I consider the role of the villa and the notion of community that it enables. In "Brown Mythologies," I focus on Kip's and Hana's romance and how it might affirm the potential of affiliation across nation and race. Then, in "Aestheticization," I argue that aesthetic representation *secularizes* religion: it empties objects of their religious "content" and focuses instead on their beautiful elements. That stroke of aestheticization *affiliates* different religious traditions, in particular Christianity and Sikhism, with one another. As a result, Ondaatje admires both Christian tableaus and the Golden Temple for their aesthetic beauty, with the aesthetic emerging as that new "universal." In the final section, "Four Bombs," I present in detail a neglected historical influence on *The English Patient*: the greatest act of mass murder to-date in Canadian history, the bombing of Air India Flight 182 by Canadian Sikhs in 1985.

1.1 The Desert

By invoking desert as place, Ondaatje allows for a contrast between nation as easily mappable and with boundaries, and the desert as that which stands outside nation, where "it is easy to lose a sense of demarcation" (18). The desert becomes for Almásy a place of renewal and regeneration, away from the constructs and ideologies of nation. Ondaatje represents the desert as a space of escape, a kind of utopia that is empty of time and space, becoming for Almásy a substitute for religion. One of Almásy's flashbacks:

> May God make safety your companion, Madox had said. Good-bye. A wave. There is God only in the desert, he wanted to acknowledge that now. Outside of this there was just trade and power, money and war. Financial and military despots shaped the world.
>
> (250)

Almásy believes in the desert as a place where he has the freedom to contemplate nation and religion. He gains insight and knowledge only after the struggles and challenges of his life in the war—with its trade, power, money—and his life in the desert, which gives him some sense of belief away from his earlier skepticism.

In the context of an older Almásy's soliloquies to a younger Hana, he attains a guru-like status as he reminisces about his time in the desert. Almásy reads to Hana a passage from desert explorer Hassanein Bey's 1924 article "Through Kufra to Darfur." Bey lavishly describes a sandstorm in the desert, as though it were *"underlaid with steam-pipes* [. . .]. [. . .] *[A]s though the whole surface of the desert were rising in obedience to some upthrusting force beneath"* (137; italics original). The dynamic tropes, reinforced by Ondaatje's italicization of the entire passage, make this an unsurprising choice. In this next passage, he admires the desert as resisting any fixed human naming:

> The desert could not be claimed or owned—it was a piece of cloth carried by winds, never held down by stones, and given a hundred shifting names long before Canterbury existed, long before battles and treaties quilted Europe and the East.
>
> (138)

David Whetter has argued that the desert functions as a character and as an "unfinished companion" that encourages a "communal identity" (Whetter 1997: 446). By "unfinished companion," I would argue that Whetter senses the plenitude offered by a companion that is always "open"—in the desert's case, always open to the literal arrival of others, always already prepared to host them. The desert especially resists "nation":

> All of us, even those with European homes and children in the distance, wished to remove the clothing of our countries. *It was a place of faith.* We disappeared into landscape. [. . .] Erase the family name! Erase nations! I was taught such things by the desert. [. . .] I wanted to erase my name and the place I had come from. By the time the war arrived, after ten years in the desert, it was easy for me to slip across borders, not to belong to anyone, to any nation.
>
> (139; italics mine)

Why is Almásy so resistant to nation? He has seen its violent effect on his friend Madox, who commits suicide after hearing a pro-war sermon: "Yes, Madox was a man who died because of nations" (242). Almásy observes the artificialness and violence of mapping and geography, as practices of the nation:

> On one side servants and slaves and tides of power and correspondence with the Geographical Society. On the other the first step by a white man across a great river, the first sight (by a white eye) of a mountain that has been there forever.
>
> (141)

Ondaatje strongly develops the binary between an institutional colonial apparatus—servants, slaves, correspondence, Societies—and its literal parallel on the other side, on the ground. The contrast between the two is sharpened by the proliferation of sibilants in the first sentence, whereas Ondaatje consolidates the sense of the second sentence through the repetition of "first" and "white." The concluding word "forever" is enough to subvert the religiosity of national, colonial institutions and their "tides of power." This idea of the desert is reminiscent of Percy Shelley's sonnet "Ozymandias" (1818) and its image of the ruined statue of a once-mighty king, another tide of power having succumbed to the natural power of the desert.

Ondaatje is careful to demonstrate that the absence of nationality does not mean "lack," as in the following line: "A man in a desert can hold absence in his cupped hands knowing it is something that feeds him more than water" (155). Moreover, "absence" can be the site for the emergence of something new and creative, a possible sensibility and affect outside nation. Here is a passage illustrating the creativity of absence:

> It was as if he [Almásy] had walked under the millimeter of haze just above the inked fibres of a map, that pure zone between land and chart between distances and legend between nature and storyteller. [. . .] The place they had chosen to come to, to be their best selves, to be unconscious of ancestry. Here [. . .] he was alone, his own invention. He knew during these times how the mirage worked, the fata morgana, for he was within it.
>
> (246)

Ondaatje has connected the gap between signifier (map, chart, legend) and signified (land, distances, nature) with agency. Pure creativity can be born in this mirage, the ability to invent oneself as one wishes, free from the control of ancestry and history. By placing such a self-affirming recollection toward the end of the novel, Ondaatje heightens its affirmative quality. Ondaatje's Almásy is a subject affirmed and empowered by knowledge of this space between signifier and signified, a subject of "his own invention" who can refuse and paradoxically "escape" from the terms represented to him (signifier/signified) by imagining himself to be *within* the space between those terms. Such invention becomes especially significant in contrast with the "English patient" whose history is unknown and unmastered. The label "English," designating a nationality to the anonymous man, could represent a failure of invention—even *colonial* invention—in that it misses the mark of who Almásy knows *himself* to be. Qadri Ismail has argued that part of *The English Patient*'s postcolonial intervention is that it challenges the very idea of disciplinarity, such as the disciplines of "history" and even "literature":

[D]isciplinarity is premised on a relation of the subject to its object homologous to that predicated about empiricism by Althusser: both understand the object as possessing evidence; methodologically, they are about the recovery of this evidence from the object; about the discovery of knowledge "in its most literal sense [. . .] removing the covering" (p. 37). And discovery, of course, is how colonialism troped itself.

(Ismail 1999: 433)

Compare Ismail's idea of "discovery" with Ondaatje's description above of the sight of a mountain by a (white) eye, and how that act of seeing can differ from the great tides of institutional power as expressed in the Geographical Society. To want to *become* the fata morgana is to reject not only the distinction between, but the very concepts of, subject and object, with the former as the master of the latter, which must be disciplined into a "discipline."

When Almásy states that the desert is "a place of faith" (139), we can examine how such an affirmation is made possible within the space of interstice and absence by considering the views of negative, or apophatic, theology. Joseph Zornado explains:

Apophatic thought provides a kind of key to those moments of silence, not that we might fill them in but rather that we might more fully experience the gaps between vehicle and tenor, between signifier and signified, as a silence [. . .].

(Zornado 1992: 119)

The desert represents a substantiation of the gap between vehicle and tenor, between signifier and signified, a "no man's land" which precedes and stands outside signification and territories. Such a semiotic and philosophical status is similar to apophatic theology's concept of the "mystery" that lies beyond signification:

Apophatic theology, like poststructural notions of text, demonstrates a radical skepticism regarding metaphor, and it holds that any truth claims relying on metaphor as a vehicle are, at best, provisional. The reader looking for truth [. . .] should not confuse metaphor, iconography, symbolism, liturgy, and the like with the ineffable mystery they attempt to signify.

(Zornado 1992: 118)

The difficulty in signification expressed by this passage is one which Ondaatje also faces at both the thematic and aesthetic levels.

Almásy becomes resistant to forms of identity or description that are misleading and false. This is reflected in his approach to describing his two loves, the desert (he is "a lover of the desert" [240]) and Katharine:

"The fear of describing her presence as I wrote caused me to burn down all sentiment, all rhetoric of love. Still, I described the desert as purely as I would have spoken of her" (241). Ondaatje establishes the desert where other representations—of subjectivity, love, relationships—seem rhetorical or sentimental. The following passage appears at the conclusion of a flashback in which Almásy attends to Katharine's injured body after removing it from her husband's suicidal plane crash. He takes Katharine to the sanctuary of a cave before walking to the nearest settlement in search of petrol for the plane:

> He looked up to the one cave painting and stole the colours from it. The ochre went into her face, he daubed blue around her eyes. He walked across the cave, his hands thick with red, and combed his fingers through her hair. Then all of her skin, so her knee that had poked out of the plane that first day was saffron. The pubis. Hoops of colour around her legs so she would be immune to the human. There were traditions he had discovered in Herodotus in which old warriors celebrated their loved ones by locating and holding them in whatever world made them eternal—a colourful fluid, a song, a rock drawing.
>
> (248)

By describing Katharine's beauty, Ondaatje develops the distinctions that will inform Almásy's reverence for the desert. The desert is "pure" and natural, and the "ritual" through which Almásy consecrates his lover's fragile body reflects some of that purity, away from any artifice—like the purity of the desert celebrated by T. E. Lawrence. The "religion" Almásy invokes is of old warriors (not saints), and there is no doctrine except "whatever" makes the loved one "eternal." There is "faith" here, but it is located in the world, and it is neither overtly religious nor a return to the religious; we may think of it as postsecular. Almásy's lover becomes *of* the world, the secular here-and-now world of the desert. Through my use of the word "worldly" I also intend to associate it with Said's notion of "worldliness," as he applied it to literary texts: "worldliness, circumstantiality, the text's status as an event having sensuous particularity as well as historical contingency, are considered as being incorporated in the text, an infrangible part of its capacity for conveying and producing meaning" (Said 1984: 39). Worldliness—in the historically contingent form of the rich cave colours in all their sensuous particularity—becomes literally incorporated into Katharine's body, allowing Almásy to express his love for her and the desert. Through the trope of the desert, Ondaatje is able to link colonialism, conventional religion, and nationalism as artificial. If the passage above emphasizes and privileges Katharine's beauty, then it also emphasizes—through its heightened poetry—Ondaatje's aestheticizing presence. For both Almásy above and for Ondaatje, such aestheticizing is constitutive of a postsecular faith.

1.1.1   *The Body without Organs (BwO)*

What would a religion look like without its doctrinal and dogmatic facets? What would it mean to secularize Christianity? What would it mean to question nation? How can Ondaatje re-signify nation—and race? *The English Patient* contains a series of Almásy's reminiscences on his time in the desert: his present, burned body is like a body without organs, with his memories emerging and departing like spectral traces. Almásy also seems to be the inverse: organs without a body—the fantastical "organs" of past selves and memories existing without a functioning body. If the desert represents the absence of social and institutional structures—the markers of cultural and national identity—then we can read Almásy's having "lost" his body as a metaphor for a similar "loss" of nation, of national affiliation and identity. Although his accent remains a possible identifier of his nationality, even that is misleading, acting as a kind of simulacrum of nation.

Ondaatje's literary representation of these concepts of body and nation can be complemented by Deleuze's and Guattari's theorization of a "body without organs." In imagining their concept of the "body without organs" (their shorthand is BwO), Deleuze and Guattari draw upon the case of a paranoid patient who suffered delusions that his body had no internal organs such as a stomach, bladder, or intestines (Deleuze and Guattari 1987: 150). They describe the BwO as follows:

> [T]he BwO is not a scene, a place, or even a support upon which something comes to pass. It has nothing to do with phantasy, there is nothing to interpret. [. . .] The BwO causes intensities to pass; it produces and distributes them in a *spatium* that is itself intensive, lacking extension. It is not space, nor is it in space; it is matter that occupies space to a given degree—to the degree corresponding to the intensities produced.
> (Deleuze and Guattari 1987: 153)

Why the metaphor of a hollow body? By emphasizing the lack of organs (or "organ-machines"), Deleuze and Guattari emphasize the lack of organization, the particular ways in which flows and intensities are condensed, controlled, and limited. Where Freud might categorize the schizophrenic as a clinical anomaly, Deleuze and Guattari exalt the position of the schizophrenic as one of creativity, free of social norms and ideologies. The BwO is not God, but the energy through it is "divine." This unique body serves as the "enchanted surface" upon which energy is transformed into particular forms, disjunctions, and territorializations, resulting in the creation of (a) subjectivity. The site of the BwO is characterized by "flows," "energy," "desire," "desiring-production," or "disjunctive inscription" (Deleuze and Guattari 1987: 13).

It is in *place* of nationalism and its inscriptions on and of the body that Almásy can sense the liberation—the energies and flows—of postnationalism.

His memories of Katharine, in the freedom of the desert, give him a sense of "enchantment"; Ondaatje's prose style becomes lyrical and poetic in these flashbacks. When Deleuze and Guattari define "God" as the "master of the disjunctive syllogism" (Deleuze and Guattari 1987: 13), we can read this in the terms of *The English Patient* as enchantment and wonder, represented by love, which produce specific disjunctions that animate the body without organs. Hana inspects Almásy: "She looks in on the English patient, whose sleeping body is probably miles away in the desert" (35). Almásy's body, though literally present, becomes "hollowed" of any subjective presence. Almásy is away in the enchanted space of the desert, where he feels most free. When the disjunctions of memories produce within Almásy that enchanted sense of self away from any national identity, those disjunctions build up to affirm this liberated self, so that Almásy's body contains "information like a sea" (18). Just as Deleuze and Guattari emphasize that the BwO is not God, so too is Almásy's body *itself* not the site of any postnational liberation. The flows, energies, desires inside the body—instead of the conventional "organs"—are important.

Those flows and energies of "information" and this sense of self have a certain "body" (or bodiness) that can influence and affect others. For example, at the end of the novel, after he receives the devastating news of the atomic bombs, Kip dramatically abandons the villa. He speeds away on his motorcycle, but he is not alone:

> He [. . .] carries the body of the Englishman with him in this flight. It sits on the petrol tank facing him, the black body in an embrace with his, facing the past over his shoulder, facing the countryside they are flying from, that receding palace of strangers on the Italian hill which shall never be rebuilt.
>
> (294)

Even *this* trace of Almásy remains with Kip. Because Almásy's body is without organs, it is easily "transportable," and it represents the force of associations, memories, and emotions that has so intimately influenced Kip. This sense of easy motion represents a kind of boundary-crossing, across bodies, which also represents a motion across the constructs of nationalities. If the racialized body is a secular construct of nation—and perhaps vice versa—then the body without organs represents a postsecular re-formation of the secular constructs of both race *and* nation. The idea of BwO can help us conceptualize how an aspect of Almásy intimately informs Kip—made vivid through literary metaphor—and vice versa.

The body as container and record of experiences is affirmed again in Ondaatje's description of Hana: "Moments before sleep are when she feels most alive [. . .]. The day seems to have no order until these times, which are like a ledger for her, her body full of stories and situations" (35). Extending the metaphor even further, we might view the villa as a large body without organs. It is without organs because the rooms, furniture, and walls have deteriorated, but the flow and enchantment of friendship, affection, and the small community that animate the villa become the new energy, the new "organs." Building upon my argument in the Introduction that postsecularism is caught in a double bind between secularism and religion, the concept of the BwO could give us another conceptualization of this relationship. The postsecular could be like a BwO, with the positive qualities of secularism and religion—the flows and enchantments—animating the postsecular.

The "faith" represented by the desert is framed by Ondaatje in terms that also inform the faith represented by the destroyed villa. Just as the desert is removed from trade, power, money, and war, the villa is also removed from them, as a kind of sanctuary. In these "emptied" spaces, there is the opportunity to look everywhere, to consider what Ondaatje terms the "choreography" of things. I want to emphasize, however, that the desert and the villa are not ahistorical or removed places. They are ultimately implicated *in* the world so that any gestures toward a postnational sensibility or community that they might inform are not "transcendent" to material reality. Rather, such gestures emerge from and are enabled by the domain of lived experience—passage through crisis and war. Although the desert may be "read" in different ways by being given different names, Ondaatje's aesthetic vision focuses on the foundational ability of the desert to *allow* for a range of names. The desert and the villa become privileged "sites" where Ondaatje can explore the emergence, from lived secular experience, of forms of belief.

1.2   The Politics of Friendship and the Problem of Nation

An array of different nationalities informs *The English Patient*: those of the characters and also the Sri Lankanness and Canadianness of Ondaatje. What is the effect of bringing together such different nationalities in the setting of the villa? The destroyed villa, with missing walls no less, has become literally and metaphorically open to the arrival of anyone. The physical state of the villa reflects the deterritorialization of its inhabitants, each removed from their original nation and community. Hana is away from Canada and the hospital community, grieving over her deceased father; Caravaggio is also removed from Canada, in a state of constant movement as a thief going through others' homes, but recovering now from the loss of both his thumbs; Almásy is no longer in Africa, Hungary, or the barracks; Kip is away from India, his life in a state of perpetual risk through his work as a bomb sapper. Through the idea of the villa, Ondaatje literalizes the tropes of hospitality and home. I would like to put this literary representation of hospitality and home in dialogue with some theorizations of these concepts.

In arguing for the concept of affective communities constituted by differing subcultural groups united against imperialism, Leela Gandhi explores the idea of an "anti-communitarian communitarianism" (Gandhi 2006:

26). The elements of this utopic community, driven by friendship, include "affective singularity, anarchist relationality, and other-directedness" (Gandhi 2006: 20). I want to invoke a vivid example from Gandhi to illustrate her concept of affective community. Mohandas ("Mahatma") Gandhi, living then in South Africa, asked the Anglican priest Charles Andrews, based in New Delhi, to come support his cause for indentured labourers. Upon seeing Gandhi on the docks, Father Andrews fell to the ground and touched the Mahatma's feet. The visuality of this moment is striking, for it defiantly and succinctly reverses the hierarchy of empire. This encounter occurred in 1914. The Mahatma and the Father's relationship, including at least its optics, serves as an important precursor for our now twenty-first-century theorizations of the role of affect, relationality, and otherness in forming communities across real and imagined divides.

How do we arrive here? Some philosophical foundations. Gandhi draws upon Kant's idea of the "self-sufficient" agent, a self-identical essential subject that is "constitutively free from the heterogeneity of consciousness and the distractions of experience" (Gandhi 2006: 21). In contrast to this subject that is "austere and 'stripped down'" (Gandhi 2006: 23), Gandhi presents the privileged postmodern subject. Defined by an affluence attentive only to its own insatiable desires, this subject is free to pursue its whims, but also risks, in Charles Taylor's words, a certain stagnation: "a being in face of a world which offers him no effective resistance tends to sink back into a stupor of self-coincidence. He approaches the stagnant pole where I = I" (quoted in Gandhi 2006: 23). Such self-coincidence merely mimics the solipsistic quality of the Kantian self-sufficient agent from which it originally sought to distance itself.

Hegel offers an alternative.[3] He moves the solitariness of the autonomous subject to a sociality manifest at the level of community, where the solidarity of the community becomes most important. For Hegel, the community consists of a mutual, intersubjective recognition that sees one's own "I" present in the "I" of the other, a relation of "Same with Same" (Gandhi 2006: 25). How could a Kantian autonomy of the *subject* be preserved without collapsing it into a Hegelian *communal* homogeneity? This leads Gandhi to the notion of an "anti-communitarian communitarianism," which she arrives at by turning to Maurice Blanchot's concept of "subjective 'insufficiency'" (Gandhi 2006: 24). For Blanchot, the subject's awareness of personal *insufficiency* inspires his or her openness to the risky arrival of unknown, asymmetrical "others" and socialities that are outside the domain of his or her safety and security, such as home, nation, community, race, gender, sex, skin, and species. Gandhi argues that this open predisposition can lead to a "genuine cosmopolitanism," with self-insufficiency allowing for the important concepts of hospitality and "guest-friendship" (Gandhi 2006: 31).

Gandhi draws upon contemporary work on community by scholars including, among others, Judith Butler, Donna Haraway, Jean-Luc Nancy, and of course Jacques Derrida. I would add to this list Julia Kristeva's *Strangers to*

Ourselves (1991), particularly Kristeva's following prescient question: "As a still and perhaps ever utopic matter, the question is again before us today as we confront an economic and political integration on the scale of the planet: shall we be, intimately and subjectively, able to live with the others, to live *as others*, without ostracism but also without leveling?" (Kristeva 1991: 1; italics original). Kristeva's recognition of the other within ourselves does not reproduce Hegel's Same = Same. Rather, it shows the potential within us each to *constitutively be* an other, *the* other. Ostracism and leveling extend this idea of difference, by envisioning a utopic community of otherness that *accepts* otherness (no "ostracism") without demanding its homogenization (no "leveling"; leveling policies like "assimilation" or "integration" could simply be ruses for perpetuating sameness and cultural narcissism). Kristeva knows well that this community is utopic. Gandhi shares this attentiveness to the unknown and experimental, so that an anti-communitarian communitarianism echoes the concept that "if the very idea of community is, from a postmodern perspective, inevitably unworkable, inoperative, negative, then we can only speak, under erasure, of an impossible community: perpetually deferred, 'indefinitely perfectable,' yet-to-come" (Gandhi 2006: 26). And in a telematic, multisensorial, globalized world—think Facebook, Twitter, Tweetbot, MySpace, LinkedIn, YouTube, Flickr, AIM, MSN, Yahoo IM, GTalk, Google Buzz, Foursquare, Yammer, among others—must not the ethical aspirations of global compassion and empathy *require* bodies without organs, enabling translation between and across bodies?

Gandhi's imagination of a deferred community, as something only partially complete, is symbolized by the destroyed villa, almost an anti-structure structure. The villa is physically incomplete, but the characters in the novel suffuse it with a sociality. This becomes another device Ondaatje employs to underscore liminality and hybridity. Each of the characters is somewhat insufficient, seeking something—which might be offered by others in the villa. And though that villa might offer temporary safety and security, it is really *the war* that has so deeply shaken everyone out of a basic safety and security. None of the characters is a host, they are all guests—the hosting is done by a friend with no human agency or speech, the villa. But affect and tenderness are, of course, present in the novel. For example, Hana's process of becoming restful culminates in "[t]enderness towards the unknown and the anonymous, which was a tenderness to the self" (49). Ondaatje collapses the self-other opposition, but the small villa community is by no means a Hegelian community bolstered by a sense of Same with Same.

Ondaatje's experiment brings together different nationalities, and sees what emerges among them—affective, relational, conflictual, and otherwise—within a war that has affected each of them. From the hundreds of patients in the unit, Hana chooses to take care of the English patient, for she imagines in him something that can quell her feeling of insufficiency: "There was something about him she wanted to learn, grow into, and hide in, where she could turn away from being an adult" (52). The metaphor of the other as outside oneself and with its own interior life stresses the dialogism inherent in a politics of friendship and hospitality. Ondaatje will push this further: *"all parts of the body must be ready for the other, all atoms must jump in one direction for desire to occur.* I have lived in the desert for years and I have come to believe in such things. It is a place of pockets. The trompe l'oeil of time and water" (259; italics mine). Almásy's affirmation of love occurs after years in the desert. Ondaatje again constructs the desert as a magical place, one that can host *trompes l'oeil* that challenges notions of time by presenting mirages of it. Almásy's soliloquy has a sermon-like quality. The phrase "I [have come to] believe" occurs no less than three times in this two-page passage. Why such affirmation, after the desert, after the war, toward the end of the novel, and almost after his life, and all to an international audience?

Such movement—rising above the insecurities and fears about the other, rising out of the controls and pretences of a colonial era, surviving the violence of war, moving away from nationalism and all its consent-producing hegemonies of solidarity and homogenous communalism, the kind of hegemony of nationalism that can lead people to follow Nazism—is prefigured in the conditions of *The English Patient*'s production. Ondaatje himself is removed from the violence of the war and is situated in a postcolonial time; geographically, he is removed from Sri Lanka, and is writing in the metropolitan, multicultural context of Toronto.

The hospitality of *his* historical circumstance has opened itself to allow for the affirmational gestures of Ondaatje. But hospitality is not a controlling mechanism: the guest is not permanent, and can leave. The villa might exist, but it can also be abandoned—its presence and others' need for it is ephemeral. This resonates with Deleuze's and Guattari's idea that, for the nomad, the point of arrival is simply momentary:

> [E]very point is a relay and exists only as a relay. A path is always between two points, but *the in-between has taken on all the consistency and enjoys both an autonomy and a direction of its own.* The life of the nomad is the intermezzo. Even the elements of his dwelling are conceived in terms of the trajectory that is forever mobilizing them.
>
> (380; italics mine)

An intermezzo Ondaatje. The war is burned into Almásy's skin, but Almásy has left that time and place, disavowing nationalism. For the characters in the novel, history is of course a very real "point"; they are surrounded by nothing less than a world war. But for Ondaatje's creation of the world of *The English Patient*, history itself becomes a point and a relay. This attitude toward history is necessary for Ondaatje to emphasize—and to add consistency to, make autonomous—the in-between that will allow his characters, while in the "thick" of circumstances, to be, as Deleuze and Guattari state above, "conceived in terms of the trajectory that is forever mobilizing them" (Deleuze and Guattari 1984: 380). Which trajectory? The flow that causes their deterritorialization from specificities. Almásy's body is of the war, but he is not, his memories and stories moving beyond the present; Hana and Kip are of different nations and are of different "sufficiencies," but they enter a certain friendship and intimacy; Katharine and Almásy also are mobilized by the trajectory of love. Love, humanism, art, and beauty become the trajectories mobilizing the text and thus *themselves* become affirmed by Ondaatje in the process.

What condition or conditions predispose the characters to being open to the arrival of the unknown other? As I argued earlier, none of the characters is a host in the proper sense; they are all guests, and of circumstance. Expressing tenderness for the other and taking care of the other are provoked when the other is damaged, either physically or psychically: Almásy's burns, Hana's psychological wounds, Kip's daily risking of his life, Caravaggio's destroyed hands. This taking care of the other emphasizes the affective dimension of the relation, and in the process Ondaatje affirms service and vocation. In characterizing Kip's relation with his ayah, Ondaatje emphasizes their mutual affection, stating such a relationship has conditioned Kip to look for love outside his family (226). Such similar openness is demanded by a *politics* of friendship. Gandhi explains the unknown friend for which the agent must be prepared: "the open house of hospitality or the open heart of friendship can never know guests-friends in advance, as one might a fellow citizen, sister, or comrade" (Gandhi 2006: 31). Though one cannot, of course, know the particular identity of guests or friends in advance, it is an attitude of *predisposition* that allows for the creation of the category of "guest" or "friend."

It is circumstance that creates in Ondaatje's characters a willingness to be open to possible future others. Thus an assemblage that might appear to be beyond the particulars of identity markers like nation, family, or society must emerge from the real crises of material realities, including violence. At the same time, the villa comes to function as an "enchanted" space, where all its inhabitants are removed from their personal and national ties and thus have the privilege of "creating anew" some form of affective community. When Gandhi states that the open heart of friendship "can never know guests/friends in advance," such unknowability is also reflected in Deleuze's and Guattari's notion of affect:

> Only in the black hole of subjective consciousness and passion do you discover the transformed, heated, captured particles you must relaunch for a nonsubjective, living love in which each party connects with unknown tracts in the other without entering or conquering them, in which the lines composed are broken lines.
>
> (Deleuze and Guattari 1987: 189)

Like Ondaatje, Deleuze and Guattari turn to love—"living love"—as the tool for exploring possibilities of affective transformation. When Deleuze and

Guattari caution against the "entering" or "conquering" of tracts within the other, they could very well use the term "colonize." Such colonization is something that Ondaatje resists in this novel, a point he belabours through Almásy's impassioned criticisms of nationalism and imperialism. The villa itself might exist as critique: it is a non-space and a non-place, and such a marked physical feature is inseparable from the special form of conviviality it generates and "hosts" for its temporary inhabitants. In Deleuze's and Guattari's view, any composed line between one party and another that is fixed is also tragically territorialized. A broken line represents a state of perpetual exchange between two parties, a mutuality that is open to the uncontainability and unpredictability of the other, but guided, importantly, by an ethic of "lived love." It is an exploration of *this* notion of community—enchanted, not religious; cosmopolitan, not national—that constitutes Ondaatje's experimentation with postsecular possibilities.

1.3 Brown Mythologies

In this section I consider how Ondaatje's representation of skin—in effect, deconstructing and reconstructing race—can be part of his exploration of the postsecular possibilities of friendship and love. Gil Anidjar asserts that "with the rise of secular science"—and Anidjar next quotes Edward Said—"race, color, origin, temperament, character, and types overwhelmed *the distinction between Christians and everyone else*" (Anidjar 2006: 68; italics Anidjar's). In this context, the undoing of religion is an undoing of "race." That undoing is not absolute or one-directional. Literary space allows for an experimental multiplicity of representations which the biases and limitations of other discourses—whether legal, political, or religious—will not allow.

The relationship between Hana and Kip allows Ondaatje to create various descriptions, particularly poetically-charged ones, of Kip's skin colour. For example, Hana "places a leaf across his brown wrist" (127). Appearing nearly half-way into the novel, this description of Kip's skin as "brown" gives no new information, just as the gesture of placing the leaf represents no practical use. Ondaatje's poetic description continues:

> She learns all the varieties of his darkness. The colour of his forearm against the colour of his neck. The colour of his palms, his cheek, the skin under the turban. The darkness of fingers separating red and black wires, or against bread he picks off the gunmetal plate he still uses for food. Then he stands up. His self-sufficiency seems rude to them, though no doubt he feels it is excessive politeness.
>
> (127)

Kip's behaviour, in Hana's (and Ondaatje's) western eyes, maintains itself within the bounds of its logic, unspecified to its audience. Hana cannot possess him, as much as she also fears losing him. But in Kip's (and Ondaatje's) perspective, the behaviour is a form of acknowledging Hana and of the circumstance between him and her (expressed as "politeness"). Another scene, following the one above:

> They talk, the slight singsong of his voice within the canvas smell of their tent, which has been his all through the Italian campaign, which he reaches up to touch with his slight fingers as if it too belonged to his body, a khaki wing he folds over himself during the night. It is his world. She feels displaced out of Canada during these nights. He asks her why she cannot sleep. She lies there irritated at his self-sufficiency, his ability to turn so easily away from the world.
>
> (128)

This poetic passage is filled with sensory imagery in which Kip metaphorically "becomes animal": his tent is nothing less than an extension of his body, a wing (the word *khaki* originally from Urdu). Such tropes seal Kip from the outside, consolidating the self-sufficiency that irritates Hana, the concept of self-sufficiency appearing twice within two pages. Kip's autonomy underscores Hana's self-*insufficiency*, for she feels a lack from being removed from Canada, and removed from the love of her deceased father. Kip's apparent emotional distance shows the courage needed by Hana—for self-completion—as part of the ethical openness to the risky arrival of others. Blanchot states that a being achieves its "awareness of [. . .] insufficiency [. . .] from the fact that it puts itself in question, which question needs the other or another to be enacted. *Left on its own, a being closes itself, falls asleep and calms down*" (Blanchot 1988: 5; italics mine). Kip is thus foreign once again: foreign to Hana's country, her body, her love, and her complete comprehension. Ondaatje constructs otherness based on race and nation, but then shows how race, nation, and otherness can be challenged through the postnational possibilities of affect, intimacy, and love.

The most tender moments between Hana and Kip are given especially poetic description by Ondaatje: "As she finished she moved the lip of the jug over Kip's hand and continued pouring the milk over his brown hand and up his arm to his elbow and then stopped" (123). The poetry of brownness continues, Kip's arm becoming a river: "She likes to lay her face against the upper reaches of his arm, that dark brown river, and to wake submerged within it, against the pulse of an unseen vein in his flesh beside her" (125). If Kip's work demands close attention, linking his body with a vocation that prevents violence, then that intimacy of connection becomes a simile forging an intimacy of connection between Kip and Hana: "She enters his tent and puts an ear to his sleeping chest and listens to his beating heart, the way he will listen to a clock on a mine" (130).

Could a poet like Ondaatje resist fetishizing brown skin? Is Ondaatje fetishizing his own skin? Such exoticism could be a sign of Ondaatje's at least diasporic situatedness. Nostalgia, alienation, and exoticism can involve concepts of separation and distance, underscoring Ondaatje's situatedness outside Sri Lanka. Kip is intriguingly brown not just to a Canadian Hana but also to a Canadian Ondaatje, which can also include Ondaatje's Sri Lankan influences, themselves informed by European colonial influences. It seems apt that Ondaatje has set his novel in Italy, its connotations of beauty and aesthetic richness allowing for Ondaatje's own aestheticizations, both thematic and formal. Hana's repeated observations on Kip's brownness might be viewed as her form of aestheticizing him. Ondaatje thus underscores the cognitive value of the aesthetic, especially as it is linked with affect and the ability to encourage friendship between people.

But Ondaatje is also aware of the material implications of skin colour. The only Indian among Lord Suffolk's bomb squad, Kip becomes one of the best sappers, but the others ignore him: "It was as much a result of being the anonymous member of another race, a part of the invisible world" (196). In a novel like *The English Patient*, colonialism might be something to resist or re-evaluate, but Ondaatje cannot *not* have a relation to it. Ondaatje seems sensitive to this relation, and certainly the text reproduces, not always unproblematically, the very terms it seeks to deconstruct or challenge. But given the text's status *as novel*, it will be subject to processes of inference about at least its content and the agency of its author. Ondaatje cannot control this. What is indubitable is that Ondaatje is writing in a postcolonial moment, situated in Canada, removed geographically and historically from the novel's setting of World War II. Critics could argue that Ondaatje reproduces the ignorance and discrimination of colonial agents. Such a dynamic certainly exists as a palimpsest, the spectre of past orientalizations. Yet Ondaatje's semiotic manoeuvres are distancing and almost, I would argue, renunciatory: Almásy has left the desert battles, Ondaatje is born after the war; Almásy has left Africa, Ondaatje has left Sri Lanka; Almásy has left the society of the English colonials, Ondaatje is writing in a moment of postcoloniality.

Such distancing devices allow for the "flattening" of violent and politically complex spaces and times—their representation in literary space, the making of tropes—in order to explore some affirmative values. Ondaatje's diasporic gaze toward Kip's brownness is one of aesthetic fascination, not subjugation and reductive judgment. These are the devices informing the text's gestures toward love and friendship. Ondaatje invokes the east/west thematic, as he does the religious symbols of a church and a Sikh *gurdwara* (temple), but he is interested in their "beautiful" aesthetic elements as they serve his explorations of the heterodox "religion" of a community outside nation. Canadian Hana stands in place of diasporic Canadian Ondaatje when she observes Kip's washing his hair and "imagines all of Asia [. . .].

The way he lazily moves, his quiet civilisation" (217). The phrase "all of Asia" could represent Hana's wonder and intrigue, so that the beauty of Kip's gestures reflects the civilizational beauty of Asia. Hana's observation could also be essentialist and sentimentalizing. Could it be the brown man's burden to represent all of Asia? Just as easily as Kip could be a beautiful Asian, he also could be a negative and inferior Asian—both contain processes of construction.

Such a methodological and epistemological manoeuvre is not simply the replacement of one code by another. It can certainly be problematic, as we shall see in the case of *Anil's Ghost*. In the act of "translating" historical phenomena—World War II, colonialism—into the mode of art, and with a view toward imagining forms of community "outside" nation, the process will be palimpsestual. Analogous to this process of offering a possibility which contains the terms of a previous system but then translates them to a different set of concerns and interests, consider William Connolly's assertion that "[b]oth the celebration and the lament of the (precarious) victory of the secular underplay the degree to which the Christian sacred remains buried in it" (quoted in Robbins 1994: 35, note 10).

For Kip, Hana's observations on his brownness reach a point where they shift from the aesthetic to the offensive. The racializing, alienating gaze of the English—Lord Suffolk's group—toward Kip is "buried" within him, and Hana's comments can remind him of this history. When at the end of the novel Kip turns away from the villa because of the west's violence against Hiroshima and Nagasaki, Hana pleads that she, Almásy, and Caravaggio do not inhere in *that* white west. But Kip is unpersuaded, and leaves. In the intimate affective economy between Kip and Hana, Kip's brownness will of course remain a fact but it is Hana's (and Ondaatje's) wish to explore how racist white mythologies can *possibly* be replaced with affirmations of friendship and love. Lilijana Burcar argues that Almásy's burned body can "be seen as not only offering a profound meta-commentary on the permeability of national borders, but as also exposing the precariousness of such identificatory schemas as nation or race that impinge upon the construction of subjects and their bodily material" (Burcar 2008: 104). The missing link here is the secular: to deconstruct the secular—to *postsecularize*—is to deconstruct nation and race.

The "precarious victory," to echo Connolly's term (quoted in Robbins 1994: 35, note 10), of an emergence of postsecular commitment to friendship and love will underplay the degree to which worldly gazes and histories are embedded within it. White mythologies might risk becoming replaced by brown mythologies: what is "Asia"? What is Asia's "civilization," let alone its "quiet civilization"? As we will see in Chapter 3 on *Anil's Ghost*, a similar challenge occurs for Ondaatje when representing the values of renewal and regeneration using a reconstructed Buddha statue in Sri Lanka, with its possible connotations of violent Sinhalese nationalism.

1.4   Aestheticization

The English Patient as a whole is like a painting. The visual and painterly qualities of phenomena appeal to Ondaatje's writerly sensibility, yet he will invoke
them not simply for their "beautiful" aspects but also for their heuristic or cognitive value. Ondaatje, sometimes self-consciously, frames relations between
his characters through an aesthetic trope ("a tableau of"). Such framing often
occurs when he is trying to bridge differences between characters and to establish and affirm some friendship and affect between them. Ondaatje will also
invoke the aesthetics of the church and of the Golden Temple of the Sikhs but
he will *secularize* such institutions by emptying them of their religious meaning.
He will also aestheticize them, and such aestheticization is *itself* a secularizing
move, "mere aesthetics." But beauty becomes a kind of religion, provoking
religion-like feelings such as awe and enchantment.

For instance, the tableaus and frescoes of the church are commented upon
by Ondaatje in terms of their aesthetic qualities. In the film adaptation, Kip
takes Hana at night to see the large frescoes in the local church, lifting her
toward the ceiling using a rope-pulley and illuminating the interior using
a flare. As the scene progresses, the main soundtrack of the film plays in
the background, eventually accompanied by Hana's joyful laughter. In the
novel, Ondaatje animates Kip's Sikhism by also drawing out its aesthetic
elements. It is again night and Kip and Hana are in a tent, lying gently,
in an embrace. Kip guides her to the Golden Temple or *Harmandir Sahib*,
the holiest shrine for Sikhs, located in Amritsar, India. The temple is covered in gold and situated in the middle of a large pool of water surrounded
by a perimeter of intricately-patterned white marble. Kip evokes the temple
grounds in rich detail, describing for Hana the early morning mist, the smell
of fresh fruit in the temple gardens, the day-long singing of the hymns of the
saints—Ramananda, Nanak, Kabir—with the narration then switching to the
third-person to describe their entering the inner chamber where the Holy
Book is kept:

> "The temple is a haven in the flux of life, accessible to all. It is the ship
> that crossed the ocean of ignorance." [. . .] Hana is quiet. He knows the
> depth of darkness in her, her lack of a child and of faith. He is always
> coaxing her from the edge of her fields of sadness.
>
> (271)

What appeals to Ondaatje's gaze is the ability of aesthetic experience to
bridge differences, in this case at least the national and religious difference
between Kip (Asian other: Indian, Sikh) and Hana (western observer: Canadian, non-believer), to say nothing of the emotional distance between them.
The structures of conventional religion are present, but they are emptied
of their doctrinal meanings, and instead exist insofar as they aesthetically

enable the affirmation of affect. A ship crossing the ocean of ignorance is among the Sikh teachings of its founder guru, Guru Nanak Dev, the teachings enshrined in the holy scripture *Guru Granth Sahib*. The idea of crossing an ocean—whether an ocean of nescience, of the material world, or of ignorance, depending on the translation and interpretation from Sanskrit—also appears in Hindu texts, such as *The Bhagavad Gita*. Interestingly, Ondaatje does not explicitly credit these Sikh and Hindu intertextual sources, both of which are based on the doctrine of reincarnation, of liberating one's soul from the cycle of birth and re-birth. Instead, Ondaatje secularizes them into an aesthetic language of affect between Kip and Hana.

If religious rituals enable the affirmation and consolidation of religious belief, then in this novel the domain of the aesthetic—the aesthetic imagining of another world, rich in pleasant sights, smells, sounds—enables the affirmation of friendship and affect, especially between individuals with marked differences. There is also an embedded indictment here by Ondaatje against the caste system of majoritarian Hinduism in India. Each of the three saints he cites—Ramananda, Nanak, Kabir—were avowedly critical of caste, especially of the Hindu Brahmanism they observed around them. Teaching instead the fundamental equality of all peoples, these three saints welcomed everyone from all religions and walks of life. Shauna Singh Baldwin also invokes the teachings of the Sikh gurus on the fundamental equality of men and women, in her indictment of gender inequality, one situated no less within an Indian state secularism that has yet to adequately represent the Sikh community, as I discuss in Chapter 4. Ondaatje's turn to a caste-free spirituality is echoed in a similar gesture by Rushdie. Rushdie invokes the egalitarianism of the Bhakti movement to describe and aestheticize a subaltern secularism, which I discuss in Chapter 5, and which I argue has implications for a kind of postsecular magical realism. In the hands of these writers, religion emerges as something which they can intimately negotiate and work through by translating a concept like "equality" into aesthetic form.

The following passage is another example of aestheticization. Almásy states:

> "It is assumed that the face of David is a portrait of the youthful Caravaggio and the head of Goliath is a portrait of him as an older man, how he looked when he did the painting. Youth judging age at the end of its outstretched hand. The judging of one's own mortality. I think when I see him [Kip] at the foot of my bed that Kip is my David."
>
> (116)

The aesthetic emerges as that space in which individuals can negotiate the categories of nationality and difference, possibly affirming connections among themselves. Using Caravaggio's example, Almásy understands Kip (again, the other) as a younger version of himself, seeing part of himself in him, affirming some commonality between them. The aesthetic imagining allows for a kind of acceptance, an acceptance of Kip that Lord Suffolk and his bomb squad could never achieve because of their rigid belief in race. In such descriptive processes, Ondaatje's prose exhibits poetic qualities, self-consciously becoming "artistic" like the artistic metaphors it seeks to convey.

Toward the end of the novel, Caravaggio, Hana, and Kip gather in the evening and Caravaggio relays the story of Hana's having previously sung the Marseillaise, the French national anthem. Kip attempts to sing the song, but Hana demonstrates the proper way of singing it, with full force and life. She removes her shoes, stands on top of a table, and sings "up into darkness beyond their snail light, beyond the square of light from the English patient's room and into the dark sky waving with shadows of cypress" (269). This description's painterly qualities are evocative of Van Gogh's *The Starry Night*. This "affirmation" of life recognizes the tenuousness and fragility of any sense of hope. The faith in the future that Hana expresses here emerges from an ongoing *worldly* context of danger and uncertainty. Like Said's notion of "worldliness" as he applies it to literary texts, these characters are also very much situated in their circumstance. This is demonstrated in the description of Hana's singing:

> There was no certainty to the song anymore, the singer could only be one voice against all the mountains of power. That was the only sureness. The one voice was the single unspoiled thing. A song of snail light. Caravaggio realized she was singing with and echoing the heart of the sapper.
>
> (269)

Ondaatje explores the above affirmation of hope and life with tentativeness. He situates it in its thoroughly worldly setting by showing how the circumstances of Hana's life have changed since the last time she sang the song, when she was sixteen. Yet Ondaatje also calls this song a "new testament" (269), a kind of religion which is able to emerge and gesture toward affirmations, however small and hesitant. The song also brings Kip closer to Hana—she echoes "the heart of the sapper"—and it also draws Caravaggio closer, creating some community among them. Where categories of race and nation might exist like "mountains of power," here is a small gesture toward some mutual understanding, "one voice"—Ondaatje's voice—in spite of such deeply entrenched categories. Hana's hope is entirely *this*-worldly and Ondaatje uses music (as a form of art) to "articulate" this hope. The hope might also be seen to consist in a sameness. There is the song of the Sikh gurus; there is Hana's song of the Marseillaise. There is an element of secular knowledge-sharing in both, secular in that it emerges from experience, from material encounter of others. Kip teaches Hana the Sikh customs and singing; Hana teaches Kip how to sing the Marseillaise. The interior darknesses of Hana that Kip imagines—lack, loss, absence of faith—are structurally paralleled in the exterior darknesses of the war-torn night. The "circle of light"—of understanding, of affective connection—that emerges between Kip and Hana and among the small villa community is no absolute, triumphant proclamation, but modestly "tentative," a "snail light." And so too the posting of the secular.

Tableaus and murals fill Ondaatje's artistic gaze. A metafictional moment:

> Lightning falls upon the steeples of the small alpine chapels whose tableaux reenact the Stations of the Cross or the Mysteries of the Rosary. [. . .] [L]arger-than-life terra-cotta figures carved in the 1600s are revealed briefly, depicting biblical scenes. The bound arms of the scourged Christ pulled back, the whip coming down, the baying dog, three soldiers in the next chapel tableau raising the crucifix higher towards the painted clouds.
>
> (277)

The description then culminates with: *"Perhaps this villa is a similar tableau, the four of them in private movement, momentarily lit up, flung ironically against this war"* (278; italics mine). Flung, no doubt, by Ondaatje also. Ondaatje offers a direct religious parallel to the scene he has created. Yet the "religion" of the villa, in opposition to the conventional Christianity of the Stations of the Cross, is that of friendship and community. This "affirmational" value is a tenuous one ("momentarily lit up"), for Ondaatje reminds us that his characters are situated against a war. The four characters in the Biblical scene—three soldiers and Christ—become in *The English Patient* the four characters in the villa. In such a one-to-one "translation," the frame of the aesthetic remains, but the relations are different; instead of persecution because of religious differences, there is an affective community in *spite* of national differences. Ondaatje's is a veritable United Nations, with Ondaatje subtly translating religion into nation via an historical image of artwork. Here is another passage using the metaphor of a tableau:

> She [Hana] was surrounded by foreign men. Not one pure Italian. A villa romance. What would Poliziano have thought of this 1945 tableau, two men and a woman across a piano and the war almost over and the guns in their wet brightness whenever the lightning slipped itself into the room filling everything with colour and shadow as it was doing now every half-minute thunder crackling all over the valley and the music antiphonal, the press of chords [. . .].
>
> (64)

Angelo Poliziano (1454–1494) was a poet, philologist, and humanist. Ondaatje again "stylizes" the romance in the villa by using an artistic metaphor of a tableau, and continues by surmising what a poet would have thought of such a "scene," like words arranged in a poem. The aesthetic becomes a heuristic device, and Ondaatje *believes* in his ability to create and explore such frames. He will especially exercise this belief when exploring love in this novel: among Hana and Kip, among Almásy and Katharine. Love holds this kind of enchantment and wonder for Ondaatje, as does his ability to frame it aesthetically, and in that sense both love and the ability to create art constitute a kind of faith for him.

Consider Ondaatje's negotiation of a religious aesthetic in light of Almásy's and Katharine's growing affair:

> Sometimes when she is able to spend the night with him they are wakened by the three minarets of the city beginning their prayers before dawn. He walks with her through the indigo markets that lie between South Cairo and her home. The beautiful songs of faith enter the air like arrows, one minaret answering another, as if passing on a rumour of the two of them as they walk through the cold morning air, the smell of charcoal and hemp already making the air profound. Sinners in a holy city.
>
> (154)

Ondaatje's trope that the minarets spread rumours of adultery, rather than emitting songs of faith, could be read as blasphemous. His description of the muezzin's call to prayer (*adhan*) focuses on Islam's aesthetic, "beautiful" form, and he invokes this aesthetic element and translates it into a simile that expresses an intimacy between Almásy and Katharine. Where a critic could read the above passage apolitically as a tender recollection of a love story (Comellini 2008: 192), I would argue that Ondaatje privileges affect as the "new" "religion," and the aesthetic as its frame, so that the couple's "sinning" is constituted not just by adultery, but by thinking that the call to worship is communicating *their* affair, privileging them at the centre. This narcissistic privilege could also be a colonial attitude: that the minarets are *about* and *for* them, and not about and for Islam.

Later in the same passage, Almásy's desire for Katharine expresses itself as follows: "He wants only her stalking beauty, her theatre of expressions. He wants the minute and secret reflection between them, the depth of field minimal, their foreignness intimate like two pages of a closed book" (155). Ondaatje emphasizes Katherine's beauty and uses the artistic metaphor of a theatre to describe her expressions. Like pages in a book, a sameness exists with difference. Like the respective darknesses, songs, and didacticisms of Kip and Hana, all the pages are different but, by connecting with one another, constitute a tentative whole greater than themselves. Aesthetic elements allow for a kind of intimacy and witnessing of the other so as to reduce the "foreignness" of the other. It is interesting that Ondaatje uses the word "foreign" here, which includes the connotations of "foreigner" as the cultural other. The realms of affect and the aesthetic are able to bind both senses of "foreign"—the cultural and the philosophical (a subjectivity other than one's own)—thereby allowing affirmations of friendship, love, and community.

Deleuze's and Guattari's concept of "faciality" might offer some further insight into this relation between the religious and the postsecular as it operates in this novel. Deleuze and Guattari theorize the face as, broadly, that which signifies the uniqueness of the human by existing at the intersection of both subjectivity—consciousness, passions—and the medium through which that subjectivity can be expressed—signs. The desert in *The English Patient* explores the removal of the "clothing of [. . .] countries" (139), the erasing of family names and of nations: "We disappeared into landscape. Fire and sand" (139). Such "disappearing" is akin to Deleuze's and Guattari's *becoming-non-human*. Burned beyond recognition, Almásy has "lost" his face, becoming in place "the English patient." Is it a coincidence that such a physical transformation accompanies his wish to move beyond nations, erase (family) names, and disappear "into" the landscape which has become for him a "place of faith"? Deleuze and Guattari argue that movement into such newness, something radically different from present convention (represented by the face, or faciality), occurs through "life lines" that require "all the resources of art, and art of the highest kind. It requires a whole line of writing, picturality, musicality [. . .]. But art is never an end in itself; it is only a tool for blazing life lines" (Deleuze and Guattari 1987: 187). Faciality is not for Deleuze and Guattari something merely to be transcended by blazing life lines, but rather a *tool* that can be used for a political purpose, for inventiveness:

> If the face is a politics, dismantling the face is also a politics involving real becomings, an entire becoming-clandestine. Dismantling the face is the same as breaking through the wall of the signifier and getting out of the black hole of subjectivity. [. . .] Such dismantling of faces is a way of drawing "lines of flight." [. . .] The white wall of the signifier, the black hole of subjectivity, and the facial machine are impasses, the measure of our submissions and subjections; but we are born into them, and it is there we must stand battle. Not in the sense of a necessary stage, but in the sense of a tool for which a new use must be invented.
>
> (Deleuze and Guattari 1987: 189)

Similarly, the struggle for Ondaatje is how to use elements and resources of art in order to explore the relation in this novel between conventional religion and postsecularism. The latter will strive to become a "line of flight" from the religious, dismantling the face of the religious. Religion's signifiers become dismantled when they no longer signify the doctrines, narratives, and dogmas of conventional religion, or expect their believers to believe or follow them as such. For example, a representation of a crucifix would be admired for its formal beauty rather than followed as a symbol of sacrifice and indebtedness; Guru Nanak's portrait would be seen for its beautiful form rather than as encouragement for selfless service to others. Deleuze's and Guattari's "tool" for which a "new use must be invented" is the aesthetic and also the ethical challenge for Ondaatje. His tool is literature and, within the world of *The English Patient*, the domain of the aesthetic. The new way in which Ondaatje uses such tools is to gesture toward "non-secular secular" affirmative values. The tool is still present—it is here, it is "secular"—but a new use must be made of it: "non-secular." It is the political face of religion that Ondaatje wishes to dismantle, like the literally crumbling face of a Renaissance fresco, and in its place explore a "real becoming." The postsecular possibility that might emerge is a becoming, a tenuous exploration of the possibilities of friendship and hope in the middle of violence, a war. The process will affirm not only the values that might emerge—friendship, love—but will also *affirm the tool*, the aesthetic: art, music, literature.

1.5 Four Bombs

Literary criticism of *The English Patient* has demonstrated its ability to historicize the text by theorizing, for instance, the role of Herodotus, a well-known "historical" figure no less (Brittan (2006), Harrison (1998), Curran (2005), Hilger (2005)). In addition to Hiroshima and Nagasaki, another pair of bombs writes through *The English Patient*, hitherto largely neglected in criticism of the novel. These are the 1985 bombing of Air India Flight 182, originating in Montreal and destined for Mumbai; and the bomb that exploded the same day in an Air India passenger bag at Tokyo's Narita Airport. These 1985 bombings by Sikhs, and the subsequent twenty years of trials and public investigations by the Canadian government, represent important historical factors at play in Ondaatje's writing of *The English Patient*. The politicization of Sikh identity across India and Canada at the time raises compelling questions about nation and citizenship. Who counts as Indian or Canadian? What does it mean, in each country, to be a minority? What guarantees can there be of just citizenship, across Indian secularism and Canadian multiculturalism? I want to explore the 1985 bombing in order to show the depth of Canadian Sikhness writing through *The English Patient*. In this context, I prefer *Sikhness* to *Sikhism*, to move away from the religious connotations of the latter.

In 1984, Sikh separatists in India, who had been demanding the separate state of Khalistan, occupied the Golden Temple, and were suspected of amassing weapons inside the temple. In June of that year, Indira Gandhi ordered a military strike against the Golden Temple, in what came to be known as Operation Blue Star. The military confrontation on the temple grounds lasted several days. Although the Indian Army was ultimately victorious, the consequences were devastating. With the attack on their most holy site, coinciding no less with the annual commemoration of Guru Arjan Devji's martyrdom, some Sikhs took it as an affront against their religion. On October 31, 1984, Indira Gandhi was assassinated by her two Sikh bodyguards. That same day, massacres against Sikhs erupted across New Delhi, lasting four days.

Operation Blue Star also had violent repercussions in the Indian diaspora. June 23, 1985, marked the bombing of Air India Flight 182, which was scheduled to fly from Montreal to Mumbai via London and New Delhi. The airplane crashed near the western coast of Ireland, leaving all 22 crew and 307 passengers dead. The bag containing the bomb had been loaded in Vancouver, onto a Canadian Pacific flight destined for Toronto. The bag was then transferred onto an Air India flight from Toronto to Montreal, which then connected with Air India Flight 182, which departed from Montreal. The changing of bags across different airlines was one of the errors committed in the case. The same day as Flight 182's demise, two Japanese bag handlers at Tokyo's Narita Airport were killed when an Air India passenger bag exploded, in a flight that had arrived from Vancouver.

Talwinder Singh Parmar, based in Vancouver and founding chief of the Sikh terrorist group *Babbar Khalsa International*, was a prime suspect in the bombings. Charges against Parmar were dropped due to insufficient evidence. He died in 1992, in a gun battle with Indian police. To-date, only one person has been convicted: Inderjit Singh Reyat. In 1991 Reyat received a ten-year sentence for manslaughter in the Narita Airport bombing, and in 2003 he received a five-year sentence for helping build the bomb that destroyed the Air India flight. The Royal Canadian Mounted Police's investigations lasted from 1985 until 2001. There was a trial from 2003 to 2005 of two further suspects, Ajaib Singh Bahri and Ripudaman Singh Malik, but both were acquitted due to insufficient evidence. The Canadian government then undertook a public inquiry, which lasted from May 2006 until June 2010. The inquiry was headed by former Supreme Court justice John Major, who states in his subsequent report that the Air India bombing "remains the largest mass murder in Canadian history." In the same sentence, he states that the tragedy was "the result of a cascading series of errors" (Major 2010: 21), including inadequate responses by Canadian agencies.

The Air India investigations and subsequent inquiry together took over twenty years to conclude. Canadian Prime Minister Stephen Harper delivered an official apology on June 23, 2010. On the issue of nation, Major states:

> [B]oth the Government and the Canadian public were slow to recognize the bombing of Flight 182 as a Canadian issue. This reaction was no doubt associated with the fact that the supposed motive for the bombing was tied to alleged grievances rooted in India and Indian politics. Nevertheless, the fact that the plot was hatched and executed in Canada and that the majority of victims were Canadian citizens did not seem to have made a sufficient impression to weave this event into our shared national experience.

(Major 2010: 38)

Where Almásy wishes for the erasure of family names and nations, here is Major keen to spread the Canadian name, in the name of justice and equality. But the victims of the families, like Almásy, know all too well the perniciousness of nation, whether through an imagined nation like Khalistan, the violence of India's Operation Blue Star, or the exclusions of "nation" in Canada. Major's use of the word "our"—in the phrase "our shared national experience"—raises interesting questions. Who would constitute the "our" of Major's imagined community, before and after the tragedy? They could be three letters forward toward inclusivity. They could also be three letters backward, naming the "our" that has not meted justice to the victims and their families. Where will the arc of inclusivity bend? We have yet to see.

Where Major's political text will not or cannot fully represent or recognize orientalism, literary space allows Ondaatje to present a multiplicity of perspectives. The bombing of Hiroshima and Nagasaki becomes for Kip the turning point, a catalyst in his development of racial awareness and self-awareness. Japan is not a white nation. The experimental community of the villa then becomes undone in a sense, and there seems no going back for Kip. As Andrew Shin states: "Kip turns his back on the community [. . .] where the vector of race returns with a vengeance, a group irredeemably bound together in Kip's consciousness by its whiteness, their Englishness" (Shin 2007: 225). He feels betrayed, having grown up with English traditions: "Your fragile white island that with customs and manners and books and prefects and reason somehow converted the rest of the world. [. . .] How did you fool us into this?" (283). The bombs have made Kip self-conscious of his brownness, and thus self-conscious of an alienating "difference" between him and the others in the villa.

In the case of Almásy, he moves from a blackness to a whiteness. The English patient begins the novel by being black; on the very first page, we are told Hana regularly washes his "black body" (3). After the bomb, Almásy becomes, in Kip's eyes at least, white—politically white. Almásy dies, whereas Kip returns to India, becomes Kirpal, trains as a medical doctor, gets married, has a daughter, wears spectacles, and dons the traditional *kurta pyjama*. A similar process occurs at the end of *The Satanic Verses*: Saladin becomes Salahuddin, returns to India, and agrees to the Islamic burial rite for his father. Let me anticipate the arguments I make in Chapter 4. Is a return to one's native land—through, in this case, such constructions as a nativized first name, an Indian male stereotype as qualifying as a medical doctor, having one's patriarchy amplified through a wife and children let alone a daughter, and donning national attire—the only way that Ondaatje can represent otherness to racism, hegemony, and ideology? What would be informing such orientalism in Ondaatje's diasporic gaze?

Aestheticization continues strongly. Kip leaves the villa, unturbanned and wearing a *kurta*—the "native." When we are told that Kip "carries nothing in his hands" (287), this expresses a genuine nothingness, in contrast to

Almásy's earlier observation that in the desert he could literally hold absence in his hands. But this is no mere nihilism, for Ondaatje's aestheticizing vision continues strongly, if subtly. Kip "walks alongside the outline of hedges," his body "standing on the edge of a great valley of Europe" (287). "Outline" and "of Europe" are the giveaways. "Outline" flattens the scene, as if it were a visual work, a painting or drawing. "Of Europe" is redundant, giving no new information, but it frames Kip's actions within the discourse of geography, indeed cultural geography, emphasizing that he is *in Europe*, and not any another continent, certainly not—and this is useful for Ondaatje's racializing purposes—*in Asia*.

Europe is not home for Kip. Even the real community that formed at the villa is now *resignified* to have been false, re-oriented (re-occidented?) at the level of the imaginary by race, by the history of previous racist significations and the racial violence of the present bombing. Even as Hana insists that her, Almásy's, and Caravaggio's whiteness is not the whiteness of the bomb, Kip is unpersuaded. He leaves the villa, and when he later enters a church and sees a statue surrounded by scaffolding, he "wander[s] around underneath like somebody unable to enter the intimacy of a home" (291). Not even the space of the aesthetic can be a sanctuary for Kip, as when he and Hana had visited the frescoes.

Hana experiences a similar nostalgia for a sanctuary, a home. After learning of the bombs, she writes to her friend Clara in Canada: "*I am sick of Europe, Clara. I want to come home. To your small cabin and pink rock in Georgian Bay*" (296; italics original). Ondaatje again refers to "Europe," now in contrast to North America. The contrasts continue, but aestheticization continues even more. Here is the closing passage of the novel, improbable in the real world: "Her shoulder touches the edge of a cupboard and a glass dislodges. Kirpal's left hand swoops down and catches the dropped fork an inch from the floor and gently passes it into the fingers of his daughter [. . .]" (302). An older Kirpal catches not just his daughter's fork but possibly also, the text suggests, Hana's glass, the two characters connected across space and time, connected *aesthetically*. In spite of the undoing of any community, there remains a certain enchantment, that of aesthetic connectivity. As Raymond Younis has observed, Ondaatje is "interested in the mysterious link that is perpetual; in the sense in which the being of one affects the being of the other" (Younis 1998: 7). If a Marxist critic might argue that the novel is merely trivial fiction, no more than a sentimental romance, it is at least interesting which *terms* Ondaatje invokes, and how he invokes them. Among the oppositions he invokes are white/black, Europe/Asia, Europe/North America, nation/community, present/past, present/future—across which inversions and oscillations occur.

In theorizing human rights, Rajeswari Sunder Rajan has argued that "a symmetry can never be satisfactorily achieved between a wrong and the compensation for it, but such an equivalence is the horizon against which it is transacted" (Sunder Rajan 2007: 167). Sunder Rajan's concepts of symmetry and equivalence are interesting in the context of *The English Patient*, for Ondaatje is trying to strike a symmetry and equivalence between Kip and Hana, through love and intimacy. A "Canadian" tragedy, the "English" patient. I want to revisit Andrew Shin's argument that Almásy, Hana, and Caravaggio become connected in Kip's eyes by their whiteness, which is their Englishness. Kip equates whiteness with Englishness because the Americas were once colonies of England. But for Ondaatje, Hana's *Canadianness* is important. As a nurse, she represents compassion and care, some hope that white Canadians *can* understand Indians and Sikhs and non-white Canadians. It is significant that Kip defuses bombs instead of manufacturing them. In the context of the crisis of Air India, this again represents a certain hope. Given the politics of Sikhness in Canada when Ondaatje wrote *The English Patient*, Kip is in one sense also *Canadian*. The Canadianness of Kip reflects Ondaatje's minority concerns about equality of nationality and citizenship, that Ondaatje *too* is Canadian, an affirmation he can rehearse and assert for himself within the realms of creativity, expression, and freedom most precious and intimate to him: the craft of literature.

Kip's Sikhness allows for a minority critique of not just violent Khalistani and Indian nationalism, but also Canadian nationalism. The actually-narrated Kip might be Indian, moving from a whiteness to a brownness. But in Ondaatje's imaginary, the contemporary Canadianness linked with Sikhness is what allows Ondaatje to create a Sikh character who, as a bomb sapper, *prevents* violence instead of undertaking it. Yet, Kip is not perfectly free of violence, just as the postnation does not and cannot perfectly "empty" itself of the idea of nation, as indeed the postsecular is not "empty" of the secular and religious.

With the sudden idea that Almásy, in Kip's eyes, *inheres* in the whiteness that led to the bombing of Hiroshima and Nagasaki, violence attains a certain temptation for Kip, and he almost shoots Almásy. After a tense confrontation, Kip does not, in the end, release the trigger, but he does conclude: "American, French, I don't care. When you start bombing the brown races of the world, you're an Englishman" (286). Is this a version of Almásy's earlier exhortations to "erase nation"? Where Almásy sought the erasure of nation as a means of freedom, notice how Kip's erasure occurs as its inverse: as an indictment, homogenization, and reduction ("x, y, and z *are all* n"). Kip's homogenizing continues: "The weeping from shock and horror contained, seeing everything, all those around him, in a different light. Night could fall between them, fog could fall, and the young man's dark brown eyes would reach the new revealed enemy" (284).

The phrase "revealed enemy" reminds me of Ashis Nandy's powerful concept of the "intimate enemy." Nandy argues that the colonizer's successful hegemony in the mind of the colonized must be carefully extricated and removed by the colonized, with determination, will power, perseverance.

Kip's anger toward Almásy is inevitably anger toward himself, upon recognizing the depth of the enemy's intimacy. "Intimate" here can even now, tragically, exist in the positive affective sense, a closeness which can be not just pernicious but a marker of trust. That trust is now betrayed, however imaginatively, just as Almásy's body accompanies Kip without its organs. As precariously as Ondaatje establishes a sense of community in the villa, that community can also be undone.

In the sense that Kip is Canadian, we could imagine that Hana is *Sikh* and *Indian*, the latter because Kip is an Indian Sikh (one could argue Kip is a diasporic Sikh now in Italy, but the majority of his life has been in India, where he returns, and it is Sikhism's religious practices in India that Ondaatje depicts). Hana exemplifies the Sikh virtue of *seva* ("service"): compassionate, selfless, voluntary care for the other, whether for the community or an individual, without any expectation of return. Hana performs *seva* toward Almásy throughout the novel. It is not enough that Hana is a nurse. She is a *good* nurse, someone exemplifying her profession and its ideals. Nowhere of course does Ondaatje name this as a "Sikh" practice. In the same spirit, Hana's visit to the Golden Temple must be aesthetically-charged, emptied of the violence of Khalistan and India, her ethic unnamed within the discourse of (a) religion. In the same spirit, we could even read Kip's Canadianness and Hana's Indianness as bodies without organs (BwO), a kind of "other" national body existing parallel to their full, organized embodiment, an openness to "otherness" achieved through their shared physical contact: the beauty of Kip's brown arm; the tenderness Kip feels toward Hana, imagining her personal history and its pain, perhaps even empathizing with her.

By establishing an intimacy between Kip and Hana, Ondaatje postulates even more some movement beyond the confines of nation, in the wake of the crises of Khalistan, India, and Canada. The space of the villa allows for this mutual understanding, and aestheticizations within literary space allow Ondaatje to experiment with such possibilities. This is part of the postsecular gesturing in the novel, moving away from the limitations of the Indian state secularism within which Operation Blue Star unfolded; and moving away from the Canadian multiculturalism that neglected and racially harassed its own citizens.[4]

I do not write "its own" as a matter of surprise; citizenship of course does not necessarily guarantee equality of treatment. But the values and idealism that have produced *the idea* of citizenship are the certain measure of value and idealism Ondaatje experimentally structures *within* this novel. As I discussed in the Preface, it is the idea and ideal of civic virtues that inspired Benjamin Franklin to affirm these as the foundation for a nation. In *Anil's Ghost,* there is a poignant passage in which Anil is with Sarath and Ananda, and feels "citizened by their friendship" (Ondaatje 2000: 200). Political citizenship is one matter; but in the wake of the failure of the state, its secular ideals seem best realized through the lived, private domain of its peoples, through friendship and, in Leela Gandhi's words, anti-communitarian communitarianism. It would be incorrect to say that the state's secular ideals are *deferred* into the domain of the people, for that would privilege the state as the source of such ideals. In a postsecular paradigm, it is the people who have their own "indigenous" epistemologies and ways of being, quite apart from the pretensions, hegemonies, and constructs of the state. Novelists are *of* the people—they are not necessarily cadres of the state—and they turn to literature as their craft through which to represent that which the state, either native or diasporic, cannot or will not. In this spirit, I agree with Gil Anidjar's assertions that

> [s]ecularism continues to be fostered by the same institutions and structurally identical elites, who work out of the same centers of power that earlier spread their "civilization" and continue to expand their mission, be it economic, military, cultural, humanitarian even. It still has the bigger bombs—it *is* the history of bombing—and the bigger police, security, military, and financial forces. It builds the bigger walls. It leads the war on terror.
>
> (Anidjar 2006: 64)

That secularism has continued to write itself through literary criticism, producing walls between Canada and India. This section, by focusing on Air India, is an effort to write that wrong. If the bombing of Hiroshima and Nagasaki is a product of secularism, then Kip's return to India is in this sense a postsecular move. The return of course could also mark a turn to the religion of nation, as succour and source of identity. We do not know how Kip matures upon his return to India: his views could become, among others, postsecular; they could lead to Khalistan; they could make him return to Europe.

If there has been a secularization of religion in *The English Patient*, through tropes focusing on the beauty of Christian tableaus, hymns of the Golden Temple, and aestheticized church frescoes, then the moment of the bomb—at the end of the war, at the end of the novel, and as the last section in this chapter—disrupts the postsecularism of the tentative villa community. Symmetry and equivalence are the horizons against which understanding across nationalities might occur. In the discourse of political theory, we could consider this as citizenship, the postulation of equivalence, protection, and symmetry at the national level. Like the bombs and the subsequent institutional and personal racism that disrupted citizenship for Canadians "of Indian origin," Ondaatje *structures* the dilemmas of history and the actual, instead of simply "representing" them. As I said in the Introduction, the form of fiction allows Ondaatje to *engage* with the historical and the actual, even if as a form of experimentation. If the families of the victims have waited for justice, equivalence, and symmetry for more than twenty years after the bomb, then *The English Patient* views history as itself something yet-to-be-justiciable: it is the history that precedes the bomb, both temporally in the plot of the novel, and historically as far back as Herodotus. The time of the villa allows for the experimental visiting of other times by memory, and for intimacy and community, however precarious. But the time of the bomb—the *timing* of the bomb—introduces a worldly time, the time of the undeniable secular present.

1.6   Conclusion

Responding to his interviewer's statement that critics have taken *The English Patient* to be "an allegory of imperialism and the world at a crossroads of political and spiritual change," Ondaatje states he has found this disturbing: "I really think I write on a very small, intimate canvas. To me, the book is about four characters in a very small corner of time and place" (Brown 1992: 17). But the novel *is* implicated in the crossroads of imperialism and politics.

For example, what remains problematic is the extent of the real Almásy's involvement with the Nazis during World War II (Tötösy de Zepetnek 2005). A German operative during the war, Almásy eventually enlisted as a lieutenant with Erwin Rommel's Afrika Korps, leading a two thousand–mile expedition into Libya with two German spies. Living in Budapest during the final days of the war, Almásy sheltered several Hungarian Jewish families. He was ultimately tried in a 1946 Hungarian war-crimes tribunal, though charged only with propaganda, given his expertise in geographic research. Edward Said has observed that the concept of "agency" has roots in the idea of the Orientalist agent: "the Orientalist could be regarded as the special agent of Western power as it attempted policy vis-à-vis the Orient. [. . .] [A]s a kind of secret agent inside the Orient" (quoted in Anidjar 2006: 68). As a double agent, was Almásy really undoing nation?

Elizabeth Pathy Salett's father was Consul-General for Hungary in Egypt and was posted at Cairo before World War II, where he met Almásy. Salett called the film adaptation of the novel ahistorical and amoral, objecting to the film's minimizing Almásy's negative qualities by casting him instead as a romantic hero (Salett 1996: C6). Ondaatje immediately published a reply in the Canadian newspaper *The Globe and Mail*, stating that "the film version is not a documentary," and concluding: "If a novelist or dramatist or filmmaker is to be censored or factually tested every time he or she writes from historical event, then this will result in the most uninspired works, or it just might be safer for those artists to resort to cartoons and fantasy" (Ondaatje 1996: C5). His reference to inspiration shows the value of art for Ondaatje. It reflects Ondaatje's strong adherence to an aesthetic manifesto, but can also become an alibi. As we shall see in Chapter 5, this will become similar to Rushdie's defense that *The Satanic Verses* is "fiction."

It is as if throughout *The English Patient* Ondaatje has been stressing the importance of history and of place, but the importance even more of being critical of the ideologies of history and place, of learning to affirm one's personally negotiated place among such worldly circumstances. Almásy "arrives" at such a position—the "post" after his "secular"—after he has witnessed Katharine's death in the Cave of Swimmers. He marks her dead body using pigments from the cave's paintings, affirming the richness of life, and concludes, "I believe in such cartography—to be marked by nature, not just to label ourselves on a map like the names of rich men and women on buildings. [. . .] All I desired was to walk upon such an earth that had no maps" (261). Almásy affirms a cartography which is his, not one which he has uncritically adopted through the orthodoxies of nationalism and religion, but one which he has personally negotiated and come to believe in from the world, being literally *marked* by that world.

The problem with postsecular affirmative values is that they hover precariously between the newness they envision and the risk of becoming another ideology. The beliefs and affirmative values with which Ondaatje experiments in *The English Patient*—love, friendship, community—must emerge *from* the world, be gained through experience *in* the world, through service *in* the world—the good nurse, the good explorer, the good thief, the good sapper. They must emerge *through* secular concepts like nation and race, and cannot mark a return to the violence of nation, race—and religion. Yet a writer like Ondaatje is aware that any affirmation cannot be an absolute one, signaling an easy new logic. This "logic" is similar to Leela Gandhi's idea of an anti-communitarian communitarianism that is perpetually deferred, yet-to-come.

Similarly, nation to postnation cannot be a simple one-way process. The postnation will be in a double bind, between nation and its others. It is that *boundedness* that can also be expressed as *oscillation* between nation and postnation, secularism and religion, race and affect, a body and a body without organs, and between law and literature. The enemy is intimate precisely because its logic is not one-dimensional: deracination is one of many roots, and routes. The postsecular is the sign in *The English Patient* of a possible unrooting, even un-routing. We can see the secularism of Edward Said in this novel, as skepticism toward nationalism. We can also see the wonders and enchantments arising from the aesthetics, not teleologies, of Christianity and Sikhism, and of the desert as a creative space. This combination of secularism and religion is postsecular, diasporically enabled in this novel.

Figure 4   View of the Himalayas at Shimla, India. Photograph by the author.

2 Minority's Christianity

Allan Sealy's *The Everest Hotel*

What would Christianity secularized within India look like? After exploring how Ondaatje in *The English Patient* experiments with the idea of nation by setting the novel within a transnational context, in this chapter I consider a writer who focuses on a particular nation. I examine Allan Sealy's *The Everest Hotel: a Calendar* (1998) and its representation of the challenges faced by secularism in India. Sealy's understanding of Indian secularism is informed not only by his location within India, but also by his English background, as an Anglo-Indian. How would an Anglo-Indian writer imagine postsecular possibilities? What would be the secular and religious influences in such a process? In this chapter I argue that there *is* a similarity between *The Everest Hotel* and *The English Patient*. I establish such a similarity in order to further argue that both texts paradoxically secularize religion *and* nation. For Allan Sealy, such secularization consists in challenging the narratives about a "pure" India and a "pure" Christianity. In place of such constructs, he turns to the enchantment of describing nature, as part of the land that is named "India," and explores what ethics might emerge that are independent of religion.

In *The English Patient*, Ondaatje empties churches and frescoes of their religious meaning, thus secularizing them, in a literary act that comes to admire beauty. Ondaatje secularizes nation by detranscendentalizing it: the religion of nation acts like a transcendent law that can command its followers to turn to violence. Ondaatje represents a diverse range of nations, with the luxury to explore what might come "after" nation. In the wake of the crisis of nation, what precariously emerge as postsecular values in *The English Patient* include love, friendship, and community, across the divides of "nation" and "race." In the case of *The Everest Hotel*, one of the critical differences between it and *The English Patient* is that whereas the latter's postsecular gestures are cosmopolitan in scope, *The Everest Hotel*'s affirmations emerge from within a single nation-state, India. Ondaatje's fifty years of continuous residence in Canada have made him more diasporically removed from Sri Lanka than Allan Sealy has been from India; hence the former's greater ease with experimentations, at times highly aestheticized, with postnationalism.

Sealy is a part of India's minority Anglo-Indian community, the hybrid descendents of the British and Indian encounter during colonialism. Sealy's minority consciousness within the nation-state informs his search for affirmative values in several ways. In *The Everest Hotel*, Sealy represents, with a few exceptions, a great diversity of characters that can constitute India. This is in order to secularize the transcendent story that says India is purely, naturally Hindu. How do ideologies construct categories of "majority" and "minority"? The opposition of "pure" and "impure" gives rise to differences between "religion" (as pure) and "secularism" (as impure). Similar to these distinctions, a connection can be drawn between the purity of religion and the purity of majoritarianism, the latter "purely" reflecting the nation. In the process, the secular and the minority become "impure," especially if the minority is racially hybrid. For example, colonial ideologies of superiority and inferiority can combine with religious ideologies, including those of Hinduism, to create and reinforce the Anglo-Indian as simply and only "inferior," "impure," and "hybrid." The Anglo-Indian exists between Englishness and Indianness, being both while simultaneously greater than the sum of those two parts.

The religious elements in this novel have their secular counterparts, and vice versa. Both processes borrow from the terms of the other, making themselves intelligible through the other terms, but then gesture to their own values. As I stated in the Preface, the postsecular is caught in a double bind between religion and secularism, informed by the best aspirations of both—such as faith, awe, and wonder, as well as political equality, recognition, and respect—while simultaneously greater than the sum of those two parts. It is greater because it opens an epistemic space, pointing with hope to an-other future yet-to-come. That future is unpredictable, and to affirm it requires a certain faith, one which is postsecular. The intermingling of the religious and the secular is reflected through Sealy's secularization of Christianity's rigid concept of charity: the young nun Ritu's understanding of charity is challenged by the real struggle and suffering of Brij in a world that is unjust and unequal.

Such a mirroring of the secular and the religious is a metaphor for the Anglo-Indian's situation and location as minority counterfaced against a religious and ethnic majority of India. This counterfacing can be reflected as follows: Christianity "is not" Hinduism; hybridity "is not" purity; and minority "is not" majority—and whatever other terms may reify and perpetuate themselves hegemonically, legally, constitutionally, and nationally. Yet there is more to one's self and one's life. That "more" is the interesting "otherness" to which Sealy gestures in *The Everest Hotel*. To secularize India is to detranscendentalize religious and ethnic majoritarianism. To re-enchant "India" is to turn to the beauty and majesty of the literal land and nature, using literary artifice to *craft* that beauty, naming it wonder. To secularize India is to demonstrate that it is constructed as "India," and that that same process of construction can create an-other possible "India" and, crucially, "Indian."

Before deepening the points above through readings of the novel, I would like to offer some background information about Allan Sealy, because neither the novelist nor *The Everest Hotel* enjoys as great a recognizability as others among the body of Indian writing in English. Born in Allahabad, educated in Lucknow, and having worked in the US, Canada, Australia, and New Zealand, Allan Sealy resides in Dehradun, capital of the northern Indian state of Uttarakhand, formerly known as Uttaranchal. *The Everest Hotel: A Calendar* (first printing, 1998) is his third novel. Sealy's first novel, *The Trotter-Nama: A Chronicle* (1988), is an epic tale of an Anglo-Indian family across seven generations; in its narration of history and use of magical realism, it is similar to Rushdie's *Midnight's Children* (1981). Sealy's second work, *Hero: A Fable* (1991) is a satire about Indian political life. Both it and *The Trotter-Nama* are irreverent and mocking in their challenge of the ideologies of nation and belonging, a challenge that continues in *The Everest Hotel*. Sealy has also published a travelogue, *From Yukon to Yukatan: A Western Journey* (1994). And in 2003 he came out with *The Brainfever Bird: An Illusion*, a love tale involving a Russian man in New Delhi. This was followed in 2006 by *Red: An Alphabet*, another love story with a Russian element, frequently referring to the world of visual art, with sections named after each letter of the alphabet.

The Everest Hotel is set in a former hotel turned convent-shelter situated in Drummondganj, a fictional town in northern India close to the Himalayas. Forming the backdrop of the novel is the political turmoil of a movement for a separate state, and protest against construction of a dam in the region. The central character, the young nun Ritu, stays in the convent for a year, providing care for the elderly eccentric owner of the hotel, Jed. Sealy presents a range of characters in the novel, including a Sikh bookstore owner, a Nepalese watchman, a Tibetan nurse, a deaf-mute goongi, a Latvian, a German visitor, the hills peoples and the plains peoples, and the city peoples and the rural peoples. As the novel progresses, Ritu is compelled to re-think Christian values such as charity and compassion, particularly through her conversations with the frequent Hindu visitor to the hotel, Brij. A small girl is left abandoned at the doorstep of the hotel; Ritu takes care of the girl, whom she names Masha. The novel concludes with the two on a train to New Delhi, where Ritu hopes to adopt Masha legally.

There are numerous similarities between *The Everest Hotel* and *The English Patient*. These include a small, eclectic community set in a sanctuary-like space in the hills, in the context of violence (World War II; agitations for the envisioned state of Akashkhand; and the environmental devastation caused by a dam). A young woman, whether a nurse or a nun, takes care of an old man, eccentric and on the verge of death, who carries a special book (Almásy's copy of Herodotus's *Histories*; Jed's *The Drummondganj Book of the*

Dead). That young woman develops affection for an Indian man, across ties of religion. There are several similarities toward the end of the novels: a bomb explosion; Kip's name reverts to the full version Kirpal, as does Brij's name to Brijeshwar; and a scene of the young nurse or nun heading toward an open, unknown future.

In *The English Patient*, Kip's reaction to the bombing of Hiroshima and Nagasaki dismantles the affect in the small villa community, but it is that turn away from affirmation which allows affirmation to re-emerge, virtually: the closing scene of Kip and Hana linked across time and space by the coincidence of an object dropped, and simultaneously picked-up elsewhere. In *The Everest Hotel*, Brij's bombing of the dam results in his death, but this also heightens affection, across a distance, with Ritu. She feels tremendous remorse and regret, and blames her naive ideas of charity. Whereas for Kip the bombing shows the brutality of the religion of nation, for Ritu, at the very least, it shows the violence of the nation of religion, that the Christianity with which she has so affiliated, as to a nation, has produced its own deprivations and controls, like the "empty salute" of Inge, devotee to Nazism: "her pursuit of purity, the black uniform, the blind salutes" (Sealy 1999: 217).[1] This element of Nazism also echoes the Nazism of World War II that forms the backdrop for *The English Patient*–a representation, in both novels, of violence and intolerance.

The idea of rewriting is also important in both novels. Jed's cherished book, the *Drummondganj Book of the Dead*, follows in the tradition of the Egyptian, Hindu, and Tibetan books of the dead. Sealy's other work also demonstrates his rewriting of former texts, such as the epic *The Trotter-Nama*'s rewriting of Kipling's *Kim* (see Crane (2008), Ganapathy-Dore (1997), Nair (2002)). In the same vein, critics have observed Ondaatje's rewriting of *Kim* in *The English Patient* (see Ismail (1999) and Randall (1998)).[2]

Like the Parsee minority community in India, the Anglo-Indians are largely urban-dwelling, in the major metropolises. Sealy's residence outside those metropolises undoubtedly informs his critiques of tradition, as represented for instance by Christianity's orthodoxies, and of modernity, as represented by the limitations of secularism. It is precisely the sense of constructedness that intrigues Allan Sealy in *The Everest Hotel*. Rohit Chopra argues that the novel "exemplifies the philosophical position that Anglo-Indian identity is both reflective of and beyond the conditions of hybridity and marginality" (Chopra 2006: 55); I extend this argument to state that the novel reflects and goes beyond the condition of the *secular*.

By "secular" I mean the secular of the Indian constitution, in its inability to fully and adequately recognize all minority groups, whether linguistic, ethnic, or religious. Minorities can feel excluded by the nation, that they do not count as either citizens or meaningful contributors to the state's policies, aims, and values. Minority provisions for Anglo-Indians, such as for employment, were gradually phased out by the state following Independence. The community has suffered violence, such as attacks against its English-medium schools. Akashkhand, the envisioned separate state in *The Everest Hotel*, functions as a symbol for the dissatisfactions with the nation-state. The novel also gestures to that which lies beyond the disenchantment of philosophical secularism: there are moments of mystery and the unknown, ones which lie beyond the grasp of conventional knowledge. Love, care, compassion, the power of nature, and the power of writing exist, independently of religion, as the postsecular values in *The Everest Hotel*.

2.1   The Anglo-Indian Community in India

Before offering a reading of the novel, I would like to present some political and historical information about the Anglo-Indian community. I do so because the community's minority position within India is one that is reflected in *The Everest Hotel*, particularly through the novel's diverse cast of characters which, by virtue of its diversity, challenges stories of an India that is naturally, purely Hindu.

The Anglo-Indian community in India insists on its minority identity: its biological connection to the British, English as its native language, and its Christian faith. Yet the community is also insistently secular, due to its location within an India that is predominantly Hindi-speaking and Hindu. During colonialism, the Anglo-Indians were given comfortable positions in government posts in the railway, customs, postal, and telegraph services. After Independence, these positions were afforded special provisions in the constitution, albeit for a limited time. Once the guarantees had lapsed, members of the community pursued opportunities in trade, business, and other professions (Anthony 1969: ix). The constitutional recognition of the Anglo-Indians was in some instances even greater than that received by larger minority groups. Some of these recognitions, such as appropriate recognition of the English language in the face of an Hindi hegemony, were hard-won by the community, led by Frank Anthony, President of the All-India Anglo-India Association (Anthony 1969: 289–351).[3] Other recognitions included guaranteed seats in the Parliament, and special protection of Anglo-Indian English-medium schools. In fact, in the new constitution, the Anglo-Indian community was the only one given a special definition, emphasizing its British descent (Anthony 1969: 5). But Anglo-Indians were the only group whose designation was removed from the 1961 census. Religious groups, however, were listed in that census, thus counting Hindus, Muslims, Sikhs, Parsees, and Christians (Anthony 1969: 9). The post-Independence period has seen large numbers of Anglo-Indians leaving India, emigrating to countries such as Britain, France, Australia, and New Zealand.

The Anglo-Indian community's hybridity has resulted in the above facts of special constitutional recognition, being privileged as descendents of the British. But the community has also faced rejection and exclusion, again owing at least to its British ancestry and its minority status (it is not "Indian" enough, Hindi is not its native language, is it really loyal to India?). Both the "indigenous" Indian communities and the British communities could accept or reject the Anglo-Indians by construing hybridity (e.g., miscegenation) as containing a "trace" of something either positive (e.g., pure) or negative (e.g., impure). The fact that I can frame the reactions and attitudes in such a formal schematic indicates their arbitrariness and constructedness. It is exactly this idea of constructedness that Sealy exposes in *The Everest Hotel*.

2.2 Reading *The Everest Hotel*

The Everest Hotel grants Christianity its positive aspects, such as care and compassion. But the novel also criticizes certain expressions of Christianity, such as its austere inflexibility, represented by the head nun, Sister Cecelia, and its rigid concept of charity, especially when the religion's virtues in the abstract collide against the material realities of inequality and injustice. Amid this Christianity, and amid the failures of the state, Sealy gestures toward and sketches moments of mystery, awe, and wonder. It is not that these moments are merely escapes. Instead, they are enmeshed within the urgent, and insurgent, presence of the political that runs throughout this novel. Sealy politicizes Christian and Anglo-Indian identities against a dominant Hinduism, and against the environmental destruction that continues under the banner of scientific modernity.

Sealy introduces each chapter with a rhapsodic, lyrical description of nature: mountains, leaves, flowers. Death, disease, and despair also pervade the novel: the sick, the elderly, and the infirm in the hotel; the leper colony; the economic frustration and hopelessness of the residents of Drummondganj; the goongi; the hills people watching their land being destroyed; the death of Brij. As Meenakshi Ganguly has noted, "one condition runs through the book: death and dying" (Ganguly 1998). In contrast to this is the highly formalized, elegant, symmetrical structure of the novel: Kalidasa's calendrical rhythm of the seasons, with summer serving as the opening and closing chapters. I agree with Manju Jaidka's view that such ordering is "part of the narrational strategy, part of the design, of the cyclic motion controlling the entire narration" (Jaidka 1998). Extending Jaidka's argument, the particular content and overarching form of the novel become a *metaphor* for the novel's tensions between the secular and the postsecular. The thematization of death, disease, and despair, combined with a novel structure that is contrived and creative, becomes a metaphor for Sealy's ability to both identify and critique contemporary dissatisfactions with the state, and also to allow creative scope for affirmations. Those affirmations are postsecular because they preserve a commitment to political secularism's ideal of equality (Ritu as an Indian Christian citizen looking to adopt an abandoned child, likely Hindu), and are born of the secular everyday (daily life in the uneven, asymmetrical nation). But those affirmations are also animated by ethics and values either informed by or similar to, but independent of, the religious ethics and values in the novel (through Brij and Masha, Ritu re-thinks Christian ideas of charity, undoubtedly including "love thy neighbour"). Nature/beauty, the literary/artifice, and the ethical (love) are independent of religion, and offer an alternative to it: hence "postsecular."

Caught between "Anglo" and "Indian," Allan Sealy would be especially compelled by the semiotic flexibility of fictional, literary form in order to critique and re-think concepts that fix ideas of what constitutes the ethical and political, whether in the terms of nation or religion. The combination of the plot's extremes of death with a highly contrived narrative structure demonstrates, albeit exaggeratedly, the flexibility of the literary sign at work, the sign showing its power, affirming itself, registering aesthetic form *as* affirmation of creativity. That literary sign is no accident, but falls within Indian narrative and representational traditions, which I discuss at the end of this chapter, showing that there can be productive engagements with the nation, so long as they are sanctioned by the politics of aesthetic space. Here are some of the thematic corollaries to the above tensions between content and form, between critique and creativity: an order of Christianity animates the hotel, but Ritu leaves it; modernity constructs the dam, but the dam is bombed; Jed is on the verge of death, surrounded by bodies in the cemetery, but he also speaks of the wonders of the soul; Ritu joins the hotel convent, but she unlearns and re-interprets the Christian ideas of charity, even love.

The distinctions represent a supporting structure, but Sealy gestures toward that which might lie beyond those distinctions. Sealy can paradoxically signify these phenomena or states of experience, ones which his characters might not fully understand, such as a re-thinking of themes or leitmotifs like nature, awe, wonder, mystery. Care and compassion emerge as postsecular ethical values in the wake of Christianity, and nature, awe, wonder, and mystery emerge from the crisis of the nation-state and the violence of its scientific modernity. The bamboo shoots all miraculously flower at the same time. There is the mysterious, elusive creature Ramapethicus: is it magical or real? The hill monkeys have a special burial ritual for their dead, placing flowers over the corpse. As Jed narrates the monkeys' story, Ritu stares at the mountains "with a look of wonderment" (157). Jed states he observes the goongi "[w]orshipping with a force [he] can only salute.

A force [he] would trade Everest for" (82). We could read "Everest" as both Everest the physical mountain and "Everest" as a marker of prestige on the global stage, an ultimate symbol of conquest (who can climb the tallest mountain in the world?), and perhaps even self-referentially as the novel itself, with Sealy's gesturing to the mystery involved in the process of writing.

Sealy stated in a 2006 interview that the writer is immersed in another world: "The process of writing a book gets you to a higher, greater intensity than almost anything I can think of [. . .]. Your world for the duration of that book, the writing of it, is truly other. [. . .] Writers are addicted to that other world in the way that a drunk is to his booze" (Roy 2006). As another example of awe and mystery in the novel, Brij, like Jed, is fascinated by the goongi, by her epileptic fit, and she returns "awe for awe [. . .] gazing at him as if he were a god" (109). The novel also refers to the practices of tantra, and the cult-like sacrifices of the cemetery goat, the mongoose, and the cat's paw. The abandoned young girl Masha, left at the convent's doorstep, is "*a mystery: a seashell on a mountain*" (275; italics original). The small bag that Masha never lets go is "[h]er treasure. A mystery, like her name. Like her. Nobody's child. Everybody's child" (233). Mystery is exactly this: belonging to nobody, and enigmatically open for everybody to witness, or represent in/as a novel, like land open to anyone wishing to name it, "Akashkhand." This process is similar to the passage in *The English Patient* of "the first step by a white man across a great river, the first sight (by a white eye) of a mountain that has been there forever" (Ondaatje 1992: 141). Nature, awe, wonder, and mystery stand outside secular human constructs. They gesture toward realities beyond the complete grasp of secular knowledge, and thus stand as a metaphor for the writer's ability to write, secularize, and make less transcendental the nation's hegemonies and their "natural" stories of community and belonging.

Sealy shows his recognition of the mystery of the process of writing. The mysterious circumstances of Inge's death prompt a detective narrative within the novel. Bisht undertakes the investigation, and the process of search and reconstruction becomes a trope for Sealy's larger deconstruction of religion and nation. Bisht has a dream of the sequences that might have led to Inge's death, but "[i]n the morning he lies there pining for the vanished dream, looking for crumbs of inspiration. [. . .] But it's gone, and with it those tantalizing revelations, promissory glimpses, intimations of complete knowledge" (219). The list—revelations, glimpses, intimations, inspiration (Latin *inspirare*, "to blow into," linked to divine breath)—suggests a religious register, but the context is thoroughly secular. What is the heaven-like corollary in this secular context? Bisht sees a book drawing "of a garden, the wicket-gate open. Hollyhocks along a stone wall and, in the beds on either side of an arch, dahlias. Bisht feels the sting of sudden tears: that is where he'd like to go, through that gate. Even if it meant never returning" (221). Because of the closeness of the above two passages, the inspiration, revelations, glimpses, and intimations of the first can be seen to find their fulfillment in the second, thus suffusing the world of nature, even if in a drawing, with religious-like animations.

Again: is that nature, that *land*, "India"? Is that animation, that *inspiration* "Christianity"? Not necessarily so. Sealy's Anglo-Indianness shapes his understanding of both the land and the religion. This minority situatedness allows Sealy to perceive the various limitations of both India as a political nation (that constructs "minorities") and of Christianity as an organized religion (that is controlling and dogmatic, represented by Cecelia's authority and power over Ritu). In the face of such limitations, Sealy turns to the *everyday* struggles of living in (a part of) India, inviting readers to understand and empathize with the day-to-day struggles of a simple man like Brij. Yet Sealy does not offer a mere description of facts. He animates his novel with moments of inspiration, as in the above passage of Bisht's looking at a peaceful garden gate that is beautifully adorned with flowers: that is where he wishes to go. It is in this intimate combination of the everyday secular (in "India") with an inspiration not unlike that of a religion ("Christianity") that we could see Sealy pursuing a space and possibility that is postsecular.

Ritu has a similarly rapturous relation with the natural world, as she crosses the riverbed and enters the forest on her way to the leper colony. It evokes memories of her "forest childhood" (256). She is troubled by the fading of her memories, "[o]f certain heightened moments when the world was transfigured, when it seemed she was truly alive. Every day there are fewer left. Some mornings a fragment will return, glowing to bewitch her as she wakes, more a feeling than a memory, and leave her mourning its loss" (257). Sealy links a childhood state of innocence and wonder—heightened moments, transfiguration, liveliness, glow, bewitchment—with a forest. The phrase "forest childhood" is suggestive. Is there a literal forest from Ritu's childhood days, or does this phrase imagine her childhood itself as a forest? In either case, Sealy intimately links the two, once again signifying the plenitude and wonder of nature, and the ability of literature to create, affirm, and represent such wonder, such creativity mirroring the plenitude of nature itself.

Just as Ritu's academic knowledge of *Shorea robusta* is challenged by the robustness and power of the actual forests, her idea of charity is challenged by her daily life in the convent and Drummondganj. About one-third of the way into the novel, Ritu and Brij discuss charity. She insists charity should be given to all, based on what they need. Brij counters with skepticism, even suspicion, mentioning that people and the world can be dangerous, against which one needs to protect oneself. He asks her: should charity be given to those who build dams that drown villages? Here are Christianity's values confronting the daily, secular life in the postcolonial nation under the local, regional, national, and international pressures of modernization. Brij attempts to bomb the dam, but he is unsuccessful, and tragically dies from his own miscalculation. At the end of the novel, Ritu reflects on their earlier discussion of charity, which begins with a comment by Brij: "'The world is full of dangerous people.' Her saying something about charity. She winces. Charity! [. . .] His confusion, her stubborn silence. Charity" (289). Ritu has unlearned some of the pieties of Christianity, through a thoroughly secular, worldly process. She has maintained her ethics of care and compassion, and now expresses them through her love for Masha, informed by her love for Brij. The postsecular moment emerges in Ritu's pursuit and practice of a personal ethics that is independent of religion's dogma and control.

Sealy thus establishes an intimate link between the challenges of both religion and nation. In the process, religion paradoxically becomes secularized, and so does nation. The concepts that can link both religion and nation are purity and hybridity. If India in its "pure" form is as a Hindu nation, then both Christianity as religion (other to Hinduism) and the Anglo-Indian as citizen will challenge that idea of purity. Taking this further, if the secular, in contrast to the purity of religion, is seen as "profane" or devolved, an impure reality, then that causes the secular to be seen to attain some of the qualities of hybridity, as an amalgamation of the diverse heterogeneities of the here-and-now world (think of this when the Anglo-Indian demands that the Indian constitution be politically secular; in the eyes of the intolerant purist, such an odious demand is seen as hybridity demanding *more* hybridity, thus polluting pure "India"). The paradox is that the Anglo-Indian community might be religious (inhering in a form of purity), but because that religion is Christianity (that is, non-Hindu, minority), it is tainted with impurity. In addition, the community's racial and cultural hybridity also degenerates it through the touch of impurity, making them un-national and un-Indian. The opposition between purity and hybridity reinforces the distinction between the religious and the secular.

This link between purity/religion/nation and impurity/secularity/hybridity can provide the theoretical underpinning for Rohit Chopra's argument that "redemption is offered outside the ambit of what is recognizable as the frame of the nation and beyond the conceptual terrain of opposing notions of purity and hybridity" (Chopra 2006: 68). In the preceding quote, for "the nation," substitute "the secular," "religion," or "Christianity." Like the secular and the religious, the concepts of purity and hybridity simply define and determine each other oppositionally. They are not "pure" *a priori* concepts. The hegemony of "purity" seeks to assert and replicate itself across both its content and form (as if as a concept it had "pure," uncontaminable edges and limits). And it is with such hegemony that it can at times dominate "hybridity" (any victory on hybridity's part is always already dictated by purity, e.g., the insecure Anglo-Indian's self-esteem as vulnerable to the vicissitudes of

British and Indian approbation and rejection). But the theoretical manoeuvre here is to recognize *both* categories as constructs with agendas. It is precisely constructs that Sealy is so keen to challenge, expose, and deconstruct
in *The Everest Hotel*.

Whereas Christianity was featured in *The English Patient* as the majority religion, in *The Everest Hotel* it becomes the minority religion. Sealy,
however, engages with Christianity more closely and politically than
Ondaatje, moving beyond Ondaatje's aesthetic raptures over Italian frescoes and tableaus. Sealy demonstrates awareness of minority status by
defining Christianity contrastively against Hinduism, as in the "not x, but
y" descriptive logic of the house that is "[w]hitewashed not in October,
for Diwali, but in December. Christians" (17). This is not to suggest that
Sealy privileges or prioritizes Hinduism, for when describing the watchman Thapa's pictures of two Hindu goddesses, he does not name them,
but only describes them as sitting on a tiger, or wearing a necklace of
heads (37). This is a subtle manoeuvre, for to dismantle the name—*Durga,
Kali*—also dismantles some of the connotations released by those names:
the hegemony of majoritarian Hinduism and Indianness, the "authentic,"
"correct," "Indian" "religion."

Like Ondaatje's aestheticizing vision, Sealy structures his novel through
highly visual terms, terms which contain certain cognitive value, giving perspective in all senses: "The hills, Ritu's hills, have shrunk to cardboard cut-outs
propped against black velvet" (70). Compare this with Hana's watching Kip in
the hills: "Each morning he would step from the painted scene towards dark
bluffs of chaos. [. . .] She would see the khaki uniform flickering through the
cypresses" (273). Consider also a consistency in tropes. The bougainvillea is as
"red as the sun" (23), Inge's hair is red, so is the "red carpet of fallen lychees"
(42), and so is the "[r]ed polished cement" (24) of Ritu's room. The morning
leaves are *"edged with a thread of crimson"* (151; italics original), and the red
stone that Inge carves varies in shades of red throughout the day, transforming
from mauve to oxblood to mulberry to puce (139), illuminated by the same
light that brightens Thapa's bottle of "red hair oil into a smoking jewel" (37).[4]

If Sealy's aesthetic formalism has linked the world of nature with the
secular constructs of society, then this becomes the secular corollary to the
words spoken by Padre Mishe at Inge's funeral, when he quotes from the Old
Testament, Isaiah 40:6, "All flesh is grass [. . .] and all the glory of man as
the flower of grass. The grass withereth and the flower thereof falleth away"
(253). All flesh is grass, all concepts are metaphors, all metaphors are red,
all concepts are constructs, and all concepts can be deconstructed. Deferred
among these are "Anglo-Indian," "India," "Europe," "Christianity," "Hinduism," "modernity," "secularism," "tradition." Compare this with Isaiah 40:8,
"The grass withereth, the flower fadeth: but the word of our God shall stand
forever." I am not suggesting that Allan Sealy's word has staying power like
the word of God, whether in form or in wisdom, but that a writer's ability to

construct metaphor from the worlds of nature and people shows a "faith" in secular creative power, one which I explore at length in Chapter 5 on *The Satanic Verses*.

Sealy's idea of constructedness as a mark of the secular is also revealed when Brij asks Inge why Christians bury their dead, contrasting it with the Hindu practice of cremation. Inge replies,

> "I don't know, I'm not a Christian."
> He is surprised, but sees she's speaking of faith. He had meant Christians, the group. The rituals they are born to.
> "But my uncle's grave, yes. It is important. He was a poet."
> Earth, leaf and air swim at the word. The marble slabs briefly leavened. Brij, who seldom reads, reveres those who write.

(131)

The tension between Christianity as a faith and Christians as a group (with rituals) reflects Ashis Nandy's distinction between religion-as-faith and religion-as-ideology, the former a way of life, the latter a form of identification for controlling various interests: political, economic, and otherwise (Nandy 1998: 322). The statement here, informed by Sealy's British background, is that not all Europeans are Christians, countering any naive or racist assumptions on Brij's part. At the same time, the distinction demonstrates Sealy's deconstruction of religion, contrasting individual choices of faith and belief with any overarching idea of "religion." That sense of the personal engaging with the wider world becomes clear by the end of the passage, when Brij expresses reverence for the role of the poet and the writer. This metafictional moment in the text parallels Sealy's ideas throughout the novel about the constructedness of categories. It also avoids any nihilism or despair in the wake of such critiques, quietly affirming the act of writing as creative, fecund, and (re)generative, and that such qualities are not the provision of religion alone, whether Christianity, Hinduism, or any other religious tradition and practice. Throughout this book, I will consider writers' affirmation of the creativity of literature, of the generative qualities of writing, as part of my argument on the importance of the aesthetic as a form of postsecular resolution.

Consider the closing scene. Ritu and Masha are on a train, heading for New Delhi, where Ritu will attempt to adopt Masha. Ritu has great love for Masha, and draws her close to her, with an affection richly informed by her memory of Brij, "Her [Ritu's] eyes say, My love, and then, my dear love" (297). We do not know what will happen to them. As both the narrative and the afterword to the novel state, Christians in India, at the time of writing (the novel was published 1998), could not fully adopt children. In 2000, however, the Juvenile Justice (Care and Protection) Act was passed by the Indian parliament. With the amendments added in 2006, this Act allows equal adoption rights to all Indian citizens irrespective of religion, for children falling under the Act's purview, such as those that are orphaned, abandoned, or surrendered.[5]

For Ritu and Masha, both the journey and how they have arrived at that journey are significant, moving through the controlling distinctions *through* which Ritu has emerged: Christian charity, secular charity, Christian care, adoptive care. Ritu has "always risked the world" (297). Ritu's secular journey and its secular risks have allowed her to re-think and rediscover the virtues of care, compassion, love, and charity *on her terms*. Even Masha has transformed from her original Hindi name Asha to her present Russian name, a secular mingling of different cultures. This closing scene suggests that Ritu must make a certain investment in the nation, turning to the state for legal adoption rights. Throughout the novel, Ritu has learned her own forms of care, learning to care for both Jed and Masha. But she must also function within the secular life of the nation, and its legal structures: Ritu feels Masha *"needs a mother, not mothering"* (276; italics original). But *mothering*, as a kind of *adopting*, represents forms of love and care that can continue without depending on the legal status of "mother" or "adoption." That is to say, there are other ways of adopting, away from the state and its laws. The secular legal future is unknown: it would only be eight years after the publication of the novel that Ritu and Masha could enjoy legally recognized full rights as parent and child. Yet that factor of the unknown is significant, indicating a certain courage on Ritu's part. As I stated in the Preface, re-thinking the secular and its juridico-legal structures will not be cause for immediate change, certainly not to those juridico-legal structures themselves, but it can open an epistemic space whose trajectories are unpredictable.

2.3 Indian Secularism and the Form of *The Everest Hotel*

If *The Everest Hotel* demonstrates ways in which secularism challenges and reimagines the purity of religion by re-thinking the latter's values, then the form of the novel also exhibits a similar dialogue of inspirations. A diverse set of Indian historical forms and practices informs the structure of Sealy's novel. By being inspired by such different forms, Sealy demonstrates a commitment to secularism, a metaphor for the Anglo-Indian community's commitment to Indian secularism. By commitment to secularism, I mean that although Anglo-Indians might be constructed in the national imaginary as "minorities," "hybrids," or even as "citizens," their lives in the nation are not just ones as objects waiting for state recognition and validation. Rather, they can be subjects of their own lives, and subjects of *their* idea of India. They can do so by building upon India's history, and re-imagining its present and future, by approaching different cultural traditions within India in a secular spirit of equality and respect.

Drawing upon specifically Indian literary forms was among Sealy's commitments as he prepared his first novel, *The Trotter-Nama*: "I needed to discover a form that belonged here [India]. [. . .] Indian modernism need not be a wholesale imitation of foreign objects" (Sealy 1993: 29). In the afterword to *The Everest Hotel*, Sealy states that he has structured the novel using the *baramasih* or twelvemonth folksong tradition. Sealy demonstrates this influence not just in the ordering of chapters by seasons, but also through the subtitle of the book, "A Calendar." The *baramasih* folksong tradition based on seasons is Bengali, the *bāromāsī*, with songs describing the passing of months from different perspectives: a religious perspective; a working perspective, from farmers' fields; a narrative perspective, as part of a larger poem; a woman's perspective, as she awaits her beloved's return; or as a test of chastity (Zbavitel 1976: 137). The seasons themselves, again as stated by Sealy in the afterword, emerge from Kalidasa's well-known Sanskrit poem *Ritusamhara* (*ritu* means season; *samhara* means compilation or abridgement), the title translated as "Garland of Seasons" or "Medley of Seasons."

These Hindu, Bengali, and Sanskrit influences are ones that Sealy then re-works into a Christian and Anglophone form and content: the story of Ritu, sharing a name no less with Kalidasa's poem. Assuming the logic of the *bāromāsī*, who is Ritu's awaited beloved? Apart from the obvious choice of Brij, with whom she had never paired, and who, having died, will tragically never return, we could invert the *bāromāsī* logic and state that Ritu is waiting for a love she does not yet know, a love informed by her Christian faith secularized by her year in Drummondganj, informed by Brij, and informed by Masha, a postsecular mixture pointing to a future yet-to-come, a train journey into the unknown. Ritu's openness to the future, one which she hopes will contain Masha, echoes Leela Gandhi's notion of an anti-communitarian communitarianism that I presented in Chapter 1, a form of affect that, because it is unknown and asks a courageous openness toward it, is "'indefinitely perfectable,' yet to come" (Gandhi 2006: 26). The *bāromāsī* also features in another Indian tradition, that of miniature paintings during the Mughal period, in various schools such as the Kangra school and Baramasa paintings, some of which depict the story of Krishna's and Radha's love throughout the seasons.

In addition, the idea of a calendar combining different religious and cultural influences has secular roots in a specifically Indian tradition, as demonstrated by Amartya Sen (Sen 2005: 330–333). Here I want to read syncretism or multireligious amity as being similar to the Indian version of secularism. It is well-known that the Mughal emperor Akbar (1542–1605), respecting the fact that he was ruling over a religiously diverse group of peoples, had welcomed to his court philosophers from many religions for debate and discussion. This influence of Hindu, Muslim, Christian, Jain, Buddhist, and Jewish religious traditions inspired Akbar to propose a new syncretic religion, the Din-ilahi. To accompany this new religion, Akbar created a calendar, the Tarikh-ilahi, or God's calendar, the year zero of which began, suitably, with the beginning of his reign, 1584 CE in the Gregorian calendar. This calendar was influenced by Hindu, Parsee, Christian, Jain, and Muslim (Hijri) elements. Although the Tarikh-ilahi fell out of use not long after Akbar's death, its secular, integrative vision influenced another calendar, the Bengali San. In the late sixteenth century the date of the San was moved back to coincide with the Hijri calendar, which was based on the lunar cycle. But the San continued in a fashion similar to the solar cycle of the Hindu Saka calendar (longer than the Hijri lunar cycle), explaining why the Hijri calendar is now "ahead" of the San.

How does this calendrical secularism connect with *The Everest Hotel*? It is an historical example of a secular mixture of several Indian influences on Sealy's text—Hindu, Muslim, Christian, Sanskrit, Bengali, musical, and painterly—ones which mark the text as uniquely Indian and secular in ethos. I make a similar argument in my criticism of *The Satanic Verses* in Chapter 5, demonstrating Rushdie's syncretic, secular use of historical Indian influences, such as images from the poetry of the medieval Bhakti saint Akkamahadevi and the Islamic and Urdu tradition of love songs, or *dastan-e-dilruba*. I also revisit Akbar in Chapter 6, in my focus on the role of art, secularism, and religion in Rushdie's writing after the *fatwa*, seeing Akbar as a secular, syncretist figure—one derived from an Indian, not western, historical context.

2.4 Conclusion

I want to conclude by reading a brief excerpt, about Brij. He is a man of rural India, angry at the city people and the foot-soldiers of modernization that are building the dam. He is unsuccessful in his attempt to bomb the dam, and tragically dies:

> "[Brij] was from here, local man. One funny thing. He was wearing a life jacket."
> "What, in case the dam burst?"
> Muffled military laughter.

(285)

What do those men know about Brij? What do the state's self-styled secular elites know about so-called subaltern faith? The postcolonial moment of laughter is made metaphorical in multiple ways: a simple, rural, "local" man (in Hindi, *aam admi*) mocked by the professional prestige of "military men." The laughter of the profession is the laughter of the nation, both groups constructed and sustained by the opium of imaginary affiliation. It is Ritu's naive Christian charity against Brij's worldly skepticism of charity, the latter risking his life for an imagined state; it is the face of prejudice as the Indian and British public laugh at each other and at the Anglo-Indian; it is the harassment of Hindu chauvinism against Christians; it is the anxious superiority of the Anglo-Indian Christian over and against Hindoo Indians; it is Jed's patriarchal, sexist taunting of Ritu and Inge. It is the laughter forever frozen in the half-complete mask that Ritu attempts to construct of Jed's face, believing him to be dead; the mask comes instead to resemble Commedia.

But postcolonial laughter is no laughing matter, for there's the creative postsecular rub: to write a novel, to construct a mask, to make art, to infuse life with inspirations that stand apart from the violence of nation and religion. How does Sealy understand such violence? He draws upon the histories and concepts of purity embedded within religion, in this case Christianity and Hinduism, links those concepts with the insurgencies of the political, in this case the postcolonial and national, and then *dismantles* the orthodoxies of all such constructs. Among postcolonialism's constructs is "hybridity" and its constraining ideas, just as western "multiculturalism" (whether in Australia, Canada, New Zealand, places where Sealy has worked) can reinforce the hegemony of the dominant group.

The Everest Hotel was largely well-received by Indian critics and writers, including Shama Fatehally, Meenakshi Mukherjee, Bulbul Sharma, and Khushwant Singh, with Sharma commenting that "never before has an Indian author of our time painted such a vivid, joyous, powerful and heartrending picture of our ever changing seasons" (Behal 1998: A37).[6] As I stated in the Preface and Introduction, if nation has become a kind of religious object, then what are the alternatives to such an orthodoxy? The move by writers like Ondaatje and Sealy seems to be to secularize the nation, exalting nature and the land, whether through the desert or through the hills. They have the privilege of literary aestheticization, and this comes with its own responsibilities, whether real or imagined, whether thrust upon them or disavowed by them in a marketing and marketed world in which they and their texts become signifiers of South Asia. The peoples living in the hills of northern India, such as the women of the Chipko movement embracing trees in order to prevent their destruction, cannot aesthetically rhapsodize about nature through the privileged means at Sealy's disposal, to an international audience eager to consume beautiful, aesthetically-pleasing (non-threatening) images of India. Would the courageous Chipko activists give quite such an excessive signification of nature, when fewer or even no words is more? Sealy's rapturous turn to nature is similar to Rushdie's frequent invocation of beautiful women as plot drivers and resolutions, risking a flat, blind creation and worship of the beautiful. What would it look like if Ondaatje, like Sealy, focused his writerly attention on a particular nation-state? Would the nation be secularized? One such secular expression could be the idea of human rights, and it is the various potentials, and limits, of human rights that I explore in the next chapter on Sri Lanka and *Anil's Ghost*.

Figure 5 Maharaja Lena (Cave of the Great King), Golden Temple of Dambulla, Sri Lanka. Photograph by the author.

3   Postsecularism and Violence
Michael Ondaatje's *Anil's Ghost*

How can we not want human rights? The question might seem intuitive, perhaps even naive in a world where injustices and violations occur with alarming inexorability. There is an ethically-based demand for human rights, even a romantic one that envisions, in Upendra Baxi's words, a "revolution in human sensibility" (Baxi 2002: 41). But the implementation of human rights legislation is no simple affair. The seeming universality of their ethical intuitiveness—the rights fought for by various grassroots movements around the globe and encoded in such treaties as the Universal Declaration of Human Rights and the Geneva Conventions—strikes crudely against their judicial enforcement in differing cultural and state contexts. Who decides when and how to intervene on behalf of human rights? How is intervention received? If the discourse and politics of human rights have emerged through solidly secular foundations—based on ideas of the "universal" and "human"—then what happens when that discourse and politics break down? If we were offered a gift, of say freedom or justice, would we expect any violence to be attached to it? Are gifts not supposed to be singularly benevolent? Pheng Cheah theorizes it elegantly: "rights are not, in the original insistence, entitlements of intersubjectively constituted rational social agents but violent gifts, the necessary nexuses within immanent global force relations that produce the identities of their claimants" (Cheah 2006: 172).

Here is an example of identities that can be produced by national and international forces. On December 2, 2010, WikiLeaks released a cable sent on January 15, 2010, by the US Ambassador to Sri Lanka, Patricia Butenis, indicating Tamil politicians' feelings of vulnerability if they insist on governmental accountability for alleged war crimes and human rights abuses ("Sri Lanka War Crimes Accountability: The Tamil Perspective" 2010). Butenis advised that the US should not pursue the accountability issue, in case it plays into the Sri Lankan government's effort at depicting itself as heroically withstanding a conspiratorial international community. Between Sri Lankan President Mahinda Rajapaksa and Patricia Butenis, who constructs and critiques the so-called "First" and "Third" Worlds? The words of Pheng Cheah again resonate: "each voice of human rights discourse claims to be the pure voice of reason representing genuine universality and to serve as an external check on particular interests and material forces" (Cheah 2006: 161). It is this idea of the universal and the rational, so intimately linked with secularism, that *Anil's Ghost* will represent, complicate, and question in its search for some affirmative values alternate to the limits of human rights.

Words such as the Sri Lankan "ethnic war" or "interethnic conflict" have tremendous emotive power, provoking strong responses from those inside and outside Sri Lanka. Ondaatje has written "to" Sri Lanka through his 1982 memoir, *Running in the Family*; his 1998 collection of poems, *Handwriting*; and *Anil's Ghost* (2000), his first novel-length treatment of Sri Lanka, through realist narrative mode no less. *Anil's Ghost*, like *The English Patient*, depicts war, but in this case, at the time of its writing, the war was ongoing, and not an historical re-creation. The ethical stakes therefore are elevated, and the stakes through which Ondaatje explores affirmative values are also elevated, raising dichotomies such as Sri Lanka/the west, Buddhism/secularism, writing/reception, violence/peace, and observer/informant. Ondaatje states that through his writing he discovers "a responsibility to diverse voices," and realizes that he owes them "the deepest intricacy. *Anil's Ghost*, of all my books, was the one where I felt that responsibility the most" (Ondaatje 2008: 90).

Anil's "in-between" location facilitates the ethical and aesthetic problems reflecting Ondaatje's diasporic nationalist concerns. How can he respectfully represent Sri Lanka? The process of representing Sri Lanka allows for a rich convergence between human rights as a politico-legal discourse, the aesthetic space of the novel form, and the historical moment of postcolonial Sri Lanka. What are the violence and terror that devastated Sri Lanka for over twenty years? What is Sinhalese majoritarianism? What is Tamil minoritarianism? Ondaatje invokes the discourse of human rights in order to elicit ethical, perhaps even political, responses to Sri Lanka, and to show how that secular discourse breaks down and becomes frustrated in its application to a particular nation-state context. The novel undoes Anil's naive ideas of human rights. In doing so, it abandons the political, so that the political is neither the solution nor opposition that Anil seeks. Ondaatje pre-empts some of this criticism of human rights discourse by making Anil open to unlearning her views and learning the "reality" of the "Third World," which includes Gamini and Sarath. These two characters become problematically the representative voices of Sri Lankan humanism: "them." Can the Sri Lankan—whether a character in a novel, or a critic in the world—gain, or be granted, agency only as a witness? The question of the witness, as much as the "truth," is deeply problematized in the novel. But to pursue those problems without falling into cynicism requires the sort of "faith" that is postsecularism.

It is that undoing and unlearning that I argue is the posting of the secular of human rights. If nation becomes a religious object, then secularizing nation by finding its alternatives can include human rights. But, as I have been arguing, even those human rights will not remain unproblematic, containing

their own potential for missionary-type ideas of salvation, redemption, and a patronizing benevolence. As Ashis Nandy has stressed: "the ancient forces of human greed and violence [. . .] have merely found a new legitimacy in anthropocentric doctrines of secular salvation" (Nandy 1983: x). Apart from the obvious "liberatory" ethics, the discourse of human rights also entails a liberal faith, as in Joseph Slaughter's words: "the international legal formulation of the right to public expression is premised on a liberal faith in the capacity of free speech to facilitate the realization of a collective, or communal, rationalism that is nonfascist, nonracist, and nonsexist" (Slaughter 2007: 152). The novel represents human rights within the space of literature, contesting and re-thinking their politico-legal secular limits.

The posting of the secular also occurs transnationally. Ondaatje's diasporic situatedness in Canada is informed by the secular multiculturalism which has circulated there as a state policy since 1971. That is the secular of Canada that Ondaatje brings to this novel, especially from as multicultural a city as Toronto, his home city and home to the world's largest diasporic Sri Lankan Tamil population. This is not to suggest that Canadian multiculturalism unproblematically informs *Anil's Ghost*. For instance, Qadri Ismail has demonstrated the novel's underrepresentation of Tamil characters (Ismail 2000a). But Ondaatje's minority situatedness in Canada should at least make him sensitive to minority concerns in Sri Lanka. In fact, Ondaatje also would be a minority in Sri Lanka, as a Burgher, a descendent of the colonial Dutch diaspora, and thus part of a diaspora in the "other" direction. Standing outside the Tamil-Sinhalese opposition, Ondaatje might feel this lends him a certain fairness toward both groups. But when he is also liable to being viewed, in Chelva Kanaganayakam's words, "as both the agent and victim of colonial hegemony" (Kanaganayakam 1992: 35), one must wonder what degree of acceptance Ondaatje could expect from the larger groups.

Ondaatje's Canadian and Burgher influences could also inform his understanding of Buddhism in Sri Lanka, particularly as he explores what forms of affirmation could emerge through Buddhism. As I stated in the Introduction, the Sri Lankan constitution privileges Buddhism, although there are articles stating citizens have the freedom to believe and practise the religion of their choice. The Sri Lankan state *should* be secular, in the name of equality, democracy, minority rights, justice, and peace for all its citizens. Ondaatje animates secularism by placing it in dialogue with Sri Lankan Buddhism.

But Ondaatje does not turn fully to religion, to Buddhism. Instead, his is a sort of "multicultural" Buddhism that he represents through the novel's closing image of a re-constructed Buddha statue. Ondaatje shows a *range* of Buddhisms informed at least by Hinduism and the Mahayana and Theravada Buddhist traditions. Minoli Salgado, referring to critics who charge Ondaatje for either not sufficiently laying claim to a long Sri Lankan Buddhist tradition (Suganasiri 1992) or, conversely, for being a Sinhala Buddhist nationalist (Ismail 2000a), has demonstrated how "reductive, hegemonic conceptions

of a singular and exclusive Buddhism are used to demarcate the boundaries of belonging and acceptance and how literary texts are caught in these exclusionary cultural registers" (Salgado 2007: 145). Literary texts are certainly caught in such registers, just as the postsecular is caught in a double bind between secularism and religion, as demonstrated by critics' varied responses to Buddhism and its aestheticization by Ondaatje. By re-thinking a Buddha statue, Ondaatje posts the limits of human rights through the affective and ethical intensities of *specific strands* of religious thought and practice: peace, hope, renewal, regeneration. That dynamic interface between the secular and the religious is what makes *Anil's Ghost* so rich—and so provocative. Euro-American-formulated human rights, Canadian multiculturalism, and Sri Lankan Buddhism: where is Ondaatje's text among all these?

This chapter has four sections. In the first section, "Representing Sri Lanka: Theoretical Considerations," I explore the role of aesthetics in trying to understand and represent phenomena resistant to representation, such as catastrophe and violence. The domain of the aesthetic emerges as that which facilitates a witnessing and sharing of the catastrophic so that the ties of affect and community can be formed, which I elaborate through close readings in the second section, "Affect." Aesthetic space allows for the representation of catastrophe, for a multiplicity of human voices. How those human voices, and their moments of silence, participate in certain ethics is where affect comes in, as a form of positive relation where the political forms of human rights have failed. The postsecular affective values that emerge are care for the other, friendship, understanding gained through one's vocation, all in fragile, small contexts: conversations on Galle Face Green, Gamini healing traumatized patients in fraught, precarious conditions. In the third section, "Buddhist Mythologies," I focus on the eye-painting ceremony of the Buddha to argue for Ondaatje's negotiation between a *religious* aesthetic and a *postsecular* aesthetic, and the perils and promises of such a negotiation. The final section, "Representing Human Rights," explores how human rights, as a response to violence and crisis, can inform, with success and failure, a search for the affirmative values outside the constraints of the political, the national and the transnational, and the juridico-legal.

3.1 Representing Sri Lanka: Theoretical Considerations

In this section I present the work of a series of intellectuals, from Sri Lanka and the west, whose writings can converge in understanding what is Sri Lanka, and which can provide some framework for theorizing the challenges of representation faced by *Anil's Ghost*. This section seeks not only to address the enormity of the challenge presented by politics and war, but also to unsettle the enormity of the existing discourses "about" Sri Lanka.

The creative and flexible space of literature, one with which Ondaatje has experimented throughout his works, allows Ondaatje to give dimension and voice to those affirmative aspects of human rights that might not

always be expressed through what Ranajit Guha has termed the "abstract univocality" of law. In his article "Chandra's Death," Guha describes how in a Bengali village in 1849, a young woman, Chandra, eventually dies from medicine administered by her sister to abort an unwanted pregnancy (the consequence would have been life expulsion from her village due to the illegitimacy of the child). Chandra's brother and two male relatives disposed her body at night. When the "case" came before the colonial courts, however, Chandra's death became a "murder," with Chandra's mother, sister, and the local producer of the medicine all becoming arrested. Guha argues: "a matrix of real historical experience was transformed into a matrix of abstract legality, so that the will of the state could be made to penetrate, reorganize part by part and eventually control the will of a subject population" (Guha 1987: 141). Could the state truly hear Chandra's mother and her sister, let alone recognize their humanity? The court decided only one relation was possible between the expression and the content of the depositions—guilt—which tragically became "the *truth* of an event already classified as crime" (Guha 1987: 141; italics mine). Fixing the "judicial evidence" in place then allowed the "stentorian voice of the state to subsume the humble peasant voices which speak here in sobs and whispers" (Guha 1987: 141). Subsumed under what? Under the control of an "abstract universality," one which "insists on naming this many-sided and complex tissue of human predicament as a 'case'" (Guha 1987: 141).

It is the abstracting voice of the state that Ondaatje challenges through the space of literature and in particular through the genre of the novel, one which, through a realist narrative mode, promises the offer of the "real" and the "particular." With the thematization of human rights *within* literary space, the empire of the sign becomes coextensive with an empire of ethics, a twinning I shall express through the concept of the "semioethical." Representing law through literature allows for a form of witnessing—characters universalize, particular identities become represented—that challenges the limits of the law's abstract univocality. That witnessing is not simply, in Ondaatje's *literary* case, detachment, or detached legal formulation, but rather a kind of participation. The novel presents us with, and takes us along, a process. Ondaatje begins the novel with human rights on the scene of the international, referring to human rights abuses in Guatemala, and then focuses on Sri Lanka. Anil moves from the US to Sri Lanka; she moves toward greater understanding of the Sri Lankans with whom she works, and at the same time gains insight into herself.

Before presenting some background on the civil war in Sri Lanka, I would like to offer a deconstructive moment. The "story" that I shall tell in giving "background" to Sri Lanka will participate in the very problems of representation addressed by the Sri Lankan intellectuals Valentine Daniel, Qadri Ismail, and Pradeep Jeganathan. These are also the problematics that Ondaatje faces in his effort at setting a novel within the "Sri Lankan civil war."

reader and written," as something which is multiple and textual (not empirical), a cluster of readings produced by multiple readers (Ismail 2000b: 304). These approaches free Sri Lanka from existing as a passive, subaltern object controlled by the uncritical, objectifying representations of anthropology or nationalist histories. Recognizing such a "subjectivity" in Sri Lanka sees it as having agency, an "internal" logic that resists easy translations and misrepresentations, indeed *any* form of representation that seeks to fix one authoritative meaning for readers, such as "place of violence." This readerly, textual, semiotic, and literary approach emphasizes "the singular, [the] unverifiable, [and] the minority perspective" (Ismail 2005: xviii). What some might configure from outside Sri Lanka as "culture" and "violence"—as if some essential property of culture *causes* violence, as if violence were *inherent* to Sri Lankan culture—in fact perniciously perpetuates the dominance of the west, through the filter of anthropology as a hard, transparent, empirical social science.

Sharing Ismail's deep skepticism toward anthropology and the western knowledge discourses it hegemonically sustains, Pradeep Jeganathan notes that violence "is an analytical name for events of political incomprehensibility" (Jeganathan 2000: 41). Namely, the misunderstanding that emerges for those located outside Sri Lanka is that the violence in Sri Lanka is due to culture, not politics. Jeganathan argues that violence as a distinct category in Sri Lankan anthropology emerges only after the violence of July 1983, an event which produced "a rupture in the narration of Sri Lanka's modernity" (Jeganathan 2000: 41). "Violence" thus commits its own violence, as a form of sealing off from a distance the knowability of Sri Lanka.

In *The English Patient*, Ondaatje explores forms of microcommunity and friendship which can be constructed in deterritorialized "non-places": among national identities; in physically deterritorialized spaces such as a ruined villa or a desert; among cultures; and among historical events and subsequent situation in the space of reflection upon those events. The aesthetic for Ondaatje functions as that which enables the "diagramming" of such affirmational possibilities: the fresco-murals in the church, the metaphors of tableau, the four characters "flung" against the villa. Each instance of aestheticization gives the reader, and undoubtedly also Ondaatje, a "frame" for understanding such moments of affirmation. When the space of the aesthetic becomes suffused with the forms of affect—for example, the love between Hana and Kip being enacted by Kip's taking her imaginatively to The Golden Temple, and literally to the Italian churches—the aesthetic emerges as that which enables Ondaatje to challenge the categories of nation and difference in order to affirm a form of humanism.

The aesthetic space of literature allows Ondaatje to present a certain subjectivity as opposed to a static objectivity, most obviously by creating "characters" with individual voices that the writer can juxtapose against one another. The emergence of an identity for the skeleton "Sailor" could be read as a metaphor for the emergence of gestures toward the humanistic. Given the insistence of Sri Lankan intellectuals on certain forms of representation, coupled with the creative potentials of literary representation, how can Ondaatje respond in ways that permit the exploration of humanistic values?

3.1.1 Aestheticization

As a process of representation, aestheticization might qualify as a discursive practice within the purview of Ismail's arguments about representing Sri Lanka. The ethical implication of this for Ondaatje is that he searches for various means to represent Sri Lanka in order to gesture toward its "infinitude of significance" (Ismail 2000b: 304).

Consider the aestheticization by Ondaatje of the up-country house (*wala-wwa*) where Anil and Sarath find refuge as they continue pursuing the mystery of Sailor's death. Anil finds a drawing there: "This simple series of lines of a naked water carrier, say, and the exactly right distance of his figure from the tree whose arced trunk echoed the shape of a harp" (202). Ondaatje is struck by the beauty of the house, the simplicity of his description reflecting the simplicity of the house and the drawing—a series of lines, calm shadows, and quiet, harmonious proportions. In contrast to such secluded simplicity is the fact that Anil, Sarath, and Ananda have gathered here to hunt "a public story" (203). Ondaatje concludes this brief passage by quoting the poet Robert Duncan: "'The drama of our time [. . .] is the coming of all men into one fate'" (203). Just as the house brings the three together, the canvas of the novel encompasses the private and the public, the simple and the complex, the harmonious and the violent—all men, all women. These distinctions fascinate Ondaatje, especially as they are played out in the "scene" of Sri Lanka, and he commits to the aesthetic in order to gain understanding of such secular, worldly phenomena.

As another example of aestheticization, here is a passage portraying Sirissa, the wife of the artist Ananda, as she reminisces on being able to walk outside, in the streets, past the curfew:

> *She'd turn a page and find a drawing of her by Ananda on a frail piece of paper he had tucked into the later reaches of the book's plot. [. . .] She would have preferred to walk into the streets after dinner, for she loved the closing up of stores. The streets dark, the fall of electric light out of the shops. It was her favourite time, like putting away the senses one by one [. . .]. And a bicycle riding off with three sacks of potatoes balanced on it into even purer darkness. Into the other life. That existence. For when people leave our company in our time we are never certain of seeing them again, or seeing them unaltered. So Sirissa loved the calm of the night streets that no longer had commerce in them, like a theatre after the performance was over.*
>
> (173; italics original)

Ondaatje turns to the aesthetic in order to gain some perspective, to *give* some perspective to the scene. There are references to the aesthetic within the aesthetic, to Ananda's drawings of Sirissa and of an insect. From that

domain, Ondaatje moves his gaze to the "local" of Sirissa, her engagement
with the "calm of the night streets." In the phrase "bicycle riding off," where
is the person riding it? This is an objectification, a distancing. The distancing
is achieved also in the references to other objects, "putting away the senses":
the shops, the stores, the vegetables. Each of these phenomena becomes "flat-
tened" and it recalls the device of "making a tableau" that Ondaatje uses in
The English Patient, when he writes that the four characters in the villa form a
tableau, flung against the war. Sirissa is also flung against the war, of course
by Ondaatje, and is in a private moment, alone. The perspectival shift that
Sirissa makes from this life to "the other life, [t]hat existence," is accompanied by a shift in visual perspective so that the deictic "this" becomes significant: here is what "this" life looks like.

This could be a belletristic, even charmingly pastoral scene, but the tragic
irony is that this is not sentimentalization, certainly not with a line like *"when
people leave our company in our time we are never certain of seeing them again, or seeing
them unaltered"* (174; italics original). Rather, it is the giving of some perspective,
the *creating* of some perspective into "everyday life," and hence another instance
of the aestheticization of Sri Lanka for the sake of understanding: art as cognition for Ondaatje, his readers, and for his characters. This might appear to be
a small passage of the novel, but in the compactness of its aestheticization, it is
representative of Ondaatje's position throughout *Anil's Ghost* of using the aesthetic as a cognitive device, in two senses: as a form of understanding, as *praxis*;
and "meta-cognitively," as a commentary on the process of cognition itself.

The aesthetic is healing. And healing—like the historicization of individuals and the metonymization of the nation—has a reductive quality, reducing pain—rupture, disruption—to the containable, and thus understandable,
domain of the present, and presence. It is a form of cognition, especially ret-
roactively. The problems of memory and its role in making sense of history—
rather, *a* history, *my* history—are perhaps what constitute the most pressing
task of any therapeutic process. An understanding of history can be achieved
in the domains of one's own life, and in the history of one's nation. The
genre of the novel allows Ondaatje to collapse the personal and the political. He represents the behaviour of his characters, Anil, Palipana, Lakma,
and Gamini, each of whose actions might initially seem incomprehensible to
readers. But it is through the narrative device of entering the histories of each
character—after their actions are presented—that readers can understand the
"deep structure" producing that behaviour.

Is Ondaatje's view of Sri Lanka, or Ondaatje's response to violence, therefore a *structural* one, one which says that history *is* important, that there
are indeed unique histories, and that they critically inform present-day
behaviour? Ondaatje recreates not just a "national" history (by "national" I
mean a reading of "Sri Lanka," as opposed to an individual) but also a personal, *human* history. When those people are Sri Lankans, it is the contiguity
between them and the surrounding war that allows for a "humanization" of

catastrophe and disaster. The link between the two, the extrapolation of patterns from historically-constituted individual lives, exhibits an affirmational quality. Encompassing these humanizations and affirmations is perhaps the greatest manoeuvre of them all: the act of producing "characters" within a novel. The genre of the novel and the larger space of literature enable these gestures, both formal and thematic, again indicating the space of the semio-ethical: the sign exists simultaneously with the ethical.

As I argued in the Introduction, the space of the postsecular is palimpsestual. In its affirmations, it might bear a resemblance to the religious, but it is not the religious, just as the religious is not the postsecular. The postsecular idiom might "borrow" elements from religion, such as its aesthetic expressions, as I will demonstrate in the section "Buddhist Mythologies," but translates and secularizes them into worldly contexts so that writers can pursue and affirm ethics, not doctrine. Ondaatje's interest in representation, the space of what I have termed the semioethical, is present throughout the novel. Each of these problems of representation is a facet of, and is implicated in, that larger phenomenon—semiotic, ethical, literary, institutional, philosophical—of giving shape to affirmation, of positing humanistic beliefs. Such postsecular affirmations *emerge* from material circumstances—disaster, catastrophe—which become the very conditions of possibility, or impossibility, of those affirmations.

3.1.2   Catastrophe and the Aesthetic

Mieke Bal has argued that the catastrophic nature of an event and the resulting trauma create a special interest in viewers toward the work of art and, ultimately, toward the artist. In contrast to Kant's and Shaftesbury's insistence on the "disinterestedness" necessary in forming aesthetic judgment, Bal argues for what she terms *interestingness*: an interest in the suffering caused by the catastrophe, an interest that undermines the public-private divide. Such commitment results in a form of witnessing, or sharing of the trauma. It is the catastrophic, overwhelming quality of the initial "event" that elicits and rivets such committed interest. The dealing with catastrophe *as* a cultural community reinforces the ties that create the community. The gravity of trauma and of catastrophe makes an *ethical* demand on a viewer or reader to more than "merely contemplate" the work of art. Bal states: "Whenever disaster happens, the secondary disaster of witnessing the primary disaster bursts the bubble—of, precisely, the self-evident preoccupation with those everyday miseries that keep our backs turned to real catastrophe" (Bal 2006: 172). Within Bal's notion of bursting the bubble (which subsumes "everyday miseries") is a notion of history such that the witnessing of a disaster—through art or otherwise—actually *defamiliarizes* the viewer-reader from an established version of history, the history that might be constructed by convention, norms, or otherwise.

Three dichotomies emerge in Bal's arguments about aestheticizing catastrophe: between experience and representation; between everyday life and

the catastrophic; and between the catastrophic and its isolated and traumatized subject. Ondaatje has gone home to Sri Lanka via *The English Patient's*
deserts of North Africa: we can read in Almásy the nomadic, deterritorialized, international Ondaatje. I believe distance in time, since at least *The
English Patient*, has given Ondaatje the strength to attempt representing the
Sri Lankan war, if even from a distance. This entire "act of literature" is
Ondaatje's effort at bringing the catastrophic to awareness and attention,
perhaps to the comforting ordinariness of the everyday. Ondaatje's matura-
tion is not just personal but also professional, bringing us to the third of Bal's
dichotomies: between experience and representation.

In light of this connection between disaster (as experience) and history (as
representation), we could consider Maurice Blanchot's views in his *The Writing
of the Disaster*:

> What about the *other* history, wherein nothing of the present ever hap-
> pens, which no event or advent measures or articulates? [. . .] It is a
> history in excess, a "secret", separate history, which presupposes the end
> of visible history, though it denies itself the very idea of beginning and
> of end. It is always in relation with an unknown that requires the utopia
> of total knowledge because it exceeds this utopia—an unknown which
> is not linked to the irrational beyond reasons or even to an irrationality
> proper to reason, but which is perhaps the return to an *other* meaning
> in the laborious work of "designification". The *other* history would be a
> feigned history [. . .] it is always calling forth the void of a nonplace, the
> gap that it is, and that separates it from itself.
>
> (Blanchot 1986: 138; italics original)

I read Blanchot's concepts of an "other history," of the "unknown," "excess,"
"utopia," "the void," and the "nonplace," as attempts to represent that which
has so overwhelmed—*excessively* signified—the subject that has experienced
the disaster. This is similar to Qadri Ismail's concept of post-empirically
reading Sri Lanka, to speak to Sri Lanka, to stand beside it, to try to capture that which is outside the realms of anthropology and western epistemological structures.

In a postcolonial context of violence, the resignification of self, in the
wake of catastrophe and disaster, is not without danger and caution. What
terms, deeply historicized, are always ready to construct the Tamil, the Sinhalese, the Sri Lankan? Here I want to turn to David Lloyd's theorizing of
recovery within the Irish context. Lloyd has argued that the collective, social
understanding of a violent and traumatic colonial history becomes deeply
problematic when it is construed as analogous to the therapeutic process that
must be undertaken by an individual recovering from a personal trauma
(Lloyd 2000: 213). For Lloyd, any correspondence between the private (the
subject) and the public (the social) is always already ideological. The subject

envisioned by modernity is one that is "fully-formed" and thus co-operative, a good worker: "the overcoming of loss is achieved by the direction of the subject towards identification with the state (or with the aesthetic disposition that prefigures it) as the representation of a restored wholeness and harmony" (Lloyd 2000: 218). As opposed to a simple process of "mourning," Lloyd affirms the more complex process of "living on," one that offers conditions for a subjectivity that is "subdued but not subjected" (Lloyd 2000: 227). Ondaatje's varied prose style and acknowledgments to the reader, however subtle and however direct, can be read as indications of the "considerable onus" of making sense, both personally and through literature, of a civil war. Lloyd states that the Irish Famine's meaning "does not lie in itself as an event, but in how it comes to signify within a set of practices through which the confrontation of incommensurable social formations produces new and again differing formations" (Lloyd 2000: 226). "Differing formations" expresses the possibilities of resistance and transformation. The reconsideration of the "event" by *living on*, by making sense of it and narrating it, constitutes the possibilities of new formations, "newness."

The aesthetic is not only spatial, but urgently *temporal* in its concern with, and eventual affirmation of, a hopeful future. It recognizes the historical formations of the present but also embraces an ethics that seeks an alternative to such history, to both the contents of that history and to the axis of that temporality. In doing so, the narrative drive of the postcolonial novel is temporal not just as an object (the novel unfolds in time), but also as an affirmation of a future, perhaps even a utopia—of community, of understanding, of love—*yet-to-come*. Radhika Coomaraswamy, in her response to Qadri Ismail's criticism of *Anil's Ghost*, defends the humanism in the novel, arguing that there are affirmational dimensions within all religions, and that we must direct our attention to those affirmational qualities, in spite of the political dimensions to which all religions are suspect. Coomaraswamy's response is interesting in that she twice uses the phrase "at this historical juncture" (Coomaraswamy 2000: 29, 30). Coomaraswamy is a former director of the International Centre for Ethnic Studies, established in Colombo in 1982. Her views on Ondaatje's novel are affirmational, showing the novel's impact on civil society in Sri Lanka. Coomaraswamy recognizes the historicity of the civil war in Sri Lanka, a recognition that although time will reveal the course of the civil war, there is hope that time will also encompass its end.

I have placed into dialogue intellectuals from different disciplines and locations. From broadly the "west" there is Mieke Bal, Maurice Blanchot, and David Lloyd; from Sri Lanka there is Qadri Ismail, Pradeep Jeganathan, and Radhika Coomaraswamy. They are concerned with the issue of signification, as reflected in their concepts that I have discussed: Bal's "interest," Blanchot's "writing," Lloyd's "formations" and "living on," Ismail's "subjectivity," Coomaraswamy's "humanism," and Jeganathan's "violence" (as a construct in the anthropology of Sri Lanka). In their configuration of the space between signified (event, object, society, violence) and signifier (representation, narrative, theory), these concepts can be viewed as deeply concerned with the ethics of the relation between signified and signifier. *This* is catastrophe, violence, and disaster doing *their* writing, through criticism, through theory, through this book. Such an impact can produce an ethical responsibility, one which like a "shriek in the dark" catalyzed Valentine Daniel's commitment to understanding violence (Daniel 1996: 105). In the following sections I examine the particular thematics through which Ondaatje represents violence.

3.2   Affect

Joseph Slaughter has argued that Anil functions "as a narrative device to study the mechanics of sphere-making and the discursive conditions of possibility for forming democratic, paranational collectives in the absence of both a legitimate democratic-state formation and an operative egalitarian national public sphere" (Slaughter 2007: 187). It is in this sense of the "paranational" that I want to explore how relations of affect—love, tenderness, care—can offer forms of belief outside the failures of human rights, nation, and organized religion.

Lakma, traumatized by the murder of her parents, is sent to live in a government ward run by nuns, but understands "the falseness of the supposed religious security around her, with its clean dormitories and well-made beds" (103). This is Ondaatje's method of indicating his criticalness toward (institutionalized) religious belief. The rest of his character development of Lakma will demonstrate his belief in the healing ability of love and tenderness. *Anil's Ghost* presents us with the challenges involved in intimacy and trust. Can Anil and Sarath trust each other? Can any family, Sinhalese or Tamil, trust a public mourning for their lost ones without fear that their families will be targeted? Can Anil trust the love of Cullis? Can the government be trusted? The following passage illustrates the growing trust between Lakma and Palipana, based on an ethics of care for the other:

> Every morning she wet his face with water she had boiled over a fire, and then shaved him. [. . .] In the late afternoon the girl sat between his legs, and his hands were in her long hair searching for lice with those thin fingers and combing it while the girl rubbed his feet. When he walked she steered him away from any obstacle in his path with a slight tug of the sleeve.
>
> (106)

Lakma's care for Palipana is similar to Hana's care for the dying Almásy; the makeshift, deterritorialized space of the villa in *The English Patient* has now become a forest grove. Palipana's blindness stands as a metaphor for his physical withdrawal and ascesis, representing another kind of retreat, from grand narratives and conventional notions of truth. He says to Lakma: "'We are, and I was, formed by history [. . .].' 'But the three places I love escaped it. Arankale. Kaludiya Pokuna. Ritigala'" (105). These are all sites of ancient Buddhist monasteries in Sri Lanka, and it is in Kaludiya Pokuna, near the ancient monastic city of Anuradhapura, where Lakma finally cremates her uncle. She carves on a rock face one of the phrases that Palipana had first uttered to her, "Not his name or the years of his living, just a gentle sentence once clutched by her, the imprint of it now carried by water around the lake" (107). This sentence appears roughly one-third of the way into the novel, after meditations on whether it is possible to represent all aspects of Sri Lanka, such as through the National Atlas (39–40) or a list of the dead (41). Ondaatje has presented us with the difficulties of preserving history and lost lives. Only rock and stone can memorialize phenomena. Palipana's phrase on the rock serves as an anchor for Lakma, as an affirmation of tenderness, of the possibility of love and trust, of the memory and persistence of a certain faith beyond the forces of history.

In *Anil's Ghost*, it is forms of a "new" language that enable, through trauma, possibilities of friendship and of microcommunity, as we saw in *The English Patient*. After Ananda has modelled the face of Sailor to resemble that of his dead wife, Anil suddenly understands Ananda's wish for peace and reconciliation. In response to Sarath's questions, "'*Who were you crying for? Ananda and his wife?*'" (186; italics original), Anil replies,

> "Yes" [. . .]. "Ananda, Sailor, their lovers. Your brother working himself to death. There's only a mad logic here, no resolving. Your brother said something, he said, 'You've got to have a sense of humour about all this— otherwise it makes no sense.' You must be in hell if you can seriously say things like that."
>
> (186)

Ananda's response:

> He moved two steps forward and with his thumb creased away the pain around her eye along with her tears' wetness. It was the softest touch on her face. [. . .] Ananda's hand on her shoulder to quiet her while the other hand came up to her face, kneaded the skin of that imploded tension of weeping as if hers too was a face being sculpted [. . .]. This was a tenderness she was receiving. Then his other hand on her other shoulder, the other thumb under her right eye. Her sobbing had stopped. Then he was not there anymore.
>
> (187)

The space of the aesthetic manifests in several ways here. It expresses itself as an aesthetic object: Ananda had previously sculpted the face of Sailor, which ultimately bore a very peaceful, and therefore unlikely, expression. The passage functions as an aestheticization by Ondaatje: he has created these two characters, and poeticized a fleeting moment. There is also a dimension of metafictional aestheticization here. When Ondaatje states, "This was a tenderness she was receiving," we readers of course already know this, but the self-consciousness on his part foregrounds the literary space through which *we* are receiving constructions of that tenderness. The aesthetic also appears as a form of "knowing" (cognition) by the body, because Ananda and Anil cannot speak a common language.

This passage might be read as sexual, with "active" male gestures toward the "passive" female. But to underscore the importance of "tenderness," Ondaatje shifts perspective so that instead of "this was a tenderness he was giving," he puts us actively in the position of Anil, one "she was receiving." Like the lights flickering in the train as the thug lifts the dead body to throw it out the window—"*he might have been a tableau in somebody's dream*" (31; italics original)—Ananda is also "not there anymore," fading out of the scene. But the memory remains for Anil. As Patricia Chu states, "Ananda's suffering and his compassion for Anil open her emotionally and restore to her a sense of membership in an imagined community she had forsaken, that of Sri Lankans seeking justice" (Chu 2006: 99). Such an emotiveness may risk becoming merely sentimental, but the wider political climate prevents such an easy elision. I agree with Hilde Staels's argument that "the expression of embodied experiences (affects and drives) [. . .] play[s] a significant part in what may be regarded as Ondaatje's ethics of love" (Staels 2007: 980).

Anil's equation of Ananda's tenderness with that of her mother's love takes us from the possibility of the sexual and into that of the affectionate. Notice Ondaatje's significant phrase "sexuality of spirit" used in an earlier passage when Gamini is overwhelmed by the pain and suffering he witnesses in the hospital:

> He turned away from every person who stood up for a war. Or the principle of one's land, or pride of ownership, or even personal rights. All of those motives ended up somehow in the arms of careless power. One was no worse and no better than the enemy. He believed only in the mothers sleeping against their children, the great sexuality of spirit in them, the sexuality of care, so the children would be confident and safe during the night.
>
> (119)

"Sexuality" emphasizes some essential, perhaps even primal quality, a careful and caring, not careless, power flowing between mother and child, outside of such abstractions as land, ownership, and rights—each vulnerable to the vanity and violence of power. Ondaatje configures spirit and care as sexual; the alliteration of sibilants in "sexuality of spirit" no doubt appeals to the poet in Ondaatje.

But Gamini's belief is contrastive, *against* the other motives listed above, so that caring for the other can be seen as an ideal. Ondaatje thus invokes again—in the now familiar sequence of violence, trauma, affect, affirmation—an "other" space, non-linguistic and unnameable. In *Anil's Ghost*, we also witness a physical space not unlike the villa of *The English Patient*: Galle Face Green, well-known in Colombo as a space for gathering. It is the site where Sarath, Anil, and Gamini are able to have a friendly late-night conversation, with Gamini eventually resting his head against Anil's thigh, unconsciously it seems to Anil.

The non-verbal also appears again in the context of a crisis: Anil saves Ananda from trying to commit suicide. The knife is still in his hand as Anil tends to Ananda's stabbed neck: "She felt she could speak in any language, he would understand the purpose of any gesture. How far back was their moment of connection, when his hand had been on her shoulder? Just a few hours earlier" (197). Moments of crisis contain the potential of creating affective bonds among characters, emphasized by Ondaatje's use of the metaphor of "citizening": "She was with Sarath and Ananda, citizened by their friendship—the two of them in the car, the two of them in the hospital while a stranger attempted to save Ananda" (200). Writing about *Anil's Ghost*, Victoria Burrows laudably argues that trauma theory should widen its western ethnocentric scope to recognize the suffering of those in postcolonial nation-states (Burrows 2008). The caution here is that trauma theory should not reproduce the limitations of an anthropological discourse that would only see Sri Lanka as a place of "violence"—and thus, potentially in trauma theory, as a place only of "suffering"—and its inhabitants only as victims without agency. Instead, intellectual discourses can seek to understand, as Ondaatje does in this novel, the fullness of "other" experiences, recognizing that such experiences can productively inform, shape, and enrich epistemological imaginations.

From a different context (affective, social, cognitive), consider the space for contemplation made possible by a large fresco: the figures are literally larger than life (recall the frescoes in *The English Patient*), so that life itself becomes offered—made static—for contemplation. Both these processes, traumatic and visual aesthetic, operate significantly in *The English Patient* and *Anil's Ghost*. The worldliness of trauma, what Lloyd terms "initiating terrorization," will inform not a detached contemplation, but rather, in Bal's terms, an *interested* one. And it is the interestedness driven by such an urgent worldliness that will *affirm* the affective relations and microcommunities that can be possible in such contexts. The aesthetic itself becomes a form of reconstruction and healing in the wake of the crises of nation and postcoloniality; the particular "themes" and "characters" it creates become metaphors of healing, and vice versa. As Gillian Roberts states, *Anil's Ghost* "presents hospitality and its embodiment in healing as necessary to the process of reconstruction, both personally and nationally" (Roberts 2007: 962). The affirmative values of friendship and community, explored also in *The English Patient* through the crises of worldliness, form part of Ondaatje's postsecularism.

3.3   **Buddhist Mythologies**

In a 1992 interview, Ondaatje tells Eleanor Wachtel that Sri Lanka's "landscape, politics, and religion affected [him] on a subconscious level," and that
his interest in the religion of the island had increased since writing *Running in
the Family* (Wachtel 1994: 259). In this section I examine the function in *Anil's
Ghost* of the aesthetic as "aesthetic object," the conscious fashioning of aesthetic
form. The aesthetic, along with human rights, becomes a way of structuring
violence. The artist Ananda reconstructs the face of Sailor, using clay. The face
bears a calm and peaceful expression, and resembles Ananda's wife, who had
disappeared from their village. This passage then concludes as follows:

> Anil rose and walked back into the dark rooms. She could no longer
> look at the face, saw only Ananda's wife in every aspect of it. She sat
> down in one of the large cane chairs in the dining room and began
> weeping. She could not face Sarath with this. Her eyes grew accustomed
> to the darkness, she could see the rectangular shape of a painting and
> beside it Ananda standing still, looking through the blackness at her.
>
> (185)

The reconstructed face (and head) as aesthetic object not only structures a
response to a violent event but its very act of structuring is suffused with an
intention, even an ethics (how one *ought* to structure), which converts trauma
into healing, using the domain of the aesthetic.

What is interesting about this passage is the presence of Ondaatje also as
"artificer." Anil gazes at Ananda, who returns her gaze. The transaction is
wordless. Ondaatje emphasizes this wordlessness, his act of emphasis itself
aesthetically-charged, on two levels. On one level it involves art objects, and on
another level the novel's status as *aesthetic structuring* of violence is made significant by the "painterly" scene, again returning readers, as in *The English Patient*,
to Ondaatje's cinematic gaze. Anil can finally see Ananda in the darkness.
He is standing next to a painting, "standing still" as if in a mural. Embedded
within Anil's view, although not made explicit by Ondaatje, is the rectangular-
ity of the wall against which Ananda stands, its shape repeated in the shape of
the painting. Perhaps Anil "could not face Sarath with this," but her interaction with Ananda is a direct facing. Ondaatje places Anil and Ananda in view
of each other, coming to know of the other, allowing Anil to feel compassion
toward him, and thus affirm him. In the process, Ondaatje affirms the ethic of
accepting the other, of feeling compassion toward the other.

Though the scene is largely "static," what rivets it is the emotion, creating an
unambiguously serious scene; there is not a trace of irony in Anil's recognition
of Ananda's having to cope with loss, indeed violence. Consider also the young
girl Lakma, who has witnessed the murder of her parents: it "touched everything within her, driving both her verbal and her motor abilities into infancy.

This was combined with an adult sullenness of spirit. She wanted nothing more to invade her" (103). Could we imagine any ironizing of such a state? This lack of irony is also in Ondaatje's gaze, and *his* form of looking at readers is constitutively aesthetic, from across the darkened rooms of time and space. The aesthetic is co-extensive with the ethical. Because both methods structure violence (or its consequence: trauma), the very fact of the aesthetic having a relation with readers-viewers (the "interest" of Bal) marks it as fundamentally humanistic, making it possible for it to create affirmations.

Before delving into the specifically Buddhist imagery in *Anil's Ghost*, I would like to read another passage demonstrating the aestheticization of violence. I had earlier referred to this passage—it is one of the first descriptions of violence in the novel. As a train passes through a tunnel, a man quickly strangles a passenger and then hurls the dead body outside the window:

> *He had a minute left. He stood and lifted the man into his arms. Keeping him upright, he steered him towards the open window. The yellow lights flickered on for a second. He might have been a tableau in somebody's dream.*
>
> (31; italics original)

This passage continues for a page and a half and is entirely in italics, set off from the rest of the text both typographically and as an independent section, as a kind of tableau itself. This "making static" of violence is a form of "containing" it, of making it comprehensible. The word "dream" condenses the metafictional angle of this passage. Several senses of "dream" are possible: the aesthetic as dreamlike (removed from the "real world"); the aestheticization of the everyday and fleeting, but punctuated by violence; the traumatized subject's reaction of being in a "dream," an unreality and a denial.

The aestheticization of Buddhism in *Anil's Ghost* consists not just of an object but also of an ethics, thus instantiating the semioethical via a particular ethics: religious ethics. In the closing image of the novel, Ondaatje presents the eye-painting or *nētra mangala* ceremony performed on a large reconstructed statue of the Buddha. This ceremony represents the confluence of literary and philosophical meditations on alterity, with recognition of the other as necessary for affirming community. Among the problems here is that Ondaatje situates this religious ceremony at the end of the novel, thereby presenting a sort of "resolution" to the various themes marking the text. And because it occurs in a semioethical space, the admiration that the characters might have for the reconstructed Buddha statue, as an aesthetic object, could also stand as an admiration for the ethics represented by it. Although Ondaatje might be seen to be affirming the ethics, he does so at the risk of privileging Buddhism. Such a possible privileging can be problematic, given the political context of Sri Lanka. I elaborate upon this below, but first I trace some relations between a Buddha statute and the ethics it might represent.

Ondaatje's literary representation of the Buddhist eye-painting ceremony bears a resemblance to the reciprocal alterity that Emmanuel Levinas conceptualizes in a western philosophical context. Levinasean ethics, with its intellectual debt to Martin Buber's I-Thou philosophy, rests upon the reciprocity of a self-other relation. Ondaatje represents this reciprocal relation and also represents the possible tensions within it. The artist Ananda becomes key to Ondaatje's markings of the ambivalence possible in such a dialogical ethics. In re-creating the Buddhist eye-painting ceremony, Ondaatje refers to the work of Ananda Coomaraswamy, author of the landmark study *Medieval Sinhalese Art* (1956).

Levinas argues that the condition of ethics emerges from the transcendent outsideness of the other, and that it is the reciprocity of respect between self and the other that conditions that ethics:

> Transcendence is what turns its face towards us. The face breaks the system. [. . .] The interlocutor appears as without history, as outside the system. I can neither fail nor vindicate him; he remains transcendent in expression. [. . .] The face that looks at me *affirms* me. [. . .] The term respect can be taken up again here; provided we emphasize that the reciprocity of this respect is not an indifferent relationship, such as a serene contemplation, and that it is not the result, but the *condition of ethics.*
>
> (Levinas 1979: 36; italics mine)

"Transcendence," for Levinas, may be glossed as "outside of," something outside a system and with the potential to break a system. What is important for Levinas is a reciprocal respect that, in Bal's terms, is "interested," not indifferent. Levinas's "serene contemplation" is similar to Bal's view of "disinterestedness." For Bal, interestingness is a condition for participation—empathic, conceptual, social, historical—in a work that aestheticizes catastrophe. For Levinas, such interestingness becomes the very *condition* of ethics, of an ethics yet-to-come, like Leela Gandhi's notion of an anti-communitarian communitarianism signaling a community yet-to-come (Gandhi 2006: 26). It is probable that the art-object for Levinas could also qualify as a "face," the presence of something so other yet also containing the ability to *affirm* its viewer or reader, to engage the viewer-reader in a dialogue.

Ondaatje's looking at his history is a condition of such ethics and one that affirms Ondaatje as both Sri Lankan and Canadian. In fact, one could argue that *Anil's Ghost* is constructed as a looking glass for Ondaatje. The mutual gazing is not therefore "merely" a contemplation but integral to the process of affirming the other, an affirmation which conditions the possibility of there being an ethical relation between the two. What is critical is that, like Levinas's interlocutor, the art-object only *appears* "as without history." *Anil's Ghost* is not just connected with a history, a crisis of violence, but in fact will come to constitute part of that history, as a product, as a text in the world. Thus, what is problematic is that *Anil's Ghost* is not "only" an aesthetic object. It is also unavoidably political. Although Ondaatje might privilege the philosophical and abstract aspects of Buddhism, he does so at the risk of underprivileging the material, present facets of violence implicated in Buddhism's practice.

A striking contrast between the philosophies of Levinas and the narrative world of *Anil's Ghost* is that the face of the other in Ondaatje's text is that of a statue. The eyes of the Buddha exist at the interface between artifice and real presence: they transform the raw material into a sacred object. Palipana explains the significance of painting the eyes, the *nētra mangala* ceremony: "'Without the eyes there is not just blindness, there is nothing. There is no existence. The artificer brings to life sight and truth and presence" (99). Ananda Coomaraswamy explains that the ceremony was necessary for any image of the Buddha, whether in a statue or painting: "The [*nētra mangala*] ceremony had to be performed in the case of any image, whether set up in a vihāra or not" (Coomaraswamy 1956: 47). Richard Gombrich describes the transformative moment: "The very act of consecration indicates that the statue is being brought to life" (Gombrich 1966: 24).

The eyes thus veritably bring the Buddha to life. In Buber's terms of I-Thou, the eye-painting ceremony enables the Buddha to become a "whole being," whom one could understand as a "Thou" (Buber 1958: 31). Re-cognition of the other, through seeing, is enabled by art. Ondaatje's understanding of the aesthetic might therefore also be informed, however consciously or not, by this embedded notion of the aesthetic as a form of understanding (cognition) conveyed through materiality and affect, through the domain of the body. There could thus be a parallel between "aesthetics" as a somatically-based form of understanding and the Buddhist importance of aesthetic "seeing" as a bodily-based process. Human bodies suffuse the world of *Anil's Ghost*—murdered bodies, painted bodies, emaciated bodies—underscoring the 'thing itself' that can be the site of both violence and peace, like rocks that "could hold one person's loss and another's beauty forever" (104).

The act of painting the eyes of the Buddha affirms Ananda's faith in artists and their work: "He stood over what they had been able to re-create of the face. It was a long time since he had believed in the originality of artists" (303). What might this belief signify? Ananda Coomaraswamy describes art's ability to humanize and spiritualize one's labour, whether in the ornamentalization of an everyday object or in religious art, the latter aiming toward "the revelation of the divine," with Buddhism serving as the chief patron of the fine arts (Coomaraswamy 1956: 47). As a parallel to creating artwork as a connection with the divine, consider the characters throughout *Anil's Ghost* and *The English Patient* in their dedication to their vocation: Gamini's devotion to his medical duties, travelling to work in the fraught conditions of the northeast; Hana's care for Almásy; Kip's commitment to the art of sapping; Almásy as accomplished cartographer. Each of these examples of devotion to one's work is not unlike religious devotion. What is common to both "devotions" is a practical, hands-on ethics. Ondaatje stated in an interview that "'[t]o me, the book is dedicated to people like that [forensic anthropologists] and to doctors, who tend to be unsung heroes in these situations'" (Kanner 2000). As Jon Kertzer has noted, these forms of work "elicit all the virtues that Ondaatje treasures: patience, tact, curiosity, encyclopedic information, daring speculation, rigorous logic infused with a sense of wonder" (Kertzer 2003: 121).

In *Anil's Ghost*, if there is any humane devotion to one's work, there is also its inverse, violence: "[Ananda] knew if he did not remain an artificer he would become a demon. The war around him was to do with demons, spectres of retaliation" (304). Ondaatje places these observations *after* Ananda performs the ceremony. For the artist, the secular immersion in creating art, in using one's body to literally give shape to one's work—worldly practices, and not just mere contemplation—allows for affirmations to emerge. This resonates with the aesthetic significance of the frescoes in *The English Patient*, with art serving as cognition: painting the Buddha statue allows for Ananda to see within himself, and to have insight into the war around him.

Having presented the ambivalence of faith and violence, Ondaatje's extraction of "non-religious" elements from a particular religious practice—in invoking the space of *affirmation*—risks conflating the affirmational dimension of the *postsecular* with the doctrinal space of the *religious*. Elements of a religious practice like painting a Buddha statue might be aesthetically attractive, but, as I have already been suggesting in this section, what becomes problematic is when elements of that religion also have political dimensions, implicated in a decades-long civil war, becoming symbols of ethnic majoritarianism. Stanley Tambiah describes a trajectory in the Sri Lanka of the 1980s that moved from a Buddhism that "fit" the traditional expectation of advocating non-violence, to a Buddhism emptied of its humane ethics (compassion, tranquility) and constituted by monks engaged, sometimes violently, in "Sinhala-religio-nationalist and social reform goals" (Tambiah 1992: 92). The space of the aesthetic is not something transcendent of the political and the historical; it would be disingenuous to claim so. The consequence of this for Ondaatje is that his text *as text*, as textual representation of conflict, occupies a position that is both political and historical in ways that could partly undermine his ethical aims.

The political and violent dimensions of Buddhism are the "ghosts" haunting Ondaatje's novel, especially its reception. Marlene Goldman has argued that Ondaatje's portrayal of Buddhism is not one that simply equates it unproblematically with a homogenous, unified Sinhalese nationalism (Goldman 2005). She highlights Ondaatje's examples of the suffering endured by Buddhists: monks beheaded, relics looted by colonial powers. She argues that the Buddhism that Ondaatje presents in *Anil's Ghost* might first appear unproblematic, but historical analysis reveals the fractures running through that Buddhism. Radhika Coomaraswamy has made a similar argument about the layers of Buddhism in *Anil's Ghost* (Coomaraswamy 2000). Joining this conversation, Salgado explains that the reconstruction of the Buddha statue is inflected by strands of Hinduism and the Mahayana Buddhist tradition, the latter away from the dominant, state-sanctioned Theravada Buddhism of Sri Lanka (Salgado 2007: 137–146). Moreover, the Hindu notion of *darsan*— that seeing a deity relic would give one that deity's blessing, coming into contact with its divinity—extends back to the Vedic period, which formed part of the religious-cultural milieu in which the Buddhist tradition was manifest (Trainor 1997: 177). A hybrid religiosity is thus actually present, literally inscribing across the fractured statue of dominant Buddhist traditions. The postsecular implications of this are fascinating. Ondaatje seeks to show the range of Buddhisms, in the same sense that Rushdie in *The Satanic Verses* seeks to show a range of Islams, which I discuss in Chapter 5. But each writer's intimate negotiation and struggle with exploring these new forms of "secular faith" will not always be readily perceptible by readers.

What remains problematic for Ondaatje is that his novel circulates among an international readership that might not have at its disposal, or perhaps even interest, the critical historical material that Goldman, Coomaraswamy, and Salgado invoke. As with a layered Buddhism, the apparently dichotomous ethnicities of "Sinhalese" and "Tamil" have also had their historical interconnections; in Steven Kemper's words: "today's Sinhalas are yesterday's Tamils" (Kemper 1991: 13). In an interview about *Anil's Ghost*, Ondaatje stated that Sri Lanka is "'not just a culture of death, it's an intricate, subtle, and artistic culture[.]' [. . .] 'I wanted to celebrate it. In a way, the archaeology was there for that purpose, as well [as the closing Buddha image]. I allowed that to represent the country, not just generals and politicians'" (Kanner 2000). Ondaatje's research trips to Sri Lanka, including his seminar at Colombo's International Centre for Ethnic Studies, indicate he was clearly interested in offering a sensitive portrayal of the country. But was it all just "fieldwork" for him? Ondaatje could not have *not* known what a closing Buddha image might mean to progressives, especially those in Sri Lanka. Although worship of the Buddha statue exists in both Buddhist and Hindu practices, the hegemony of the Buddha symbol circulating in the Sri Lankan public sphere as part of Sinhalese majoritarianism overrides the more subtle, hybrid religious practices.

Perhaps if Ondaatje were not so diasporically removed from the daily life of Sri Lanka he might have chosen a less politically charged symbol. The difficulty for Ondaatje is that although he might wish to celebrate the artisticness of a culture in his exploration of affirmative values, this individual process also risks being liable to political insensitivity. Such insensitivity has provoked strong critical responses from the Sri Lankan intellectuals I have already discussed in this chapter. This same set of readers has observed the novel's lack of specific names, such as through underrepresented Tamil characters (Ismail 2000a). In addition, Tariq Jazeel highlights the novel's unnamed agents of violence: "Throughout the novel the narrative does not distinguish between political/mob violence committed by the LTTE, the JVP or the government. In the humanist analysis, political violence is a universal" (Jazeel 2009: 143).

In contrast to the "divine transcendence" represented by the Buddha statue, Jon Kertzer focuses on the image of Gunesena's body nailed to the road in the shape of a crucifix, and the image of Gamini's holding his brother Sarath's dead body in the tableau of a "pieta." For Kertzer, these images show a "reverence" based on the "intermeshing" of lives, affirming that "the meaning of life is life" (Kertzer 2003: 135). What could be more secular than the here and now of life *as* life? The Buddha statue and the Gamini-Sarath "pieta" are postsecular symbols, affirming reverence and devotion in the wake of the failures of dominant state Buddhism and of Christianity, while preserving secular values of peace and democracy. The use of Buddhist and Christian imagery shows several national, and transnational, influences on Ondaatje's part, informed by his years in Sri Lanka, the UK, and Canada. Ondaatje's combination of such symbols—affirming their ethical elements— demonstrates the transnationalism of his postsecular position. I thus endorse Sam Knowles's argument that Ondaatje's use of western religious symbols in *Anil's Ghost* "opens up the possibility of a Western act of recognition, while at the same time emphasising the Sri Lankan specificities of the scenes" (Knowles 2010: 434). Even human rights themselves can be seen to have their origins in western seventeenth-century Christian thought, so that the posting of human rights, as a secular religion, also contains the posting of Christianity (Freeman 2004: 375–400, esp. 387–389). The conceptual and critical vocabulary of postsecularism obviates distinctions of an "either/or" between the Buddha and the pieta, between "transcendence" and "life is life." We can read *both* images as intimately negotiating religion while emerging inextricably from fraught secular circumstances.

3.4   Representing Human Rights

In addition to aesthetic space, the discourse of human rights serves as a way of structuring violence in *Anil's Ghost*. Anil functions as an emissary of human rights, but hers is no simple intervention. Returning "home," she undergoes a process of learning, of revising her beliefs, of developing humility. The abstract univocality—criticized by subaltern historians as a limitation of the letter of the law (Guha 1987, Baxi 1987)—that previously signified itself as "violence" becomes translated and aestheticized by Ondaatje within the polyphony of the novel form. Human rights become conceptualized as a process, thus raising questions about the legal application and enforcement of such rights. A paradigm of a "universal" human rights enables the structuring of the novel's plot like that of a detective novel. The narrative motor becomes an investigation, a search for the truth of how Sailor died, possibly implicating the government, which is already suspected in an organized campaign of killing and the use of mass graves to dispose of the "disappeared."

A universal human rights enables a "crime detection" structure because in the values of such a human rights, the state is held accountable, necessitating intervention by an international visitor. Sri Lanka has signed the Universal Declaration of Human Rights, Article 5 of which states: "No one shall be subjected to torture or to cruel, inhuman or degrading treatment or punishment" (United Nations 1948). What is particularly significant for the plot of *Anil's Ghost* is that Sri Lanka has signed the Convention against Torture and Other Cruel, Inhuman or Degrading Treatment or Punishment, acceding to the Convention on January 3, 1994. Anil's UN-sponsored visit to Sri Lanka is made possible by Article 20 of the Convention, which stipulates that a confidential inquiry may be made to a nation-state, with the agreement of the State Party, if there is sufficient ground to believe that torture is being systemically practised in the territory. The co-operation of the State Party would be requested at every stage, with the final stage being the inclusion of the findings in the annual report of the Committee against Torture to the General Assembly.

An inquiry into Sri Lanka was initiated by the UN due to information submitted to the Committee on July 21, 1998 by the following non-governmental organizations based in London, which alleged systematic practice of torture in Sri Lanka: the British Refugee Council, the Medical Foundation for the Care of Victims of Torture, the Refugee Legal Centre, the Immigration Law Practitioners Association, and the Refugee Legal Group. A UN-sponsored visit to Sri Lanka took place from August 19, 2000, to September 1, 2000 (the confidential inquiry itself began in April 1999 and ended in May 2002), almost exactly contemporaneous with the publication of *Anil's Ghost* (2000). As a result of the UN's recommendations, the Permanent Inter-Ministerial Standing Committee (PIMSC) on Human Rights Issues was established by the government of Sri Lanka on November 20, 2000 in order to "consider issues and incidents relating to human rights, in particular the prohibition against torture, and to take policy decisions in this regard" (United Nations 2002: Article 20, Section 4, Paragraph 138). At the same time, an Inter-Ministerial Working Group on Human Rights Issues, connected to the UN Committee against Torture, was established to monitor the implementation of decisions taken by the PIMSC. Overall, the UN Committee was satisfied that the government of Sri Lanka implemented nearly all the Committee's recommendations and concluded by stating that "the fight against torture is an ongoing process which requires the vigilance of the State party" (United Nations 2002: Article 20, Section 7, Paragraph 195).

Such vigilance is enabled by Sri Lanka's Human Rights Commission, established in 1996 under the Human Rights Commission of Sri Lanka (HRCSL) Act No. 21 of 1996. The website of the HRSCL contains reports highlighting its strategic plans. In the most recent annual reports uploaded (covering the period 2001–2009), among the Commission's objectives is to focus on internally displaced peoples (Human Rights Commission of Sri Lanka 2012). In 2006, the Ministry of Disaster Management and Human Rights was established in Sri Lanka. Its tasks have included co-ordinating with the office of the UN High Commissioner for Human Rights. On May

15, 2010, President Rajapaksa appointed the Lessons Learnt and Reconciliation Commission (LLRC), influenced in part by South Africa's Truth and Reconciliation Commission and the UK's Iraq War Inquiry. Apart from expected roles of promoting national unity and interethnic reconciliation, it is also among the LLRC's objectives to "identify mechanisms for restitution to the individuals whose lives have been significantly impacted by the conflict" (Lessons Learnt Reconciliation Commission 2012). However, Amnesty International, Human Rights Watch, and the International Crisis Group have charged the Sri Lanka government with lack of transparency.

Allegations of human rights abuses continue against the government, from organizations including the International Committee of the Red Cross, *Médecins Sans Frontières*, and UNICEF. How many innocent civilians were captured and killed in the final crossfire? For those who fled, what were the conditions in the refugee camps? Where, when, and how will the thousands of internally displaced persons (IDPs) be resettled? What is the extent of the war crimes? In May 2009, UN Secretary-General Ban Ki-moon visited Sri Lanka to view the human rights records, such as the rehabilitation of IDPs. In June 2010, Ban appointed a three-member panel for an independent inquiry into the government and accountability issues. Following protests at the UN offices in Colombo, Ban recalled his envoy to Sri Lanka. In December 2010, President Rajapaksa stated his government would co-operate with the UN to allow the inquiry to proceed. But the government has also insisted throughout on protecting Sri Lanka's sovereignty. Opponents of the inquiry have stated that the UN has double standards in aggressively examining the human rights records of some states over others; in July 2010, Kalyananda Godage, former Ambassador and Head of the Mission of Sri Lanka to the European Commission, published an article to this effect (Godage 2010).

Dayan Jayatilleka, former Ambassador of Sri Lanka's Permanent Mission to the UN and a Vice President of the UN Human Rights Council (HRC), argues that the best way forward, after the war, is power sharing, recognizing that in Sri Lanka "the culture, language and civilization of its majority [have] built-in preference" (Jayatilleka 2010: 53). He recommends fully implementing the Thirteenth Amendment to the Sri Lankan constitution, which emerged from the Indo-Lanka Accord of 1987: "devolution of power and provincial autonomy within a unitary framework" (Jayatilleka 2010: 54). Jayatilleka frames the challenge suggestively: with the defeat of the LTTE, Sri Lanka is now territorially united, but what political steps can it take to ensure the peace?

In September 2010, the Sri Lankan parliament approved the Eighteenth Amendment, the most recent, to the constitution. Among the changes effected by the Eighteenth Amendment, they have removed the article that stipulates the President can only hold office for two terms. These enactments also now state that when appointing members to the Sri Lanka Human Rights Commission (among other commissions), the President must seek observations of the speaker, the leader of the opposition party, the prime minister, and two members of parliament, each recommended by the prime minister and the leader of the opposition. These changes, achieved because of the present government's success in ending the war, make the presidency of the country stronger and more centralized than before, and a threat therefore to minority representation and thus democracy (Keethaponcalan 2011: 31). What degree of representativeness and justice these amendments can provide for all citizens of Sri Lanka remains to be seen.

Anil's investigation, her search for the "truth," parallels the forward-moving narrative of the novel. Her official intervention allows for multiple significations within the text, such as comments on the "west" and how it might differ from "Asia" (Ondaatje tends to prefer the latter term to "Sri Lanka"); reflections on what constitutes "truth" and the "true"; and the various forms of epistemology emerging from the above set of terms. These three facets of Anil's intervention allow for the intersections between an international or "universal" value or culture of human rights and a particular national culture, a space of intersections within which Ondaatje can explore his postsecular affirmations.

Some of this affirmational sense is captured in the Preamble to the United Nations Declaration of Human Rights, which states that the recognition of the "inherent dignity" of all members of the "human family" is foundational to "freedom, justice and peace in the world" in the promotion of "social progress" (United Nations 1948). Upendra Baxi argues that human rights consists in "positing peoples' polity against state polity" (Baxi 2002: 41). It is the positing of a people's polity—the idea of the "universal human"—over state polity that enables an outside intervention via Anil. The idea of a universal humanness also can enable the recognition of minority rights. July 29, 1999, marked the death of one of Sri Lanka's greatest human rights activists, Neelan Thiruchelvam, killed by an LTTE suicide bomber. Among his many activities, Thiruchelvam had served as the Chair of the Minority Rights Group, an international human rights organization based in London, and in 1982 he had founded the Law and Society Trust, a non-governmental organization in Colombo whose mission includes advocacy for human rights. In his memorial speech for Thiruchelvam at the International Centre for Ethnic Studies in 2001, Amitav Ghosh cited Ondaatje's poetry (Ghosh 2001). Ondaatje himself might have been aware of Thiruchelvam's death.

A notion of a people's polity begs the question of what constitutes "people" and, moreover, what constitutes the human. Ondaatje seems aware of this also, and once again uses the character of Anil as a site upon which to enact differing notions of the human, almost always cultured along the east/west divide. Elements of Anil's western culture include her love for western literary classics (*Les Misérables*) and her Euro-American education. In contrast, Ondaatje establishes the Asian other through Sarath, as someone inscrutable to Anil, no less in a land that Anil can access only through "one arm of language" (54). The following exchange between them, beginning with Sarath, divides "truth" along cultural lines:

"I don't think clarity is necessarily truth. It's simplicity, isn't it?"

"I need to know what you think. I need to break things apart to know where someone came from. That's also an acceptance of complexity. Secrets turn powerless in the open air."

"Political secrets are not powerless, in any form," he said.

"But the tension and danger around them, one can make them evaporate. You're an archaeologist. Truth comes finally into the light. It's in the bones and sediment."

"It's in character and nuance and mood."

"That is what governs us in our lives, that's not the truth."

"For the living it is the truth," he quietly said.

(259)

Sarath implies that the problem of epistemology is not merely an intellectual one. Rather, it has serious implications for the lives of Sri Lankans, in that, for instance, misrepresentations of them by the foreign media can provoke violence, stirring hatred between groups and inciting feelings of injustice and oppression.

In a later section, Palipana takes Sarath to see rock paintings, using rhododendron branches for light. And then this reflection:

> Half the world, it felt, was being buried, the truth hidden by fear, while the past revealed itself in the light of a burning rhododendron bush. Anil would not understand this old and accepted balance. Sarath knew that for her the journey was in getting to the truth. But what would the truth bring them into? It was a flame against a sleeping lake of petrol. Sarath had seen truth broken into suitable pieces and used by the foreign press alongside irrelevant photographs. A flippant gesture towards Asia that might lead, as a result of this information, to new vengeance and slaughter.

(156)

Ondaatje contrasts the aesthetic and the violent through the seme of a common image: burning. "Burning rhododendron bush" is set against a sleeping lake of petrol. The visual similarity of the morphemes in the former phrase (the symmetry of "b/r/b" creating an aesthetic nicety) and its alliteration establish it as a unit of signification against the petrol, itself established as a unit through the metaphor of sleeping. Whereas the bush is a cause, the lake is an effect, reactive; whereas the bush is fixed in one place, the lake has potential for agency, to emit flames that can spread uncontrollably. The latter—violence—is a fantastic "other," a sleeping agent of petrol that can be easily ignited into ferocity, like the unfolding of "vengeance and slaughter" whose causal flame can be a flippant photograph from abroad. Of course, Ondaatje is ethically saying here, "But my gesture is not flippant." His wish is for *Anil's Ghost* to be illuminating.

But an illumination set against which horizon? Not only can the framework of human rights help us understand this question, but also, within the novel, what Ondaatje sees as one form of western aestheticization. Toward the end of the novel, there is a flashback featuring Anil and her forensic scientist friend Leaf, in Arizona. The two spend evenings watching Westerns. One particular Western captures their attention as they try to locate where in his body one of the actors was shot, ultimately writing to the director for clarification. Anil says, "'You know, Leaf, we should do a book. *A Forensic Doctor Looks at the Movies*'" (237; italics original). Ondaatje places this Western passage toward the end of the novel, by which point we readers have had exposure to the particular, "local" logic of the violence in Sri Lanka. We could read this placement as Ondaatje's ethical sensitivity to Sri Lanka, to show how "real"—and unreal—Anil's immersion is in the politics of Sri Lanka. Her immersion is real because now the violence is not in a film but all around her, and unreal because she is not familiar with its particular "logic."

In the end, her human rights work is not "just another job." Sarath says to her: "'You should live here. Not be here just for another job'" (200). Anil defends herself, saying that she *chose* to come back. At the end of the novel, as she presents her findings to the assembled audience, Anil states: "' think you murdered hundreds of us'" (272). Sarath's response: "*Hundreds of us.* [. . .] Fifteen years away and she is finally *us*" (272; italics original). The trauma of the war allows Anil to feel a sense of community and belonging ("us") that, at the start of the novel, she was aware of only through *lack*, as the self-conscious outsider. Ondaatje shares a similar position. He too is an "outsider" to Sri Lanka and Sarath's comment might serve to pre-empt, as mediated by Anil, any accusations of being an outsider, and hence indifferent to or ignorant of the politics of Sri Lanka. I believe this is an insufficient gesture on Ondaatje's part, leaving both the gesture and the author liable to being read as disingenuous.

The horizon against which Ondaatje situates such thematics foregrounds the problem of "perspective" and "framing." Ondaatje takes pains to show us that he is aestheticizing "both ways," toward Sri Lanka, toward the west. It is this distancing strategy that is consonant with his ethical position. It is a semio-ethical gesture, with particular aestheticizations in the text as signs of the ethics that generate them. The trope of human rights serves as a powerful sign of this ethico-structural relation. Its narrativization *into* the text allows Ondaatje just enough space to tell us so, or at least for criticism to recognize it as such.

Ondaatje's ethical wish is for *Anil's Ghost* not to be a flippant gesture to Sri Lanka. He thus represents the "lush" particularity of Sri Lanka, and he lets us know it—we might even call such attention a sign of diasporic guilt. Anil must go *to* the "particularity" of Sri Lanka in order to see the limits of the universality of "her" discourse of human rights. It is not only Anil who brings the human rights of the west to Sri Lanka. So does Ondaatje. Yet Ondaatje also brings Sri Lanka to the west, prompting a relation, not necessarily dialogue, between the west and those states that are the "beneficiaries" of globalization, particularly when "human rights issues" can so often become a shorthand for representing and witnessing the Third World. It is the aesthetics of Ondaatje's literary human rights—formal and also thematized—that allows for the happening of, the revealing of, "that" "particular" "system" "of" "rights." These literary human rights are independent from the "universal" (global), but they are also semantically and ontologically dependent *on* that system—a palimpsestual relation I must resort to expressing through scare quotes. Explorations of postsecular values can exist—tenuously, riskily—on the edges of such systems.

3.5   Conclusion

Ondaatje's gaze in *Anil's Ghost* shifts from the public and political to the private and personal, from large, encompassing narratives about nation to local, intimate narratives about the love between two people. Such movement would suggest a "humanization" of the political, to show that "big" phenomena can find their parallels, or even origins, in the "small": the problems of unrest in the nation in the problems of unrest in the family; the violent in the personal; the traumatization of a peoples reflected in the traumatization of one girl, who has lost both her parents, seeing them murdered. Perhaps such humanization would suggest a humanism in Ondaatje's gaze, to show that "they" are just like "us," that "we" are just like "them," and, concurrently, that "I" am just like "them." Ondaatje's diasporically-conditioned inquiry into Sri Lanka is also an inquiry into himself. As Ashley Halpé has observed, "Anil speaks for Michael, I think; at least for the Michael who wrote the novel" (Halpé 2010b: 92).

These humanistic affirmations are given a special urgency by Ondaatje's framing them within the context of an ongoing civil war; it suggests that an awakening—his, ours—to such violence can catalyze ethical responses. The "semioethics" I sketch in this chapter could apply especially to contexts that demand close witnessing attention. Referring to *The English Patient*, Ondaatje has stated that he was working with "four characters in a very small corner of time and place" (Brown 1992: 17). It seems that in *Anil's Ghost*, ironically, he wishes to work in a kind of timelessness. Ondaatje visits a particular time, a particular place, but his craft—framed through the discourses of aesthetics, religion, and human rights—wishes to universalize identities embedded within this locus.

A small but potent marker, expressible in three letters, one word: "set." Qadri Ismail has taken issue with the author's note at the front of the novel that the novel is "set" against the backdrop of 1980s and 1990s. For Ismail, this makes Sri Lanka and its politics merely *incidental* to the novel, which is not *of* Sri Lanka (Ismail 2000a: 24). Moreover, Ananda Abeysekara argues: "to depict the war in generalized, *humanist* fashion is to deny the politics of the war" (Abeysekara 2008: 59). This is because, for Abeysekara, at the same time that Ondaatje neglects the political dimensions of the violence, Ondaatje assumes a kind of peaceful historical past, replete with beautiful ancient monastic cities: "an effort to sugarcoat contemporary violence and atrocities in Sri Lanka" (Abeysekara 2008: 59). The problem that emerges here is that of at least referentiality. Joseph Slaughter argues that, in *Anil's Ghost*, forensic anthropology, medical diagnostics, archaeology, paleontology, reconstructive history, imaginative sculpture, and psychobiography can be viewed as "variations on the theme of reading" (Slaughter 2007: 188). In that respect, we can consider Slaughter's list to be examples of what Ismail would consider postempirical, textual Sri Lankas (Ismail 2000b: 304). But so too as Canadian multiculturalism secularly envisions its ideal citizen polity, it becomes offensive when reality falls short of the imagined picture. If the final Buddha statue is a hybrid of Hinduism, Mahayana Buddhism, and Theravada Buddhism, then that is a secular imagining, just as "Michael Ondaatje" is an historical product of Canadian multiculturalism and of Sri Lankan colonialism and postcolonialism. For the purpose of this book, I "set" Michael Ondaatje inside Canada and Sri Lanka, inside a transnational secularism.

What is the postsecular *Anil's Ghost?* The values of peace, hope, and regeneration are "set" inside the Buddha statue; the Buddha statue is "set" inside Buddhism; Buddhism is "set" inside Sri Lanka; the novel is "set" in the historical moment of 1980–1990 in a geographical region named Sri Lanka. As Ondaatje imagines and performs such setting, he affirms his literary craft. He *believes* in his literary craft when describing the *nētra mangala* ceremony.

Anil remembers "Clyde Snow, her teacher in Oklahoma, speaking about human rights work in Kurdistan: *One village can speak for many villages. One victim can speak for many victims*" (176; italics original). One speech can envillage many speeches. Speech as habitation, as communal habitation, as dwelling. To dwell inside the voice of Sri Lanka is to abide by many speaking Sri Lankas. The postsecular is similarly universalizing. Its particular brand of "human rights" includes the aesthetic elements of religion—the music, the painting, the sculpture, as we have seen in both *The English Patient* and *Anil's Ghost*. The postsecular becomes a "religion" by virtue of its occupying the same epistemological and ethical space of (a) religion. Yet it does not necessarily exhibit the same content as (a) religion, for it seeks to avoid the dogmas and ideologies of religion, although the relation might be palimpsestual. This is the palimpsestual feature of the postsecular that allows critics to demonstrate that Ondaatje, however subtly, problematizes the politics and internal conflicts of Sri Lankan Buddhism while still using a Buddhist symbol in order to "gesture toward the ideals of transcendence, wholeness, and unity" (Goldman 2005: 36). Ondaatje's search for ethical values is tenuous, and he makes no effort to "erase" the history literally fractured across the surfaces of the reconstructed statue. The "interestingness" that *Anil's Ghost* elicits from its readers—through the space of the aesthetic, the discourse of human rights, the unironic representation of violence, and the paranational possibilities of affect—allows for and affirms forms of witnessing. This is a postsecularism driven not by following religious doctrine, but by exploring—with courage, with risk—worldliness.

Figure 6 Sri Harmandir Sahib (The Golden Temple), Amritsar, India. Photograph by the author.

4 If Truth Were A Sikh Woman
Shauna Singh Baldwin's *What the Body Remembers*

Supposing truth is a woman—what then? It is Friedrich Nietzsche's famous question in *Beyond Good and Evil*, where he wonders whether the methods for discovering truth might be as inexpert and awkward as those used to win a woman's heart (Nietzsche 1998). In *What the Body Remembers*, Shauna Singh Baldwin tells the story of Partition from a woman's perspective and from a Sikh perspective—among the central characters is a woman, Satya, whose name means "truth" in Sanskrit. I argue in this chapter that *What the Body Remembers* challenges the myth of "secular India," which entails the ideas of the "secular" and of "India." Both of these ideas are political and national constructs: they might seek merely to reflect a reality, but they also create a reality, at the cost of exclusion and misrepresentation. By challenging these constructs, Baldwin narrates the story of women and of Sikhs, stories that show there were and there are alternatives to the idea of nation presented as a "succour" to the violence of ethno-religious conflict.

What the Body Remembers presents the case that the oppression of women is not unlike the oppression of Sikhs in India, as religious minorities. Baldwin's linking of women's experience with the experience of the Sikh community is not unproblematic, but the parallel is suggestive in opening a space of understanding and insight—and yes, even truths—neglected by sanctioned stories and histories of the secular nation. How could Baldwin explore representing these truths? The mutable, flexible space of fiction allows Baldwin to undertake her explorations of truth, giving her the creative freedom to juxtapose different voices, points of view, and ways of knowing. As I discussed in Chapter 3, this creativity and flexibility of literary representation is what also allows Ondaatje in *Anil's Ghost* to pursue and represent diverse epistemologies.

In this chapter I explore the similarities, variously representational and theoretical, between *What the Body Remembers* and *Anil's Ghost*, but will now turn to discussing the relations among Partition, secularism, and gender. Robert Young has observed that the paradox of India is that it emerges as a secular state based on "a partition made on religious grounds" (Young 2001: 321). Although leading to the creation of the Indian nation-state, Partition has also been seen as a loss for India, imagined as the loss of a limb. For Pakistan,

Partition becomes a founding moment, of creation and of beginning, the "origin story" of the "land of the pure." No matter how "pure" the land or how "Islamic" the nation, the *idea* of nation still prevails, with the idea a secular concept, one constituted by legal and political autonomy and sovereignty. One way for propagating the concept of nation has been through the Two-Nation Theory, the theory that the Hindus and Muslims constitute two different nations based on religion alone. An interpretation of this theory is that the two groups require *separate* territories that are politically autonomous and sovereign. Yet, challenges to this theory include the fact that not all Muslims in India moved to Pakistan (how many of them had the means and wherewithal to do so?). In addition, the secession movement that created Bangladesh from East Pakistan in 1971 further proved that religion alone was not sufficient for uniting Muslims as a nation, and that differences in language can in fact be divisive (Bangla in the former East Pakistan, Urdu in the former West Pakistan).

If the nations that are "Pakistan" and "India" are secular entities, enacted through a secular distinction, then *What the Body Remembers* is postsecular in showing the crises and injustices resulting from such a separation. Violence in this novel becomes the marker of the inadequacies of the national "border." If secularism in India is the succour to the violence produced by the Two-Nation Theory, then the vulnerable position of the Sikhs, caught between the Hindus and the Muslims, with their rights not fully protected, shows the limitations of secularism, no matter how symbolic an achievement it might be to have a Sikh currently installed as the Prime Minister of India. How well can the secular Indian state know and represent the lives of those who constitute the nation?

If Ondaatje in *The English Patient* looks at what comes *after* the nation and nationalism, then Baldwin in *What the Body Remembers* gestures to the criticism, writing, and visions that can come *instead* of and in the *wake* of the inherited history of the secular. This is the secular articulated by Gandhi and the Congress Party before the days of Independence, which, as the novel states, did not adequately represent the Sikhs: "[t]he Mahatma raised the national flag of a free India and it did not have a strip of deep Sikh blue as he promised" (Baldwin 2000: 91).[1] It is also the secular integrated in the Indian constitution after Independence. Sikhs were underrepresented in the Parliament. Moreover, in 1984 the Indian state bombed The Golden Temple as a result of a confrontation between the Indian Army and the Sikh militants sheltering inside the Temple. The 1984 bombing led to Indira Gandhi's assassination by her Sikh bodyguards, which then sparked the massacre of Sikhs in New Delhi and other parts of India. Sikhs have certainly been allowed a connection to the political by serving as invaluable members of the Indian and British Armies. But the degree of participation and influence they have had within the realms of political power, especially after Independence, and particularly after 1984, has been comparatively low. To be sure, Nehru appointed Sardar Swaran Singh to his cabinet in 1952. Singh remained there until he resigned in 1975, becoming the longest-serving cabinet minister in India. But his appointment could also be viewed as a token one.

Any majority will like to believe, either overtly (such as through declarations) or covertly (such as through attitudes and assumptions), that it is just, equitable, tolerant, reasonable, and fair: it is in its interests to do so, for the sake of protecting its power. Also, such belief is comforting at the very least at the psychological level, as the majority manoeuvres to preserve its self-image. In the process, the majority *secularizes* itself. In the case of India, it makes the story of "secular India" appear natural, everyday, a part of normal reality, "the way things are" in the secular here-and-now. In the words of Sardarji: *"One should never trust a teetotalling Baniya* [Gandhi] *or a Kashmiri pandit* [Nehru]. *Or anyone who builds a realm only from words"* (438; italics original).[2]

The stories of Sikhs and of women show different points of view. The novel states that "[o]nce Hindus forget to remember the word 'secular,' Muslim men throughout India know they will be forced—along with Sikh men, Christians, Buddhists, Jains, Jews, Parsis, tribals and animists—to accept the whims of many gods not of their choosing" (141). "Forced" and "whims" could so easily translate into violence. When earlier Sikh reformist scholars translated Sikhism as a "world religion" within the shadow of Christian theology (and as "religion" and "Sikh theology"), they construed Nanak as pacifistic, quietist, transcendental, and detached from the world. In turn, this constructed Sikhism as something static and immutable. Arvind-Pal Mandair argues that these conceptions of the religion characterize "later Sikhism's entry into violence [e.g., 1984] and politics as a *deviation* from the pacifistic subjectivity of Nanak" (Mandair 2009: 34; italics original). This characterization then allows for "the ironic injunction that if Sikhs are to exist in modern secular society they must return to its pacifist origin, a move which, in the context of the modern nation-state, imposes a *legal* injunction that effectively forecloses Sikhs and Sikhism from any connection to the political" (Mandair 2009: 34).

This is an example of how the secular becomes secularized: the political secular tries to show itself as everyday and normal, as part of the ordinary here-and-now, by fixing Sikhism within a narrow, prejudiced definition, even though it is secularism itself that is narrow and prejudiced, but it will never reveal itself as being so—after all, it is state secularism, seeking to respect all religions. To further deconstruct this sense of the secular secularizing itself, I build upon Gyan Pandey's argument that "[r]eason, progress, organization, discipline, (history itself?), belongs to the state and the ruling classes; violence belongs to the Other, those left behind by history" (Pandey 1994: 193). The delimitation of Sikhism's subjectivity is similar to the delimitation of women's subjectivity. If "the violent Sikh" is a construction of the religious prejudices within Partition and a "secular India," then *What the Body Remembers* is postsecular in moving beyond these limiting constructs and telling the stories of those unrecognized and unrecognizable by history.[3]

Gendered experience works as an indictment of the discourses and ideologies of nation, whether before or after Independence. Baldwin affirms in
her novel that Sikhism is one of the few religions in the world that advocates
the fundamental equality between men and women, with the gurus teaching that women should be addressed as "princesses" (*kaur* in Punjabi). Yet
the practice has hardly been so. The violence of colonialism can easily be
understood as one nation systematically exploiting another, but how readily
can people understand that a similar violence, colonial and postcolonial,
occurs across the divide of gender? Gendered violence, such as the violence
of the elder, resentful Satya toward the younger, beautiful Roop, allegorized
as the pair of fighting partridges kept divided in a single container, becomes
a metaphor for the inadequacies of nation.[4] By intimately, almost inextricably, linking gender with nation, Baldwin shows the violence and injustice
suffered by both. Where reformist scholars translate Sikhism into a religion
that is merely passive and pacifistic (in the shadow of Christianity), then that
subjugated subjectivity is similar to the patriarchal control and subjugation
of women's subjectivity. If we are only ever as free as the "least" among us,
then this novel shows that the postcolonial, post-Partition nation is only ever
as self-determined, dignified, and free as its women.

What the Body Remembers is not an entire abandonment of religion and
Sikhism. It shows instead the hypocrisies in society, that some people living
life under the name of Sikhism—and that name can mean the difference
between life and death—in fact do not truly practise the teachings of the
gurus. Some Sikhs want the freedom and self-determination of a nation they
imagine as Khalistan or Sikhistan, but what will it take for that same society
to treat Sikh women with the freedom and equality taught by its gurus?

If truth were a Sikh woman, what then, in India? How justifiably could
the nation-state proclaim the successes of secularism's history, present, and
future? Baldwin's novel exemplifies Sangeeta Ray's call to "account for the
repressed gendered subject that allows a masculinist nationalist discourse to
flourish" (Ray 2000: 147). Yet Baldwin does not merely deconstruct nationalist and religious mythologies and stop there. The gendered critique of the
masculinist, and I would add *secularist*, nationalist discourse would still operate within the sign of that dominant discourse. To move beyond that secular
discourse, to a position within the imaginary of *postsecularism*, is not just to
launch a gendered critique (the secular *non-x* "to" the secular *x*), but to enter
within and explore the array of diversity, experience, and richness of wom-
en's lives, and the *affirmations* those lives contain, ones that flourish outside
of and that do not need the validation of the nation-state, the masculine, or
the secular. This is Roop's love and care for her children. It is the love and
devotion that Gujri shows by following Roop for five miles, so that Roop is
not alone. It is Satya's belief in a "higher law" within Sikhism. Satya's Sikhism is *her* Sikhism, a woman's individually-negotiated Sikhism, away from
fixed constructions of Sikhism. Through Satya, Baldwin "restores" agency

and subjectivity to Sikhism and its founding guru, Nanak, seeing the religion and Nanak as immanent and personal. In Sikh practice, Nanak's immanence is affirmed through the repetition of his name, the "devotional practice of meditating on the Name initially through vocalized repetition and eventually through interiorized repetition" (Mandair 2009: 487), called *nām simaran* (*nām* = name; *simaran* = meditation). In the process, language fascinatingly exhibits its own agency and aliveness rather than simply conveying human speech.[5] Baldwin's novel shows the strength of the written word, as a literary parallel to Sikhism's conception of the sovereignty of language (it can speak itself), thus offering the novel as a secular equivalent to the immanent enchantment of speaking Nanak's name.

The novel's message is not to meditate on Nanak, but to remember Partition, as a textual parallel to the immanence of bodily memory. Would there be a novel without readers repeating its words, without readers reading it? Readers' repetition of Baldwin's words immanently conveys the call to remember Partition, to internalize and empathize with the lives that Baldwin represents. Like Sikhism's conception of the sovereignty of language, the novel is also alive, as a meditation within its author, and living through its readers, its agency extending through readers' increased knowledge of, and perhaps even empathy with, Partition's victims.

4.1   Situating *What the Body Remembers*

Because Shauna Singh Baldwin's work is not as well known as Ondaatje's and Rushdie's, I would like to begin this section by providing some context for *What the Body Remembers*. Baldwin currently resides in Milwaukee, Wisconsin, where she obtained an MBA degree from Marquette University. She was born in Montreal, grew up in northern India, and studied for a Master of Fine Arts degree at the University of British Columbia. Her first book of fiction, *English Stories and Other Lessons* (1996), chronicles the lives of Indian women, especially Sikh ones, in India, Canada, and the US. *The Tiger Claw* (2004) continues Baldwin's interests in gendered critiques of majoritarian religious systems by drawing upon the real-life experiences of Noor Inayat Khan, who worked against the Occupation after the Nazi invasion of France. *We Are Not in Pakistan* (2007) is a collection of stories exploring Canadian and American multiculturalism. Her most recent book, *The Selector of Souls* (2012), is a story intertwining, among other concerns, the issues of women's rights, infanticide, and adoption, set in 1990s India against the backdrop of nuclearization and Hindu fundamentalism. Baldwin has also co-authored a piece of non-fiction, *A Foreign Visitor's Survival Guide to America* (1992).

What the Body Remembers (1999) is set in India between 1895 and 1948, and follows the lives of two Sikh women, Roop and Satya, and their husband, Sardarji, a high-ranking engineer working with the British administration in India. Because the relatively older Satya is unable to bear children, Sardarji weds Roop, a young woman from the village of Pari Darvaza. Roop gives birth to a daughter and two sons. Satya is resentful of Roop, and once she accepts Sardarji's decision to privilege Roop and their children over her, she turns to suicide, but on her terms, thus preserving her personal honour. The novel concludes with a graphic description of the days leading to Partition. On the fateful night when Pakistan officially becomes a separate nation, Roop must travel by car from Lahore to Delhi, where Sardarji has promised he will meet her.

I have placed this chapter after the chapter on *Anil's Ghost*. Baldwin's and Ondaatje's novels share numerous similarities, particularly in that these writers struggle with representing the multifaceted nature of "interethnic violence" in India and Sri Lanka respectively. Like *Anil's Ghost*, *What the Body Remembers* makes use of the space of fiction to allow for multiple, rounded representations of experience where other discourses cannot, or will not, allow such representation, such as discourses of law (e.g., "human rights") and politics (e.g., "nation"). Anil must unlearn the biases of human rights, and Roop must unlearn the dogmas of patriarchy, in the process gaining self-confidence. The process is not easy, one-directional, or complete, but the effort is parallel to deconstructing the dogmas of nation, religion, and law. Baldwin shows the heterogeneity, even contradictions, in women's imaginaries and lived experiences, a faithfulness of representation where law cannot recognize "woman." This limitation of legal discourse is captured in Nivedita Menon's argument that the law "functions by fixing meaning, by creating uniform categories out of a multiplicity of possibilities, by suturing open-endedness. The experience validated by feminism as 'real', on the other hand, acquires meaning precisely through an interplay of contexts, and may be rendered sterile within the rigid codification required by legal discourse" (Menon 2000: 68).

Whereas Ondaatje in *Anil's Ghost* meditates on whether different maps of Sri Lanka can truly represent the country, Baldwin's novel is an alternative representation of the "boundary" between India and Pakistan, telling stories of pain, loss, dispossession, and violence. The act of telling stories, as *action* and as oral histories, attains a special power and responsibility to preserve cultural memory. How many people in the world know about Partition, let alone how it impacted women and Sikhs? Who knows the real injustices and illegalities that unfold in Sri Lanka outside what is recognizable and sanctioned by the agendas of official human rights investigations, international media reports, and the Sri Lankan state?

This sense of telling stories echoes Mieke Bal's argument, which I discussed in Chapter 3, that aestheticizing catastrophe reduces the gap between the artist and the community, inviting the community to understand the artist's trauma by having an *interestedness* in the art and artist. *What the Body Remembers* also exemplifies what I explored in the context of *Anil's Ghost* as the "semioethical." The creation of the literary sign (*semio-*) constitutes an ethical act, putting representation in the service of calling and drawing attention to all the faces of struggle, pain, and suffering of a nation and its peoples. The novelists invite their readers to join them as witnesses to others' experience, with ethical messages that urge understanding, sensitivity, respect, empathy, compassion, and remembrance. The force of the semio-ethical runs throughout *What the Body Remembers*: to awaken readers not just to the violence of Partition, but to demonstrate that such violence is simultaneously violence against women.

4.2   Reading *What the Body Remembers*: Gender, Nation, Class

I would like to read *What the Body Remembers* along the dimension not just of nation, but also of class and gender. Why these three dimensions? As I argued in the opening of this chapter, Baldwin seeks to tell stories "other" to the ones sanctioned by secular India. Her logic is not a reactionary one that posits the unheard stories as "virtuous," "pure," and "unproblematic." Rather, Baldwin presents nuanced and layered perspectives of almost infinite inequalities and blindnesses *within* inequalities and blindnesses. Sardarji rails against racial inequalities, but he cannot see the patriarchy that he embodies. Satya rails against sexism, but she cannot see her own attitudes of class superiority. She can speak the truth to Sardarji about his internalized colonialism, but will she so easily give up the violence of her class contempt for Roop, and her servant Jorimon? (The contempt might be driven by jealousy of Roop, but why can Satya summon class so easily in an attempt to alienate Roop?) Even as some Sikhs are critical of the prejudices of the majority Hindus, those Sikhs hold prejudices against Muslims, and vice versa. Even as some British feel superior to poor Indians, there are unequal class divides within England, forcing some poor English, like Ms. Barlow, to seek work in India—and when she arrives there, she delivers orders "as if born to command" (334). Similarly, Roop and Satya can order their servants because "*It's easy to give orders when people are trained to obey*" (461; italics original), colonial subjugation thus finding a parallel with class and caste subjugation.

What the Body Remembers holds a mirror to the multiple, layered inequalities and hypocrisies of everyday life, and then tells its own stories, other stories. In its refusal to postulate any "one" position that is free of prejudice and contradiction, the content of Baldwin's novel reflects the semioethical act of writing the novel itself. That is to say, the act of *telling* other stories *demonstrates* that there are other stories apart from those sanctioned as national mythologies. In turn, however, Baldwin does not write just a "pure" story, for that would make her story no more representative than the mythologies she seeks to expose. Instead, she does want her story to be representative, because then it would be closer to the "truth." I place "truth" in quotation marks to signal that this truth is deeply embedded in the material thickness of circumstance and location and not easily understood or representable as "national history." Recall in *Anil's Ghost* when Sarath tells Anil that he thinks truth is located in nuance, character, and mood (Ondaatje 2000: 259). *Representing* the multiple contradictory faces of everyday life requires a certain measure of belief, in one's own ability to represent. That belief must also be affirmed in the face of circumstances that can so easily lead anyone to cynicism and despair, especially with a crisis as destructive as Partition. Striving to represent the national, class, and gendered dimensions of a situation—historical, ongoing, contradictory—allows both the writer and her readers to understand and see the multiple sides of a situation.

There is a constant paralleling of nation, gender, and class throughout the novel, so that the inequalities present at the level of nation are apparent also at the level of gender. For example, Roop's father, Bachan Singh, explains to his son Jeevan that it was "ordinary" (50) Sikhs, not privileged ones, who became martyrs in the Jallianwala Bagh massacre in order to expose for the entire nation the true intentions of the British and their greed. Bachan Singh then praises Gandhi and the Congress Party for not saying, "'These martyrs follow the ten Gurus, we will not claim their long-haired dead as our martyrs'" (50). Shortly after this statement, however, Roop remembers that her father will not allow Revati Bhua to practise Hinduism, concluding with the observation, repeated often in the novel, that "men only see women from the corners of their eyes" (51).

Similarly, the British can see Indians only out of the corners of their eyes. Mr. Farquharson predicts that Partition will be the "biggest bloodless handover in history" (398), by which he means English blood. Some British characters do not even look at the "bloody natives" (398), such as Ms. Barlow not looking at Roop, or the European women at society functions, who ignore Satya as soon as they discover she cannot speak English. But Satya is also empowered on her own terms, challenging Sardarji's naive ideas of "merit." Educated at Oxford, Sardarji believes in scientific modernity as progress, and the linking of that modernity with and as rationality, a mindset which he hopes will win him British acceptance and recognition based on his intelligence, talent, and discipline, summarized as "merit." He receives promotions, but Satya says he might only be "another bone the British can throw before Mahatma Gandhi and Nehru, hoping to appease the non-cooperators and all the self-rule agitators, justify the blood spilled and pain endured by protestors" (171). It might be that Sardarji, despite his rationality, cannot understand or accept Satya's insight, perhaps wishing that she, like Roop, would be the praising, celebratory wife. (Even if Sardarji can intellectually recognize that Roop's submissive role involves a degree of performativity, he might deny that, ignoring it.) Satya states even further: "you may be excellent at engineering, but you may not be worthy of the freedom fighters' sacrifices" (171). This is a stark indictment not just of the stranglehold of colonial rule, but of Sardarji's alienation from the common man (Punjabi: *aam bundha*), the men like Brij in *The Everest Hotel* who are willing to risk their lives in the name of political autonomy and self-determination. If the British have difficulty seeing Indians, how well can Sardarji see himself and his fellow Indians?

Turning again to class, Baldwin expresses class alienation through the brilliantly succinct description of New Delhi on the day of Indian Independence, marked by "Celebrities celebrating Independence" (469). What do celebrities know about the pain, loss, and suffering of those who had to walk across the unmarked "border"? Contrast the city celebrations with the suffering and innocence of the old Sikh farmer who collapses against Roop's car on the Grand Trunk Road and asks, "Beti, do you know how far is Sikhistan?" (439). The farmer and Sardarji could not be more removed on the social scale of privilege, but is not Sardarji also always asking "Do you know how far away is the next promotion?" Kavita Daiya argues that *What the Body Remembers* demonstrates that "sexual violence was not always about nationalism or ethnicity" (Daiya 2008: 86). An example of this is when a group of Muslim thugs attempts to rape the Muslim servant Jorimon. These men become less aggressive once Roop asserts her class status, remembering Satya's confidence.

Baldwin also shows the strength of colonial and national mythologies in cutting across all strata of the nation. "Pakistan" may be the "land of the pure," but the novel has no uncritical (pure) reverence for purity, for Pakistan can also be seen as the "land purified of Sikhs, Hindus and maybe Christians, too" (508). Although Baldwin can be critical of the idea of "nation," that resistance extends to all groups, not just the idea of Pakistan, for Roop hears that violence against women is "always by *them*—never by *us*" (473; italics original). This is part of a self-secularizing ideology, whether colonial, national, or gendered: "other people's beliefs, their principles and the things they hold dear, are always called superstition, when someone is manufacturing differences" (498). As Gyan Pandey states, when historians from Pakistan and India would describe Partition violence, their attitudes and stories would stress "the essential humanity of the 'host' nation [. . .] through examples where *the minority was protected, mercy displayed, and 'secularist' principles were upheld*" (Pandey 2008: 115; italics mine). We could also view such bias from a gendered perspective, as in Urvashi Butalia's words: "Pakistan came to be represented as the communal, abductor country, refusing to return Hindu and Sikh women, while India was the reasonable, and civilized non-communal country, fulfilling its moral obligations" (Butalia 2000: 152).

Gender might yet represent one of the most powerful sites through which Baldwin communicates the various degrees of knowability and unknowability across differences. As if it were not demeaning enough to know that Sardarji has married her for the main goal of having children, and particularly a son, he asks Roop to give her newborn children to Satya. Roop wonders: *"What has this giving to do with my faith? No, don't doubt. Don't think this. Mama always said to give to those who need. Satya needs this baby more than I"* (201; italics original). What indeed does it have to do with faith? Patriarchy demands that Roop put her own desires and needs second to others', even erasing them, under the ruse of "giving." Ritu from *The Everest Hotel*, as I discussed in Chapter 2, might try understanding this as a form of "charity," but the more secular-minded Brij would not.

If patriarchy succeeds when women begin to police themselves and other women using patriarchy's values, then this is what happens when Roop shapes her young daughter Pavan into becoming diffident and demure, less bold. Roop remembers the lesson that others had been teaching her for years: "the greatest love-gift an elder can give a daughter is to hurt her lovingly, gently, for-her-own-good, before a cruel world brings longer lament. [. . .] Roop knows she has made a hole like her own within Pavan, a hole that cannot be embroidered away" (259). The hole is not embroidered away, and Roop knows that it is there, and how it came to be, rather than accepting it as natural.

Could she challenge that patriarchy? Just over half-way into the novel, the following realization dawns on Roop, upon her visit home from Sardarji's haveli: "*My Papaji is no different from any other Punjabi man. He may be a God-praising Sikh, he may be lambardar, he may be dipty of all Pari Darvaza, but in the end, he is just a poor, ordinary Punjabi village man*" (290; italics original). This represents a detranscendentalizing of her father. How? Bachan Singh might be God-praising (himself thus taking on some divine qualities, seen for example as the law of the father), and he might have the status of being the village head and its deputy, but at the base of it all, he is just poor and ordinary. We could translate "ordinary" as the everyday, and thus as secular. Roop can similarly secularize the patriarchy that her father represents, seeing it as a system that is everyday and ordinary rather than something transcendental in the sense of being "above" criticism, understanding, or challenge: she becomes "so weary of everyone's explaining to her, they explain everything but their reasons for explaining" (290). Why would ideology explain its reasons for explaining? Patriarchy will not explain its real reasons, and so too colonialism will not explain its real reasons. To ask the very question of explaining allows Roop to begin deconstructing those systems as she sees fit, of building confidence in her ability to make her own choices for herself and her life.

The hopeful element in this novel is that Baldwin *does* posit that "other" which is empowering and made out of human choices that are not governed entirely by the ideologies of patriarchy and colonialism. Baldwin is keen to assert that Sikhism is one of the few world religions that teaches the equality of men and women. When those teachings become perverted and misunderstood in the hands of patriarchy (subjugating women) and colonialism (seeing "native" religion as superstitious and barbaric), what alternatives might emerge to the religion, including alternatives to the secular concept of "nation"? One of the most tender moments in the novel is when Roop is cradling her infant daughter Pavan, knowing that she has to give her up to Satya:

"This is my smell," she tells the baby. "Remember it. This is the taste of my body. Remember it. This is the touch of my hands, feel it. This is my tongue, suck from it all the words it should have spoken, the words it wants to say." *Say them for me.*

(199; italics original)

If there were ever a moment in literature of tenderness, dignity, and love, it is here.[6] *Say* the words, *repeat* the love of mother, this here is a secular form of *nām simaran*, as the affirmation of a personal ethics, a child affirming her absent mother's love: the mother, like Nanak, is outwardly absent but present within her child. This is part of the "power" of love as ethics, one that emerges in the wake of the violence of nation, which *What the Body Remembers* translates through (not *as*) the violence of colonialism, and again translates through (not *as*) the violence of patriarchy.

Baldwin places Punjabi words throughout the novel to signal some of the worldview, epistemologies, and differences that lie outside English and outside, in her words, "Judeo-Christian symbols" (Baldwin 1999: 2). She makes the excellent point that, were she concerned with "complete authenticity," she would not have written her novel in English (Baldwin 1999: 2). The above passage between Roop and her daughter Pavan is evocative in English. Had Baldwin presented it in Punjabi, some of us readers could have accessed still other poignant, emotionally evocative dimensions of the exchange:

Yaad rakhi, e meri khushbooh ve. Yaad rakhi, e mere sharir da swaad ve. Mehsoos kar, mere hath da chchuna ve. Eh meri jeeb ve, jere lafaz ehde vichon nikelne chahi de sun, jere oh kehna chahndi eh, oh meri jeeb to choos ley. Oh tu mere vaste bolin.

(translation mine)

The Punjabi syntax is slightly different from English, with the verbs "remember" (*yaad rakhi*) and "feel" (*mehsoos kar*) working better stylistically at the beginning of their sentences, giving those verbs a certain emphasis.[7] Here is the secular *nām simaran*, secular because it passes from mother to daughter: say these words for me, *oh tu mere vaste bolin*, this language is alive inside of me and passes to you, so that my subjectivity and spirit can animate yours. The above Punjabi translation can give emphasis to Edward Mallot's argument that the novel presents the body as "an intentional instrument of personal agency" (Mallot 2006: 165). At the same time, the connection across bodies shows that the personal agency of the mother *becomes* the agency of her daughter.

Just as Punjabi might represent a universe of meaning and form other to English, so too Satya turns to a form of empowerment outside the sway of patriarchy. Satya makes a choice on her terms, which is the choice to end her life, literally imbibing the tuberculosis infection from the mouth of Mamta (349). She asserts:

"I grow stronger. I dig within me and when I clear away weeds and leaves and loose earth, I hit bedrock, smooth as the truth I am named for, elegant. Heart-solid, extent unknown. This is mine, this simple hardness that moves from life to next life, impervious to any man's whims. Because there is a higher law."

(339; italics original)

That higher law is not only impervious to men, but if we continue reading the novel as translating among nation, gender, and class, then that higher law can also exist outside the reach of nation and colonialism. As reincarnation, that law stands outside Christianity. As a form of belief and knowledge of the self, we can even call it a form of self-governance, not needing the structures and laws of politics and the nation, and being able to dismiss constructs like "the violent Sikh." Here is an active, dynamic Sikhism: this is neither a Satya nor a Nanak that is pacifistic and quietist.

But how accurately could we translate between the inequities of gender and race? This is among the questions Jenny Sharpe pursues in *Allegories of Empire*. I introduce race here because it is a salient feature of the difference in nation between India and England. In thinking through how British women in the Victorian age would seek to assert their racial superiority over Indian women while trying to challenge their gendered subordination to British men, Sharpe states, "the British feminist argument for equality appeals to the idea of social progress on which modern colonialism is founded" (Sharpe 1993: 11). That notion of colonialism as progress was based in part on race, so that English women's "bid for gender power passes through a colonial hierarchy of race" (Sharpe 1993: 12).

The voice from the non-west would be one that rejects this colonial idea of "social progress," refusing to privilege men and also "racial" "whiteness" as embodying some kind of superior rationality or enlightened civility. Satya aspires toward self-realization; I want to avoid Sharpe's word "bid," for its connotations are too secular, political, and materialist in this context. Satya's aspiration passes through the sign of *religion*, one emphatically not Christian. She rejects trying to be "equal" to men, to Sardarji, and to the British, for "there is a higher law." Her wish is not for "social progress," but for self-realization and self-knowledge. This self-realization is the site of a belief, not simply by dogmatic creed, organized indoctrination, or a religion caricatured through political reactionism. After the politically-charged violence of 1984, dominant Hinduism caricatured Sikhs as "the violent Sikhs." Instead, this is a belief which Satya internalizes on her terms, through personal struggle. Like the challenges of translating between gender and nation, Satya's (or anyone else's) passage through religion is not without struggles against controlling mechanisms, whether of patriarchy, nation, class, or otherwise. But Satya is not meekly waiting to inherit the earth. Her very name indicates her intelligence, one unimpressed and unduped by the shams and ruses of ideology. Satya's knowledge of an inner strength is something that she has discovered within herself, not one which she has learned entirely from Sikhism. Why? Because the "[g]urus tell how to reach the divine but offer her no guidance for her pain" (345). The gurus cannot understand women's pain as indeed ordinary men cannot understand women's pain.

Similarly, Roop knows that her father cannot understand the pain she suffers from having to give up her children to Satya: "[men] need to be told of her pain in words or they live in oblivion. [. . .] *Read between the lines, Papaji, read around them, past them, between them. In the spaces between the words is your daughter. In the unspoken, in the unwritten, there is Roop*" (284, 285; italics original). Continuing my translation between gender and nation, just as Roop's pain and experience lie outside her father's understanding—the metaphor of existing between words is especially illustrative—Sardarji must translate for the British the "infinite variation in shades of brown" (148). Otherwise, all Indians or natives are easily pigeonholed by British administrators in coarse categories like "Maratha, Gurkha, Sikh" (148). Translating again between gender and nation, the "body" of India—whether gendered or not, and with all its memories, pains, joys, struggles, and lived experiences—lies around, past, and in the spaces between the new India-Pakistan "boundary" and "nations." Sardarji knows well this challenge of representation, for he must make a recommendation to the Punjab Border Commission: "How can he think upon issue, every canal, weir and headwork, every generating station, every reservoir, every embankment, every barrage, their locations, their connections by road and rail, their history, and their dependants in the same moment?" (420). Baldwin does well in repeating "every," and mirroring it with the repetition of "their," this symmetrical enumeration gesturing toward the enormity of what it cannot represent, and which cannot be easily understood. Sikhs and women of course constitute real, integral parts of India and Pakistan. If India in particular has *yet* to be representationally secular, in the sense of truly recognizing and *seeing* (juridically, politically, democratically) the fullness of the lives of Sikhs and women, then how can it begin to undertake the necessary understandings? Baldwin does not just tell the stories of Sikh women, she also tells us the difficulties *of* telling.

That demonstration of the difficulty is in itself instructive, and I want to return again to my translational readings, showing the "micro" of ordinary lives against the "macro" of nation. In the above senses of Roop's father not knowing her pain, and the colonial administrative bodies (such as the Border Commission) not knowing the complexities of Indian ethnicities and the land, how could pain be understood, if at all, across gender and nation? In arguing for the agency of the subject in pain, Rajeswari Sunder Rajan states that "to prevent [the] conceptual split between body and consciousness," we should see pain as constituting part of a subjectivity, and that the consequences of such a holistic view are "to see pain as a *stage* rather than a *state* and to regard the subject in pain as a *dynamic being* rather than a *passive 'space'*" (Sunder Rajan 1993: 23; italics mine). Among the messages here is that the subject in pain is "human," but not as a reaction to ideologies (colonial, white-privileged, and otherwise) by saying "they *too* are human," for that would fall into the classical traps of "humanism" (which Christianity is keen to missionize). We could also phrase Sunder Rajan's above sentence as: "to regard the object as a *subject* in pain, as a dynamic, active being rather than as a passive 'object.'"

A postsecular inflection can arise at this juncture of subjectivity and humanness, as follows. Let us not see Sikhism, as a sign of religion, as some passive space—a homogenous, empty object-religion, which could be homogenously construed as a "violent religion"—into which people become indoctrinated or fixed, losing their sense of autonomy, rationality, and subjectivity. Satya's Sikhism is very much *Satya's Sikhism*. She is *dynamically being* within Sikhism, in a stage of self-knowing. I will make a similar argument in the next chapter that Rushdie's Islam is one through which he intimately negotiates a sense of himself, so that it is very much *Rushdie's Islam*. Satya commits suicide—like the middle-class Bhubaneswari Bahduri that inspired Spivak's question "Can the subaltern speak?"—but on *her* terms, not to preserve the honour of Sardarji, but to preserve *her* honour. Bhubaneswari does send a message after death, through a letter, and with her menstrual blood serving as a sign that hers was no submissive suicide out of sexual shame. But Satya speaks after "death," *as* spirit, and ultimately of course as a character in Baldwin's novel. Satya does not speak as a "good good girl," the phrase with which patriarchy indoctrinates and rewards Roop, but as a woman who animates herself through her Sikh faith. The subaltern (in British eyes) has not died, but has continued as spirit. That spirit's awaiting reincarnation is a sign of postsecular difference against the feminist, classist, and religious prejudices of imperial ideology. Traces of Satya's strength embolden Roop. Satya lives on, and here too Baldwin engages intimately with Sikh teachings as the spirit of Satya waits to experience the realms described by Guru Nanak, the *khands* (planes) of *dharam* (duty), *gian* (knowledge), *saram* (beauty), *karam* (actions), and *sach* (truth).[8] Baldwin has written this novel not simply to "write back" to nations, colonial powers, and men, but to explore the inherent dignity and dynamism of women and Sikhs. Baldwin's semioethical message seems to be, "These lives too are part of 'India,' part of 'Pakistan,' part of 'woman,' part of 'Sikhism.' Look at them, respect them, try to understand them."

But the experiences of gender are not those of nation, and vice versa. Jenny Sharpe cautions against direct translations between women and the colonized/colonizing nation, that we could derive the exploitations of one from the exploitations of the other. Instead, she argues that the two are inextricably connected, with "woman" referring to women in both England and India: "the English woman as the *sexed subject of* colonial discourse and the Indian woman *as her subaltern shadow*" (Sharpe 1993: 12; italics mine). Sharpe syntactically prioritizes the English woman, and although that woman is a subject, she is "sexed" and "of" colonial discourse. The Indian woman is more an object ("as her"), demoted *as* a "subaltern," one reinforced by the image *as* a "shadow." Form meets content, and both meet argument: in this single sentence, Sharpe's description critically exemplifies the rhetorical strategies she seeks to deconstruct, for she explains that her use of "woman" as a figure emphasizes "the rhetorical strategies of the dominant discourses from which we derive our counternarratives" (Sharpe 1993: 12).

Accepting history as a grand narrative would result in a project that would reactively and regressively become a recovery of "lost testimonies" (Sharpe 1993: 12). "Lost" assumes something to be lost inside (such as a grand narrative), within which "testimonies" are produced by an always already pre-dicted and controlled subject. We can appreciate how and why Sharpe would resist privileging and accepting a dominant discourse, for although "woman" is, according to Sharpe, "becoming deessentialized in the West, she is being reconstituted elsewhere in the voice of non-Western women [i.e., let's empty the West of dominant discourses, but then displace them onto the non-West]. Because it implies the self-presence of living speech over writing, 'voice' can all too easily efface our roles as mediators, translators, indeed, as writers" (Sharpe 1993: 15). Yet a writer like Urvashi Butalia has clearly been motivated by a desire to record, preserve, and honour people's experiences and memories of Partition, which led to her volume *The Other Side of Silence: Voices from the Partition of India* (2000).

Where does the subject lie—whether gendered, classed, racialized, or nationalized—between the theorist's productive skepticism and the writer's enriching compassion to tell? There is of course merit to both, of course overlapping: Sharpe writes out of a commitment to expose and challenge ideologies, Butalia writes accepting that her project can never fully represent the depth, multiplicity, and agency of those who experienced Partition.[9] Butalia does not seek to create a grand new narrative that would report a full catalogue of "lost testimonies," but carries instead a respect for silence. To think that "silence" would be one-way, constituted only as the silenced "other side" of (state-)sanctioned histories, would be intellectually and ethically misguided. It would be akin to Rajeswari Sunder Rajan's argument above to see the subject in pain as having agency instead of as something constituting a passive space (Sunder Rajan 1993: 23). Butalia arrives at the negatively-created silences (those silenced by dominating discourses), but also recognizes that there are active silences constituted by agency, the decision to speak only as one wishes.

Here is where the theorist ("Jenny Sharpe" as the proper name) and the writer ("Urvashi Butalia" as the proper name) working in the interstices among at least "non-Western," "woman," "colonialism," and "postcolonialism" can productively contribute to one another's work, through shared semi-oethical sensitivities to understand—stand under, respect, abide by, honour, *see*—the subjectivities of silence. We can think of this in terms of the liberal theorization of freedom as negative freedom (absence of obstacles) and positive freedom (autonomy, self-fashioning, self-determination). Thus: negative silence, positive silence. It is Sita's positive silence when she asks the earth to swallow her to prove she had remained faithful to Ram while held captive by Ravana. In Satya's words, Sita "countered all aspersions on her worthiness with absence" (344).

Where is the novelist positioned in this? Could we charge Baldwin with essentializing women's experience? The semioethical force of Baldwin's novel is to tell the story, not to construct and theorize an abstract figure of woman. With lived knowledge of Indian, Canadian, and American cultures, it is probable that Baldwin would have a sense of feminism's aims, limitations, and commitments in both India and North America. In her criticism of *What the Body Remembers*, Priya Kumar argues for "the crucial importance of a feminist mode of cultural recall in defamiliarizing and rendering uncanny our sanctioned group memories and national mythologies" (Kumar 2008: 120). I have extended this call by showing that there is a defamiliarization not only of secularism as national mythology, but, in its wake, an affirmation of the ethics of love and of self-realization, especially as the latter can be aspired for through Sikhism.

4.3   Postsecularism and the Untranslatable

What the Body Remembers presents us with the limitations of understandings, whether those understandings try to occur across overlapping categories like "religion," "culture," or "politics." I want to explore in this section how untranslatability can feature in the limits of understanding, and how untranslatability is part of the postsecular possibilities caught in a double bind between the secular and the religious.

If colonizing agents represent themselves as the acme of rationality and intelligence, and if masculinity tells the story of itself as the embodiment of rationality and intelligence, then Cunningham, the inner voice of Sardarji taking root through his years of education in England, literally represents the internalization of a colonial mindset. Sardarji is grateful for this voice, because he thinks, despite evidence to the contrary, that it gives him a toehold on "the inner sanctum where the real chess game is played" (147). Does Cunningham have a symmetrical access to Sardarji's inner sanctum? To challenge and refute the not purely rational but biased voice of Cunningham would be to undertake Ngugi wa'Thiongo's call to decolonize the mind. If it is not quite decolonization, there is an unknowability that Sardarji holds onto, keeping from Cunningham his "'ten percent,' his turban, his faith, the untranslated, untranslatable residue of his being" (147).

This literary representation of the untranslatability of faith converges elegantly with Arvind-Pal Mandair's theorization of untranslatability across religion:

To allow the "untranslatable" would be to refuse the ruse of transparency that allows religion (for example) to be translated perfectly; that is, to refuse the false belief that it is possible to pass from one language/culture to another and back again without being contaminated, a ruse/belief that constitutes the enunciation of religion as a universal.

(Mandair 2009: 429)

This belief that religion, namely Christianity, should and *could* be made universal was of course one of the constituent features of imperialism. But the fact of untranslatability (not "intransigence," for that would affirm the logic and presence of a source language and idea) disrupts imperial Christianity's assumptive arrogance. Arvind-Pal Mandair explains that religion's untranslatability "bring[s] into relief the enunciative modality that exists prior to every decision, the nonconvergence of discourses" (Mandair 2009: 429). Such nonconvergence allows one to expose, and here Mandair quotes Judith Butler: "the 'ruptures of narrativity, the founding violence [sic] of an episteme'" (Mandair 2009: 429).[10]

This is the epistemic violence that translates (and thinks it *can* translate) Sikhism via Christian theology as "Sikh theology" and as a "world religion," as I discussed in the opening section of this chapter. It is the violence of the English tutor who teaches the Indian child to say the phrase "little pagan baby" (365). It is the epistemic violence that can see women only as passive and as objects—they are assumed not to feel pain. It is the violence that constructs refugees as "Indian" or "Pakistani." As Lenny, the narrator in Bapsi Sidhwa's *Cracking India* states, "'I am Pakistani. In a snap. Just like that. A new nation is born'" (Sidhwa 1991: 150). It is the patriarchal, nationalist Hindu violence that constructs Sita as a model of piety and virtue, completely faithful to her husband Ram's wishes. But Satya's re-telling of Sita's story restores Sita's agency, and secularizes Sita by connecting her with Satya's experiences. Satya emphasizes, quite apart from the patriarchal Hindu-sanctioned versions of the story, that Sita chose to die of her own will, and thus "shamed [Ram] for all time" (282).

Mandair, working within the sign of religion, uses "enunciative modality" and "nonconvergence" to describe dominant discourses. Jenny Sharpe, working within the signs of gender and nation, identifies the "codified interpretative systems" always already shaping readings and interpretations (e.g., of history), systems that are constructed, as in Mandair's analysis, by dominant discourses. Combining Mandair's and Sharpe's analyses, the *untranslatability of gendered religion* would be exposed by, and in turn expose, the nonconvergence (between man/woman, Sikhism/Christianity, religion/secularism) and enunciative modalities (who is speaking? how and why?) of discourses. If we see Satya's belief in a higher law as "Sikh theology," among the codifying interpretive systems here is "Christian theology." Satya has a form of belief, but it is not entirely shaped by Sikhism.

Satya's is a unique belief arising from her unique lived experience and unique understanding of Sikhism.

Everyone's experience is of course uniquely theirs, but how well can we truly see and understand others? The postsecular is the sign of not just the limits of translation (Sikhism can, to a *degree*, be understood as "religion"), but also of untranslatability itself ("Sikh theology" is *not* "Christian theology"). The postsecular is the sign of a call for a new form of interpretation, one which does not recode prior interpretive systems, and one which does not attempt a convergence of systems where it knows there can be none. Satya's belief is not simply in "Sikh reincarnation." Nor is it a "woman's superstition," avoiding easy, assumed convergences of "woman," "subaltern," "religion," and "Sikhism." Her belief is caught in a double bind between the religious ("Sikh reincarnation") and also secularity (she knows the gurus cannot understand her pain). This is the sense of "neither"/"nor" that Saba Mahmood pursues in *Politics of Piety*, questioning the distinction between secularism and religion, which I will revisit in the conclusion of this chapter.

Baldwin does not assume that her representations in the novel are unproblematic. One way she thematizes this caution is through her acknowledgment that no tale can be reliable, and this is where the postcolonial novelist can join the work of critics and theorists in understanding how discourses codify interpretation. The end of the novel concludes with Roop's father and her brother Jeevan each describing Kusum's dead body. Roop knows that these men will tell the story as they see fit, to preserve both their and the dead women's *izzat* ("honour"; *izzat* itself difficult to translate into English): "Papaji is the teller of Revati Bhua's tale and he tells it as he wishes it repeated" (502).[11]

4.4   Conclusion

By challenging the idea of "secular India," and therefore the idea of the nation, Shauna Singh Baldwin presents those other voices not so easily available or known. This is similar to the academic re-theorization of the non-western woman in pain, trying to restore some subjectivity and agency to the woman. Baldwin shows the agency and subjectivity of Sikhism through Satya and also through Roop. As the novel progresses, Roop gains self-confidence, consciously modelling herself on Satya's assertiveness and self-command. Roop takes perhaps her greatest risk at the end of the novel, telling Sardarji that she is deaf in one ear. This is a risk because he might disown her, and thus dishonour her family. Instead, Sardarji promises to help her. The disclosure demonstrates Roop's strength not only because she has undertaken a large risk, but also because she knows it will empower and re-masculate Sardarji after the losses of Partition: "*Something must be sacrificed for his haumai, his self-ness, to return, rise and move forward*" (512; italics original). Roop's declaration allows for Sardarji's sense of agency to be restored, as a potent, empowered, consequential agent and subject in the world.

This is also a demonstration of Roop's agency and subjectivity. Roop knows well the patriarchal oppressions around her, but chooses to remain within the system of which they are a part, for that larger system gives her a connectedness with others, which assuages her fear of being alone. Referring to the women's mosque group in Cairo that on its surface shows women supporting a system that subordinates them, Saba Mahmood has argued that "what may appear to be a case of deplorable passivity and docility from a progressivist point of view, may actually be a form of agency" (Mahmood 2005: 15). Mahmood defines agentival capacity in this context as something "entailed not only in those acts that resist norms but also in the multiple ways in which one *inhabits* norms" (Mahmood 2005: 15; italics original). The key word here for me is "multiple," and it is that multiplicity of inhabitations that Baldwin shows in her novel, a multiplicity which the mutability of literary representation *allows* her to represent. Satya could be more easily read than Roop as showing the signs of agency envisioned and endorsed by Euro-American feminism, like ideals of self-autonomy based on assumptions of liberalism and individualism.[12] Satya's sense of subjectivity is not entirely autonomous, nor is Roop's entirely passive.

Waiting for several days at the Delhi railway station for Sardarji to join her from Lahore, Roop sheds her clothing as a challenge and affront, to show others a woman respecting her body, on her terms and under *her* gaze, without shame, diffidence, and effacement: "*See me, I am human, though I am only a woman. See me, I did what women are for. See me not as a vessel, a plaything, a fantasy, a maidservant, an ornament, but as Vaheguru made me*" (479; italics original). As we will see in the next chapter on *The Satanic Verses*, Rushdie alludes to the Bhakti tradition as he narrates the story of the young prophet Ayesha, strikingly beautiful and so immersed in her divine revelations that she feels no need for clothing, becoming covered by a sari of butterflies. Among Rushdie's historical and literary influences here is the medieval Bhakti poet Akkamahadevi, who became so enraptured by her love for her divine lover Shiva that she shed all her clothing, feeling united with and protected by divine omnipresence. In Rushdie's text, Ayesha becomes an object of desire and lust, of beauty objectified.

This passage demonstrating Roop's agency can also find echoes with Sojourner Truth's famous speech "Ain't I a Woman?" Because Sojourner Truth was a former slave, an African American, and a woman, her speech contained a special capacity to challenge slavery, racism, and sexism in the early twentieth-century American South. I also discuss this speech in the next chapter on *The Satanic Verses*. Shauna Singh Baldwin has stated that she was influenced by African American women's writings as she wrote *What the Body Remembers* (personal communication). The following quotation by Toni Morrison, about slavery, was particularly influential as Baldwin wrote her novel: "You only have to write it—they had to live it." Baldwin interpreted this within the context of Partition.

Shauna Singh Baldwin's characterization of both forms of subjectivity, one that challenges the distinction between "passive" and "active," shows her diasporic feminist influences across India, Canada, and the US. From within a Canadian context, we could see similarities with Margaret Atwood's *The Handmaid's Tale* (1985), also an indictment of patriarchy, one using the genre of dystopic fiction, and how women negotiate agency when their only social function is to work as concubines. As another Canadian perspective, Prabhjot Parmar has observed that *What the Body Remembers* could be influenced by the potential partition of Canada, through the separation of Quebec (Parmar 2008). Baldwin's diasporic situatedness could be her strength, but it could also be her weakness. With an historical trauma where even oral histories are difficult to record, and even then unreliable, here is an author with the luxury to aestheticize the living-on of a woman's spirit, and how it might speak. The semioethical drive of Baldwin's novel is clear, but her privilege of aestheticization, from a distance no less, would be vulnerable to the charge of insensitivity.

The postsecular challenge is to witness the closing gesture by Roop and see not patriarchy, but love, choice, and agency. This is similar to the difficulties in interpretation provokable by the closing Buddha image of *Anil's Ghost*. The postsecular challenge here is to look at the Buddha and see not the violence of Sinhalese majoritarianism, but instead peace, hope, and regeneration. These moments in both novels highlight the presence of the novelist. This presence is underscored even more through a metaphor appearing in both *What the Body Remembers* and *The English Patient*. In *The English Patient*, Ondaatje describes the villa and its inhabitants as forming a tableau, as a scene "flung" against the war (Ondaatje 1992: 278). Atop the haveli, Satya sees Rawalpindi stretched all around her like "a child's painted wooden toys flung in the lap of the Margalla Hills" (329). These passages resonate with a scene in *Anil's Ghost*, of Sirissa's riding her bicycle at night, the shops closing *"like a theatre after the performance was over"* (174; italics original). All three passages demonstrate aestheticization, overt gestures by novelists to render figurative everyday scenes. Ondaatje and Baldwin seem to be fascinated by how something that could be as innocuously comforting as children's toys or an evening bicycle ride through a community could also be a site of violence. Among toys and a bicycle and a villa, the signification of the unrepresentability of violence is at the same time a *representation* of violence, thus serving as a cognitive device for the author, as part of the author's work at understanding violence.

To deconstruct the mythology of "secular India" is to tell the fullness of the lives of Sikhs, which will include telling the fullness of the lives of Sikh women, which will include telling the fullness of the lives of women. As Baldwin has stated, "I wasn't interested in the 'Freedom At Midnight' view of Indian history, and read between the lines and against the grain, often telling stories told by one class or community from another point of view, using educated guessing and imagination" (Ranjan 2011). Representing such fullness of experience will include contradictions, so that where a Sikh man might feel unjustly treated by the British, he will himself act unjustly toward his wife, who in turn could mete out unjust treatment toward her servant. Baldwin does not explicitly link these injustices, as indeed she does not homogenize experiences within gender, nation, class, and religion. Instead, her interest is in helping us see injustice itself, how it works and what motivates it. This could invite reflections on how we ourselves might embody parts of the very system, discrimination, or practice that we criticize, especially across divides in postsecular societies, secularized societies now facing religious diversity within their borders, a concept that I discussed in the Introduction using the work of Habermas. Baldwin helps us see injustice by making the figure of "woman" central to this novel. She shows the ways in which religion (Christianity, Hinduism, Islam, Sikhism), nation (England, India, Pakistan), class, and men cannot understand women.

Just as Allan Sealy in *The Everest Hotel* affirms elements of Christianity like care and compassion, Baldwin affirms elements of Sikhism, such as its teachings on the equality of men and women, and its teachings on the higher self through the doctrine of reincarnation. The power of Baldwin's novel lies in its portrayal of agency within Sikhism, that Sikhism is a dynamic, active religion, in turn constituted and animated by the agency of women. I invoke Arvind-Pal Mandair's theorization of untranslatability to demonstrate its convergence with the special semioethical force and multiplicity of perspectives offered by the postcolonial novel. The fact that both productions are occurring on a world stage demonstrates the significance of the historical shift in the thinking of secularism and religion, a world where "the other" is not simply an ethnographic curiosity but an integral part of oneself. The postsecularism of *What the Body Remembers* is marked by untranslatability (for example, men must respect women's choice to be silent), a heightened sensitivity to the enunciatedness of modalities (for example, "secular India" is a mode of story enunciated politically, but it is not representative of Sikhs and women), and the nonconvergence of discourses (for example, "oppression of Sikhs in India" *is not* "oppression of women by Sikhs" *is not* "oppression of subalterns by elites"). Through the character of Satya, Baldwin shows one woman's agency through religion: Satya's affirmations are a part of *Satya's postsecular Sikhism*, not as markers of uncritical belief, but as markers of active negotiation with the immanence and teachings of Guru Nanak (more untranslatabilities: "Guru Nanak's teachings" *are not* "Sikh theology"; and "Sikh theology" *is not* "Christian theology"). It is in this sense that I explore in the next chapter how Rushdie's agency through Islam is a sign of *Rushdie's postsecular Islam*, a critical, active negotiation with the enunciative modality that is "Islam."

Figure 7 Morning fog over Panch Mahal, Fatehpur Sikri, India. Photograph by the author.

5 Postsecularism and Prophecy
Salman Rushdie's *The Satanic Verses*

Salman Rushdie is, emphatically, not dead. But his death has existed in
virtual reality for over twenty years: threatened, imagined, deferred. As
flames burned *The Satanic Verses* in the UK, the *fatwa* set literary and cultural criticism ablaze, sparking a set of oppositions that seemed to replicate
infinitely, such as freedom vs. oppression, religion vs. secularism, modernity vs. tradition, and the west vs. the non-west. The now common phrase
"clash of civilizations" (Huntingdon 1993, 1996)—used in the crisis of 9/11, of
Iraq, of Afghanistan—first appeared a year after the *fatwa* in Bernard Lewis's
1990 article entitled "The Roots of Muslim Rage." After the weight of the
fatwa, and the *fatwa*'s resounding impact throughout the world, how can
we read Rushdie now with some distance from it, without its long shadow?
How can we make the novel born again, as if the *fatwa* never happened? As
if the novel had its own forms of belief and commitment? Several volumes
have offered meditations on the novel and the *fatwa* from the vantage, and
advantage, of historical distance (Gurnah 2007; Herwitz and Varshney 2008;
Mishra 2007). In this chapter, I build upon and depart from this scholarship
by exploring what a *postsecular* possibility of belief might look like.

Rushdie creates a range of representations in this novel in order to approxi-
mate and understand that which resists representation: faith. What constitutes
faith? How does it emerge? What *is* faith? The Oxford English Dictionary
defines faith as "confidence, reliance, trust [. . .] in the truth of a statement or
doctrine," and as "belief proceeding from reliance on testimony or authority"
(oed.com). The OED states that, in its theological sense, faith is "the spiritual
apprehension of divine truths, or of realities beyond the reach of sensible
experience or logical proof" (oed.com). It is this idea of confidence, reliance,
and trust, especially in that which is beyond sensible experience or logical
proof, that fascinates Rushdie. He is fascinated with Islam in particular and
with religious faith in general. Although some representations of the novel
might be taken as blasphemous—and there is tremendous insensitivity in
such gestures, which I shall address—there are "believing" impulses that generate Rushdie's text: faith in his literary powers. But there is a confrontation,
between faith-in-art and faith-in-religion, between a much-guarded aesthetic

autonomy and an equally guarded belief in religious thought and practice. That confrontation is paralleled in Rushdie's emphasis on the diversity and range of beliefs and practices within Islam. That emphasis allows him to critique fundamentalism in Islam, simultaneously showing the diversities of religion itself.

In his essay on the *fatwa* and its aftermath, Talal Asad investigates the double standards at play in the dominant, middle-class, liberal British reaction to the Rushdie Affair. Blasphemy laws in the UK have extended to Christianity, but not to Islam. There was no public outcry against the burning of immigration laws, or against the burning of Rabbi Kaplan's prayer book re-defining Judaism. But when *The Satanic Verses* was burned, it became an affront to nothing less than the foundations of western civilization, in part because it represented a burning of *literature*, of the sacred role played by literature in modern western culture. Yet when ordinary British citizens suffer racial harassment, there is no corresponding outcry about a civilizational threat, only "dismay at the violent intolerance of [the] lower classes" (Asad 1993: 302). All of which leads Asad to ask: "If the freedom of public criticism is in fact restricted by laws that protect the sensibilities only of the rich, the famous, and the majority, what happens to the rest, those who are always Others in liberal society?" (Asad 1993: 278).

What about when the subject, however real and imagined, is somewhere between the privileged and the Other? Vijay Mishra has argued that "[w]hat is missing from diasporic theory is a theory of the sacred based not on the idea of the sacred as a pathological instance of the secular, in itself defined along purely modernist lines, but as a point from which interventions can take place" (Mishra 2007: 233). By "interventions," Mishra means that the sacred becomes a "source for metaphors of empowerment easily available for ethnic mobilization" (Mishra 2007: 233). It is here that the diasporic narrative of the sacred is "constructed as a defense mechanism or as a means of connecting the impossible world of the here-and-now with the lost, ideal world of the there-and-then" (Mishra 2007: 235). For Mishra, standing in contrast to the diasporic narrative of the sacred is the diasporic narrative of the "hyphen" or fractured. The hyphen narrative, of which Rushdie's work is emblematic, describes hybridity, the subject in the process of change, re-definition. Islam sacralizes that which exists as other in the British nation-state—in this case an illiberal, demonized ethnic and religious minority. For fundamentalist Muslims, Rushdie's novel demonizes the Qur'an as a whole, calling it satanic. Let us read the title anew: *The Satanic Verses*. As Vijay Mishra succinctly and powerfully states it, "Racialized politics meets its sacralized Other here as the title horrifies" (2007: 233).

With the postsecular *The Satanic Verses*, I would re-conceptualize Mishra's argument as follows: "Othered politics meets its racialized sacred as the title mollifies." Rushdie others the politics of the UK liberal state by sensationally introducing into the public domain—however (un)intentionally, as subject and object of the Rushdie Affair—debates and controversies about a religion other to Christianity: Islam. He does so by racializing, and thus secularizing, the sacred of Islam, by presenting a postcolonial, diasporic Islam informed by the unironic realities of his lived experience as an "ethnic" "minority" "migrant" in the UK (the scare quotes do not doubt the reality of the lived experience; they indicate the hegemonies behind the terms; one could go further: "in" "the" "UK"). The entire creative act is a pleasurable one for Rushdie, reinforcing his faith in his ability to create forms and narratives as he wishes. In the act of creating such forms—*what is newness?*—the novel affirms itself, in spite of the cadres of fundamentalism rushing everywhere to obliterate it.

Rukmini Bhaya Nair has observed that "[l]oyalty, the effective emotional ingredient in the definitional makeup of faith in religion or love for one's country, is redefined in Rushdie's text as the capacity to tell" (Nair 2002: 249). Nair's observation is one that I flesh out and extend in this chapter. How exactly does the text demonstrate Rushdie's affirmation of his capacity to tell? The novel gestures toward and affirms forms of belief, however tenuous, in the wake of the violence of religious fundamentalist belief. The postsecular values that emerge include affirmations of hybridity, the migrant's eye-view, literature, newness, and love. Where Rushdie sees *verses*, the state and the offended religious believers see *versus*: antagonism, mutual suspicion, good confronting evil, oppositional thinking, odious difference. *The Satanic Versus The Satanic.* Rushdie is caught in a double bind, yet trying so hard to find the newness of something outside such duality. After the *fatwa*, there is no reversing of the versus, only a continual re-versing of the verses. Talal Asad has identified the faces of the *versus*, whereas Vijay Mishra tries to find the *verses* in the sacred of the diasporic co-religionists, adding depth, layers, and subtlety to their motivations for burning the book: the well-wrought burn.

The story continues. Criticism joins the reversing. Mishra's reading can also be placed alongside Akeel Bilgrami's argument that the post-publication backlash by Muslim immigrants against the UK state occurred due to "a prior refusal on the classical *liberal* state's part to acknowledge that the migration of cultural difference into one's midst should have the effect of laying it [the state] open to internal argument, which the state must use its conceptual and other resources to provide" (Bilgrami 2008: 50; italics original). Liberalism here means freedom of speech. By internal arguments, Bilgrami means that the state should look within British Muslim populations, particularly non-fundamentalist or non-absolutist Muslims, to see that they too might have values which guide them to value freedom of speech. But, according to Bilgrami, the state's refusal of internal argument—reflected, for example, in its rejection of the Bradford Muslims' demand for implementing blasphemy laws—is in part because the state believes its truths and values to be universal, and therefore applies them to others with self-justification.

For Homi Bhabha, this unwillingness of the state also undermines liberalism's claims that tolerance and egalitarianism are available and accessible to

everyone (Bhabha 1996). Secularism becomes closely linked with this liberalism. The British state might not be constitutionally secular, but in Bhabha's
view, the equation of secularism with modernization is what allowed "spokes-
persons for the Eurocentric liberal 'arts' establishment [. . .] to characterize
the 'backwardness' of migrant communities" (Bhabha 1996: 209). This is
parallel to the sense of secularism that I discussed in the introductory chapter; postsecularism challenges secularism as ideology, where only secularism
is seen as the preserve of reason and progress. As demonstrated by the frus-
trations of the British migrant communities, the idea of liberal secularism as
rights applying equally across all citizens in a spirit of egalitarianism and free
choice—the subject conceived here as rational, good, commonsensical—is a
fantasy. Bhabha turns to "subaltern secularism" as the truly progressive vantage point from which to ensure more representative and equal citizenship
and rights, for the subaltern perspective identifies and takes its inspiration
from the *limitations* of liberal secularism.

What *The Satanic Verses* therefore provokes is a posting of *this* unequal
sense of secularism and its attendant liberalism, using the vantage points
of diaspora and a "minority" religion to challenge the state, and its ossi-
fied orientalism, to be introspective about the actually existing limits of its
tolerance for and accommodation of "other" points of view. This posting
is not an abandonment of the best aspirations of Indian secular principles
in and with which Rushdie grew up, especially not after the violence of
Gujarat and Ayodhya, and the rise of Hindu fundamentalism in his native
Mumbai. Instead, it is an attempt to re-think and move forward, furthering
the capacity of the state to recognize and accept difference, whether religious, racial, ethnic, or otherwise. The book burning therefore ironically
helped Rushdie. The protesters were offended most in the name of religion,
but ultimately they drew attention, thanks in part to the inexorable commentary they provoked, to the injustices of racism and unequal citizenship
that the novel itself addresses.

Rushdie's writerly access to liberal secularism, especially in the wake of
the enormous success of *Midnight's Children* as both "great literature" and
native informancy, was the deep divide between him and the novel's protestors. Vijay Mishra sees a diaspora of the whole and a diaspora of the
hyphen; I want to extend this and state that Rushdie's liberal secularism
itself is hyphenated. His secularism is both elite, giving him the privilege
of acceptable high art expression and the luxury of representing an array
of Islams as he wishes, but it is also informed by his knowledge of the limits
of that secularism, as racial "other" in the UK state (of course, not every
"other's" experience is homogenous, just as that of every "same" is not homo-
geneous). Rushdie's knowledge of Indian secularism allows him to confront
the orthodoxies of Islamic fundamentalism and its self-rationalizations. How
can Rushdie post *the religion of religion*, while still affirming some sense of
belief? The post *to* the secular in this sense represents a search for belief in

the wake of an acute recognition of both the ideals and failures of hyphen-ated secularism and of the violence of religious fundamentalism.

The postsecular values that emerge for Rushdie do not emerge from facile abstract imagining. They are hard-won. They are achieved through secular struggle, across the inequalities I have sketched above: inequalities of lib-eral secularism, citizenship, lived experience itself. What also emerges for Rushdie is the presentation of a worldly Islam: Islam on *his* terms. This is a postcolonial, diasporic Islam embraced not because of ideology or politi-cal pressure—faith (in religion) conceived here as "reliance on testimony or authority" (OED)—but because of the real, unironic challenges and crises which consolidate and affirm the believer's sense of self-constitution, espe-cially when he or she is so deeply challenged by the real pressures of immi-gration, relocation, racism, classism. Who am I? What should I believe? The Islam that Rushdie presents in *The Satanic Verses* as his own is one he opposes to what he has termed "Actually Existing Islam," describing the latter as "the political and priestly power structure that presently dominates and stifles Muslim societies" (Rushdie 1991: 436). The catastrophes and crises so fre-quently marking this novel—death, a plane crash, physical transformation, Partition, to name only a few—serve as modes of provocation for the exami-nation and consolidation of self-constitution. Subsequent affirmations of such self-constitution can avoid the vacuity and "bad faith" of sentiment, or the vacuity of an uncritical acceptance of religious ideology.

I divide my analysis of this complex novel into two main sections. The first focuses on the chapters that depict the life of Muhammad, entitled "Mahound" and "Return to Jahilia," the parts of the book which attracted controversy. It is here that Rushdie has most perceptibly re-narrated the life of Muhammad, not only secularizing it but also infusing it with the enchantment of literary re-creation. The second section focuses on the chapters "Ayesha" and "The Parting of the Arabian Sea." I explore here the possibilities of a "new" post-secular magical realism, where magical realism becomes the secular equiva-lent of the religious miracle. Narrating the story of the female prophet Ayesha from the perspective of the subaltern, these chapters also could be considered blasphemous, though they did not spark as much controversy as the Mahound sections, and have received relatively less critical attention.

5.1 Representing Muhammad: Ain't I a Prophet?

In his effort to understand religious faith and its origins, Rushdie takes great effort in *The Satanic Verses* to historicize Muhammad. In light of Islamic teachings that state Muhammad was a mortal, a messenger of Allah, and not God or the religion itself, Rushdie asks: who was Muhammad the person? What story can I tell about him? The surface result came to be read as sen-sationally blasphemous. At a more subtle level, Rushdie uses the framework of a novel, as literature—the ability to create characters, to use tropes—in

order to explore the nature of faith, of which "disbelief" would be too easy
an opposite:

> Question: What is the opposite of faith?
> Not disbelief. Too final, certain, closed. Itself a kind of belief.
> Doubt.
>
> (Rushdie 1988: 92)[1]

How does Rushdie introduce this doubt? How does Rushdie historicize and
represent Muhammad and Islam by interpreting them through postcolonial
migrancy? Finally, how does Rushdie explore the philosophical dimensions
of religion, as represented by the question throughout the novel, "What kind
of idea are you/is this?" I select these aspects because they constitute and
emphasize the writerly "craft" of Rushdie.

"Mahound" and "Return to Jahilia" are dream sequences dreamt by
Gibreel, who becomes not just dreamer-observer, but also participant-actor
as Angel Gibreel to Muhammad. This use of dreams and of magical realism
problematizes the realist mode through which it is so easy to read, and respond
to, these controversial sections. Yet the very delusions that distress Gibreel can
mirror the precariousness of the narrative status for readers, especially readers
who might not be as faithful to the reading process as Rushdie, or any novelist,
might wish. Rushdie straddles the discourses of history, religion, and literature
in one single ambition. Most evanescent among these discourses will be the
literary, for the other two are conventionally constituted by realist modes of
narrative. Thus, the belief with which Rushdie imbues the literary will be so
subtle that its competing discourses will inscribe their realist modes, beyond
Rushdie's control, into the "sacrosanct" literary. The craft of the literary that
Rushdie exercises includes the mutability of forms—for example, changing the
historical Muhammad into the character "Mahound." Rushdie appropriates
the master narrative that is the historicized, ritualized Islam into the Islam that
is his, an urgently, irrepressibly postcolonial Islam. *The Satanic Verses* is a novel
whose events include, among others, a hijacked airplane crashing in mid-flight;
a young man who transforms into a devil; scores of people who become crea-
tures of various distortions and disfigurations; an entire village that walks to
its death into the sea; ethnic riots that grip a city, replete with fires, thefts, and
murders. By invoking such violence, crisis, and catastrophe, Rushdie commands and provokes readerly attention toward that which is so important to
him, is beyond doubt, and which is real: migration and the migrant's eye-view,
postcoloniality, ethnicity.

Although it might not appear so on the surface, and this was evidently the
case for readers who felt the slings and arrows of blasphemy, faith for Rushdie is a serious business. Rushdie makes a series of equations and connections in order to underscore that seriousness. Both Gibreel and Saladin are
Indian, they are immigrants to England, and they experience magical realist

transformations. One hallucinates becoming an angel; the other literally becomes the devil. Gibreel dreams the prophet Muhammad who is given the name "Mahound," the Satan-like creature into which Saladin transforms. Why does Rushdie so intimately intertwine the narrative of a religion with that of a fantastically-portrayed migrant experience? Rushdie seeks to show readers the diversity of Islam, and in particular *his* Islam, one which confronts us and challenges us to witness its varied inflections and translations by the postcolonial migrant experience. Thus his equation: the expression of religious selfhood is inextricable from the culture—national, political, historical, ethnic, and otherwise—in which one is situated. Who am I? What am I? Where is the self situated? These questions can construe the self as both subject and object, as something that asks questions and about which questions can be asked. This sense of self can obtain insight and perspective into such questions from the outside, from the promise of moving radically and totally outside the terms of a system. This is what Rushdie envisions as "newness." It is what Rushdie relentlessly attempts to represent throughout the novel with his question, "What kind of idea are you?" Religious thought intrigues Rushdie because of its promise of this newness. But it also frustrates and disappoints him because of its hypocrisy. In its pretense toward newness, religion can codify and prescribe its ideas through orthodoxies, rationalizing itself so that it conditions people to believe in a particular brand of newness, which might not be newness after all. If catastrophe is particularly resistant to representation, then so too are newness and "ideaness." It is this hesitant, momentary search for an enchanted sense of newness, but one that is other from religion and firmly situated within the secular present, that is among the postsecular possibilities in this text.

The paradox then emerges: how to represent this unrepresentability? We might recall the problem faced by Ondaatje in *Anil's Ghost*. The fantastic other for Ondaatje, that which so relentlessly resists representation, is Sri Lanka in general and violence in particular. Ondaatje asks: can a National Atlas map represent Sri Lanka? Is the capacity for violence resident in each of us, like a sleeping lake of petrol? Is a succinct, italicized list of victims sufficient to represent violence? Ondaatje's diasporic location adds another dimension to these questions, perhaps one of urgency, because he sees and participates in Sri Lanka from both the "inside" and the "outside," through both spatial and historical distance.

Rushdie is similarly positioned. Rushdie's emigration from Mumbai to London allows for the duality of the secular Islam of his family in Mumbai and the Islam which is the object of his critique: the inflexible, fundamentalist Islam he sees around him in London. But the vanity, and failure, of Rushdie is that he wishes the prophet Muhammad's experience to be his own. If the prophet Muhammad had been a postcolonial migrant to London undergoing such foundational and catastrophic transformations, would Rushdie still champion and explore, with such dedication, his brand of newness? Although diasporic situatedness enables such a questioning, it also handicaps Rushdie's sensitivity to the locations in which such questioning is a matter of violence, of life and death. And those locations are not simply the so-called "Third World," with the Italian translator and the Norwegian publisher attacked, and the book burned in the UK. This is not to privilege the west as the criterion for legitimizing suffering. Instead, it is to show that the stakes—the crises of secularism—are transnational.

I would like to begin my reading of the novel with the passage in which Muhammad's wife Khadija reassures him that he is the messenger of God. Gibreel plays a dual role: the sections "Mahound" and "Return to Jahilia" are dream sequences of his, but he is also the Angel Gibreel, connected to Muhammad not just through the evanescence of a dream but also as the divine revealer of the Qur'an. Such an extraordinary position as the messenger of God overwhelms Muhammad, who becomes distressed by his visions of the Angel Gibreel:

> He can't stop walking, moves around the courtyard in a random sequence of unconscious geometries, [. . .] a series of ellipses, trapeziums, rhomboids, ovals, rings. [. . .] [H]er husband walks in pentagons, parallelograms, six-pointed stars, and then in abstract and increasingly labyrinthine patterns for which there are no names, as though unable to find a simple line.
>
> (118, 119)

There is method to Rushdie's "blasphemy," and the method shares a similarity with religion's six-pointed star: patterned and aesthetic. This could be the six-pointed star appearing in the cosmologies of a range of religions, including Buddhism, Christianity, Hinduism, Islam, Jainism, and Judaism. Leaving the star unnamed could be a secularizing move on Rushdie's part, but also blasphemous in its combination of different religious epistemologies. The patterns are first simply "acted" (walked), and then their posting is labyrinthine, unpredictable, not "a simple line." After removing the star from particular religious traditions, the posting that follows—the tentative explorations of the boundaries of the present and the religious—is abstract, labyrinthine, something for which no names exist. Given the number of shapes represented in so short a passage, there is a certain speed here, and it provides a textual example of Sten Pultz Moslund's notion of the relatively fast speeds of becoming and change represented by the transcultural-hybrid novel, of which, for Moslund, Rushdie's works are exemplary (Moslund 2010: 19). Where will such cultural change lead us? As I stated in the Preface, if the postsecular is a process, then we do not know where it will lead us, but the change it constitutes and inaugurates can occur epistemically, as in the gesturing afforded by the literary imagination. We could also read the above patterns of walking as a metafictional comment, as a gesture to the patterns that constitute the literary qualities of the novel, reflected, for example, in the short but revealing phrase "allgood allahgod" (92). The succinct, playful, and self-conscious combination of the visual with the phonetic in this phrase demonstrates Rushdie's turn to the literary in order to enact his "doubting," posting critique.

There is a similar combination of terms in the novel's plot, in that the life of the fictional "Mahound" closely parallels the life of the historical Muhammad. Yet it is not merely the unfolding of events that Rushdie relays to readers. His ambition is literary in that he presents nothing less than Muhammad as a "character." Rushdie puts into place what Donna Haraway terms a "trickster figure." This is a figure who, according to Haraway, occupies an "excessive critical position [. . .] attained through practices of political and personal displacement across boundaries between sociosexual identities and communities, between bodies and discourses, by what I like to call the 'eccentric subject'" (Haraway 1992: 98). Rushdie is able to create his own eccentric subject and proclaim, "Can't I be a believer too?" The result threatens the very boundaries and ideologies which seek to keep a single, fixed notion of Islam and a fixed notion of Muhammad, both surface features of a deeper fixed notion of belief. It is not just Rushdie's idea which is a threat to the idea of a prophet; it is also the means through which he expresses that idea.

When Rushdie continually asks throughout the novel, "What kind of idea are you?," he is taking the position of Sojourner Truth's famous question: "Ain't I a woman?" Born into slavery, the abolitionist and women's rights activist Sojourner Truth delivered her now popular question in a speech at the 1851 Women's Convention in Ohio (Gates Jr. 1991: 134). Rushdie chimes in: "Isn't my Muhammad a prophet also?" The miraculous in Rushdie's case consists of the fact that he *can* make a subject, that he *can* craft an eccentricity. Rushdie gives to Haraway that other shape of history, an other imagination of humanity, his humanity: a postcolonial, diasporic humanity. In creating his Muhammad, Rushdie essentially is saying, "Where did my Islam come from? From Mahound and me. And ain't I wonderful?" In the process, Rushdie fashions himself as an *eccentric* figure, so that his very obliteration through the *fatwa* is an imperative to obliterate all those other histories, other imaginations, other interpretations, other stories, and other humanities that, like the irreverent intelligence of Sojourner Truth, threaten the self-rationalizing narrative—and shatters the confidence—of a single kind of Islam.

What does it mean to believe in religion? *A* religion? Gibreel and Saladin and the form of the novel constantly raise the concept of "ideaness." What kind of idea are they? Rushdie directs this question to Muhammad and thus in one swift move ascribes to the prophet a relativism and a doubtability: "the businessman-turned-prophet, Mahound, is founding one of the world's great religions; and has arrived, on this day, his birthday, at the crisis of his life. There is a voice whispering in his ear: *What kind of idea are you? Man-or-mouse?*" (95; italics original).

Such a historicizing challenge was also applied to the life of Jesus Christ by late eighteenth-century and early nineteenth-century scholars in a movement that came to be called "Higher Criticism." A group of German scholars that was part of the German Protestant rationalist theological movement—Friedrich Schleiermacher, his student David Friedrich Strauss, and Ludwig Feuerbach—analyzed historical records of the Middle East from Christian and Old Testament times in order to find scientific parallels to the Biblical account of the life of Jesus. Strauss became the first to fully describe the "historical" Jesus in his *Das Leben Jesu* (1835–1836), translated by George Eliot in 1846 as *Life of Jesus* (Eliot also translated Feuerbach's *The Essence of Christianity* [1854], a form of theology continued by Ernest Renan in his *La Vie de Jésus* [1865]). By applying "myth theory" to the life of Jesus, Strauss treated the Gospel narratives as any other form of historical narrative, thereby denying any of their supernatural elements. Strauss argued that such miraculous events as walking on water, stilling storms, raising the dead, and healing the blind were myths added to the narrative to construct the divine origin of Jesus. Strauss's controversial work shocked some Christians who believed the very idea of undertaking such research—a secularizing move—was disrespectful toward the status of the Bible as the revealed truth of God.

Similar to Strauss's effort at historicizing Jesus, Rushdie's effort is not only to historicize Muhammad, but, as novelist, to offer a historicization informed by his own experiences. The crisis that is Muhammad's is the crisis that is also Gibreel's and Saladin's—and Rushdie's. It is the crisis of geographical and cultural displacement. Such displacement produces delusional, physical, and cultural transformations that frame the other, previous life: "my history." These transformations also, by definition, expose that which stands outside the frame: the new present, the uncertain future. At such a juncture, Rushdie asks, "What kind of idea am I?" Mahound agonizes over the status of Al-Lat, Manat, and Uzza, the three goddesses who will become the subjects of the so-called satanic verses. Are they the angel Gibreel's sisters? Can Allah accept them? We can remember also that this is all a dream sequence of Gibreel, so as both witness and participant, Gibreel also becomes agonized, wondering how he can "answer" Mahound.

The crisis about God—*what kind of idea is he?*—becomes for Muhammad a crisis about himself. Not only does Rushdie's characterization enable a depiction of Muhammad's inner life, but, more radically, it introduces an element of doubt squarely against faithful venerations of the prophet. Rushdie's representation is thus at least doubly offensive, as relativization of Muhammad, and *as* representation, *from* the inside no less. The historical Muhammad states in the Qur'an that he is only a man (see Soorah Al-kahf, or The Cave, Aayah 110); Rushdie pursues this point by introducing that in which Rushdie has faith: fallibility, doubt.

Annemarie Schimmel states that "[i]t is natural that in a religion that prohibits the representation of living beings, particularly of saintly persons, no picture of the Prophet could be legitimately produced" (Schimmel 1985: 36). In place of such visual representations, what is permissible are verbal descriptions of Muhammad. A *hilya* (variously glossed as "description" or "ornament") is a short description of the Prophet's external and internal qualities. Muhammad is believed to have said, "For him who sees my *hilya* after my death it is as if he had seen me myself, and he who sees it, longing for me, for him God will make Hellfire prohibited, and he will not be resurrected naked at Doomsday" (Schimmel 1985: 36). Muhammad's grandson Husain is thought to have asked his uncle Hind for a description of the Prophet. His uncle replied:

> Muhammad was middle-sized, did not have lank or crisp hair, was not fat, had a white circular face, wide black eyes, and long eyelashes. [. . .] His face shone like the moon in the night of full moon. He was taller than mid-dling stature but shorter than conspicuous tallness. He had thick, curly hair. The plaits of his hair were parted. His hair reached beyond the lobe of his ear. His complexion was *azhar* [bright, luminous]. Muhammad had a wide forehead and fine, long, arched eyebrows which did not meet. Be-tween his eyebrows there was a vein which distended when he was angry. The upper part of his nose was hooked; he was thick-bearded, had smooth cheeks, a strong mouth, and his teeth were set apart. He had thin hair on his chest. His neck was like the neck of an ivory statue, with the purity of silver. Muhammad was proportionate, stout, firm-gripped, even of belly and chest, broad-chested and broad-shouldered.
>
> (Schimmel 1985: 34)

In place of an image of Muhammad, a *hilya* serves as a token of protection and good fortune. Here is Rushdie's "*hilya*":

> The businessman: looks as he should, high forehead, eaglenose, broad in the shoulders, narrow in the hip. Average height, brooding, dressed in two pieces of plain cloth, each four ells in length, one draped around his body, the other over his shoulder. Large eyes; long lashes like a girl's. His strides can seem too long for his legs, but he's a light-footed man. [. . .] [H]e is nei-ther Mahomet nor MoeHammered; has adopted, instead, the demon-tag the farangis hung around his neck. To turn insults into strengths, whigs, tories, Blacks all chose to wear with pride the names they were given in scorn; likewise, our mountain-climbing, prophet-motivated solitary is to be the medieval baby-frightener, the Devil's synonym: Mahound.
>
> (93)

"MoeHammered" and "farangi" (Hindi for "foreigner"), the literary and the postcolonial: the signatures of Rushdie's faith. Himself originally a *farangi* in the UK, Rushdie seeks here to show his support for persecuted minorities—whigs, tories, Blacks—and hopes to extend this minority status to

Muhammad. But, again, this seemingly generous gesture is obscured by the *hilya* that surrounds it. This other *hilya* of Muhammad—representations of the migrant sufferings of Gibreel and Saladin—will be too subtle in contrast to the tradition of venerational representations of Muhammad that precedes *The Satanic Verses*. Sara Suleri Goodyear has argued that the above description of Muhammad is Sufistic, but how many ordinary readers—or non-readers—would recognize that resemblance (Suleri Goodyear 2008: 117)? The history of religious representations of Muhammad asserts itself, and blasphemy emerges as the dominant marker of this text. The postsecular is thus caught in a double bind between the two, between the history of self-rationalizing religious practice and the secularism of blasphemy.

5.1.1   Secular Blasphemy

The novel might have been burned, and it might have been banned, but it was also written. The "blasphemy" that is Rushdie's is not simply constituted by religious offence. I have been arguing that Rushdie seeks both to humanize and to "culturize" Muhammad. The humanization of Muhammad shows him as fallible, even having selfish motives. The culturization of him places him in the same set of experience that is Rushdie's, Gibreel's, and Saladin's: migration, crisis, transformation. Rushdie "believes" in the "real" of the crises of his experiences. For him, that belief is extended through the sanctity and sanctuary of the literary, that craft which in its aesthetic malleability and creative potential can gesture toward the nuances and subtleties—newnesses—of the history that he unironically takes as his own.

Gauri Viswanathan links blasphemy with migration, arguing that the latter functions as a "textual code for blasphemy, that is, for conditions of estrangement and loss of community that would place any utterance, innocent or malicious, outside the framework of known, familiar, and acceptable meanings" (Viswanathan 1998: 243). The elegance of Viswanathan's conceptualization lies in its twinning of phenomena—postcolonial migrancy and religion—that so deeply enable the production of *The Satanic Verses*. The subsequent challenge is to theorize how such a twinning—a twinning not just of images, or other such "literary devices," but, more fundamentally, of conceptual paradigms—marks the text as one that is deeply, irrepressibly committed to the historicization of belief.

Viswanathan's rhetorically-driven concept of blasphemy resonates with that of Sara Suleri Goodyear and Homi Bhabha. After praising Suleri Goodyear's insight that "a postcolonial desire for deracination, emblematized by the protagonist Saladin Chamcha, is equally represented as cultural heresy" (Suleri 1992: 226), Homi Bhabha argues that blasphemy

> is not merely a misrepresentation of the sacred by the secular; it is a moment when the subject-matter or the content of a cultural tradition

is being overwhelmed, or alienated, in the act of translation. Into the asserted authenticity of continuity of tradition, "secular" blasphemy releases a temporality that reveals the contingencies, even the incommensurabilities, involved in the process of social transformation.

(Bhabha 1994: 226)

If we push Bhabha's vision of a "social transformation" and the temporality that reveals it, then that temporality can also release a sense of "newness," a newness that can be threatening to a tradition which has an "asserted" authenticity. The temporality is of course historical, just as democracy as a concept and ideal is constantly worked and re-worked, the ideal as something yet-to-come. Similarly, state secularism in India continues to be worked and re-worked in an ongoing process. When Muhammad emigrated to Medina from Mekkah and effectively founded Islam in 622 A.D., that year became the marker of a "new time," the beginning of the Muslim calendar (Schimmel 1985: 13). The conceptualization is profound, for it releases a newness. If Muhammad's migration to Medina constitutes the beginning of a new time, then Gibreel's and Saladin's crashing onto the coast of England also constitutes the beginning of a new time, "passionate as always for newness" (131). This newness is expressed by Rushdie through magical realism, a narrative device within the text inaugurated by Gibreel's and Saladin's fall. It is this "newness" that fascinates and eludes Rushdie.

Are Islam and the life of Muhammad antecedents to Rushdie that enable the production of his "new" text? Whatever Rushdie's response to this grand narrative, whether ironization, blasphemy, ridicule, reverence, allegorization, or irreverence, he is ineluctably situated—intellectually, aesthetically, historically, personally—in relation to this "presence." This is the presence in which he has belief, the basic, indubitable relation in which he participates. The two elements of the relation—the grand narrative of Islam and Muhammad; and Rushdie—do not completely determine or predict the other. Rushdie is not simply a reactionary figure to Islam and Muhammad. That would be too simplistic a proposition. Conversely, Islam and Muhammad do not totally contain or predict Rushdie, certainly not proleptically. That would be blasphemous. Rather, the relation is at least dialectical, and constitutes a fundamental belief for Rushdie, a commitment that is intellectual and aesthetic, one that informs his critique and his craft. His craft *becomes* critique. Saladin's and Gibreel's migrations are Muhammad's migrations. The crisis that was the mid-air explosion of Saladin and Gibreel's plane is the crisis of Muhammad fleeing Mekka for Medina. Saladin's and Gibreel's transformations and quests for newness are those of Muhammad.

The literary in *The Satanic Verses* allows Rushdie to affirm the history of his migrant, postcolonial experiences. It is the twinning of Muhammad's life and *his* life, as represented by the English experiences of Gibreel and Saladin, which constitutes for Rushdie an inviolable presence, an act of representation in which he has belief. The "blasphemy" that Rushdie applies to the life of Muhammad would be blasphemous—to Rushdie—if someone applied it to his life and its real difficulties and struggles, experiences which undoubtedly have been sources of insight for *The Satanic Verses*. In one sense, we can view racism as blasphemy against migration. Would Rushdie trivialize or dismiss racism?

Farzaneh Asari argues that Khomeini's *fatwa*, while seeking of course to punish Rushdie for blasphemy, was also engineered by Khomeini to send a message to diasporic Muslims that Islam remained a homogenous, strong ideology with "continued hold on the Iranian people" (Asari 1989: 11). I agree with Asari. Khomeini's *fatwa* was very much *Khomeini's fatwa*, the product of its geography and history (Iran, 1989) and not simply the product of some transcendental, incontestable Islam. Khomeini sought to reinforce the complete identification of the Muslim world with the Qur'an, forcing that community to *become* the text, simultaneously marking Rushdie as outside the text, as transgressor. Talal Asad has argued that Rushdie's "self-fashioning through a particular kind of individualized reading and writing" (Asad 1993: 287) would be recognizable to western middle-class readers because of the great value they give to such self-fashioning. But Khomeini reads and creates his own kind of Qur'an (this suggestion would doubtless be offensive to him and his followers, especially with its western inflection); he forces such readings and interpretations onto a group of people, manoeuvring to control religion and nation—and life, Rushdie's life. Rushdie's fashioning might thus not be dissimilar to Khomeini's fashioning. Perhaps the latter's recognition of such semiotic semblance added fuel to the macho affront. Pen envy? Rushdie, as I have been seeking to demonstrate, is quite inside his own text, and has a commitment of his own which might have even pleased Khomeini had the latter undertaken a close reading, or any reading, before Gayatri Spivak's notion of "criticism by hearsay" spawned a devastating consequence for Rushdie. The *fatwa*, although officially revoked, remains a reading of the text. V. S. Naipaul has called the *fatwa* an extreme form of literary criticism; the spectre of the *fatwa*'s fulfilment will forever remain a fatal misreading for Rushdie. In an age where it is possible for theory to imagine and challenge the distinction between the word and the world, could the *fatwa* exist only literally?

When considering how blasphemy can be expressed in a secular world, Sara Suleri Goodyear argues that the term "blasphemy"

> must be reread as a gesture of recuperative devotion toward the idea of belief rather than as the insult that it is commonly deemed to be. The interpretive problem that *The Satanic Verses* poses to its readership involves, as a consequence, attention to the forms of veering narrative into which contemporary blasphemy can transmogrify. What kinds of stories, the narrative most self-consciously asks itself, will emerge out of a fidelity to disbelieving? [. . .] The figure of desecration [is] rendered coterminous with a desire to embody the continuing attractions of Islam

in history, so that the narrative can represent cultural leave-taking and homecoming as mutually interchangeable.

(Suleri 1992: 191, 192)

What Suleri Goodyear views as an "interpretive problem" contains the terms of its solution if we extend her argument about blasphemy, as a form of belief, to the domain of literary form. Suleri Goodyear astutely conceptualizes Rushdie's position as one of "fidelity to disbelieving," but the dazzling array of Rushdie's veering narratives, transmogrifications, and the twinned desecration-desire is hosted and enabled by the commitment of its literary form: "Where there is no belief, there is no blasphemy" (380). Desecration-desire also is seen in the episode of the twelve prostitutes whose names are the same as those of the Prophet's twelve wives. The "wives" attend fastidiously and lovingly to their visitors, taking care of them as if they were the Prophet himself and thus "in a thousand ways enacted the dream-marriage they had never really thought they would have" (384). This can be read as an example of Suleri Goodyear's notion of blasphemy as faithful recuperation to the idea of belief. When Mahound observes, "Writers and whores. I see no difference here" (392), this underscores the "desire" of Rushdie, perhaps a desire and nostalgia for a religiosity he never had. Such twinning of desecration and desire, along with the other fantastic forms of this novel, is what allows for the articulation of Suleri Goodyear's "interpretive problems." Aamir Mufti has argued that it is the formal ambivalence that the novel provokes—whether it is about historical religious events or just fiction—that allows it to function as a critical, public, political act. In the process, pastiche "is neither a purely formal question, nor merely the textual correlate of a hybrid 'external reality'" (Mufti 1992: 99). Let us call this the formal correlative of the question of the religious in this novel: neither purely formal (what kind of an idea is religion?), nor merely an external reality (religion as manifest in-the-secular-world).

Because the novel is a temporal art-form, the temporality that it demands and which it "releases" constructs its own logic of transformation. The novel has its own time and thus its own calendar, one which readers can possess. The novel, as a basic act of communication, is always written to at least some notion of the future, to its imagined readership and imagined comprehension, even if an author writes primarily to himself or herself. Magical realism stands as a strong sign of the author's presence. The outstanding contours of transmogrification are sensational in contrast to realist narrative, demanding the reader's faith not just in their subject-matter but in the temporal logic through which they will unfold.

Joel Kuortti argues that the novel is an "attempt at giving a fictional representation of Islamic history," that there is a "religious void in the centre of the narrative," and that it is "an attempt at retelling the history of Islam from a secular point of view [. . .] setting secular words against the absolute words

of revelation" (Kuortti 2007: 133). Re-thinking the religious-secular dichotomy in Kuortti's argument, we could view the void not as "religious," but
a void of a deeper structure, one reflecting what it means to believe and to
have faith, an epistemic crisis informed by real-world crisis. In that respect,
the novel is not simply or oppositionally the "re-telling" of Islam's history, for
it aspires and struggles to move outside the epistemic and ideological framework constructed by "Islam." The novel is more subtly a re-telling of what
constitutes history, representation, and faith. The secular and the religious
are simply two faces and possible expressions of this complex inquiry and
problem. The miraculous and the magical, which are not simply the other of
revelation, are the spectres and supplements to "secular words." The figure
of dialectic, between the secular and the religious, is insufficient in capturing
the deconstructive gesturing of the postsecular.

Sara Suleri Goodyear views blasphemy not as a "statement of religious
conviction," but as a narrative device, "as an aesthetic form that is indeed
aligned to the structure of magical realism" (Suleri 1992: 201). Both blasphemy and magical realism introduce an edge of difference, even newness,
to religion and realism respectively. Yet because there is a trace of their
connection to the "original" of religion and realism, their difference is a
posting. Magical realism is a secular phenomenon—*in* the secular world—but
its representation and thematization of the miraculous add that edge of the
posting of the secular. Wendy Faris has argued that although a magical realist text might question the assumptions of western empiricism and the binary
between the magical and the real, the assumptions and the binary persist
because "they are embedded within the conventions of realism the text
employs" (Faris 2004: 29). This is not dissimilar to the concept of palimpsest that designates the relation between religion and postsecularism. The
latter can invoke the great signifiers of religion (for example, the Prophet
Muhammad) but attempt to "empty" them of their religious, dogmatic, and
doctrinal meanings, in the process secularizing and translating them into
particular contexts (for example, 1980s London), guided by particular values
(for example, the insights of a migrant's eye-view). But the great signifiers of
religion, to echo Faris's words, will remain *embedded* within postsecular gestures. That embedment can be both fascinating—and fatal.

The similarity between the two dominant narratives of this novel that
at first appear so disconnected, the Islamic narrative of Mahound and the
migrant narrative of Gibreel and Saladin, is underscored by Rushdie through
identical proper names for their characters. What emerges, as I have been
arguing, is a postcolonial, diasporic Islam. Magical realism is of course not
only a secular literary "device," but also something paradoxically more than
just secular or a device. It can mark Rushdie's posting of the secular, his
faith in the "newness" possible when the exigencies and insurgencies of a
personal, diasporic, migrant, and postcolonial history can connect with the
religiosity and tradition of an inherited religion and "organized faith." The

literary becomes the mark and the seal of this affirmation. When the Prophet appears in his dreams, Gibreel is both witness and participant, as both cause and effect:

> Allah Ishvar God [is absent] as ever while we writhe and suffer in his name. [. . .] [W]hat keeps returning is this scene, the entranced Prophet, the extrusion, the cord of light, and then Gibreel in his dual role is both above-looking-down and below-staring-up. And both of them scared out of their minds by the transcendence of it.
>
> (111)

By referring to the "Supreme Being" by combining the Christian, Hindu, and Muslim faith traditions ("Allah Ishvar God"), Rushdie *affirms* that/a supreme being—in semiotic terms, as a transcendental signified, as something beyond particular signifiers, beyond particular faiths. The literary and dramatic scenes that keep repeating are not just the interaction between Gibreel and the Prophet, but the narrative itself. The particular significations flourishing in the novel are made contiguous with one another: "the extrusion, the cord of light." The resulting transcendence represents a merging, the comprehension and apprehension of the one by the other, sameness becoming otherness, and vice versa.

We can also read the above as the fantastical merging of secular and religious epistemologies, to simultaneously be in both, and to observe both. We can also read it as an analogy, however fantastical, representing the merging of an Indian state secularism as political ideology with an indigenous religiosity that animates everyday life, resulting in a spiritualized, humanist secularism. Such processes of narrative and thematic collapse become vivid markers in the text of Rushdie's presence, of his commitment to the literary, and of his search for newness. Rushdie uses the word "transcendence" above. His veering narrative has vividly illustrated how this "transcendence" is historically driven, as a dream emerging from worldly situatedness. The "post" emerging from within the secular is like the "transcendence"—deconstructive, hesitant, exploratory—that historically emerges through Gibreel's dream. The result can inspire awe, and also fear, as in the above passage. This resonates with the theologian Rudolf Otto's concept of the "numinous," as that mystery which stands outside of the self, and which can produce a fear, tremendum (Otto 1923: 5–30). Otto's idea of the numinous emerged from within a Christian conception of the holy. Rushdie's description above is working within an Islamic context, and can also have similarities with Sufi notions of mystical union.

Who recites the so-called satanic verses? Mahound is sure that it is the devil, coming to him in the guise of the archangel Gibreel. But the postcolonial Gibreel, dreaming this entire sequence, thinks otherwise, believing himself to be author and audience of the verses. Gibreel is both satanic and angelic. He is the source of both the narrative and the counter-narrative: "From my mouth, both the statement and the repudiation, verses and converses, universes and reverses, the whole thing, and we all know how my mouth got worked" (123). The above could very well be the voice of Rushdie. Rushdie himself is trying to unwrite the story, and what can also constitute blasphemy in this novel, apart from the obvious profanations of Muhammad, is Rushdie's postmodern configuration of Islam as a "story," and a narrative therefore that can be doubted, suspected, and deconstructed. It is no secret that narration plays a crucial role in the "writing" of the religion: Muhammad's revelations had to be inscribed. The insistence of Islamic scholars on Muhammad's illiteracy, in order to argue for the inspired and revealed nature of the recitations and their superiority over the most sophisticated contemporary writings, further emphasizes the influence of the literary that informs the religion from its inception, and thus its potential fallibility and contestability. It is this vulnerability that Rushdie is keen to manipulate, as a novelist. To launch a view of one of the world's great religions—through the elaborate form of a five-hundred-page novel no less—that exposes it, at its foundation, as a narratively-driven possibility rather than as an incontestable, *absolutely true* divine revelation ("there is no God but Allah and Muhammad is his prophet") becomes the crux of the blasphemy. What kind of an idea is Islam? What kind of an idea is Rushdie? What kind of an idea is his novel? Rushdie's flagrant display of the literary status of his text adds insult to injury. It is in this sense that we might view the use of literary form as a prolepsis for the *fatwa*. The form launched the *fatwa*, so that the actual *fatwa*, declared on February 14, 1989, lay buried within the novel, coming before the novel, as a prophesy of sorts: "rivers of blood" (97).

5.1.2 *The* Fatwa: *Ain't I a Believer?*

What does Rushdie believe in? Several weeks before the Ayatollah Khomeini issued the *fatwa*, Rushdie had stated: "Unable to accept the unarguable absolutes of religion, I have tried to fill up the [God-shaped] hole with literature" (Appignanesi and Maitland 1989: 75). Exploring and questioning Islamic faith is certainly a personal process for Rushdie. It is a feature of the struggle with secularism in this text. As a secular *form*, the novel allows for the critique of religion's—*any* religion's—ideologies. The significant autobiographical elements of the novel underscore the presence of Rushdie's personal stakes. Yet Islam in its many varieties also exists as a social, public discourse. Such a private and public dichotomy, between personal faith and public social discourse, is reflected in the constitutive mechanics of writing. Although the word is personal to Rushdie and inheres in a faithfulness that allows him to govern shapes as he wishes, each representation is also open, simultaneously, to an infinite number of (public) readers. Rushdie's post-*fatwa* declarations that the Islam of *The Satanic Verses* was particularly *his* Islam, and that he *is* a

Muslim, are ineffectual. When Islam, or indeed any religion, is represented in a public forum, it can become—literarily, commercially—everybody's and anybody's Islam and religion. In the same article from which I have derived the above quotation, Rushdie describes the reception of the text:

> [A]fter working for five years to give voice and fictional flesh to the im-migrant culture of which I am myself a member, I should see my book burned, largely unread, by the people it's about, people who might find some pleasure and much recognition in its pages. I tried to write against stereotypes; the zealot protests serve to confirm, in the Western mind, all the worst stereotypes of the Muslim world.
>
> (Appignanesi and Maitland 1989: 75)

If Dr. Aziz is, in Rushdie's view, his literary parallel of the hole at the centre of his being, then Rushdie's concerns in the above quotation can find their parallel in the childhood of Saladin Chamcha, who desperately wants to be loved and accepted by his father, who in turn only humiliates and ridicules him. Rushdie views subcontinental migrants to Britain—the readers with the ability to empathize and identify with his experi-ences and representations—as his "community." But their book burnings and protests mark their rejection of Rushdie's novel and, in this case by extension, Rushdie. Like Saladin, Rushdie wants it both ways. He seeks acknowledgment and appreciation of his migrant experience yet also is eager to publicly perform his criticism of a religion that is important to many people's lives. Is Rushdie really part of the same immigrant culture as the Bradford bookburners?

Rushdie laments that the protests of the "zealots" confirm Muslim ste-reotypes in the western mind. This of course begs the question of what and who, for Rushdie, constitute the "Western mind." His tutors at Cambridge? The Booker prize jury? Readers of *The Daily Mail*? Rushdie has lived and worked in the UK and the US; Rushdie writes in English, using the novel form, alluding to western literary sources. Is Rushdie himself not shaped by western institutional and intellectual forms? What is the "Muslim world"? With what degree of sensitivity or even empathy can Rushdie understand the experiences of those believers who are perhaps poor, perhaps illiterate, and for whom their religious faith is central to their lives? I do not intend to construe "those believers" as sentimental subalterns who have some privi-leged access to "authentic" religiosity. Nor do I wish to invoke the construct of the "moderate Muslim," which can easily be code for the "good Muslim," especially after 9/11. Instead, my assertion is a simple one: Rushdie's class privilege and the elitism of his "art" make him insensitive to those follow-ers of a religion who might not be able to appreciate or even perceive the subtlety of his postsecular explorations—or even interested in any of his literary explorations.

5.1.3   *Father, Nation, Religion: Gained*

I argued in my criticism of *The English Patient* and *Anil's Ghost* that the postsecular moments of the texts could be located in those realms that were resistant to representation. In both texts, what constitutes their postsecularism is the affirmation of affect: of friendship, of love. In the case of *The English Patient*, affective affirmation is able to emerge in a context and crisis which deterritorializes ethnic and national identities. In *Anil's Ghost*, such affirmation becomes possible in the middle of a civil war which affirms one's vocation— medicine, art, archaeology—as a form of *dharmic* devotion and commitment. In both texts, the space of the aesthetic is a creative space that points to itself—*as space*—as a forum *for* affirmation. The Buddha statue looks across the Sri Lankan killing fields not as an escapist, facile "transcendent" gesture, but as affirmation of renewal that emerges from fraught circumstances. The statue is reconstructed and brought to life by an artist traumatized by the disappearance of his wife. We might also remember the character Lakma, the young girl so shocked by witnessing the murder of her parents that she no longer speaks. Living with her uncle Palipana in the special marked place of the forest allows her eventually to regain trust in the world and people around her. Trauma comes to stand as that "unrepresentable," the domain of the real which keeps narrative in the register of the sombre and serious, distinct from irony and irreverence. It also allows, as I stated in my criticism of *Anil's Ghost*, for the aesthetic to be a healing dimension of representation, that which can allow insight into one's history.

It is deeply-embedded postsecular moments of the text such as these that I wish to locate in Rushdie's representation of the father-son relationship of Saladin and Changez. Consider the following quotation (I would like to leave the speaker, for now, unnamed): "I left my country, crossed the world, settled among people who thought me a slimy foreign coward for saving their, who never appreciated what I, but never mind that" (367). The speaker here is Salman the Persian, who emigrates to join Mahound as scribe of his revelations. Yet it could also be the voice of Saladin, who emigrates from Mumbai to London, moving away from his unloving father. It could also be the voice of Rushdie, who had himself emigrated from Mumbai to London and likely experienced the racial discrimination of which he writes. Salman the Persian says, "[t]here is no bitterness like that of a man who finds out that he has been believing in a ghost" (368). In the course of the novel, both Islam and nation become deterritorialized: India in England; England in India; Islam in Medina, Islam fictionalized, Islam postcolonialized.

After a literal passage through Dante's inferno, the novel's closure features Saladin's return to Mumbai (as metonym for India, for nation), to Islam, and to his father. As a sign of Saladin's increasing acceptance of and belief in those narratives that had earlier been so painful for him—family, origin, culture—Rushdie refers to him using the expanded version of his name,

"Salahuddin." It is the "real" of his father's death which allows for resolution. Saladin rejects the ritual motions of the attendant mullah:

"This cloth has been to Mecca," the mullah said. *Get it out!* "I don't understand. It is holy fabric." *You heard me: out, out.* "May God have mercy on your soul."

(532; italics original)

There are two belief systems at conflict in the above exchange: religious belief, postsecular belief. It is the interpretation of Islam which emphasizes elaborate ritualism that Rushdie seeks to criticize, a ritualism which seems so ineffectual and artificial, even offensive, in the wake of suffering. This is similar to the ending of *The English Patient*, when Almásy marks Katherine's deceased body with the colours of the cave, linking her with nature, away from the labels and names of maps and nations.

The renewed love that Saladin feels for his father is for him a beautiful, life-affirming experience after decades of anger, causing him to introspect:

Saladin felt hourly closer to many old, rejected selves, many alternative Saladins—or rather Salahuddins—which had split off from himself as he made his various life choices, but which had apparently continued to exist, perhaps in the parallel universes of quantum theory.

(523)

As we noticed in the relationship between Hana and Kip in *The English Patient*, and in the Buddhist eye-painting ceremony in *Anil's Ghost*, the danger of such postsecular affirmation is slippage into sentiment. What is certain from a linguistic perspective is the *presence* of such affirmation, its insertion and deployment by novelists at the closure of, and also in the middle of, narratives that examine the grand narratives that shape people—nation, secularism, religion, ethnicity, majoritarianism—often as a matter of life and death. Salahuddin buries his father, entering his grave: "*The weight of my father's head, lying in my hand. I laid it down; to rest. The world, somebody wrote, is the place we prove real by dying in it*" (533; italics original). "[W]e prove real" is ambiguous: either the world is proved real, or the subjects of "we" are proved real. Both possibilities make an affirmation. The crisis of death becomes contiguous with the affirmation of life.

Rushdie uses the loss and regaining of affect as the bookends of his dense, multi-layered novel. Early in the novel, Saladin and his father are visiting London and undertake a fast. But Saladin loses his resolve, and he finds himself purchasing chicken, hiding it beneath his jacket as he returns to his hotel room, not wanting his father to ridicule his weakness. Yet the young Saladin is painfully aware that others can see his hidden meal. This helplessness and humiliation give rise to a rage within him, a rage that will continue well after the visit to London:

> [It] would boil away his childhood father-worship and make him a secular man, who would do his best, thereafter, to live without a god of any type; which would fuel, perhaps, his determination to become the thing his father was-not-could-never-be, that is, a goodandproper Englishman.
>
> (43)

Nation, religion, and family-affect each becomes concentrated in the trauma of the public and fatherly humiliation. There is a similar seriousness of tone in another childhood episode of Saladin, when he is visiting the rocks at the Mumbai coast. An elderly man calls toward him, and Saladin follows, only to find himself in an exploitative embrace. He frees himself of the man's arms—and the man then comes to symbolize everything he dislikes about Mumbai, which he resolves to escape, "convincing himself that he could make the miracle happen even without his father's [magic] lamp to help him out" (38). The miracle, of course, does happen: Saladin goes to London, only to be miraculously transformed by Rushdie into "Shaitan." If the young Saladin feels the loss of trust and faith, then the older, adult Rushdie can trust and believe in his capacity to create narrative and to affirm a healed father-son relationship. The final reconciliatory scene between Saladin and his father does not, however, escape sentimentality. Such sentimentality appears to be the only way Rushdie can find to replace the religious with its non-religious equivalent from the domain of human feeling, that is, via filial love, return to the native land, and filiation to a community of "one's kind."

5.2   Ayesha and Postsecular Magical Realism

It is 1983, the month of February. The midnight moon shines over Hawkes Bay in the southern Pakistani coastal city of Karachi. A group of thirty-eight villagers, all Shia Muslims, is heading toward the Arabian Sea. But this is no ordinary journey. Naseem Fatima has claimed to be in direct contact with the twelfth imam of Islam, beginning with dreams and culminating in direct exhortations. Fatima lives in the northern Pakistani village of Chakwal Tehsil, population two thousand. There have been claims of miracles inside Fatima's home. People from the village come regularly to the home to pray to signs considered sacred by Shia Muslims, and to ask the imam for advice on matters both large and small. Fatima's health waxes and wanes with the passing of her fits and revelations alike. At times she loses weight, at other times she is seen to emanate a spiritual glow, *noor* in Arabic. She abandons the customary veil for women and begins to deliver public teachings, both acts transgressions for a woman in the village. The imam's ultimate message is for Fatima to gather a group of villagers and lead them to the Arabian Sea, which upon their arrival will part and allow them to walk to the Iraqi city of Basra, and eventually to the sacred site of Karbala. The imam instructs the villagers to place women and children inside locked trunks. The final procession includes six such trunks.

Fatima and her followers approach the dark sea, its surface ephemeral under the light of the moon. The currents feel cold and the water is treacherous, but the villagers' faith gives them the strength to continue forward. Some cannot swim, still others struggle. The sea remains unparted, unrelentingly powerful. The villagers reach desperately for air. Half of them drown. One of the six trunks is crashed open by waves; the women and children inside survive. Those in the other trunks are not so fortunate. In the end, the group is arrested by the Pakistani police on the charge of attempted illegal exit from the country. But the survivors are unagitated, in a deep spiritual calm. Wealthy Shias in Iraq, impressed by the villagers' faith, offer to fly them to Karbala. The imam's promise, some afterward assert, is fulfilled.

The "Hawkes Bay case," as it came to be known, provides the inspiration for the chapters in *The Satanic Verses* entitled "Ayesha" and "The Parting of the Arabian Sea." Both these chapters are dreams dreamt by the character Gibreel. The historical Naseem Fatima becomes for Rushdie the peasant girl Ayesha, who in dream-like states receives her instructions from the imam. She repeats the following message throughout the pilgrimage: "'Greatness has come among us' [. . .]. 'Everything will be required of us, and everything will be given to us also'" (225).

A maker of small crafts, Ayesha is distinguished in the small village of Titlipur by her extraordinary beauty. One of the elements of magical realism that Rushdie introduces in the story of Ayesha is the appearance of clouds of butterflies in the village which change colour to match their surroundings: the "miracle of the butterflies" (217). Ayesha comes to be associated with the butterflies through yet another magical realist act: she consumes them. As her revelations increase, she sheds her clothing and walks virtually naked, covered by butterflies that form a sari around her. Ayesha succeeds in leading a group of villagers to the Arabian Sea. In Rushdie's version, there are over a hundred villagers, and they all ultimately drown.

Unlike the chapters about Muhammad, the Ayesha episode has received relatively little critical attention. I focus on the Ayesha chapters because, as with his interest in Muhammad, Rushdie explores the nature of prophecy. These chapters can also be blasphemous, given the writing of a woman prophet into the narrative of Islam. For Rushdie, the device of magical realism becomes the secular equivalent of the religious miracle, as a kind of secular enchantment, furthering his ability to affirm his literary creativity. Rushdie's medium becomes the message. Wendy Faris has argued that magical realism "has mastered the European discourse of realism and now uses it not to curse, exactly, but to undermine some of its master's assumptions.

[. . .] Realism [. . .] does not believe in miracles, but it has given the magical realist the means to describe them" (Faris 2004: 28). What better critique of a religion's dogmas, fundamentalisms, and self-rationalizations than from the margins of subalterneity? What better critique of religious faith's potential escapism and doubtability than from the domain of the real, drawing upon a real historical event? From the vantage point of superstition, indeed *subaltern* superstition, Ayesha forces us to re-think the religious and the secular, and their hegemonies. Concurrently, Rushdie's provocations invite us to think through questions on the nature of the real and the historical—under the edge, no less, of the postcolonial.

It is here where Partition becomes important, Partition as a catastrophe in the postcolonial nation's history, as an event of unimaginable violence and suffering. I argued in Chapter 3 that, in *Anil's Ghost*, Anil's diasporic situatedness allows Ondaatje to express his diasporic nationalist concerns—what is Sri Lanka?—and that the temporal logic of an international human rights investigation provides a logic for the novel's plot, driving the novel forward. With Ayesha, it is the parting of the Arabian Sea—the *promise* of its parting—that becomes the narrative logic and the epistemological logic for these sections, allowing Rushdie to explore his postsecular concerns. How and in what to believe, in the wake of the crisis of belief? Parting the sea, partitioning a nation: such concise morphological similarity, yet such enormous differences. In both, a certain faith operates: in the latter, faith in nation and secularism; in the former, faith in religion.

As with Ondaatje's explorations in *The English Patient* and in *Anil's Ghost*, we also witness here the posting of the secular through the use of aesthetics-as-cognition, establishing variant proximities between the aesthetic field and a religious sensibility. Rushdie's historical sources for Ayesha are hybrid, from Muslim and Hindu faith traditions, thereby showing the influence of Indian secularism on Rushdie. Rushdie draws upon not only the historical case of Naseem Fatima, but also medieval Hindu poetry and the images it contains of "walking naked," a beautiful woman poet-saint so enchanted by her divine beloved that she feels no need for clothing, a literary allusion that I shall discuss toward the end of this section.

Rushdie invokes the literary devices at his disposal in order to perform doubt as the opposite of faith. The more elaborately Rushdie represents events and individuals, the more his form—literary form—exemplifies that very faith that fascinates him intellectually. The Hawkes Bay case was, of course, a constitutively historical case. The literary imagining of such a case is like the literary imagining of Muhammad. In seeking to critique the effects of religious faith by drawing upon an historical incident as graphic and sensational as Hawkes Bay, and by invoking the device of magical realism in doing so, Rushdie affirms, and asks his readers to affirm, faith-in-art.

Ruvani Ranasinha has argued that "the fictional agreement [the suspension of disbelief] is a literary judgment entrenched as normative and universal in liberal discourse. This subverts the widely received perception of the Rushdie Affair as embodying the battle between dogmatic certainties and liberal questioning" (Ranasinha 2007: 52). I would like to extend Ranasinha's argument and state that there is an opposition not only between what can be viewed as (non-western) dogmatic certainties and (western) liberal questioning, but also between belief and doubt, with liberal questioning representing a form of belief. What was hurtful for some Muslims offended by the book was that some British laws became exposed as a "fictional agreement": those laws demonstrate the flexible qualities of fiction by applying *unequally* across citizens. Was undivided citizenship only a fiction for the "illiberal other"? Rushdie embodies the questioning of belief on a transnational scale. Having grown up in the UK and having studied history at Cambridge would acquaint Rushdie with the reasoning of western European liberalism; his years in India and Pakistan would acquaint him with their literary, political, and religious traditions. Rushdie believes in the literary tools that enable him to express his doubt, that allow him to command the attention of his readers as he undertakes highly individual explorations of secular and religious forms of belief.

Rushdie invokes a "catastrophe by proxy" in order to elicit readerly attention. To foreground the role of the novel is to foreground the role of the reader, which is to foreground the role of witnessing. This in itself localizes, makes present for Rushdie a "beyond," a newness, an idea, the possibility—healing, therapeutic, reconciliatory, even sympathetic—of an "outside" to his position. In the Ayesha chapters, Rushdie presents us with at least three levels of representation: Rushdie creates the character of Gibreel, Gibreel has a dream, and the story of Ayesha unfolds in the dream. When Gibreel has a dream and wonders "what story is this?" (216), this resembles, and is likely an allusion to, Rushdie's choice question throughout the novel, which also appears in the Ayesha sections: "What kind of idea are you/is this?" It becomes yet another instance of Rushdie's fascination with newness, as something that can stand outside the realm of the existing and knowable. In this sense, it is comparable to Charles Taylor's idea of the "immanent frame," which I discussed in the Introduction, as that which secularism delimits and delineates as the realm of the true, knowable, and observable (Taylor 2007: 542).

There is also a process of gendering at play in the Ayesha chapters. Gayatri Spivak argues that the section on Mahound, in which Rushdie raises the issue of the missing so-called satanic verses from the Qur'an, "is a story of negotiation in the name of woman. As so often, woman becomes the touchstone of blasphemy" (Spivak 1993: 223). Spivak further argues that Ayesha lacks the "existential depth" of the other prophet in the novel, Mahound (Spivak 1993: 224). Whereas Mahound is blasphemized as a "businessman," Ayesha must content herself with receiving her revelations from Gibreel in the form of popular Hindi film songs. We might also consider that the historical Naseem Fatima was always under the watchful eye of her father, whose honour in the village increased considerably following his daughter's revelations and teachings (Ahmed 1986: 51).

The "superstitious faith" represented by Ayesha is tempered by Rushdie with "modern secularism" in the form of the local wealthy landowner, Mirza Saeed. Rushdie's device of linking these two characters is not just oppositional or contrastive. Although Saeed is repelled by Ayesha's belief, he is attracted to her beauty. The dichotomy thus established by Rushdie contrasts "superstition/religious faith" against "secularism/modernity." Rushdie resists advocating simply one position. It would be too simplistic to affirm either secularism or religious faith, or to reject both. Mirza's wife says to him: "Saeed, a thing is happening here, and you with your imported European atheism don't know what it is. Or maybe you would if you looked beneath your English suitings and tried to locate your heart" (238). Not only is Mirza's lack of belief westernized, but *Ayesha's* faith is linked with the heart, thus gendering the "east/west" divide as "emotional/rational."

The story continues. Mirza tries recruiting one of the pilgrims to join his secular front. The man in question is the Hindu merchant who buys Ayesha's handicraft:

> "Don't you see?" Mirza Saeed shouted after him. "We are not communal people, you and I. Hindu-Muslim bhai-bhai! We can open up a secular front against this mumbo-jumbo."
>
> (476)

"Hindu-Muslim bhai-bhai" is an allusion to Jawaharlal Nehru's slogan for Indian secularism: "Hindu-Muslim brother-brother." But Ayesha's beauty, once again, intervenes. The merchant becomes transfixed when he realizes that Ayesha and the goddess depicted in his calendar have the same face. The lustful men in Ayesha's village fail to fulfill their desire, for she is so fixed on another world that she completely ignores them. Her habit of eating butterflies also gives her, in their eyes, a frightening demon-like quality. Thus, whether she is seen to possess divine beauty or the demonic quality of destruction, both attributes inhere in an awesomeness of power. In the process, religious faith, superstition, and the miraculous each becomes gendered. The gendering of religion and secularism marks Mirza as a site of conflict. He is torn between duty and desire, between his duty to his wife and his desire for Ayesha. He also feels a duty to his beliefs: to modernity, and to the nation. Yet Ayesha continues to assert that she is "nothing," just a "messenger." This might even be a metafictional comment. Ayesha is Rushdie's messenger also, and as a product of his imagination, is unreal in the object world. But she is everything as a messenger, as a creation of literary imagination, just as, in the words of the novel, the "pilgrimage itself has been a miracle" (499).

Although the narrative of Ayesha is entirely a dream sequence of Gibreel, Rushdie's characterization of it betrays an ambivalence of form. When introducing Gibreel's entry into the dream sequence of "Ayesha," Rushdie uses language that draws upon textual sources and which is fantastically visual. In the phrase "his own image, translated into an avatar of the archangel" (216), the passive verb "translated" begs not only the question of agency, but also foregrounds the translator himself, Rushdie. Rushdie aestheticizes, Gibreel dreams, Ayesha does. The status of the visual is one that thus becomes deeply significant. It stands not only as a mode of representation (of launching, say, a film) but is a mode whose status *as mode* serves as another commenting feature of this section. The visual is not neutral, just as Ayesha's beauty is not neutral. Both speak, as it were, volumes about the agency structuring them. The visual is part of a *worldview*, a particular mode of perception and cognition.

Some of that particularity is exposed in yet another subtle phrasing (metaphor) of Rushdie. The notoriety-gaining pilgrimage attracts tourists, Gandhians, and voyeurs. These spectators become amazed when seeing Ayesha and her butterflies, and "retreated with confounded expectations, that is to say with a hole in their pictures of the world that they could not paper over" (488). Rushdie himself has painted a picture with rather broad strokes, that is, broad binaries, which I have identified as "male/nationalist/secular/sceptical/bourgeois/western" and "female/believing/miraculous/superstitious/subaltern/Islamic."

The hole is a threat. The challenge for Rushdie was to begin with the hole, and then construct a world around that which resists representation, which remains expressionless. The challenge is to "find a form," one that is concerned not with announcing its own materiality, but one that can gesture to the paradoxically dense absence that generated it. The gesture is a search and a call to witnessing, both gesture and call translated and transformed into the questions, *What is religious faith? What is the miraculous? What is newness?* In his struggle with the form of religion, Rushdie invokes numerous possibilities: religion as faith and superstition; as doubted and disbelieved; as commodification; as immanence and transcendence; as therapy, conversion, dogma, ideology. The "transcendental" and "immanent" stories throughout *The Satanic Verses* are constantly, historically intertwined by Rushdie, so that the same name is shared by characters in the religious narrative of Islam and in the postcolonial narrative of Rushdie.

Lest all these arguments become rarefied and threaten therefore to disappear into the semiotic space about which they argue, Rushdie uses a formal device of introducing a catastrophe. A single word becomes the hinge between the fantastical, superstitious, and magical, and the factually undeniable, historical, and violent. *Partition*. Ayesha informs Mirza that Gibreel says opening the sea and their hearts will allow them to move into wisdom. Mirza replies, tauntingly, "'Partition was quite a disaster here on land [. . .]. Quite a few guys died, you might remember. You think it will be different in the water?'" (501). Throughout this section, Mirza has been variously constructed by others, and ultimately by Rushdie, as a blasphemer, as a heartless atheist, and also as a progressive secularist representing the voice of modernity and skepticism. But here we gain an appreciation for Mirza's historical situatedness. Like Mirza, Rushdie, as I mentioned earlier, also is influenced by both western "rationalist" culture and Indian political secularism. Rushdie's use of Partition is potent. Partition historicizes, Partition challenges any claim of miracle or faith by replying, unambiguously and unavoidably, from the desert of the real. Catastrophe and death resist ironization. Catastrophe rivets, demands attention. If religious faith is controversial, it is because it threatens to trivialize the traumatically real—a few lives, a few million lives. Only having lived the unique history that Rushdie has lived would allow Rushdie to experiment with and explore these possibilities between catastrophe and religion. If there is any affirmation in this novel, the condition of its possibility is precisely a catastrophe like this.

The closure that Rushdie offers for these Ayesha chapters is one of collapse. Mirza finds himself in the Arabian Sea, with Ayesha. The compelling passage is worth quoting at length:

> The sea poured over him, and he was in the water beside Ayesha, who had stepped miraculously out of his wife's body . . ."Open," she was crying. "Open wide!" Tentacles of light were flowing from her navel and he chopped at them, chopped, using the side of his hand. "Open," she screamed. "You've come this far, now do the rest."—How could he hear her voice?—They were under water, lost in the roaring sea, but he could hear her clearly, they could all hear her, that voice like a bell. "Open," she said. He closed. He was a fortress with clanging gates.—He was drowning.—She was drowning, too. He saw the water fill her mouth, heard it begin to gurgle into her lungs. Then something within him refused that, made a different choice, and at the instant that his heart broke, he opened. His body split apart from his adam's-apple to his groin, so that she could reach deep within him, and now she was open, they all were, and at the moment of their opening the waters parted, and they walked to Mecca across the bed of the Arabian Sea.
>
> (506)

This "scene" is fantastically visual, and it literally collapses Mirza into Ayesha. We can read this on several levels. We can read it as fiction, that Mirza and Ayesha are both objectively "nothing," just "messengers" of Rushdie, so that their collapse into one another is only spurious—the distinction was never there to begin with. We could also read it as a collapse in epistemologies: Mirza's skepticism and secularism take a literal leap of faith. We could also interpret it as a translation in form: Mirza *becomes* the fantastic visuality of Ayesha. Such a translation could technically constitute a blasphemy. Mirza's "new" belief is blasphemous to his skepticism. We could also see it as a "happy ending," as a resolution of competing ideologies: they walk to Mecca. Finally, we could read the passage as a formally self-triumphant ending. All forms in these sections now bend upon themselves, commenting on themselves.

Rushdie shows us that although everyone might have drowned and gone to Mecca and thus reached the acme of their narrative drive, he—Rushdie—is still here, both as omniscient narrator-creator and as a person in the world. By forms "bending" and commenting upon themselves I mean that we notice a sort of materiality for materiality's sake. There is a strong visual element throughout these sections, of which Ayesha's visual beauty is the most obvious example. This final passage presents the climax of the formalizing motor driving this section forward, the climax a richly visual encounter that commands our attention, perhaps commanding readers to open. Ayesha's belief and faith bend toward Mirza's, and they meld. The hole is removed and Mirza's longing-desire might have been satisfied, not sexually, but within the terms of *Ayesha's* paradigm of belief. Represented by his ruined home, Mirza undergoes a sort of "end of history," the birth of a new self. Conjunction is the ultimate other of partition.

Yet, because the ending remains so polysemous, it might also be read as a sort of cop-out on Rushdie's part. Rushdie assiduously follows an historical catastrophe, choosing to aestheticize it. But in offering a closure which can appear as a mystification, he can be seen to be trivializing the seriousness of that original crisis. Like the reductiveness of sentimentalization, such a process could be a sudden dropping of the tragically historical, allowing the aesthetic to fold indulgently upon itself in trivialization of the crisis it takes and addresses as its inspiration. Thus, although magical realism might have its potentials for enchantment, or re-enchantment, there is also the dimension of insensitivity, a kind of aesthetic translation—especially when linked so closely with beauty, and gendered beauty—that can mute and trivialize the original violence.

Rushdie's historical situatedness within the Indian subcontinent informs the literary form of *The Satanic Verses*. Feroza Jussawalla argues that the novel fits into an Indian Islamic and Urdu tradition of a *dastan-e-dilruba*, which is a love song for a beloved, especially one who cannot be had. Jussawalla construes *The Satanic Verses* as Rushdie's "love letter" to Islam, an Islam he cannot "have" because of Indianized secular Muslim attitudes (Jussawalla 1996: 67).

These sections also resonate with another aspect of the subcontinental history that Rushdie has inherited. The image of a woman saint walking naked can be found in the life and poetry of the twelfth-century south Indian poet-saint Akkamahadevi. Her beauty is thought to have attracted the king of the land, who demanded marriage. Akkamahadevi, however, rejected any possible marriage. She discarded her clothing and set forth on a journey in search of the Hindu god Siva, seeking to unite with him as his wife. She had always felt a spiritual affinity with Siva, considering

him her lover. The contrast between the king and Akkamahadevi is similar to that between Mirza and Ayesha. Vijaya Ramaswamy states that the
"shedding of all inhibitions constituted the ultimate act of defiance by a
woman saint. It was her flagrant refusal to conform to sexual expectations"
(Ramaswamy 1997: 174). Akkamahadevi produced a series of short poems
or *vacanas*. Among them is the one in which she describes shedding her
clothing, number 124:

> You can confiscate
> money in hand;
> can you confiscate
> the body's glory?
>
> Or peel away every strip
> you wear,
> but can you peel
> the Nothing, the Nakedness
> that covers and veils?
>
> To the shameless girl
> wearing the white jasmine Lord's
> light of morning,
> you fool,
> where's the need for cover and jewel?
>
> (Ramanujan 1973: 129)

Akkamahadevi's writings and example—her flagrant rejection of religious-
societal controls—informed the spread in India of the Bhakti movement. This
movement came to mean love, sharing, worship, and devotion, and is considered to have started in approximately the fifth century, beginning in south
India and gradually spreading northward over the next thousand years, wel-
coming believers irrespective of caste, gender, or religion.

In addition to Feroza Jussawalla's argument that Rushdie's roots extend to
an Indianized, secular Islam, we may also include these secular Hindu literary sources. Rushdie is likely to have been familiar with and used the well-
known Ramanujan translation from which I have quoted the above poem.
Srinivas Aravamudan has observed that the Ayesha episode could also share
a similarity with the north Indian Bhakti poet-saint Meerabai, who abandoned her husband, believing Krishna to be her lover (Aravamudan 2006:
211). What would interest Rushdie are the transgression, subversion, and
difference that Naseem Fatima, Akkamahadevi, Meerabai, and the Bhakti
movement represent—the last as a secularized form of worship distinct from
orthodox Brahmanism. Akkamahadevi and Bhaktism translated through
Ayesha and Islam is, for Rushdie, poetry after Partition.

Some left secularists in India are keen to promote forms of worship such as Bhakti, for they avoid the hegemonies of religion while allowing space for the affective realm. Sufism is also held as an example, in its emphasis on the mystical elements of Islam distinct from the latter's more orthodox formations. Such hybridity of Hindu-Muslim identity, however, can be both secular in the specifically Indian sense of distance from both religions, but can also be blasphemous. *The Satanic Verses* can be viewed to draw upon a hybrid religiosity that informs not only the secular Islam of its author but also the posting of that secular through literary form. This is what marks the text as a product of its secular Indian place of production.

I conclude this Ayesha section by invoking a single voice. A Gujurati dalit woman boards a train destined for Mumbai in order to celebrate the anniversary of Dalit leader Dr. Ambedkar's conversion from Hinduism to Buddhism. Entering the train, the woman finds herself verbally harassed by an upper-caste businessman for her bravado in seeking a seat in his compartment. Unintimidated, she replies in the language he will understand—Marathi—and sings a song by Meerabai, on the dignity of the "poor" life. The businessman is silenced, and the woman's singing is followed by the cheer and respect of the others. She enjoys the rest of her journey unharassed. Rashmi Bhatnagar, Renu Dube, and Reena Dube see this exchange as a text, as an example of the living tradition of appropriating Meerabai's work in order to "sacralize" the everyday and therefore "craft a text of [one's] own praxis" (Bhatnagar, Dube, and Dube 2004: 46). Akkamahadevi understood and re-worked Hinduism on her terms, as indeed Naseem Fatima became immersed in a highly personal Islam. Fascinated, perhaps even inspired by these two extraordinary women and the religious faith and worldly courage they represent, Rushdie is also crafting a text of *his* own praxis.

5.3 Conclusion

It is a gripping scene, toward the end of the novel. The setting is Brickhall, the neighbourhood of London where Saladin, in devil form, has found refuge in the home of the Bangladeshi shopkeeping family, the Sufyans. The scene is of a gigantic fire resulting from race riots. The fire might also be emanating from Gibreel, who, believing or hallucinating that he is the angel Azraeel, has blown his gigantic, golden trumpet. This is the Last Trumpet to end the world, sending forth fire across the skies. The fire burns the home of the Sufyans. Hanif, the boyfriend of the Sufyan daughter Mishal, comforts her by saying, *"Stay with me. The world is real. We have to live in it; we have to live here, to live on"* (469; italics original). I read this as an affirmation. Of what? Rushdie takes pains to draw attention to the exigencies and insurgencies of the world, *his* world. It is not a sentimental or escapist gesture, but is fundamental to the act of self-constitution *in* the world. Hanif's affirmations sketch the world as Rushdie affirms it, as a kind of "secular survival": it is *real*; we have to live *in* it; to live *here*; and to *live on*. Rushdie offers such affirmations at the end of the novel. They emerge after the immanence of a literal and social demonization, of crisis, of racism, of the relentless questioning of religious faith—all from a world that inexorably confronts Rushdie with its inequalities and injustices.

Religion's possibility of discursive inflexibility, its unwillingness to permit entry of patchwork forms, can be the condition resulting in the notion of blasphemy. Yet Rushdie's novel insists on its own form of belief quite apart from the self-rationalizing inflexibility of the expressions of Islam that he seeks to challenge.

Because of the text's unrelenting concern with secular worldliness—post-colonialism, immigration, racism, metropolitanism, nationalism, family—the affirmations it offers emerge *because* of such historical secular situatedness. The posting of the secular emerges through the historical condition of the secular: we have to live in it, we have to live here, to live on. If, as Sara Suleri Goodyear argues, blasphemy is a recuperative devotion toward the idea of belief, then I argue, inversely, that the devices of magical realism are a recuperative devotion toward the exigencies of worldliness. They mark the postsecular explorations of the text precisely because they emerge from worldly and secular situatedness—and the final literary text they constitute is ultimately in-the-world. The devices of magical realism allow Rushdie to translate between Muhammad and Gibreel/Saladin—across the borderline of the religious and the cultural—in order to iterate *and thus affirm* survival: worldly, insurgent, empowered survival. The novel, as medium and message of the challenge to broaden the scope of the liberal state, has survived. The novel, as medium and message of the challenge to represent the diversities of Islam, has survived. The novel, as a searchingly internal exploration of Islam enabled both by British liberalism and Indian secularism, has survived.

I do not mean to act as an alibi for Rushdie. Nor do I mean to reward or conceptualize mere survival as an aesthetic victory (satanic *versus* satanic), certainly not survival along some teleological axis. In 1990, Rushdie stated: "one reason for my attempt to develop a form of fiction in which the miraculous might coexist with the mundane was precisely my acceptance that notions of the sacred and the profane both needed to be explored, as far as possible without pre-judgement, in any honest literary portrait of the way we are" (Rushdie 1991: 417). Toward the conclusion of the same essay, he declares that he cannot bear the "idea of the writer as secular prophet" because literature according to him can never have the perfection, abso-luteness, and finality of prophecy (Rushdie 1991: 427). As in *Anil's Ghost*, where the flexibility of literary space allows for a multiple representation and contestation of human rights, that representational multiplicity also allows for a varied exploration of religion's faces of faith, not as a secular prophet but as a subject caught in a bind between different forms of belief, religious and political.

The posting of the secular in this novel stands as a message to re-think the distinction between secularism and religion, that a group of believers—protestors and writers alike—characterized as a "minority" in both the UK and India can provoke challenges to the secular that compel the state to reflect upon and question its practices. Can a state have the charisma and largesse to truly grant to *itself*, "after" orientalism, the liberties of acceptance and tolerance that it aspires to extend to religion, to "other" religions? In an irony of history, the burning of the book considerably increased the book's afterlife, so that more than twenty years after the *fatwa* and *post*-9/11, *The Satanic Verses* is compelling us to re-think the distinction between the "secular west" and the "non-secular, non-west." Let us say that Ayesha, parting the Arabian Sea, has also, as an element of *The Satanic Verses*, helped to partition the above distinction. The hole that miraculously opens at the centre of Mirza's being is greater than the sum of the parts that seek to categorize parts into "secular," "non-secular," "religious," "west," "non-west." Rushdie's gestures toward newness, in the wake of the catastrophes and crises of politicized religion, emerge experimentally, riskily, deconstructively among the shadows of borderlines. To ask *what kind of an idea is x* is to gesture to the idea that ideas must imagine their own expressions through the perilous disjunctures between received ideologies and *as-yet-unborn* forms. In this age of postcolonial postsecularism, what then becomes the task—liberatory, excavational, secular—of the postcolonial critic finding himself or herself on the increasingly small stage of the increasingly transnational?

Figure 8 Entrance to Akbar's Tomb, Sikandar, India. Photograph by the author.

6   Art After The *Fatwa*

Salman Rushdie's *Haroun and the Sea of Stories*, *The Moor's Last Sigh*, *Shalimar the Clown*, and *The Enchantress of Florence*

In the preceding chapter, I examined how *The Satanic Verses* could be Rushdie's means of showing a range of Islams, including Islam as represented by the literary versions of Muhammad and Ayesha. Rushdie's representation of Muhammad and Ayesha, creating them "anew" in literary form, becomes the secular equivalent to the religious miracle. Such a literary figuration gestures to new creative and epistemological possibilities beyond the constraints of British liberalism, Indian secularism, and fundamentalist Islam. Rushdie seems to be saying, "Here is my postcolonial, transnational Islam," thus challenging narrow conceptions of religion and belief, and challenging the self-rationalizing religion *of* religion.

Then came the *fatwa*. The Ayatollah Khomeini of Iran issued the *fatwa* on February 14, 1989. Four days later, Rushdie offered a public apology, in which he expressed his regret for the distress caused by his novel, and professed his sensitivity to a religiously plural world (Appignanesi and Maitland 1989: 120). Religious leaders in Iran, however, remained unforgiving and unflinching, and Rushdie went into hiding, until he thought one last step could win him some flexibility. On December 24, 1989, he met with Muslim scholars and formally stated his belief in Islam (Hedges 1990). In an interview on May 12, 2008, on the British Channel 4's show *Shrink Rap*, he confesses his declaration of belief was a pretence, designed to win back his life and freedom. The *fatwa* and the responses it provoked from around the world fueled debates about the nature of censorship, blasphemy, literature, and politics, and the responsibility of a writer to both his inherited religion and that religion's meaning for its different followers. Jose Casanova has argued that "the public resurgence of Islam has been one of the main developments thrusting religion back into public view" (Casanova 1994: 10). The Rushdie Affair is part and parcel of such a public resurgence. If there are "rivers of blood" (Rushdie 1988: 97) proleptically embedded in *The Satanic Verses*—yes, the *fatwa* came before the novel—then in this closing body chapter, I examine how such rivers run through Rushdie's fiction immediately following *The Satanic Verses*, how the *fatwa* shapes Rushdie's views on secularism and Islam.

The breakdown of secularism is something Rushdie might lament as a political crisis in India, and now in the US. At the same time, he struggles to gesture toward some affirmation and belief *in spite of* the politicized and ritualized Islam and Hinduism he irrepressibly critiques. What postsecular possibilities might emerge in some of Rushdie's fiction after the *fatwa*? I examine Rushdie's work immediately following the *fatwa*: *Haroun and the Sea of Stories* (1990) and *The Moor's Last Sigh* (1995). I also look at Rushdie's most recent work: *Shalimar the Clown* (2005) and *The Enchantress of Florence* (2008), as well as *Luka and the Fire of Life* (2010). Immediately after and most belatedly after: I privilege the perspective of linear time in order to contrast how postsecular explorations can emerge across a range of Rushdie's work.

In his fiction after *The Satanic Verses*, Rushdie's stance toward religion becomes explicitly adversarial. He no longer speaks of "faith," as he did in *The Satanic Verses*, but rather of "religion," by which he means fundamentalist Islam, and also Hindutva (as we shall see in *The Moor's Last Sigh*), and now Christianity in the US. In his essay "In Good Faith," published a year after the *fatwa*, he states that *The Satanic Verses* "dissents from the end of debate, of dispute, of dissent. Hindu communalist sectarianism, the kind of Sikh terrorism that blows up planes, the fatuousness of Christian creationism are dissented from as well as the narrower definitions of Islam" (Rushdie 1991: 397). Rushdie's secularism, in turn, becomes hardened, as expressed in this passage from a March 2005 op-ed piece by him:

> Victor Hugo wrote, "There is in every village a torch: the schoolmaster—and an extinguisher: the parson." We need more teachers and fewer priests in our lives because, as James Joyce once said, "There is no heresy or no philosophy which is so abhorrent to the church as a human being." But perhaps the great American lawyer Clarence Darrow put the secularist argument best of all. "I don't believe in God," he said, "because I don't believe in Mother Goose."
>
> (Rushdie 2005)

Alongside such a secular outlook, Rushdie becomes increasingly committed in his post-*fatwa* fiction, as I shall demonstrate, to the creative and generative potentials of art and literature. In the process, the vocational aspect of literature attains a kind of *dharmic* significance for Rushdie, allowing him to pursue high humanist ideals. Rushdie expresses this position in his essay "February 1999: Ten Years of the Fatwa," where he states that literature is a rebuke to dogma and power, that it is "more resilient than what menaces it" (Rushdie 2003: 294). In the same essay, Rushdie's view of literature as a "passionate, dispassionate enquiry," captures the secular dimension of literature which Rushdie esteems as impartial and insightful, and also captures the postsecular dimension of literature, as that which affords Rushdie some enchantment and wonder. He states, "beyond grief, bewilderment and despair, I have rededicated myself to our high calling" (Rushdie 2003: 294).

Art for Rushdie, however, is not simply a forum for exploring moral and transcendent possibilities. Rushdie is aware that art can serve as the site for both an "enlightened" cosmopolitanism and hybridity, and its unfortunate opposite. Pre-*fatwa*, we witness the character of the art critic Zeenat Vakil in *The Satanic Verses* and her insistence to Saladin on the hybrid nature of Indian art and culture: "was not the entire national culture based on the principle of borrowing whatever clothes seemed to fit, Aryan, Mughal, British, take-the-best-and-leave-the-rest? [. . .]. [. . .] 'Why should there be a good, right way of being a wog? That's Hindu fundamentalism [. . .]'" (Rushdie 1988: 52). In contrast to such cosmopolitanism, art after the *fatwa* becomes liable to the opposite, vulnerable to cadres of Hindu fundamentalism who can claim Uma Sarasvati's sculpture in *The Moor's Last Sigh* as representative of a pure nationalist Hinduism. Whereas one character, pre-*fatwa*, can confidently affirm the cosmopolitan and hybrid potentials of art, another character, post-*fatwa*, laments that her art is liable to misuse by religious fundamentalists. This is not of course necessarily Rushdie's position, but the appearance of the contrast across two novels straddling a pivotal event signifies the registering in the author's imagination of art as potentially both creatively enabling and materially disabling. Discussing *The Moor's Last Sigh* in detail later in this chapter, I now turn to *Haroun and the Sea of Stories*.

6.1   *Haroun and the Sea of Stories*

Haroun and the Sea of Stories (henceforth *Haroun*) was written by Rushdie toward the beginning of his hiding and "exile" following the issuing of the *fatwa*. The book's dedicatory acrostic verse spells the name of Rushdie's son, Zafar:

Z embla, Zenda, Xanadu:
A ll of our dream-worlds may come true.
F airy lands are fearsome too.
A s I wander far from view
R ead, and bring me home to you.

(Rushdie 1990)

Although Rushdie tempers the space of dream-worlds with the "fearsome" reality of the *fatwas* that can emerge as a result of them, his emphasis remains on the power of the imagination, the capacity of the act of reading to bring Zafar's father home. Indeed, the last line of the poem demonstrates that reading—and, conversely, writing—is a matter of both life and death, something Rushdie particularly believes in after the *fatwa*. It also demonstrates Rushdie's belief in the vitality of reading as a democratic activity, one that can be critical of ideologies.

The domain of the aesthetic as the mode through which such imagined possibilities can find their expression is something Rushdie privileges throughout *Haroun*. By using the genre of the children's book and, specifically, a fairy tale, Rushdie is able to stress the space of the aesthetic, particularly post-*The Satanic Verses*, as it stands in opposition to the space of the political. The egregious display of imaginative aesthetic form—not just a story, but a fairy tale; not just characters, but fantastical ones; not just subtle oppositions, but self-consciously extreme ones like good and evil—inversely reflects the creative and historical constraints and inflexibility of the *fatwa*. Rushdie seems to be saying, both formally and thematically, "this is art, and this is my defense of art."

If Rushdie was previously insensitive to the political consequences of his writing, there can be little doubt about his heightened awareness of them immediately after the *fatwa*. At the same time, Rushdie has also insisted on art as a form of secular transcendence. In his well-known essay "Is Nothing Sacred?" Rushdie wonders whether art, in a dialogue with the material and spiritual worlds, can offer a kind of secular transcendence. He concludes that it can, must, and does offer such a possibility, stating that transcendence is "the flight of the human spirit outside the confines of its material, physical existence which all of us, secular or religious, experience on at least a few occasions" (Rushdie 1991: 420). Art and literature then become "for a secular, materialist culture, some sort of replacement for what the love of god offers in the world of faith" (Rushdie 1991: 420).

With such "replacement" in mind, I turn to the eponymous Sea of Stories, located on a distant planet and constituting the source of all creativity, to which Haroun travels in order to restore his father's gift for storytelling. The Sea of Stories is literally transcendent to the everyday material world in which particular stories exist. What is the relation between this form of transcendence and its particular instantiations or expressions? Rushdie's response, in *Haroun*, is that one possibility is "truth value." When Haroun questions his father about the use of stories that are not true, this greatly upsets his father, the Shah of Blah. This is reinforced by the fact that the Shah, when depressed, describes the Land of Moody as only a story.

The questioning in *Haroun* of whether stories might merely be fiction presents an opportunity to read *Haroun* through the distinction invoked by the critic Aron Aji, of the text as authorial biography (e.g., following Haroun's question above, we could ask: does the story truly represent Rushdie's life?) or as a formal creation. Aji, leaning more toward a formalist reading and less toward what he views as simple biographical interpretations of the text (it's not just about Rushdie), argues that *Haroun* is in fact informed by Islamic themes, such as the use of names from Islamic history and doctrine. For example, Aji states that Rushdie derives the names of the two central characters in the story, Haroun and his father Rashid, from the historical caliph of Baghdad, Haroun al-Rashid. This caliph had established ties with Christendom and the Far East, and his rule was marked by literary and artistic flourishing (Aji 1995: 109). The historical Haroun al-Rashid serves as an appropriate intertext for Rushdie, insofar as *Haroun* is concerned with reconciling "the [Islamic] faith and the inherent plurality of its culture(s) [. . . in an] attempt to articulate a universalist aesthetics firmly anchored in the inalienable human desire for self-expression, one that upholds the diversity of forms through which self-expression is possible" (Aji 1995: 127). Rushdie also alludes to the historical Haroun al-Rashid in *The Enchantress of Florence*, as a figure in the famous *Hamzanama* paintings, which I discuss later in this chapter.

Aji's reading is commendable for contextualizing Rushdie within the dynamic narrative traditions of the multiple cultures that believe in Islamic doctrines and teachings. Although I agree that Rushdie's universalist aesthetics are grounded in an "inalienable" human desire for self-expression, Rushdie's "universalist" aesthetics also stem from a particular situation. The crisis of the *fatwa* becomes the mode of provocation for a universalist aesthetic affirmation ("we should all be able to tell stories"), and in turn that aesthetic freedom ("here is a story") can lead to the crisis of a death sentence. It is the precarious, almost endless oscillation "between" the two, *between* affirmation and crisis, that can constitute a postcolonial "newness." That newness can be the space within which such oscillation occurs; that newness is the space *toward* which Rushdie can gesture. This is also perhaps the newness that has so fascinated scholars and that the plethora of academic scholarship that followed, and continues to follow, the *fatwa* has tried to understand (Asad 1990, Taylor 1989).

If Rushdie gestures toward a "universalist aesthetics," it is because he is rooted in a particular historical crisis—*his* crisis, *his* diasporic location, *his* uncertain situation between life and death—and not just because of sentimental self-expression. Zafar's reading of the book, after all, is not solely for aesthetic pleasure, but can bring his father home to him. Rushdie affirms art and self-expression, and it is the violent attack of a religion that makes such affirmation especially urgent. The enchantment of art, that which satisfies affective needs within us, becomes especially highlighted for Rushdie after a severe secular threat. The postsecularism of *Haroun* is constitutively informed by the ineluctably *secular* situatedness of its author.

Rushdie's latest work of fiction, *Luka and the Fire of Life* (2010), continues *Haroun and the Sea of Stories*' affirmations of creativity. Rushdie had promised his son he would write another children's book, and the Shah of Blah in *Luka and the Fire of Life* does not disappoint. Luka states, "gods and goddesses, ogres and bats, monsters and slimy things, is the World of Rashid Khalifa, the well-known Ocean of Notions, the fabulous Shah of Blah" (Rushdie 2010: 182). Guarding the Fire of Life is a cosmopolitan pantheon of gods, including, among others, Assyrian, Aztec, Egyptian, Greek, Inca, Norse, and Roman gods (Rushdie 2010: 171). But Luka's confidence and strength outwit the gods, whom he taunts as being extinct and dead, and he captures the

Fire of Life. He takes the Fire to the Real World and brings his father and his creativity back to life. The power of aesthetic creativity and the destructive effects of the "gods" of organized religion are themes that Rushdie of course explores in *The Satanic Verses*. When Luka defies the gods' command that the Fire of Life must not enter the Real World, this is paralleled in Rushdie's defiance of conventional understandings of what constitutes the real. Later in this chapter, I examine the intriguing ways in which Rushdie explores this mixture of the real and the imaginary in *The Enchantress of Florence*.

6.2   *The Moor's Last Sigh*

Rushdie's first major novel following *The Satanic Verses*, *The Moor's Last Sigh* (1995) takes readers to Rushdie's beloved city, Mumbai, and can be read as Rushdie's lamentation on the rise of the Hindu right in Mumbai. Much of *The Moor's Last Sigh* (henceforth *MLS*) is organized around ekphrases, through Rushdie's description of Uma's and her mother Aurora's artwork. Aurora's art helps to modulate forms of personal and social commentary. This is an example of my argument throughout this book on the function of aestheticization as cognition, and the proximities it allows between aesthetics and religion. As Dora Ahmad has observed, Aurora compensates for an "absent god as she creates a secularist art by borrowing from many religious traditions" (Ahmad 2005: 6). Aurora's painting "Palempstine" represents the hybrid mixture of Moorish Spain and her contemporary India, in search for a pluralist secular nation.

In *The English Patient*, the church frescoes allow for Kip's emotionally-charged epiphanies; the highly visual images of the imagined Golden Temple in India allow for the building of emotional intimacy between Kip and Hana, away from the barriers of (the religion of) nation. In *The Satanic Verses*, the highly visual Ayesha episode demonstrates Rushdie's inspiration from Hindu religious poetry. The Buddhist eye-painting ceremony in *Anil's Ghost* shows the visual exploration of possibilities of regeneration and hope within a politically and nationally fraught context. For Aurora, creating art is a process of understanding, both personal and social, as indeed it would be in Rushdie's own life. This intimate link between the visual and the literary is thematized by Rushdie through the fact that Aurora has friends who are literary luminaries in India: Mulk Raj Anand, Ismat Chugtai, Sadat Hasan Manto, and Premchand.

The possible interrelations among the visual, the religious, and the worldly are also expressed by Rushdie as the potential misappropriation of artwork by religious groups. The Hindu right Maharashtra Axis, led by Raman Fielding, gains influence over the city's political and social circles, undermining Aurora Zogoiby's fame and promoting in her place the young artist Uma Sarasvati, who works closely with Hindu themes and motifs. Uma's famous sculpture is entitled *Alterations in/Reclamations of the Essence of Motherhood in the Post-Secularist*

Epoch (Rushdie 1997: 261). Mumbai's ruling Hindu right uses this work to promote and valorize Hindu art and belief. The postsecular expressed in the artwork's title might be read, within the terms of the novel, as merely a political guise for the religious. The (Hindu) religiosity of the usage is especially given force because the title features emotively connotative words such as "motherhood," "essence," and even arguably "epoch," the last heralding the arrival of a "distinctive" beginning, as per the definition in the Oxford English dictionary: "the beginning of a 'new era' or distinctive period in the history of mankind, a country, an individual, a science, etc." (oed.com). In my conception, the postsecular does not have this teleological, politically driven sense, nor is it merely an uncritical substitute for the religious. But it is interesting that Rushdie uses this sense of "postsecular," showing the term's vulnerability to being glossed by the religious right as the (re)emergence of a religious identity, an identity that is itself vulnerable to fundamentalist influence.

The artistic intentions behind Uma's work are not "postsecular" but grounded in a highly personal, individual Hindu faith. This faith surprises Moor, who had been romantically involved with Uma. She explains to Moor that although she deeply values the privacy of her religious beliefs, Fielding is trying to construe her love for the Hindu god Ram as an attack against Muslims (Rushdie 1995: 262). In the same speech-like expression of her views, Uma asserts that whereas Moor might be from a relatively small religious minority, she as a Hindu must negotiate an enormous tradition, finding her own sense of truths and origins. She affirms that exploring religious belief is a personal affair, and that Moor should respect that privacy; in fact, her relationship with Moor proves to Uma that she is no fanatic (Rushdie 1995: 262). Uma's views contain an almost textbook definition of Indian secularism, as the state's respecting religious belief and practice by striving to maintain a distance from all religions, given the diversity of religions in India. It also reflects the secularization to which Rushdie would be exposed in the UK, as the relegation of religion to the private sphere. Rushdie also relativizes the Hindu subject-position as one that is not uncritical or hegemonic, but involves a struggle with origin and truths.

In terms compatible with Uma's views above, India's Hindu nationalist party, the Bharatiya Janata Party (BJP)—and in particular the ideology of Hindutva ("Hinduness")—claims to embrace the "true" secularism. Here is the description of Hindutva's secularism from the official website of the BJP:

When Hindus realized that pseudo-secularism had reduced them to the role of an innocent bystander in the game of politics, they demanded a true secularism where every religious group would be treated the same and a government that would not take Hindu sentiments for granted. Hindutva awakened the Hindus to the new world order where nations represented the aspirations of people united in history, culture, philosophy, and heroes.

(Bharatiya Janata Party 2012)

The above twinning of secularism and nationalism of course begs the question of the role of minority religions in the nation-building project. Before considering that, I would like to present the note on which Hindutva ends its self-description:

> The future of Bharat [Hindi, "India"] is set. Hindutva is here to stay. It is up to the Muslims whether they will be included in the new nationalistic spirit of Bharat. It is up to the government and the Muslim leadership whether they wish to increase Hindu furor or work with the Hindu leadership to show that Muslims and the government will consider Hindu sentiments. The era of one-way compromise of Hindus is over, for from now on, secularism must mean that all parties must compromise.
>
> (Bharatiya Janata Party 2012)

The parties in question are of course minority religious groups—and their role in becoming part of the nation must involve compromise. The "secularism" of compromise that Hindutva envisions is one built on the following principles:

> Hindutva will not mean any Hindu theocracy or theology. However, it will mean that the guiding principles of Bharat will come from two of the great teachings of the Vedas, the ancient Hindu and Indian scriptures, which so boldly proclaimed—"Truth is one, sages call it by many names"—and—"the whole universe is one family."
>
> (Bharatiya Janata Party 2012)

The above proclamations are, by definition, partisan. But when apparently religiously-neutral notions like "truth," "oneness," and "family" can only be articulated and tolerated from within an overarching Hindu context (and an extreme one at that), then that clearly goes against any strictly secular framework for the nation.

Similarly, beneath the surface of Uma's secularism lies a tragic reality, which becomes the cause of both Moor's and Rushdie's lament. Uma's love for both her god and for Moor is eventually exposed by Rushdie as a sham only to promote her commercial ambitions. Moor's mother, after all, is the leading Indian artist of her time. Uma's pretense shows the tenuousness and fragility of any postsecular values like art and hybridity. Her attitudes seemed to have reflected Indian and British secularism along with the sensitive self-vigilance of a "personal" Hinduism, but these do not represent a simple or naive teleology for Rushdie. This dual possibility, almost simultaneity, of affirmation and crisis echoes the same duality in *Haroun and the Sea of Stories*. As I argued in the section on *Haroun*, a postsecular possibility can lie precisely *in* that duality of affirmation and crisis. If Rushdie, post-*fatwa*, experiences a curtailing and loss of his freedom, then *MLS* explores precisely that loss. Moor is ultimately jailed by the Hindu right, and made to work for them. He also witnesses the Hindu right's sabotage of his mother's artwork and fame. In the end, he flees to Benengeli, a village in the south of Spain that attracts residents from around the world.

Here is where "moor" in the novel's title can be substantiated, with its allusion to the Muslim invasion of southern Spain in the eight century, establishing a civilization that lasted until the late fifteenth century. It is this manifestation of a "plural polity" which Ashis Nandy has invoked in his criticism of the failures of Indian secularism. Arguing that political secularism is a concept foreign to India and especially its non-English-speaking majority, Nandy insists on drawing upon traditions and concepts of tolerance indigenous to India. He also insists that Indian society should learn only from other cultures that have genuinely achieved a peaceful plural polity:

> And why import an idea from countries that have such shoddy records of religious, racial, cultural and ethnic tolerance? Why not, for instance, borrow the concept of *convivencia* from Medieval Islamic Spain, arguably the only truly plural polity Europe has produced in the last one thousand years?
>
> (Nandy 2004)

The novel's "ideal" Benengeli might stand as a parody of the secular ideal. The two Spanish women who are initially warm and affectionate toward Moor reveal themselves to be conspirators with the mad Gama. The *convivencia* represented by this idyllic southern Spanish location ends as a mirage. It becomes a play on pure surface where migrants from around the world spend the days walking along the promenade, appearing happy when in fact they are disenchanted. This textual structure, the bifurcation between the promised and the actual, parallels Rushdie's imagining of the disappointments of secularism. The promise of a space tolerant of all religions tragically finds its crisis in the rise of religious fundamentalism and communal violence, on the site no less of Rushdie's beloved Mumbai.

But like *Haroun*, and the inspiring artwork of Moor's mother Aurora, the promise of "secular redemption" might lie in art itself. For Rushdie, the act of writing is his means of sustaining a sense of enchantment. It is no coincidence that the sheer urgency of writing—as an act of survival, as an act of self-affirmation—provides the dramatic bookends for *MLS*. Almost inextricable from this heightened urgency is that Moor ages at twice the normal speed, thus introducing magical realism into the novel. I argued in the chapter on *The Satanic Verses* that the device of magical realism for Rushdie is one that allows him to pursue possibilities that avoid the limitations of the conventional mode of realist narrative. Yet magical realism is not simply a "device" or a "tool" that Rushdie strategically employs. Rushdie has explained that quite without a *fatwa*, death can happen at any time, which accounts for the sense of urgency in *The Moor's Last Sigh* (Rushdie 1996). Magical realism for him can capture, not without risk, some of this piquancy in life, not merely as a "trick," "acrobatics," or "fancy footwork," but as a way of expressing "human truth" (Rushdie 1996).

It is interesting that Rushdie refers to a problematic universal like "human truth" in the context of magical realism. This underscores the significance, to Rushdie, of the space of the literary as a ground upon which he can enact a dialectic between the force and crises of historical circumstances and the emergence of any sense of renewal, affirmation, and regeneration.[1] "Human truth" is a *problematic* universal because of the self-deconstructive status of any "truths," especially in a context such as the postcolonial where there is acute, traumatized awareness of the fragility of any notion or sense of "resolution" (and the human). The trauma that writes through, perhaps automatically, for Rushdie in *MLS* is the urgency produced through an acute awareness of his mortality. He states in the novel that the closer one works to a bull, the more one must be prepared to be gorged (Rushdie 1995b: 171). That bull has shown Rushdie just how deeply it can gorge. Moor's magical aging, therefore, is not merely strategic or playful. It is a site Rushdie creates to express what he believes to be true.

There is a religious trope informing Moor's account of his life through the posting of notes, that of Martin Luther nailing his 95 theses to the Castle Church at Wittenberg in 1517. Luther protested against the Roman Catholic Church's practice of selling indulgences, payments to secure remissions of punishment for sin, as a means of raising funds for the rebuilding of St. Peter's Basilica in Rome. Yet Luther did not merely revolt against ecclesiastical abuses. He also believed his was a fight for the gospel. In Luther's view, at the heart of the gospel was the doctrine of justification by faith, that Christ's own righteousness is imputed to those who believe and who thus have faith in Christ, and it is on that ground, and not through merely "good works" or paying indulgences, that they can achieve salvation. As Richard Marius has observed,

> Luther declared that since the just shall live by faith, all righteousness resides in faith and that faith alone fulfils all God's commands and makes all its works righteous. [. . .] The ritual good works encouraged by the Roman Church [. . .] were not bad in themselves, but they were fatal to piety if they became rules.
>
> (Marius 1999: 232)

If we read Rushdie's Moor as a "postcolonial Luther," then it is the corruption of Mumbai's Hindu right that Moor is reacting against: the people that literally persecute him; those from the Hindu right underworld seeking to avenge his murder of Raman Fielding; and those responsible for destroying his mother's professional reputation. The "rules" of the religious right become fatal to the particular form of "postsecular piety" that Moor espouses—the rapture of art, the enchantment of cosmopolitan living, the faith in the aesthetic.

At the time of writing *MLS*, Rushdie was himself, of course, under persecution. The act of writing enables him to affirm his presence, and to affirm
the value that writing has for him. The urgency of this novel is also informed
by a desire for something *other* than the secularism that Rushdie feels has so
failed his city. Mona Narain has observed that quite apart from critics who
view *MLS* as valorizing hybridity, difference, and multiculturalism, Rushdie
recuperates an "imaginative early modern past through the Catholic-Jewish-
Moorish antecedents of the novel's protagonists" and thus "seeks to create
an alternative allegory for the modern Indian nation state" (Narain 2006:
56). For Narain, this allegory is alternative to the polarizations produced by
the Hindu-Muslim binary in Indian political discourse. I endorse Narain's
criticism, because by turning to Catholicism, Judaism, and Moorish Spain,
Rushdie gestures to possibilities that are *other* to the failed Indian secularism
of Mumbai, and is thus postsecular, an alternative allegory being an expression of that postsecularism.

6.3 *Shalimar the Clown*

It is through this idea of the potential for creativity and open-mindedness
within religious practices that I turn to *Shalimar the Clown* (2005). In early
November 2008, Rushdie shared a public forum at Columbia University with
Gauri Viswanathan, in which they discussed the various aspects of secularism and religion in Rushdie's recent work. Viswanathan states that in *Shalimar the Clown*'s "hauntingly lyrical evocation of Kashmir, the counterpoint to
religious extremism is not necessarily secularism [. . .] but religion restored
to a more expansive and more inclusive practice" (Rushdie and Viswanathan 2008). Rushdie agrees with Viswanathan, saying he is moved by such
religious and cultural inclusiveness.

Shalimar the Clown pursues this ideal within a specific region, Kashmir,
where there can be a peaceful coexistence of Hindus and Muslims, as exemplified by each worshipping at the other religion's shrine. This possibility is
not unlike the syncretic space Rushdie imagines in *The Moor's Last Sigh* as
Benengeli in Moorish Spain. Kashmir has appeared in Rushdie's previous
works, as the opening scene in *Midnight's Children*, as the parallel to the fictional setting for *Haroun and the Sea of Stories*, and as the setting for his short
story "The Prophet's Hair" in *East, West*. In *Shalimar the Clown*, Rushdie's
most detailed engagement with Kashmir, Rushdie explores the idea of *Kashmiriyat* or Kashmiriness, the idealized notion of the coexistence in Kashmir
of peoples of all faiths, their greatest allegiance being to the land, the village,
and the region: "the belief that at the heart of Kashmiri culture there was a
common bond that transcended all other differences" (Rushdie 2006: 110).[2]
It is *Kashmiriyat* that allows the eponymous Muslim Shalimar to marry the
Hindu Boonyi, a marriage that Boonyi's father affirms: "To defend their love
is to defend what is finest in ourselves" (110). Art too emerges in affirming

Kashmiriyat. The handicraft exporter Yuvraj explains that each art-piece represents the collaboration of many artists, with each piece symbolizing that it is "not only made in but in fact made *by* Kashmir" (359; italics mine). Quite opposite to the positiveness of *Kashmiriyat*, it is the violence of American imperialism that brings Max Ophuls to Kashmir. He is the American ambassador to India, and he eventually seduces the young, beautiful, and talented dancer Boonyi. The liaison ultimately leads to Boonyi's murder by a vengeful Shalimar, who has joined the ranks of militant Islam in Kashmir. Shalimar murders Max as well, in Los Angeles, where he also attempts to murder Max's and Boonyi's daughter, who is named India by her adoptive mother Peggy (Max's wife), and is named Kashmira by Boonyi.

I would like to focus on the dramatic closing scene of the novel. It is night and Shalimar has broken into Max's home. He has looked throughout the house for Kashmira, and now approaches her unlit bedroom. He is wielding a large knife. Kashmira is inside the room, fully alert, and is watching Shalimar using night-vision goggles. Shalimar senses that he is being watched, and pauses, looking for patches of darkness within the darkness. He walks toward her. Kashmira is wielding a bow and arrow pointed directly at him. She shoots the arrow. The novel's closing lines are: "There was no possibility that she would miss. There was no second chance. There was no India. There was only Kashmira, and Shalimar the Clown" (398). There is no direct resolution to the novel: we do not know for sure whether Kashmira or Shalimar dies. But the bold tableau-like creation of the binary is its own resolution: Shalimar and Kashmira face-to-face. The arc of *Kashmiriyat* is profaned in its bending into the murder of an American public figure by a Kashmiri militant, one who has already terrorized Kashmir, wreaking destruction in such a beautiful land. Kashmira, the privileged daughter of hybridity—hybrid in race and class, growing up in England and America—is face-to-face with the subaltern. In his forum with Gauri Viswanathan at Columbia University, Rushdie states that he is no utopianist (Rushdie and Viswanathan 2008). The character of Kashmira shows some of the potential failures of hybridity, through her resentment of her adoptive American mother. Shalimar represents how a relationship generated within and endorsed by *Kashmiriyat* can transform into its violent opposite, like his own handsome face that becomes disfigured in prison.

Kashmira and Shalimar remain standing, face-to-face. Where do we go from here? Of course it is very likely that the arrow will pierce Shalimar. But the novel's statement of "no possibility" that Kashmira would miss Shalimar deconstructively opens *other* possibilities, the imagined possibility of her actually missing him, or other alternatives, ones perhaps emerging as magical realism. Examples of such magical realism could include the mullah who is made of metal, or Shalimar's escape from prison by running across the top of the prison walls and then upwards into the sky, echoing his childhood training that a tightrope is really a "line of gathered air" (394). I am fascinated by the deconstruction of the rope, for it succinctly and elegantly reconceptualizes the real with another real, one that is invisible, but just as substantive, and one that produces miracle-like effects: to walk on water, to walk on air. Rushdie is compelled by the invisible but powerful: this is the invisible world of terrorist networks that Shalimar joins. In spite of an enormous sweep of characters and cultures and places, and all the visible and invisible permutations and potentials they represent and release, the closing scene of *Shalimar the Clown* is dramatic for the simple, bold binary it presents. There is no India, the construct of her foreign adoptive mother, but the thing itself, the real Kashmira.

This face-to-face encounter raises the ethical question of how to negotiate the *fact* of the other's presence. Differing recognitions of and relations with such a fact can include possibilities like multiculturalism, secularism, racism, terror, enmity, fascism, love, acceptance, friendship, hospitality, and community. If secularism orders what counts as real in the world, and I think here of Charles Taylor's notion of the "immanent frame" that I discussed in the Introduction (Taylor 2007: 542), then in this closing image is a dichotomy of characters who have imploded and exploded the secular, through the faces of hybridity and *Kashmiriyat*.

Kashmira and Shalimar are invisible, they are bodies without faces. But they are *there*. This seems to be Rushdie's closing message, that we cannot escape the basic presence of the one and the other, the *presence of presence*, not just ours, but that of another's presence ("another" conceived in the widest possible sense, whether as another person, or as an abstraction like "history"). In Chapter 1 on *The English Patient*, I read this one-and-other relation through the work of Deleuze and Guattari, as faciality, as that which becomes the pivotal point for an array of signifiers and subjectivities, so that to dismantle the face is to break through all significations. The metaphor Deleuze and Guattari use is a line of flight, like the literal line of flight by Shalimar as he escapes from the "face" of the prison. In Chapter 3 on *Anil's Ghost*, I read this one-and-other relation through the work of Levinas and the face of the Buddha, that the face of the other represents something transcendent to the self (in the sense of being different from the self's system), affirming the self (as a presence), just as the self offers a face *to* the other, affirming the other.

6.4   *The Enchantress of Florence*

Whereas *Shalimar the Clown* pursues a syncretic ideal within a specific region, Kashmir, *The Enchantress of Florence* (2008), Rushdie's most recent novel, and one that has enjoyed the greatest critical success among his post-*fatwa* work, represents a possible syncretic ideal stretching across Europe and South Asia. Whereas *The Moor's Last Sigh* laments the limitations of secularism, *The Enchantress of Florence* (henceforth *EF*) demonstrates a reinvigoration of Rushdie's belief in the potentials of secular political organization, especially as he couples such secularism with the enchantment provided by the magical and the miraculous. Ayesha, the beautiful prophet in *The Satanic Verses*, finds her parallel in *EF* with the beautiful Qara Köz, the eponymous enchantress who inspires awe and wonder among people, whether they are in Florence or Fatehpur Sikri. As a further parallel, Mirza Saeed in *The Satanic Verses* is the secular and skeptical counterpart to Ayesha, and in *EF* the Moghul emperor Akbar is a committed secularist. But Akbar also passionately believes in the power of magic—through his *khayal* or imagination he has created his wife, Jodha.

I would like to focus on Akbar, especially as *EF* emerges on the literary landscape shortly after Amartya Sen publishes *The Argumentative Indian* in 2005. For Sen, both Akbar and another great Mughal emperor, Ashoka, are exemplars of secularism in their tolerance for and acceptance of peoples of all religious faiths. Akbar is well-known for having welcomed to his court scholars of all religions in order to debate questions of metaphysics and ethics. He would even attempt the creation of a new religion, the Din-ilahi ("God's religion"), a synthesis of all the positive qualities of different religious faiths. According to Sen, the Din-ilahi reflected Akbar's "constructive search for an overarching unity, combined with a firm acknowledgment of plurality" (Sen 2005: 41). This search for unity was not based on any naive sentimentality or blind faith, but driven by reasoning or *rahi aql* (the path of reason). Akbar argued that even the question of individual faith should be approached by the path of reason rather than by blind adherence. *EF* states that in Akbar's court "argument itself—and no deity, however multilimbed or almighty—would here be the only god" (Rushdie 2009: 80).[3] Akbar is particularly interesting as a "secular" figure because he is a product, as Sen argues, of an indigenous Indian historical context, and is not a figure derived from liberal, western, Christianized secularism.

According to Gil Anidjar, western secularism emerges from within Christianity—as a form of reinvention, reincarnation, disenchantment—and then ensures the "division of the real" around the world (Anidjar 2006: 59). In his argument, Anidjar draws upon Derrida's term *mondialatinisation*, as the construction of the world (*le monde*) in specific ways through the division and distribution of the real. Given the historical connection between Christianity and secularism, Anidjar argues that secularism *is* Christianity. Orientalism becomes one such "worlding" expression of Christian imperialism, allowing Anidjar to argue that orientalism *is* Christianity (as a product of imperial Christianity). The terms secularism, orientalism, and Christianity for Anidjar are thus interchangeable.

Akbar would appeal to Rushdie because of the secularism that he represents from within an Indian context. Akbar of course lived before the political secularism integrated in the constitution of post-1947 India. He could represent to Rushdie some hope, that a Mumbai so attacked by the cadres of the Hindu right might yet be reinvigorated and strengthened by a secularist ethos, respect, and practice like that of Akbar. The spaces and lifeworlds of

Fatehpur Sikri gesture to the opening of a secularism officially yet-to-come in India, a presecular polity. The imaginative spaces of *EF* allow Rushdie to conceive of Akbar as what I might term a *presecular postsecular* figure, *post* and other to liberal, western Christianized secularism, and *pre* to an envisioned secularism yet to be constitutionally and justly manifest in India, in letter and in spirit, especially in its major metropolises.

Among critical responses to the novel, Justin Neuman argues that *EF* "repudiates linear, Eurocentric histories of the Renaissance and conjures in their stead a synchronous world of parallel realities in which the seeds of secular humanism flower not once but twice—once in northern Italy and simultaneously in northern India" (Neuman 2008: 675). Stuti Khanna argues that conjoining different cultures and spaces allows Rushdie to "lay bare the absurdity of the premises underlying racism, the failure of the imagination that reduces the 'Other' to a reductive stereotype" (Khanna 2008: 5). Radhouan Ben Amara argues that *EF* demonstrates Rushdie's "deft reversal of the oriental gaze" by depicting Mughal India as "more tolerant, philosophical and progressive than Europe" (Ben Amara 2011).

I wonder why it would be so appealing for these critics, variously located in the US, India, and Europe, to stress the eurocentrism of secularism and humanism, Rushdie's celebration of the imaginative syncretism of an east-west dialogue, and the progressiveness of Akbar's empire. Akbar's syncretism encompassed a geographical locale designated as present-day India. Rushdie's syncretism as expressed through *EF* absorbs a wider geographical sweep, encompassing India and Italy, and also assumes an historical sweep by imagining Renaissance Florence and Mughal Sikri from the vantage point of early twenty-first-century New York City. It is part of the American liberal fantasy that there *can* be such practices of tolerance across widely differing cultures and time periods. At the same time, it is American imperial hegemonies that unimaginatively reduce the other, so often Muslim and Asian, to racist stereotypes.

Akbar in *EF* becomes the metonym not just of Islam, but an Islam in the shadow of 9/11. Renaissance Florence is pleasing to Europe's image of itself—as part of secularism as ideology, as I discussed in the Introduction—as the enlightened, creative generator of greatness in the sciences and arts, rediscovering its earlier classical glories. Akbar is also an image that mollifies European and American fear of the intolerant and religiously fanatical Muslim. Akbar's pluralist Sikri would be pleasing to those Indians, whether they identify as secularists or not, who like to imagine a progressive, inclusive future for the nation. After the violence of 9/11, here is Rushdie's novel offering succouring images of creativity, tolerance, and potential—from two historical locations of great artistic and cultural achievement—to at least American and Indian readers. When criticism identifies the syncretism and laudable heterogeneities of Rushdie's novel, it comes to *constitute* the affirmation of syncretism that the novel thematizes and inaugurates. If the *fatwa* came before *The Satanic Verses*, then syncretism continues after *The Enchantress of Florence*.

Justin Neuman has argued that the novel represents "nonsecular atheism, a modernity divorced from rationalism, and a vision of the encounter with fiction as enchantment rather than the willing suspension of disbelief" (Neuman 2008: 682). I agree with Neuman's argument about a nonsecular atheism, represented by Akbar, who in *EF* does not pray but meditates at the mosque. I also agree with the creative potentials of enchantment. I would, however, reverse "modernity divorced from rationalism" and state that Akbar represents a rationalism divorced from modernity, because modernity was always already presented as a supremely rationalist and rationalizing project in India, as has been demonstrated by numerous scholars, including Ashis Nandy. Akbar is of course not postcolonial (instead, very much colonial), but the point holds about Rushdie's postcolonial attention to an historical figure of rationality not derived from western political or philosophical traditions.

Especially for the postcolonial nation, modernity appears *as* rationality, but like western secularism hiding its origins in Christianity, and orientalism hiding its origins in secularism and Christianity, modernity hides the fact that it is simply one way of doing things, that it is not the only and exclusive site of rationality. In Chapter 1 on *The English Patient*, I argued for postsecularism as a critique of nation as a secular religion, by drawing upon Gil Anidjar's argument that secularism always has the bigger bombs and the actual weapons of mass destruction, a secularism that divides the world into what counts as real and human (Anidjar 2006: 64). In the context of *EF*, I can deepen this argument by stating that by provincializing modernity and rationality, postsecular momentousness challenges the hegemony of secularism as the only site of the modern and the rational.

This postsecularism is no mere aesthetic celebration or aesthetic nicety. The violences and tragedies of postcolonial India, and the longer histories of violence before Independence, are undoubtedly alive in Rushdie's mind (the dates alone are potent enough: 1857, 1919, 1922, 1992, 2002). Rushdie is inspired by Indian secularism to maintain a literary and creative position that respects both the Islam of Sikri and the Christianity of Florence. At the same time, the enchantment that he pursues is that of at least syncretism: the ethical possibilities of empathy, respect, understanding, sensitivity, and acceptance.

This enchantment is not simply aesthetic triviality. The unforgettable tragedies of the postcolonial, the searing violence and pain of history and of the shattered, sharded present, command seriousness and sensitivity. Each of the writers I discuss in this book has a deep connection to India or Sri Lanka, by birth or upbringing, and I do not think they would deliberately trivialize, ironize, or sentimentalize the struggles they have seen their countries endure. It is this memory (even "cultural memory" has now become too standard and anaesthetized a term) that prevents them from creating literary art that provides merely nice enchantments. And we too as readers can inhere in that seriousness and sensitivity, to witness their art, and see how enchantment can be *an* example of the work of the imagination, to remember and re-think history by re-imagining it. This is not enchantment as a merely secular, recreational form. Instead, it can be part of a search for *values*: what should we value, how should we live?

It is here that I want to turn again to Rushdie's affirmation of the syncretic potentials of art. As in *The Moor's Last Sigh*, *The English Patient*, *The Everest Hotel*, *The Satanic Verses*, and *Anil's Ghost*, the figure of ekphrasis is also significant in *EF*, through Rushdie's references to Akbar's *Hamzanama* paintings. The *Hamzanama* is an epic sweep of fourteen-hundred paintings depicting the adventures and journeys of Hamza, a figure who was part historical, part fictional. The historical Hamza was a warrior, and an uncle of the prophet Muhammad. Shortly after his death, Hamza became the fictional Amir Hamza, featuring in fantastical tales describing his heroic conquests and adventures. Some of these stories might have flourished prior to the historical Hamza, and still others might describe another Hamza, who fought against Haroun al-Rashid, the caliph of Baghdad, himself featured in fiction through *The Thousand and One Nights*.

As I discussed earlier in the chapter, Haroun al-Rashid inspired the names of the father and son protagonists—Haroun and Rashid—in *Haroun and the Sea of Stories*. Given his life and work, Haroun al-Rashid represents a synthesis of cultures and religions. To show him being attacked in these paintings is not necessarily a comment by Rushdie on the loss of culture and creativity. Quite the opposite: more significant is what the *Hamzanama* as a *whole* represents to Rushdie. Akbar had commissioned the *Hamzanama* in 1557, when he was fourteen years old. The project took fifteen years to complete. It represents the collaboration of over a hundred artists from throughout India, each bringing the best of their regional and religious traditions, and supervised by two Persian grand masters. In contrast to Renaissance Florence, there was no great emphasis on celebrating individual genius in the Mughal India of Sikri. Instead, it is Akbar himself who emerges as an overartist, what Rushdie terms a "many-headed, many-brushed composite artist" (Rushdie 2010: 190).[5] For Rushdie, the values that emerge from this synthesis and collaboration are the creative powers of dreaming, genuine and robust philosophical inquiry, tolerance, inclusivity, and creativity itself. Rushdie's respect and admiration for these aspects of Akbar's imaginative and philosophical engagement with religion and art are clear. Indian secularism is alive in Rushdie's mind, for he has stated that the *Hamzanama* stands as a brilliant counterexample against the self-victimizing complaints of the Hindu right that the historical Muslim rulers "crushed and stifled the 'true' Hindu India" (Rushdie 2010: 190).

Rushdie also affirms the secular spirit of the *Hamzanama* in *The Satanic Verses*, when Zeenat and Saladin visit Changez Chamchawala's private art collection. Zeenat admires the paintings as representations of the strengths and virtues of hybridity in Indian art. This is consonant with Zeenat's affirmation of art that I presented at the opening of this chapter: art as cosmopolitan, enabling, and pointing to possible new futures. In *EF*, Dashwanth is the gifted painter commissioned by Akbar to lead the production of the epic *Hamzanama* paintings. Dashwanth paints the beautiful Qara Köz in a series called the *Qara-Köz-Nama*. Qara Köz also comes to life through the stories told by Mogor dell'Amore. Magical realism abounds in *EF*. After completing the *Qara-Köz-Nama*, Dashwanth leaves the "real" world and enters the painting itself, appearing as a small figure at the bottom-left corner of the canvas.

Narrating stories of Qara Köz, the Mogor claims that he is Akbar's uncle. Akbar is willing to entertain this notion and listens to Mogor's stories about the fantastical and real Qaras. Some members of Akbar's court dismiss Mogor and his tales; Akbar describes those skeptics as lacking imagination and opposing "all intrusions of dreamworlds into the real" (312). This sense of the dreamworld continues within Qara Köz herself: "Qara Köz understood even while she was dreaming that she was all the people in the dream. [. . .] [S]he was floating outside herself and watching her own story as if it were happening to someone else, without feeling anything, without permitting herself to feel. She was her mirror as well as herself" (294, 295). This is strikingly similar to Gibreel's hallucinations of the Angel Gibreel. There is a cord of light that extends between the navels of the two, and Gibreel does not know who is dreaming whom (Rushdie 1988: 111). We can thus detect a certain consistency in Rushdie's affirmation of dreamworlds in *The Satanic Verses* and the novel currently the most removed in time from *The Satanic Verses*. If after 9/11 Rushdie's secularism has become hardened, so too has he continued to affirm the imaginative, open-minded capacities of dreamworlds, ones that can negotiate between and challenge the values, potentials, and boundaries of secularism and religion.

In Gauri Viswanathan's November 2008 public discussion with Salman Rushdie, she highlights Amartya Sen's invocation of Akbar as a proto-secular, syncretic figure in India. Rushdie acknowledges this, but also draws attention to the moments of oppression in Indian history, such as that of Hindus by Muslims, and vice versa. One example is the intolerance and the violence of Aurangzeb, only the third king after Akbar. So that although there might be great historical examples of tolerance, there are also its opposites, ones that continue into the present. This again informs Rushdie's secular resistance to religion, when he notes the violence in the world, "of death and bombs and destruction and hatred and distrust" (Rushdie and Viswanathan 2008). Although he is no utopianist, Rushdie agrees with Viswanathan that he has a sense of "alternative political futures," ones marked by debate and argumentation. Equally, one can imagine what one does not like: "I believe in the argument, and if you are by nature satirical in your imagination it's always easy to see what you don't like" (Rushdie and Viswanathan 2008).

Viswanathan observes that although Akbar is highly rational, he is also fascinated by the power of magic and miracles. Rushdie states that there is a mystery in the way stories are created. All religions, in answer to the question of how to live life, come to offer not just stories, but also inquisition and oppression. Echoing his skepticism in 2005 toward priests (Rushdie 2005), Rushdie states he does not want his answers to come from a priest. Instead, it is debate itself that can point to reasonable options and possibilities: "debate itself is the thing from which flows the ethical life" (Rushdie and Viswanathan 2008). At the same time, Rushdie speaks of his constant battle with feeling obliged to use language "that has been shaped by religion in order to express things that may not have a religious purpose" (Rushdie and Viswanathan 2008). The magical and the miraculous, of which magical realism is one expression, are examples of this intimacy between the religious and the non-religious.

This intimacy is reproduced in Akbar's distinction between God's ethics as controlled and promulgated by religious dogma, and ethics as derived and affirmed by the people themselves, through their secular experiences, and by their inner strength and power, such as rationality. Yet, for Akbar, magic has a power and potency that is invulnerable to the appropriations and misuses to which religion is liable. In *EF*, Akbar feels that "[God's] existence deprived human beings of the right to form ethical structures by themselves. But magic was all around and would not be denied, and it would be a rash ruler who pooh-poohed it. Religion could be rethought, re-examined, remade, perhaps even discarded; magic was impervious to such assaults" (318). Magic represents creativity, the ability to invent forms that challenge conceptions of the real and the possible. I do not think Rushdie is dismissing religion entirely. Instead, certain forms of religious practice can also open possibilities of positive expressions.

Shalimar the Clown (2005) and *The Enchantress of Florence* (2008) appear simultaneously with Faisal Devji's *Landscapes of the Jihad* (2005) and *The Terrorist in Search of Humanity* (2008), demonstrating that, especially after 9/11, literary fiction's humanization of the question of terror finds parallel efforts in academic scholarship seeking to understand and uncover the humanistic and ethical rather than merely reactive dimensions of terrorism. Such understanding finds itself in one critic's observation that *Shalimar the Clown* challenges the "orthodox interpretations" of terrorism (Kempner 2009: 53). Rushdie humanizes terrorism, and does so by delving into the life of Shalimar, investigating how a handsome young man of *Kashmiriyat* could develop (not devolve) into a disfigured militant full of lethal hate.

Similarly, Rushdie humanizes privilege, exploring how a beautiful young woman with among the best the west can offer can develop (not devolve) into murdering another person. An example of such humanizing effort is to look for something common among peoples. For Rushdie, the trope of a mirror allows him to assert, in *Shalimar the Clown*, that violence reflects and reproduces itself across places as diverse as Los Angeles, Strasbourg, Kashmir, Tiananmen Square, and Soweto (Rushdie 2006: 355). That same mirror, in *The Enchantress of Florence*, will allow for communication between dreamworlds and real worlds. In both novels, the mirror conveys the semiotic power of the binary, the one *in* the other.

For Faisal Devji, the courage and fearlessness exhibited by terrorists are, in their eyes, the expression of virtue and the voice of a humanity that is otherwise oppressed by suffering and injustice. That humanity thus "speaks" through the fearlessness and courage of violence, which points to a kind of posthuman body without organs. According to Devji, "having destroyed the body as a subject within which such human virtues [courage and fearlessness] could be grounded, and dismissed life itself as the limit of humanity, militant practices like suicide bombing open up a space for the posthuman" (Devji 2008: 221). If Dashwanth and Mogor dell'Amore can leave the real world and enter the world of paintings, then so too can terrorists enter paintings, becoming pictures of birds.

To elaborate the idea of the posthuman, Devji refers to the artwork of militants, which often contains images of birds. These birds, particularly green ones, represent the souls of dead terrorists, at times echoing the image in the Qur'an of Muhammad as a white dove, one that is protected inside a cave covered by a spider's web. Like a thousand cells relentlessly multiplying as the US wages a war against an abstract noun, what I might call the "terrorist aesthetic" always already constitutes its own abstraction through the posthuman, the abstraction of "posthuman" mirroring the abstraction of "terror" (war relies on annihilation; the posthumans say they are already dead, and then reject the distinction between "life" and "death"). To suggest such a mirroring would be an affront to the arrogance and narcissism of imperial power. But it can also be a humanization (on their own terms, not on imperialism's terms) of the other who has always already been dehumanized.

To use a term like "terrorist aesthetic" might then be an instance of strategic essentialism: the use of "terrorist" draws attention by invoking an essentializing term, which then might strategically lead toward further consideration of that work, perhaps seeing the "humanity" of such people. The raid of Osama bin Laden's compound in Pakistan uncovered boxes of poetry written by members of Al-Qaeda and the Taliban. According to Faisal Devji, "these poets criticize the idea of human rights that coalition forces are supposedly fighting to protect in their country. Instead, they voice notions of humanity that are linked to private duties like generosity, compassion and, indeed, nonviolence" (Devji 2012: SR7). This criticism of human rights resonates with my argument in Chapter 3 on *Anil's Ghost* and the limitations of human rights interventions in Sri Lanka, limitations which lead Ondaatje to explore what might constitute humanitarianism—including the generosity, compassion, and nonviolence of which Devji writes.

The secularist and humanist in Rushdie would resist any privileging of the terrorist's position. But the artist in Rushdie could appreciate the theoretical parallel between the imaginary of terrorism and that of magical realism, both entering acts of creativity that reimagine what constitutes the real and the human. This is similar to the Kashmir liberation front's understanding of freedom in *Shalimar the Clown*: "Freedom to choose folly over greatness but to be nobody's fools" (253). "Folly" here can be magical realism and the posthuman; "greatness" can be the hegemonic conventions of realism and humanity. Shauna Singh Baldwin in *What the Body Remembers* secularizes the story of Ram and Sita by not only offering parallels with the lives of Roop, Satya, and Sardarji, but also by giving voice to the neglected role of Sita's agency in choosing to take her own life. The Ram and Sita story also appears in *Shalimar the Clown*, and Rushdie also secularizes this story. Lakshman draws an enchanted line around Sita (the line here repeating the trope of Shalimar's line of flight from prison) so that no one can harm her (49). But when Ravan abducts Sita, violence breaks loose, resulting in "rivers of blood" (49). The rivers of blood in Enoch Powell's incendiary speech appear as a trope in *The Satanic Verses* (1988: 97), and in *Shalimar the Clown* Rushdie links the rivers of blood with the enchantment of Hindu mythology. The two worlds could not be more removed: the ancient enchanted world of Hindu mythology, the contemporary world of racially-charged England. Yet, Rushdie's linking is not merely whimsical or trivial. If nothing else, the novel's semioethical commitment indicates its seriousness. To rephrase in the terms of the novel's statement that freedom is being free to choose folly, but also to be nobody's fools: magical realism and posthumanity can offer postsecular enchantment, but they are grounded in and shaped by secular struggle and survival, and are thus nobody's fools.

6.5   Conclusion

After 9/11, Rushdie reaffirms his belief in secularism. At the same time, his works continue to flourish with an array of fantastical and magical representations. In the beginning of his essay "The Composite Artist," Rushdie states that he has set *The Enchantress of Florence* in an historical period of enormous change and development, in Renaissance Florence and Mughal India—and that "our own" is a similarly transformative historical moment (Rushdie 2010: 183). The Rushdie Affair has come to constitute part of the momentousness of this living history, what Casanova has called the resurgence of religion in public life (Casanova 1994: 10). In Chapter 5, the postsecular values I identify in *The Satanic Verses* include literature itself, the migrant's perspective, hybridity, newness, and love. These values continue in Rushdie's fiction after 9/11. The *continuity* of Rushdie's affirmation of such postsecular values, in spite of the terror of a death sentence, not only demonstrates his personal strength but affirms the enduring creative power of writing.

I concluded Chapter 5 on *The Satanic Verses* by reading a passage in which Brickhall is ablaze from fires fuelled by race riots. Hanif comforts his girlfriend Mishal, asking her to stay with him, because the world is real, they have to live in it, and to live on. Rushdie's fascination with secular survival continues in *Shalimar the Clown*: "*The world does not stop but cruelly continues* [. . .] . [. . .] [*Y*]*ou wonder at it, the world's capacity for continuing*" (330; italics original). *The Enchantress of Florence* is similar to *The English Patient*: both are set in historical periods, and have an enormous geographical sweep, demonstrating both authors' efforts at making sense of times of great change, and the affirmations that can emerge within and from such transformation.

By the same token, *Shalimar the Clown* is similar to *Anil's Ghost*. Both show their authors focusing on regions with great personal emotional resonance for them, Kashmir and Sri Lanka, and again searching for some form of positivity that can emerge from such particular contexts. In *Shalimar the Clown*, *Kashmiriyat* emerges as the alternative to the limitations of Nehruvian secularism. Like the semioethics of *Anil's Ghost*, there are semioethical moments throughout *Shalimar the Clown* as Rushdie calls readers' attention to how a charmed village like Pachigam could be so brutally destroyed by militants. Some passages of the novel are filled with rhetorical, compelling, compassionate questions reflecting on justice (335, 341, 343) and violence (308), whereas still others describe violence and despair by removing the names of people, cities and villages, as if they could be any village, city, or people (292–294).

Yet, the novel is also liable to insensitivity, which is one of the vulnerabilities of postsecularism that I have been addressing throughout this book. As Supriya Chaudhuri has observed, *Shalimar the Clown* is a rich, linguistically impressive representation of Kashmir, but Rushdie's "making that memory [. . .] an effect of language [. . .] sacrifices the reality of loss and suffering, and demonstrates the inability of nostalgia to reconstitute the past" (Chaudhuri 2009: 278). I agree with Chaudhuri, and also return to my assertion about *The Satanic Verses*: the novel might have been banned, and it might have been burned, but it was also written. The souls of terrorists might reincarnate as green birds, but those birds are also art. Haroun and Luka restore their father's storytelling capacity, but it is art that tells us so. If the *fatwa* comes after the art of *The Satanic Verses*, then art will also always be "after" the *fatwa*. If religion and secularism are face-to-face in the dark, whether poised antagonistically or amicably, then postsecularism is the name of the possibility of their encounter, an encounter made of human choices. That encounter signals epistemic changes—and its futures are unknown.

Figure 9   Ta Prohm Temple, Angkor, Cambodia. Photograph by the author.

7 The Known and The Unknowable

Amitav Ghosh's *The Hungry Tide* and Mahasweta Devi's "Pterodactyl, Puran Sahay, and Pirtha"

Among other works we could consider through the lens of postsecularism are Amitav Ghosh's *The Hungry Tide* (2005) and Mahasweta Devi's novella "Pterodactyl, Puran Sahay, and Pirtha" (1995). I have chosen these works despite Mahasweta Devi's being a Bangla writer, as these two writers form part of the metropolitan canon of South Asian postcolonial literature, and, as I stated in the Introduction, they are able to straddle at least two different worldviews. Ghosh wrote *The Hungry Tide* after 9/11 and diasporically from New York City, which informs his reflections on how understanding can occur across the real and imagined borders of at least nation, gender, religion, and class, including animism. Similarly, Devi represents how understanding can or cannot occur across the divides of religion, how animism can or cannot be understood by someone inside India but outside the lifeworld of the tribals. Both these texts force readers to reflect upon what it is possible to know and what might be inherently unknowable.

7.1 Amitav Ghosh's *The Hungry Tide*

The Hungry Tide is set in the Sunderbans, remote tide islands and a vast mangrove forest located in the Bay of Bengal, stretching across India and Bangladesh in the world's largest delta. Ghosh gives prominence in *The Hungry Tide* to the myth of the goddess Bon Bibi, who represents a sort of animism. The peoples living in the Sunderbans pray to Bon Bibi for protection from attacks by the islands' tigers, whom they believe are disguises assumed by a demon. The Bon Bibi myth is syncretic, representing influences from Islam and Hinduism, as well as from several languages, including Arabic, Arakenese, Bengali, English, and Hindi. This multireligious and multilingual character reflects the myth's removal from dominant, conventional forms of belief. Ghosh undertakes a certain risk by exploring the possibilities of belief that stand counter to overarching religious, metropolitan, and national beliefs and knowledges. The Sunderbans' physical separateness from the Indian and Bangladeshi mainlands stands as a metaphor for that risk.

Among the historical events that Ghosh structures in this novel is the Partition of 1947, whereby the province of Bengal in British India became partitioned into West and East Bengal, the latter becoming a province of Pakistan. The aftermath of Partition saw the resettlement of those exploited and attacked by Muslim communalists and upper-caste Hindus in East Bengal (and later Bangladesh): the poor, most of whom were Dalits (Ghosh 2005: 98).[1] They became refugees in "secular India," where they found themselves resettled by the Indian government, including in the region of Dandakaranya in central-east India (Sengupta 2011: 104). It was this settlement that the poor then fled, turning to the tide country island Morichjhāpi. "Nation" might be considered the succour for the groups that sought "Pakistan." But the people who became refugees in the nation "India" challenge the myths of the nation as protective and benevolent, and as home. Both "Pakistan" and "India" failed them. I highlight these exclusionary, violent aspects of nationalism and nation to demonstrate their parallels with the violence of religion. It is this potential for violence that can link religion with nation, and thus at least doubly afflict and oppress groups of people through negative value-judgments such as untouchability, unworthiness, and undesirability.

The island of Morichjhāpi becomes a symbol of newness, a literally and figuratively new space that is alternative to the exclusionary violence of the nation-state. Ghosh does not sentimentalize or romanticize this "newness," certainly not given the history of Morichjhāpi. The state would still attempt to control those who sought refuge in Morichjhāpi: in 1979, the peoples on the island were massacred by police cadres of the West Bengal government in a campaign to remove them from the island (Sengupta 2011: 116). Ghosh structures the dichotomy of romantic and realist perspectives through the characters Nirmal and his wife Nilima, respectively. Nirmal is the idealist, the Marxist who seeks a society where all can be equals and enjoy freedom; Nilima is the realist and pragmatist, aware of the obstacles in creating any new society. Whereas Nirmal is a secularist skeptical of religion, the idea of revolution is the "secret god" that inspires and motivates him (100). The tide country for him exemplifies, embodies, and literalizes the idea of change, flux, and permanent transformation, and thus creativity. Nirmal's secularism resembles the secularism of the landlord Mirza in the Ayesha episode of *The Satanic Verses*, which I discussed in Chapter 5. It seems writers create a dichotomy in order ultimately not only to collapse it, but to do so by positing an "in between" which allows such collapse. For Rushdie, a literal—and also magical realist—leap of faith allows Mirza at last to "enter" the lifeworlds that Ayesha had been prophesying (Rushdie 1998: 506). For Nirmal and Nilima, their attitudes might be romantic and realist, but they both dedicate their lives to creating change on the islands, toward building a just society, and it is their observable progress in doing so that continues to affirm their work.

Linked with this creativity of the tide islands is Nirmal's fascination for the syncretism of faith represented by Bon Bibi, even though he might dismiss it as false consciousness. He describes a book which contains the text of the song of Bon Bibi. The language is Arabic, but the prosody is that of Bangla folklore. Nirmal surmises that the legend must have emerged in the late nineteenth or early twentieth century, as different settlers arrived at the tide country. In contrast to Salman Rushdie's phrase "rivers of blood" in *The Satanic Verses* (Rushdie 1988: 97), inspired by Enoch Powell's racially divisive speech, in *The Hungry Tide* there is the phrase "rivers of languages" (205), describing the influence of Bengali, English, Arabic, Hindi, and Arakenese on the song of Bon Bibi. In its syncretism, the Bon Bibi faith is similar to Rushdie's use of syncretism, through Akbar, in *The Enchantress of Florence*, and Allan Sealy's use of syncretism, through the historical Indian calendar, in *The Everest Hotel*. The appeal that syncretism seems to have for these writers, including Ghosh, is that it inheres in a form of belief while simultaneously recognizing the plurality of belief, thus moving beyond divisiveness.

It is the bridging of divides that Ghosh is also able to suggest through the novel's main protagonists, Piya and Fokir. For Piya, enchantment abounds: the dolphins offer a form of awe and wonder, like the wonder offered by nature in Allan Sealy's *The Everest Hotel*, as I discussed in Chapter 2. The rhythmic breathing of the dolphins becomes a melody that is echoed in the song of Fokir. The sea is a place of escape for Piya, free of the struggles and injustices of human society, a place where "she had never known the human trace to be so faint, so close to undetectable" (72). Piya's work, her scientific study of the dolphins, becomes a form of *dharma*, an ethics governing how she should live her life. The demands of her vocation—taking her to remote locations, with minimal, unpredictable funding—are satisfactory to her; she feels no need to apologize for her choices. The joy of her work lies in the inspiration of discovery, that the site of the everyday can be the site of the miraculous. Piya and Fokir come from different worldviews—Piya's work relies on geostationary satellites, Fokir's tools are made of shark bone and broken tile—yet Fokir's knowledge of the tide country becomes essential to the success of Piya's research.

The Hungry Tide resonates in many ways with other novels I have discussed in this book. As with Ondaatje's use of the desert in *The English Patient*, Ghosh makes use of an "other" space, the tide country, which allows Ghosh, like Ondaatje, to question differences of ethnicity and nation, and indeed the *ideas* of ethnicity and nation. Nirmal and Nilima establish the Badabon Trust, and *badabon* means "mangrove" in Bengali: it combines the Arabic name for desert, *badiya* (hence the word Bedouin), with the Sanskrit word for forest, *bon* (69). Juxtaposing Piya's diasporic difference against the special space of the tide country allows Ghosh to explore the possibilities, and impossibilities, of contact and knowledge between the privileged "subject" of diaspora, one with an American cultural influence informing her virtual blindness to caste hierarchies, and the relatively unprivileged "subaltern" of a remote part of India, for whom caste is a real divide.

Like *Anil's Ghost*, *The Hungry Tide* places a female diasporic character in dialogue with "local" knowledge experts and people. As Anil's stay in Sri Lanka humbles her knowledge of the country and its peoples, and indeed her ideas of what *constitutes* knowledge, so too Piya's travel into the Sunderbans brings alive for her, and also helps her appreciate, her difference from India. Unlike *Anil's Ghost*, where Anil at the end has the privilege of boarding a plane and leaving Sri Lanka while Sarath dies, the ending of *The Hungry Tide* has Piya remaining in the Sunderbans with the aim of establishing a research centre, intending to incorporate the local fishermen's expertise. Fokir does die, but Ghosh is careful to make his an "honourable" death. Piya's and Fokir's closest physical contact occurs when they are holding each other as they struggle to survive a tropical hurricane, the eye of which is about to pass over them. It is a riveting moment of the novel—Fokir is cradling Piya from behind, his face pressed against hers, his breath on her, and she is able to hear his last words: the names of his wife and son. Fokir is thus an "honourable" man, loyal and loving until the end to his wife and son, avoiding any threat from the emotional closeness that develops between him and Piya.

I agree with Pramod Nayar's view that in *The Hungry Tide* "the myths of the place teach the metropolitan human the inadequacy of knowledge, while at the same time proposing an alternative belief system" (Nayar 2010: 99). The concept of postsecularism can flesh out what Nayar sketches as an "alternative belief system." Despite their apparent differences, Piya and Fokir are able not only to communicate successfully, but to develop a mutual trust, even love. The divides that Ghosh wishes to bridge secularly include home (the indigenous Indian characters) and diaspora (Piya, America); the mainland (represented by Kanai) and the tide country; and the privileged and the subaltern. The Indian secularist principles of equality, and even American liberal notions of the free self (as opposed to the oppressions of caste), could inspire Ghosh to have Piya reach out to Fokir. There could be a certain sentimentalism, even stereotyping, in Ghosh's gesture. Does the divide between Piya and Fokir have to be so extreme, taking in differences of gender, nation, continent, caste, and language? I am not suggesting an absolute extremeness; to be sure, Ghosh's correspondence with Dipesh Chakrabarty on the latter's *Provincializing Europe* shows his acute sensitivity to the integrity and logic of "local" cultural and religious traditions, away from the hegemonies of modernity (Ghosh and Chakrabarty 2002).

Perhaps it is that sensitivity that informs the character of Kanai. As a mainland Hindu, caste-privileged man, Kanai comes to appreciate and respect the animism of the tide country, perhaps even learning from the "faith" that it represents. Kanai losing his uncle's rare notebook in the sea storm, watching it soar away into the vast sky, could stand as a metaphor for the tide country's requiring people to think outside traditional forms of knowledge and belief. Given the enormous physical struggles of life in the tide country, Ghosh appears to suggest that such a postsecular search requires courage, the courage to grow and to test oneself, with an openness to difference—qualities that Devi affirms in her novella "Pterodactyl, Puran Sahay, and Pirtha."

7.2 Mahasweta Devi's "Pterodactyl, Puran Sahay, and Pirtha"

In her novella "Pterodactyl, Puran Sahay, and Pirtha," Mahasweta Devi situates the indigenous world of Indian tribals against the majoritarianism of the Indian nation-state and shows the stark differences between the two. If one of the failures of the Indian nation-state is its inadequacy in eliminating caste inequalities, then a similar challenge can lie in the state's inadequate recognition of India's tribal populations. Devi rigorously portrays the injustices and calamities afflicting India's indigenous tribes: lack of education and employment, socially-engineered famines, malnutrition and starvation, lack of arable land, bonded labour, and child labour, to name only a few. In an interview with Gayatri Spivak, Devi relayed the following exchange: "A tribal girl asked me modestly, 'When we go to school, we read about Mahatma Gandhi. Did we have no heroes? Did we always suffer like this?'" (Devi 1995: xi). Such difference between the tribals and majoritarian India is reflected in the main character, Puran, a journalist sent to document the conditions in the drought-stricken village of Pirtha. As Puran's familiarity with Pirtha increases, the "logic" of the tribe—its worldview, its beliefs—begins to unfold for him, and he is humbled by the extent of his *difference* from them, and his inability to fully know and understand the tribe.

The eponymous pterodactyl enters the story in the form of a cave drawing by the child Bikhia. The bird represents the ancestral spirit of the tribe. Devi's vision is not a sentimentalizing one that creates friendship and rhapsodic epiphanies between Puran and Bikhia in the special space of the cave. Instead, Devi describes their differences as being "parallel" to each other (Devi 1995: 182).[2] Although Devi's vision is steadfastly "realistic," avoiding any romanticization, it is through this drawing, through the domain of the aesthetic, that Puran can gain some insight into the beliefs of the villagers. The pterodactyl comes to represent the miraculous. The tribe also comes to impute this miraculousness to Puran, because his visit coincides with the desperately-needed rainfall. Reflecting on the differences between Puran and the tribe, the narrator presents us with the question, "How can he have faith in their faith?" (186).

Spivak states: "For the modern Indian the pterodactyl is an empirical impossibility. For the modern tribal Indian the pterodactyl is the soul of the ancestors" (204). Devi explicitly avoids representing the tribals through the discourse of "religion." In doing so, she shows the difference, perhaps on behalf of the tribals, that Indian discourses and power structures like nation and citizenship must strive to understand, acknowledge, and hopefully accept and embrace. For the tribals, their animism is not "cultural identity," which is the concept and discourse that the nation-state would impute to them, through its apparatus of "modernity." Puran states, "How can one rob a people of the supernatural, of myth, what is in their understanding an unwritten history, when the present time has given them nothing?" (178). The nation-state and its policy of secularism have, in this respect, been inadequate in addressing the plight and cultural difference of the tribes. The tribals stand as the "other" to such a state policy. In fact, Devi's lesson seems to be that such understanding of belief requires respect across unknowability, that the animism of the tribals is not reducible to "identity," but is a secret to be preserved, as a condition of its survival. Puran's journey represents an ethical encounter with the other, without rational understanding, and one that requires humility, akin to Levinas's notion of being open to the other. The pterodactyl becomes a symbol of the tribals' primordial, non-verbal identity. As literary form, it can also mark the brink of a magical realist mode—again, to show the difference of the tribals' "belief system" from conventional modes of knowledge and representation.

As the translator of Devi's novella, Spivak is aware that the western academy can be vulnerable to viewing Devi's work as the voice for a so-called Third World "culture left behind" (Devi 1995: xxiv). Devi's text might be seen, as with Ondaatje's *Anil's Ghost*, to be semioethical, a literary representation inextricable from the desire to elicit ethical and ultimately political response, a commitment woven into the texture of the story. As a resident of India, an activist alongside the tribal peoples, and an organizer of such alliances as the Tribal Unity Forum, Devi is familiar with the tribals' struggles on a day-to-day basis. Any glib representation would constitute for her a form of literally "bad faith."

Although Devi, like Ondaatje, is driven to challenge the orthodoxies of development work and journalistic reporting, the critical difference for Devi is that she does not have Ondaatje's luxury of diasporic distance and the concomitant reflection, perhaps constitutively, of such luxury within the register of the aesthetic. For example, a cave in Ondaatje's *The English Patient* can be the site for a romance; Ondaatje constructs Almásy as a romantic hero, a characterization that could be offensive to those having connections with the historical Almásy, as I discussed in the conclusion to Chapter 1. There is no similar "romance" in *Anil's Ghost*, a novel somewhat closer to "home" for Ondaatje, set in Sri Lanka, and in the civil war unfolding at the time of writing. Yet the cave in both Devi's novella and *The English Patient* is a space where difference can be appreciated, of nation (in *The English Patient*) and of religion and ethnicity (in Devi's text).

In her preface to Mahasweta Devi's stories, Gayatri Spivak argues for the inextricability of Devi's literary production from her work as an activist. Spivak concludes by advocating what she calls "ethical singularity" (Devi 1995: xxv). By this she means one-to-one encounters between people, such as leaders and subalterns, and the radicals and the oppressed, when they both inhabit normality, not a crisis. This would be an engagement in which responses "flow from both sides," inspiring individuals to "reveal and reveal, conceal nothing" (Devi 1995: xxv). Yet not every leader can engage every subaltern in such a way—for example, during a political movement—hence the impossibility of such a full engagement. Concluding therefore that "ethics is the experience of the impossible," Spivak emphasizes that she does not mean that "ethics are impossible." She argues that

for a collective [political] struggle *supplemented* by the impossibility of full ethical engagement—not in the rationalist sense of "doing the right thing," but in this more familiar sense of the impossibility of "love" in the one-on-one way for each human being—the future is always around the corner, there is no victory, but only victories that are also warnings.

(Devi 1995: xxv; italics original)

If Ondaatje affirms a reconstructed Buddha statue as the "victory" of hope, such a gesture might also serve as a warning, as I demonstrated in Chapter 3, of the dangers of such "affirmation" in the middle of a political and national crisis. By refusing to repair the statue's damaged face, its uneven stone surface remaining fractured, Ondaatje might be signaling that such a reconstruction is an experience of the impossible. In a 2001 interview, he stated: "I hope *Anil's Ghost* is seen as a communal book, in a time when there seems to be little chance of a solution to the acts of violence, on all sides. Pacifism, reconciliation, forgiveness are easily mocked and dismissed words. But only those principles will save us" (Coughlan 2001).

When Spivak speaks of an "impossible" social justice, an "impossible" communication, an "impossible" undivided world, and ethics as the experience of the "impossible," I would suggest a "possible impossible" social justice, communication, undivided world, and experience of ethics. It is that paradoxical "possible impossibility" that informs postsecular gestures toward a non-secular secularism or a non-religious religion. The space of literature makes possible the glimpsing of and *witnessing* of a possible impossibility. Where Spivak might lament the impossibility of such ethics and justices, writers will invoke an *interestedness* that will allow the literary pursuit of the possible impossible.

When Mahasweta Devi states "[o]ur double task is to resist 'development' actively and to learn to love" (Devi 1995: xxii), I endorse her skepticism and optimism. Her skepticism toward "development" is replaced by the affirmative value of love, echoed in "Pterodactyl, Puran Sahay, and Pirtha": "To build [civilization] you must love beyond reason for a long time" (195). For Spivak, such "love" is marked by a conviction of the "sacredness" of human life:

> In order to mobilize for nonviolence [. . .] one relies, however remotely, on building up a conviction of the "sacredness" of human life. "Sacred" here need not have a religious sanction, but simply a sanction that cannot be contained within the principle of reason alone. [. . .] [I]t is my conviction that the inter-nationality of ecological justice in that impossible undivided world cannot be reached by invoking any of the so-called "great" religions of the world, because the history of their "greatness" is too deeply imbricated in the narrative of the ebb-and-flow of power.
>
> (Devi 1995: 199, 200)

The skepticism Spivak expresses about the ideologies of power with which conventional religion is implicated is reflected in the skepticism and cautiousness of the postsecular. But a manoeuvre is *made* nonetheless to move beyond the principle of reason alone. And that, as I have been arguing throughout this book, requires courage and risk.

Figure 10   Connaught Place, New Delhi, India. Photograph by the author.

Coda

Into the risks of absolute night: it is Derrida's image for the journeys undertaken in imagining a faith unaccompanied by dogma (Derrida 2002: 57; italics mine). For Derrida, this faith stands outside the opposition of reason and mysticism. This book has taken its own risks, and thus travelled through its own absolute nights, as it has explored the possible and impossible forms of belief that can exist outside the opposition of secularism and religion, an opposition similar to that between reason and mysticism.

I have argued that postsecularism can designate that possibilities and impossibilities of belief that emerge through and away from the violence of organized religion, the failures of state secularism, and the disenchantments of philosophical secularism. If writers explore some affirmative values in the wake of the ideologies of nation, religion, and secularism, those values are not teleological: they remain tenuous, fragile, experimental. A negotiation with and questioning of secularism is not unproblematic—any "postsecular faith" that might emerge risks devolving into sentiment. When such exploration occurs from the vantage point of diaspora, it carries the added risk of becoming politically insensitive to the nation which the novel depicts, or in which it is set, as with *Anil's Ghost*, *The Satanic Verses*, and *Shalimar the Clown*. Such diasporic insensitivity could also result in the trivialization of politics and real-world struggles. Postsecular gestures are also vulnerable to simply taking the place of a religion unless they are accompanied by a self-consciousness of their fragile and riskful trajectories.

Given the above dangers and vulnerabilities, the quest remains nonetheless to find some values. One of the most striking features in the entire process is that such a quest and questioning are enacted through *writing*. This represents a form of "faith" for writers, especially for Rushdie in the aftermath of the *fatwa*. Writing becomes a form of sharing, of witnessing, of sustaining interest, of affirming the human forms of community that are possible or that *might* be possible through acts of writing.

I say "might" because even though literature *as* literature might not provoke an immediate difference in people's attitudes and behaviour, the writer can at least *imagine* a readership, can imagine a possible form of community, and imagine solutions to the most intractable problems of his or her time. I argued in the Preface that a postsecular endeavour requires an enormous imaginative manoeuvre, one that can creatively and innovatively try to think through the problems and potentials of realities such as nation. The postsecular affirmations I have pursued in this book include friendship, art, literature, community, nature, the migrant's eye-view, newness, love. This book has not been an argument *for* the uniqueness or newness of these values, nor have I intended it as an uncritical celebration of the transformative powers of literature. Instead, I have sought to show how writers located in the forces of postcoloniality, diaspora, nation, minority identity, gender, secularism, and religion can pursue and represent what to them appear to be creative and productive relations, ethics, and possibilities that are worth affirming.

It is in the space of affirmation that the idea of humanism can circulate as a possibility, perhaps even as an ethical value. The violence of humanism, especially historically, is undeniable. Untold projects, travels, interferences, and interventions have been undertaken, justified, and legitimized in the name of ideologies like "we are all the same" or "they should be like us" or "love conquers all" or "let us enlighten them to the greatness of being human." But if we can read humanism as an ethics—for example, as non-violence and love toward the other, with humility and awareness of historical wrongs, and a commitment to genuine openness and acceptance of "other" worldviews—then what would the process of achieving and practising that humanism look like? The postsecular position takes the risk of affirming this humanism, with acute awareness of the fragility of that affirmation.

Although holding on to a notion of humanism and ethics, one which in part drove his commitment to the cause of Palestine, Edward Said has produced some of the most philosophically insightful and politically astute ideas on how we understand and misunderstand "others." Reflecting on the reception of *Orientalism* in the afterword to the book's 1994 edition, Said stated:

> [A]mong American and British academics of a decidedly rigorous and unyielding stripe, *Orientalism*, and indeed all of my other work, has come in for disapproving attacks because of its "residual" humanism, its theoretical inconsistencies, its insufficient, perhaps even sentimental, treatment of agency. I'm glad that it has! *Orientalism* is a partisan book, not a theoretical machine.
>
> (Said 1994: 339)

Insisting on the humanism informing his work, among Edward Said's favourite quotations was the following by Hugo of St. Victor: "The man who finds his homeland sweet is still a tender beginner; he to whom every soil is as his native one is already strong; but he is perfect to whom the entire world is as a foreign land" (Said 1984: 7). Said praises Hugo's model in that it allows one "to transcend the restraints of imperial or national or provincial limits"

(Said 1993: 335). But Said is quick to emphasize Hugo's belief that "the 'strong' or 'perfect' person achieves independence and detachment by *working through* attachments, not by rejecting them" (Said 1993: 336; italics original). Such a "working through" is essential in the circumstance of the person "whose actual condition makes it impossible to recapture that sweetness [of the homeland], and even less possible to derive satisfaction from substitutes furnished by illusion or dogma" (Said 1993: 336).

Anthony Alessandrini has invoked Said's notion of "working through" in arguing for Said's *emergent* rather than residual humanism, highlighting that Said's work marked a renewed beginning for humanism rather than a derivative or weak ending of it (Alessandrini 2000: 447). In the same sense, it is the notion of "working through" which constitutes the "humanism" of the postsecularism of fiction: working *through* secularism, nation, and religion, working *through* moments of crisis, working *through* the search for some affirmative values, working *through* the literary challenge of representing that which remains resistant to representation. If Said's humanism emerges through the framework of his secular criticism, then it may find its trajectory—its deepening and its continuing emergence—through what I have been exploring as postsecular writing and criticism.

If it is the urgency of worldly crises that invigorates writers' search for some affirmative values, then that is also the urgency that has informed this book's effort at interrogating and examining how writers can affirm and represent those values. In an article in *The New York Times*, Peter Steinfels states that, contrary to expectations, as history has marched on, religion has not quietly retreated into insignificance, but has now assumed a greater public presence (Steinfels 2002). Written in the aftermath of 9/11, this article recognizes the challenge of how a secularized, highly industrialized society like the US must live with the public power of religion. As a continued sign of this recognition, the 2011 volume *The Power of Religion in the Public Sphere* brings together American and European intellectuals to debate secularism and to reflect upon its potential for newness.

It is through this potential for newness—recognizing the challenges within nations, such as the US, and the challenges across nations—that I have pursued postsecularism as a search for values that can retain the best features of religion and secularism. Arvind-Pal Mandair has elegantly argued for untranslatability, that the secular of India is different from the secular of Europe, and therefore postsecularism in both regions would also be different (Mandair 2009: 5). There are examples in this book of the postsecular in India and Sri Lanka as it has been imagined by and through literature. If literary space can demonstrate untranslatability, could scholars and leaders learn from that untranslatability? If writers take the risk of affirming an affirmation, to imagine through and beyond the divides of secularism, religion, ethnicity, nation, and culture, what lessons can emerge for aspirations toward making a valuable difference?

Two figures, to conclude: Valentine Daniel, Puran Sahay. A Sri Lankan girl who has witnessed her father's dead body dragged away by a jeep of thugs urges Daniel, who stands in her eyes as a man who has "seen the world," to write her story, to let the world know what happened (Daniel 1996: 105). Puran, finding himself venerated by the tribe for bringing rain to their village, states: "To be a *miracle man* is a grave responsibility" (Devi 1995: 149; italics original). The act of writing—of telling a story, *the* story, *their* story—from a moment and place of crisis imbues writing with the potential for "miraculousness," the ability to inspire reaction and action. It begins the process of realizing a possible impossible communication and a possible impossible social justice, tenuously affirming survival and the ethical singularity of love. Such a process is not a manifesto for a new beginning; it is a courageous and modest imagining of how to make a difference.

Notes

Notes to the Introduction

1. Different definitions will emphasize differing dimensions of the secular, secular-ization, and secularism. For example, see Taylor (2007: 1–22), Casanova (2011: 54–74), Smith (2008: 1–19).
2. Rushdie adapted this essay from his Herbert Read Memorial Lecture, which was delivered on his behalf by Harold Pinter at the Institute of Contemporary Arts in London on February 6, 1990.
3. I vividly remember such an enactment of the *Ramleela* from my own childhood in India. The scale of the production was immense (especially from my child's view-point), the characters even frightening, but all ultimately dazzling and even divine-like in their scale and splendour.
4. For a discussion of postsecularism and caste, see Ganguly (2005). For discussions of secularism and South Asian literature, see Kumar (2008), Singh (2006), and Srivastava (2008). For discussions of secularism and postsecularism in religion and philosophy, with reference to South Asia, see Abeysekara (2008) and Mandair (2009).

Notes to Chapter 1

1. See Ibarrola-Armendariz (2000), Ty (2000), Visvis (2009), and Williams (1998); for a discussion of postnationalism in the film adaptation, see Hsu (2005).
2. All further references will be to this edition and will appear in parentheses in the main body of the text.
3. Gandhi here draws upon Charles Taylor's *Hegel* (1975), especially pages 153, 154, 156.
4. For an excellent article on the relations between multiculturalism and constitu-tional secularism in Canada, including their limitations and contradictions, see Berger (2008).

Notes to Chapter 2

1. All further references will be to this edition and will appear in parentheses in the main body of the text.

2. Both Sealy and Ondaatje are children of mixed colonial parentage, European and South Asian. Kipling, although not "racially" mixed, would qualify as Anglo-Indian within the former definition as any Briton living long-term in India. In Ashis Nandy's analysis, Kipling was "a tragic figure seeking to disown in self-hatred an aspect of his self identified with Indianness, which in turn was identified with victimization, ostracization and violence, because of a cruel first encounter with England after an idyllic childhood in India" (Nandy 1983: 37). Nandy describes Kipling's childhood stay in England as a boarder with the stern Mrs. Holloway (think of Cecelia in *The Everest Hotel*), during which he remained "a conspicuous bicultural sahib, the English counterpart of the type he was later to despise: the bicultural Indian babu" (Nandy 1983: 67). By "conspicuous" Nandy means that Kip was visibly "other," with the skin "of" an Indian. A similar conflict could exist for Sealy, as a metonym of the discriminations faced by Anglo-Indians. And such conflict can stand as a metaphor for the relation between the secular and the postsecular: to have to write within, negotiate within, emerge from, and re-think the very system that has produced you, in Sealy's case as "Anglo-Indian," but which cannot understand you, producing hate and sentiment alike: a split, at least bifurcated existence (religious/secular; Indian/British; home/diaspora) which you embody but elements of which you are trying to shed, re-invent.

    With the publication of *Red* in 2006, Sealy for the first time used the full version of his first name, Irwin, on the cover of a novel, and had this to say in an interview that same year: "I've been told [my name is] not Indian enough, that the kind of English reader who would look for 'Indian writing' would put my books down. So this is my response. Fuck you. This is who I am, it's also my father's name, it's also a tribute to him" (Roy 2006). The expletive indicates the depth of the contrastiveness in Sealy's mind between Englishness and Indianness. It is this contrastiveness of categories that writes through *The Everest Hotel*, not, I conjecture, as "minority-writing" (for that simply perpetuates a minority signifier like "Anglo-Indian"), but as self-exploration, opening an epistemic space whose trajectories are unknown but whose opening and exploration, via literary craft, is satisfying.

3. Frank Anthony describes Uttar Pradesh, the state immediately south of Uttarakhand, as "the spearhead of Hindi chauvinism" (Anthony 1969: 303), and tells the story of a group of politicians disrupting a parliamentary session (they eventually had to be removed) because a Bill was trying to be passed that would allow English to serve as the language of amendments to enactments originally made in English (Anthony 1969: 303). Is it ironic that Allan Sealy is now resident in Uttarakhand, and his novel shows signs of being inspired by two actions in the same region, that is, the 1970s Chipko movement (where women would hold on to trees to stop deforestation), and the protested construction of the Tehri dam?

4. Sealy has a particular liking for the colour red, as indicated in his novel *Red: An Alphabet* (2006). Among the inspirations for the use of red images in *Red* are Matisse's paintings "The Red Room" and "The Painter's Family." If we compare Sealy's use of red with that of Shauna Singh Baldwin in *What the Body Remembers*, we can appreciate the much greater force in Baldwin of the genderedness of experience, a gendering that I discuss in detail in Chapter 4:

> *Red, colour of blood, colour of anguish. Auspicious red, colour of bad blood, lehnga red, colour of brides, vermilion red marking married women, blood-on-the-sheets red, red filling my womb, garnet-red eye of the white peacock, poppy red, clot red, red of aloneness, threatening red that says "Beware, young girl, stop before speaking." That red.*
> *Betel-juice red.*
> *"Stop, don't love yet." That red.*
>
> (Baldwin 1999: 403; italics original)

5. The Indian constitution envisages personal laws as being a secular concession, in that allowing different personal laws to prevail gives each religious community the freedom to follow their "own" religious laws. Thus it is Christian personal law which does not recognize complete adoption, not the Indian state which disallows Christians from adopting, or only to the extent that the Indian state permits Christians to be ruled by their own personal laws. If religious communities choose to reform their personal laws to allow complete adoption, they are free to do so. Since Independence, efforts have been made by the state to pass a uniform and secular bill that would apply to all citizens, but some Muslims and Parsis have objected to a "secular" adoption law, which has forestalled such a law's development. It thus happens that only Hindu personal law accepts complete adoption. Within a legal framework, the Hindu Adoption and Maintenance Act (HAMA) of 1956 grants Hindus the right to adopt children. "Hindu" here also subsumes—contentiously, as in other parts of the constitution—Sikhs, Buddhists, and Jains. This Act does not apply to Christians, Parsis, Jews, and Muslims. Members of these religious communities can apply to "adopt" under the Guardians and Wards Act (GAWA) of 1890. GAWA, however, only gives parents rights as "guardians," and adoptees are "wards." Once adoptees reach age 21, they no longer remain a "ward." These children then cannot claim any right of inheritance; instead, the blood relatives of the guardians would be legally entitled to any inheritance, such as property, unless there is a will of course (but even that could be challenged by blood relatives).

   Shortly after the 1998 publication of *The Everest Hotel*, the Juvenile Justice (Care and Protection of Children) Act (2000) was passed. Amendments to the Juvenile Justice Act were made in 2006, which guaranteed two crucial rights. Firstly, Sec. 2 (aa) of the Act defines adoption as follows: "Adoption means the process through which the adopted child is permanently separated from his biological parents and becomes the legitimate child of his adoptive parents with all rights, privileges and responsibilities that are attached to the relationship" (*Juvenile Justice (Care and Protection of Children) Amendment Act, 2006* 2006: 2). This means adopted children have the same legal status as biological children, giving them the same rights, such as inheritance. Secondly, Sec. 41 (2) of the Act states, "Adoption shall be resorted to for the rehabilitation of the children who are orphan [sic], abandoned or surrendered through such mechanism as may be prescribed" (*Juvenile Justice (Care and Protection of Children) Amendment Act, 2006* 2006: 5). This means adoption could include an abandoned child like Masha.

   The Juvenile Justice Act is a step forward for secularism, for the Act affords all Indian citizens the right to adopt children who fall under its purview, irrespective of the religion of the parent or the child. When Minister Maneka Gandhi, during Parliamentary debates, was challenged to indicate whether the

Juvenile Justice Act would conflict with the HAMA, she displaced a religious language with a secular one by arguing that it was *children's welfare* at the heart of the matter, not religious issues (Kumari 2010: 120). The Juvenile Justice Act is legislation that is *enabling*, not one that is *forcing*, adoption on peoples. A possible conflict that could arise is that Hindus having a natural child cannot adopt a child of the same sex under the Hindu law, whereas the Juvenile Justice Act allows such an adoption. If there were a conflict between two legislations, the courts would have to resolve the matter. No such conflict has yet arisen; that is, courts have not had to decide the legality of an adoption under the Juvenile Justice Act. The Juvenile Justice (Care and Protection) Act is not, like political secularism itself, without its challenges. As Ved Kumari has argued, the "cooperation of various agencies involved in the system and coordination of their activities is necessary for ensuring care, protection, and developmental opportunities to all children as envisaged in the Act" (Kumari 2010: 163). For more information, see the website of the Central Adoption and Resource Authority (CARA): <www.adoptionindia.nic.in>. For their assistance in clarifying for me various aspects of the Juvenile Justice Act, I am grateful to Pratiksha Baxi, Ratna Kapur, and particularly Ved Kumari.

6.   See this article for comments on the book by Fatehally, Mukherjee, Sharma, and Singh.

Notes to Chapter 3

1.   All further references will be to this edition and will appear in parentheses in the main body of the text.

Notes to Chapter 4

1.   All further references will be to this edition and will appear in parentheses in the main body of the text.
2.   Khushwant Singh's novel *Train to Pakistan* tells the story of Partition from a Sikh perspective, with one of the characters, the sub-inspector, also expressing skepticism toward the Gandhian theories originating from those in power in Delhi: "What do the Gandhi-caps in Delhi know about the Punjab? What is happening on the other side of Pakistan does not matter to them. They have not lost their homes and belongings; they haven't had their mothers, wives, sisters and daughters raped and murdered in the streets" (Singh 1988: 31).
3.   When later historians from Pakistan and India would describe violence, their attitudes and stories would selectively construct violence, in turn stressing, according to Gyan Pandey, "the essential humanity of the 'host' nation [. . .] through examples where *the minority was protected, mercy displayed, and 'secularist' principles were upheld*" (Pandey 2008: 115; italics mine). And in Urvashi Butalia's words: "Pakistan came to be represented as the communal, abductor country, refusing to return Hindu and Sikh women, while India was the reasonable, and civilized non-communal country, fulfilling its moral obligations" (Butalia 2000: 152).
4.   The partridges might be separated by a barrier, but they are both inside a cage. There is a similar image in Aravind Adiga's *The White Tiger*, what Adiga calls

the "rooster coop" (Adiga 2008: 175). Servants have the task of delivering millions of dollars and briefcases of diamonds across the city, but never abscond with the goods. Seen from the vantage of class, what is the invisible cage here?

5.   For another Sikh woman's negotiations of a personal Sikhism, see the paintings of Arpana Caur, in particular those from her landmark solo exhibition "Nanak," held at the Academy of Fine Arts and Literature in New Delhi in December 2003. In this collection, and in contrast to the traditionally-sanctioned conservative representations of the guru as static and immutable, Caur depicts a dancing Nanak, a slim Nanak, a Nanak active and full of joy. In one painting, Caur depicts Nanak inside a large outline of a foot, to highlight his love for undertaking long journeys by foot (personal communication).

6.   And when the female child can speak back? Here is the response from daughters and granddaughters to their grandmother Ba, in Parita Mukta's memoir *Shards of Memories*:

>   we observe the alchemical magic with which she has changed her pain into a rill of gold whose burnish draws those who have been scarred into her presence. We pay tribute to her efforts, for we know that this is the ground of her daily *puja*. We hover around her, like anxious butterflies around a precious flower. We are chary of drinking of her sweetness, fearful of depleting this, intent always to say: 'Oh, but you are beautiful.' And swift comes the reply: 'Your eyes have made me so.'
>
>   (Mukta 2002: 18; italics original)

7.   I am grateful to Shauna Singh Baldwin for her feedback on my translation of this excerpt.

8.   For a theorization going against the grain of the logic that death is the narrative closure of a subaltern's life, and that the subaltern must die, see Sunder Rajan (2010: 128–131).

9.   The volume *Can the Subaltern Speak? Reflections on the History of an Idea*, edited by Rosalind C. Morris (2010), reflexively continues this work of challenging gendered ideologies, especially the essentialization of non-western women at the service of western freedoms. See also Brinda Bose's article "The (Ubiquitous) F-word" (2007), which reflects the multiplicities of South Asian feminisms, and the challenge of representing them all. In its ethical commitment and originality, Butalia's work is consonant with Uma Chakravarti and Nandita Haksar's 1987 volume *The Delhi Riots: Three Days in the Life of a Nation*, a collection of interviews with those who witnessed the 1984 massacre of Sikhs in New Delhi, and/or were involved in relief work.

10. Butler's original text states "violences," and she would of course be keen to assert a multiplicity of violences (Butler 2000: 37).

11. Compare Bachan Singh's story with that of Urvashi Butalia's interviewee Mangal Singh, who killed seventeen women and children in his family before crossing from Pakistan to India. Singh insists to Butalia that he did not "kill" his family members but instead "martyred" them. When asked by Butalia if the women and children had been afraid of death, Singh replied:

>   Fear? Let me tell you one thing. You know this race of Sikhs? There's no fear in them, no fear in the face of adversity. Those people [the ones who had been killed] had no fear. They came down the stairs into the big courtyard of our house that day and they all sat down and they said, you can make martyrs

of us—we are willing to become martyrs, and they did. Small children too
. . . what was there to fear? *The real fear was one of dishonour. If they had been
caught by the Muslims, our honour, their honour would have been sacrificed, lost. It's
a question of one's honour . . . if you have pride you do not fear.*

(Butalia 2000: 154; italics original)

Whose honour is at stake?

12. For differences between Indian and Euro-American (particularly American)
feminisms, see Madhu Kishwar (1990).

Notes to Chapter 5

1. All further references will be to this edition and will appear in parentheses in
the main body of the text.

Notes to Chapter 6

1. Jean Franco demonstrates the similar status of magical realism for the Latin
American writers Jorge Luis Borges and Juan Carlos Onetti, "in the service
of the secular reenchantment of literature." Franco argues that these writers
dislodge magic "from its source in popular religion and [associate it] with the
power to inspire unanchored belief" (Franco 2002: 10).
2. All further references will be to this edition and will appear in parentheses in
the main body of the text.
3. All further references will be to this edition and will appear in parentheses in
the main body of the text.
4. For discussion of non-European, pre-colonial premodernities in South Asia, see
Alam and Subrahmanyam (2012) and Pollock (2006).
5. I have derived the historical facts about Hamza and the *Hamzanama* from this
essay, which is a reprint of the lecture that Rushdie delivered under the same
title at the Hay Festival in London on May 25, 2008. Rushdie also delivered
a lecture with the same title as his inaugural address as visiting professor at
Emory University, on February 25, 2007.

Notes to Chapter 7

1. All further references will be to this edition and will appear in parentheses in
the main body of the text.
2. All further references will be to this edition and will appear in parentheses in
the main body of the text.

References

Abeysekara, Ananda (2008) *The Politics of Postsecular Religion: Mourning Secular Futures*, New York: Columbia University Press.

Abeysekera, Charles and Newton Gunasinghe (eds) (1987) *Facets of Ethnicity in Sri Lanka*, Colombo: Social Scientists' Association.

Adiga, Aravind (2008) *The White Tiger*, Noida, India: HarperCollins.

Ahmad, Dora (2005) "'This Fundo Stuff Is Really Something New': Fundamentalism and Hybridity in *The Moor's Last Sigh*," *Yale Journal of Criticism* 18.1: 1–20.

Ahmed, Akbar S. (1986) *Pakistan Society: Islam, Ethnicity, and Leadership in South Asia*, Karachi: Oxford University Press.

Aiyar, Yamini and Meeto Malik (2004) "Minority Rights, Secularism and Civil Society," *Economic and Political Weekly* 39.43: 4707–4711.

Aji, Aron R. (1995) "'All Names Mean Something': Salman Rushdie's 'Haroun' and the Legacy of Islam," *Contemporary Literature* 36.1: 103–129.

Alam, Muzaffar and Sanjay Subrahmanyam (2012) *Writing the Mughal World: Studies on Culture and Politics*, New York: Columbia University Press.

Alessandrini, Anthony (2000) "Humanism in Question: Fanon and Said," in Henry Schwarz and Sangeeta Ray (eds) *A Companion to Postcolonial Studies*, Oxford: Blackwell.

Anidjar, Gil (2006) "Secularism," *Critical Inquiry* 33: 52–77.

Anthony, Frank (1969) *Britain's Betrayal in India: The Story of the Anglo-Indian Community*, New Delhi: Allied Publishers.

Appadurai, Arjun (ed.) (1986) *The Social Life of Things*, Cambridge: Cambridge University Press.

Appiah, Anthony (1991) "Is the Post in Postcolonial the Same as the Post in Postmodern?," *Critical Inquiry* 17: 336–357.

Appignanesi, Lisa and Sara Maitland (eds) (1989) *The Rushdie File*, London: Fourth Estate Ltd.

Aravamudan, Srinivas (2006) *Guru English: South Asian Religion in a Cosmopolitan Language*, Princeton, NJ; Oxford: Princeton University Press.

Asad, Talal (1990) "Ethnography, Literature, and Politics: Some Readings and Uses of Salman Rushdie's *The Satanic Verses*," *Cultural Anthropology* 5.3: 239–269.

―― (1993) *Genealogies of Religion: Discipline and Reasons of Power in Christianity and Islam*, Baltimore: Johns Hopkins University Press.

―― (2003) *Formations of the Secular: Christianity, Islam and Modernity*, Stanford: Stanford University Press.

Asari, Farzaneh (1989) "Iran in the British Media," *Index on Censorship* 18.5: 9–13.

Atwood, Margaret (1985) *The Handmaid's Tale*, Toronto: McClelland and Stewart.

Bal, Mieke (2006) "Aestheticizing Catastrophe," in Michael Steinberg and Monica Bohm-Duchen (eds) *Reading Charlotte Salomon*, Ithaca: Cornell University Press.

Baldwin, Shauna Singh (1996) *English Lessons and Other Stories*, Fredericton, N.B.: Goose Lane.

—— (1999) "What the Body Remembers" (essay). Online. Available: <http://www.shaunasinghbaldwin.com/wtbressayo99.pdf>.

—— (2000) *What the Body Remembers*, Toronto: Vintage.

—— (2004) *The Tiger Claw: A Novel*, Toronto: Vintage.

—— (2007) *We Are Not in Pakistan: Stories*, Fredericton, N.B.: Goose Lane.

—— (2012) *The Selector of Souls: A Novel*, Toronto: Knopf Canada.

—— and Marilyn M. Levine (1992) *A Foreign Visitor's Survival Guide to America*, John Muir Publications.

Baxi, Upendra (1987) "'The State's Emissary': The Place of Law in Subaltern Studies," in Partha Chatterjee and Gyanendra Pandey (eds) *Subaltern Studies VII: Writings on South Asian History and Society*, Delhi: Oxford University Press.

——. (2002) *The Future of Human Rights*, New Delhi: Oxford University Press.

Behal, Suchitra (1998) "What Caught the Eye," *The Hindu* (Dec. 20) A37.

Ben Amara, Radhouan (2011) "Frontiers and Thresholds in Rushdie's Writings," Between 1.1. Online. Available: <http://www.between-journal.it/>.

Bennett, Jane (1996) "'How Is It, Then, That We Still Remain Barbarians?' Foucault, Schiller, and the Aestheticization of Ethics," *Political Theory* 24.4: 653–672.

Berger, Benjamin L. (2008) "The Cultural Limits of Legal Tolerance," *Canadian Journal of Law and Jurisprudence: An International Journal of Legal Thought* 21.2: 245–277.

Bhabha, Homi (1994) *The Location of Culture*, London: Routledge.

—— (1996) "Unpacking my Library . . . Again," in Iain Chambers and Lidia Curti (eds) *The Post-Colonial Question: Common Skies, Divided Horizons*, London: Routledge.

—— (1997) "Editor's Introduction: Minority Maneuvers and Unsettled Negotiations," *Critical Inquiry* 23: 431–460.

Bharatiya Janata Party (2012) "Hindutva: The Great Nationalist Ideology," *Bharatiya Janata Party Website*. Online. Available: <http://www.bjp.org/history/htvintromm-1.htm>.

Bhargava, Rajeev (1995) "Religious and Secular Identities," in Upendra Baxi and Bhikhu Parekh (eds) *Crisis and Change in Contemporary India*, Sage: New Delhi, 1995.

—— (ed.) (1998) *Secularism and Its Critics*, Oxford: Oxford University Press.

—— (2007) "The Distinctiveness of Indian Secularism," in T. N. Srinivasan (ed.) *The Future of Secularism*, New Delhi: Oxford University Press.

Bhatnagar, Rashmi, Renu Dube, and Reena Dube (2004) "Meera's Medieval Lyric Poetry in Postcolonial India: The Rhetoric of Women's Writing in Dialect as a Secular Practice of Subaltern Coauthorship and Dissent," *boundary 2* 31.3: 1–46.

Bilgrami, Akeel (2006) "Occidentalism, the Very Idea: An Essay on Enlightenment and Enchantment," *Critical Inquiry* 32: 381–411.

—— (2008) "Twenty Years of Controversy," in Daniel Herwitz and Ashutosh Varshney (eds) *Midnight's Diaspora: Critical Encounters with Salman Rushdie*, Ann Arbor: University of Michigan Press.

Blanchot, Maurice (1986) *The Writing of the Disaster*, trans. Ann Smock, Lincoln: University of Nebraska Press.

—— (1988) *The Unavowable Community*, trans. Pierre Joris, Barrytown, NY: Station Hill Press.

Bose, Brinda (2007) "The (Ubiquitous) F-word: Musings on Feminisms and Censorships in South Asia," *Contemporary Women's Writing* 1.1–2: 14–23.

Bradley, Arthur and Anthony Tate (2010) *The New Atheist Novel: Fiction, Philosophy and Polemic after 9/11*, London and New York: Continuum Books.

Breckenridge, Carol A. and Peter van der Veer (eds) (1993) *Orientalism and the Post-colonial Predicament: Perspectives on South Asia*, Philadelphia: University of Pennsylvania Press.

Brittan, Alice (2006) "War and the Book: The Diarist, the Cryptographer, and *The English Patient*," *PMLA* 121.1: 200–213.

Brown, Mick (1992) "Triumph of the History Men," *Daily Telegraph* [London] (Oct. 15): 17.

Buber, Martin (1958) *I and Thou*, trans. Ronald Gregor Smith, Edinburgh: T&T Clark.

Burcar, Lilijana (2008) "Re-Mapping Nation, Body and Gender in *The English Patient*," in Zoe Detsi-Diamanti, Katerina Kitsi-Mitakou, and Effie Yiannopoulou (eds) *The Flesh Made Text Made Flesh: Cultural and Theoretical Returns to the Body*, New York: Peter Lang.

Burrows, Victoria (2008) "The Heterotopic Spaces of Postcolonial Trauma in Michael Ondaatje's *Anil's Ghost*," *Studies in the Novel* 40.1–2: 161–177.

Bush, Catherine (1994) "Michael Ondaatje: An Interview," *Essays on Canadian Writing* 53: 238–249.

Butalia, Urvashi (2000) *The Other Side of Silence: Voices from the Partition of India*, London: Hurst and Company.

Butler, Judith (1990) *Gender Trouble: Feminism and the Subversion of Identity*, New York and London: Routledge.

——— (2000) "Restaging the Universal," in Judith Butler, Ernesto Laclau, and Slavoj Žižek (eds) *Contingency, Hegemony, Universality: Contemporary Dialogues on the Left*, London: Verso.

——— Jürgen Habermas, Charles Taylor, and Cornel West (2011). Eduardo Mendieta and Jonathan Van Antwerpen (eds) *The Power of Religion in the Public Sphere*, New York: Columbia University Press.

Cameron, David (2011) "PM's speech at Munich Security Conference," *The Official Site of the British Prime Minister's Office*. Online. Available: <http://www.number10. gov.uk/news/pms-speech-at-munich-security-conference/#>.

Canadian Charter of Rights and Freedoms (1982) *Department of Justice Canada Website*. Online. Available: <http://laws.justice.gc.ca/eng/charter/page-1.html>.

Casanova, Jose (1994) *Public Religions in the Modern World*, Chicago: University of Chicago Press.

———.(2011) "The Secular, Secularizations, Secularisms," in Craig Calhoun, Mark Juergensmeyer, and Jonathan Van Antwerpen (eds) *Rethinking Secularism*, New York: Oxford University Press.

Chakrabarty, Dipesh (1998) "Postcoloniality and the Artifice of History," in Ranajit Guha (ed.) *A Subaltern Studies Reader*, Minneapolis: University of Minnesota Press.

——— (2008) *Provincializing Europe: Postcolonial Thought and Historicizing Difference*, Princeton: Princeton University Press.

Chakravarti, Uma and Nandita Haksar (1987) *The Delhi Riots: Three Days in the Life of a Nation*, New Delhi: Lancer International.

Chandhoke, Neera (2003) *The Conceits of Civil Society*, New Delhi: Oxford University Press.

Chatterjee, Partha (1993) *Nationalist Thought and the Colonial World: A Derivative Discourse?*, Minneapolis: University of Minnesota Press.

Chaudhuri, Supriya (2009) "Translating Loss: Place and Language in Amitav Ghosh and Salman Rushdie," *Etudes anglaises* 3.62: 266–279.

Cheah, Pheng (2006) *Inhuman Conditions: On Cosmopolitanism and Human Rights*, Cambridge, MA: Harvard University Press.

Chopra, Rohit (2006) "Beyond Hybridity and Purity: Anglo-Indian Marginality and the Postcolonial Condition in *The Everest Hotel*," *South Asian Review* 27.1: 53–73.

Chu, Patricia (2006) "'A Flame against a Sleeping Lake of Petrol': Sympathy and the Expatriate Witness in Selvadurai's *Funny Boy* and Ondaatje's *Anil's Ghost*," in Rocio Davis and Sue-Im Lee (eds) Literary Gestures: The Aesthetic in Asian American Literary Discourse. Philadelphia: Temple University Press.

Comellini, Carla (2008) "Bodies and Voices in Michael Ondaatje's *The English Patient* and *Anil's Ghost*," in Merete Falck Borch, Eva Rask Knudsen, Martin Leer, and Bruce Clunies Ross (eds) *Bodies and Voices: The Force-Field of Representation and Discourse in Colonial and Postcolonial Studies*, Amsterdam, New York: Rodopi.

Connolly, William (1999) *Why I Am Not a Secularist*, Minneapolis: University of Minnesota Press.

Constitution of Sri Lanka (1978) *The Official Website of the Government of Sri Lanka*. Online. Available: <http://www.priu.gov.lk/Cons/1978Constitution/Introduction. htm>.

Coomaraswamy, Ananda (1956) *Mediaeval Sinhalese Art*, New York: Pantheon Books.

Coomaraswamy, Radhika (2000) "In Defense of Humanistic Way of Knowing: A Reply to Qadri Ismail," *Pravada* 6.9: 29–30.

Coughlan, Peter (2001) "Meander, If You Want to Get to Town: A Conversation with Michael Ondaatje" (Mar. 28) Online. Available: <http://www.kiriyamaprize.org/ winners/2000/2000ondaat_interview.shtml>.

Crane, Ralph (2008) "Contesting the Can(n)on: Revisiting *Kim* in I. Allan Sealy's *The Trotter-Nama*," *Journal of Postcolonial Writing* 44.2: 151–158.

Critchley, Robert (1992) *The Ethics of Deconstruction: Derrida and Levinas*, Oxford: Blackwell.

Curran, Beverley (2005) "Ondaatje's *The English Patient* and Altered States of Narrative," in Steven Tötösy de Zepetnek (ed.) *Comparative Cultural Studies and Michael Ondaatje's Writing*, West Lafayette: Purdue University Press.

Daiya, Kavita (2008) *Violent Belongings: Partition, Gender, and National Culture in Postcolonial India*, Philadelphia: Temple University Press.

Daniel, E. Valentine (1996) *Charred Lullabies: Chapters in an Anthropography of Violence*, Princeton: Princeton University Press.

Das, Veena (1990) *Mirrors of Violence: Communities, Riots, and Survivors in South Asia*, Delhi: Oxford University Press.

de Certeau, Michel (1998) *The Writing of History*, trans. Tom Conley, New York: Columbia University Press.

Deleuze, Gilles and Félix Guattari (1984) *Anti-Oedipus: Capitalism and Schizophrenia*, trans. Robert Hurley, Mark Seem, and Helen R. Lane, London: The Athlone Press.

—— (1986) *Kafka: Notes toward a Minor Literature*, trans. Dana Polan, Minneapolis: University of Minnesota Press.

—— (1987) *A Thousand Plateaus: Capitalism and Schizophrenia*, trans. Brian Massumi, Minneapolis: University of Minnesota Press.

Derrida, Jacques (1976) *Of Grammatology*, trans. Gayatri Chakravorty Spivak, Baltimore: Johns Hopkins University Press.

—— (1978) *Writing and Difference*, London: Routledge.

—— (ed.) (1982) *Margins of Philosophy*, Chicago: University of Chicago Press.

—— (1994) *Spectres of Marx: The State of the Debt, the Work of Mourning, and the New International*, trans. Peggy Kamuf, London: Routledge.

—— (. 2002) "Faith and Knowledge: The Two Sources of 'Religion' at the Limits of Reason Alone," in Jacques Derrida, *Acts of Religion*, ed. Gil Anidjar, New York: Routledge.

Devi, Mahasweta (1995) "Pterodactyl, Puran Sahay, and Pirtha," in Mahasweta Devi, *Imaginary Maps: Three Stories*, trans. Gayatri Spivak, London: Routledge.

Devji, Faisal (2008) *The Terrorist in Search of Humanity*, New York: Columbia University Press.

—— (2012) "The Poetry of Al Qaeda and the Taliban," *The New York Times* [New York edition] (May 13): SR7. Online. Available: <http://www.nytimes.com/2012/05/13/opinion/sunday/militant-ideals-captured-inpoetry.html?_r=2&ref=opinion>.

de Zoysa, Richard (1990) "Manifesto for an Alternative Society," *The Island* [Colombo] (Feb. 11): Sunday edition.

Dhareshwar, Vivek (1993) "Caste and the Secular Self," *Journal of Arts and Ideas* 25.6: 115–126.

Duara, Prasenjit (1995) *Rescuing History from the Nation: Questioning Narratives of Modern China*, Chicago and London: University of Chicago Press.

Eagleton, Terry (1990) *The Ideology of the Aesthetic*, Cambridge: Basil Blackwell.

Faris, Wendy (2004) *Ordinary Enchantments: Magical Realism and the Remystification of Narrative*, Nashville: Vanderbilt University Press.

Farmer, B. H. (1963) *Ceylon: A Divided Nation*, London: Oxford University Press.

Feuerbach, Ludwig (1854) *The Essence of Christianity*, trans. Marian Evans, London: J. Chapman.

Franco, Jean (2002) *The Decline and Fall of the Lettered City: Latin America in the Cold War*, Cambridge: Harvard University Press.

"Freedom of Religion Bill" (2005) *Sri Lanka Department of Government Printing*. Online. Available: <http://documents.gov.lk/Bills/2005/Freedom of Religion/PL 000387 Freedom of Religion (E).pdf>.

Freeman, Michael (2004) "The Problem of Secularism in Human Rights Theory," *Human Rights Quarterly* 26: 375–400.

Freud, Sigmund (1959) *Collected Papers: Authorized Translation under the Supervision of Joan Rivière*, New York: Basic Books.

Ganapathy-Dore, Geetha (1993) "The Novel of the Nowhere Man: Michael Ondaatje's *The English Patient*," *Commonwealth Essays and Studies* 16.2: 96–100.

—— (1997) "Allan Sealy's *The Trotter-Nama*: A Postcolonial Synchronicle," *The Journal of Commonwealth Literature* 32: 67–78.

Gandhi, Leela. *Postcolonial Theory: A Critical Introduction*. Edinburgh: Edinburgh University Press, 1998.

—— (2006) *Affective Communities: Anticolonial Thought, Fin-de-Siècle Radicalism, and the Politics of Friendship*, Durham and London: Duke University Press.

Gandhi, M. K. (1997) *Hind Swaraj and Other Writings*, ed. Anthony J. Parel, Cambridge: Cambridge University Press.

Ganguly, Debjani (2005) *Caste, Colonialism, and Counter-Modernity: Notes on a Postcolonial Hermeneutics of Caste*, London, New York: Routledge.

Ganguly, Meenakshi (1998) "View From the Mountain," *Time*. (Nov. 2) Online. Available: <http://www.time.com/time/world/article/0,8599,2054128,00.html>.

Gates Jr., Henry Louis (ed.) (1991) *Narrative of Sojourner Truth; A Bondswoman of Older Time, With a History of Her Labors and Correspondence Drawn for Her "Book of Life,"* Oxford, New York: Oxford University Press.

Ghosh, Amitav (2001) *No Greater Sorrow: Times of Joy Recalled in Wretchedness. Neelan Thiruchelvam Second Memorial Lecture, July 29, 2001*, Colombo: International Centre for Ethnic Studies.

—— and Dipesh Chakrabarty (2002) "A Correspondence on Provincializing Europe," *Radical History Review* 83: 146–172.

—— (2005) *The Hungry Tide*, Boston and New York: Houghton Mifflin Harcourt.

Glazener, Nancy (2008) "Benjamin Franklin and the Limits of Secular Civil Society," *American Literature* 80.2: 203–231. Godage, Kalyananda (2010) "Ban Ki-moon and

Human Rights," *The Island* (July 5) Online. Available: <http://www.island.lk/index.php?page_cat=article-details&page=article-details&code_title=1419>.

Goldman, Marlene (2005) "Representations of Buddhism in Ondaatje's *Anil's Ghost*," in Stephen Tötösy de Zepetnek (ed.) *Comparative Cultural Studies and Michael Ondaatje's Writing*, West Lafayette: Purdue University Press.

Gombrich, Richard (1966) "The Consecration of a Buddhist Image," *Journal of Asian Studies* 26.1: 23–36.

Gourgouris, Stathis (2008) "Detranscendentalizing the Secular," *Public Culture* 20.3: 437–445.

Guha, Ranajit (1987) "Chandra's Death," in Ranajit Guha (ed.) *Subaltern Studies V: Writings on South Asian History and Society*, Delhi: Oxford University Press.

——— (1988) "The Prose of Counter-Insurgency," in Ranajit Guha and Gayatri Chakravorty Spivak (eds) *Selected Subaltern Studies*, New York: Oxford University Press.

Gurnah, Abdulrazak (ed.) (2007) *The Cambridge Companion to Salman Rushdie*, Cambridge: Cambridge University Press.

Habermas, Jürgen (2008) "Notes on a Post-Secular Society," *New Perspectives Quarterly* 25.4: 17–29.

Halpé, Aparna (2010a) "Fielding Ondaatje: A Brief Look at the 'Canadian' Response," *Moving Worlds: A Journal of Transcultural Writings* 10.2: 43–56.

Halpé, Ashley (2010b) "Anil's Ghost as Symphonic Poem: Viewed in the Context of Michael Ondaatje's Re-engagements with Sri Lanka," *Moving Worlds: A Journal of Transcultural Writings* 10.2: 92–99.

Haraway, Donna (1992) "Ecce Homo, Ain't (Ar'n't) I a Woman, and Inappropriate/d Others: The Human in a Post-Humanist Landscape," in Judith Butler and Joan W. Scott (eds) *Feminists Theorize the Political*, New York: Routledge.

Harrison, Thomas (1998) "Herodotus and *The English Patient*," *Classics Ireland* 5: 48–63.

Hedges, Chris (1990) "Rushdie Seeks to Mend His Rift with Islam," *The New York Times* (Dec. 25): "Books" section. Online. Available: <http://www.nytimes.com/books/99/04/18/specials/rushdiemend.html>.

Herwitz, Daniel and Ashutosh Varshney (eds) (2008) *Midnight's Diaspora: Critical Encounters with Salman Rushdie*, Ann Arbor: University of Michigan Press.

Hilger, Stephanie M. (2005) "Ondaatje's *The English Patient* and Rewriting History," in Steven Tötösy de Zepetnek (ed.) *Comparative Cultural Studies and Michael Ondaatje's Writing*, West Lafayette: Purdue University Press.

Hsu, Hsuan (2005) "Post-Nationalism and the Cinematic Apparatus in Minghella's Adaptation of Ondaatje's *The English Patient*," in Steven Tötösy de Zepetnek (ed.) *Comparative Cultural Studies and Michael Ondaatje's Writing*, West Lafayette: Purdue University Press.

Huggan, Graham (2010) "Is the 'Post' in 'Postsecular' the 'Post' in 'Postcolonial'?," *Modern Fiction Studies* 56.4: 751–768.

Human Rights Commission of Sri Lanka (2012). Website: <http://hrcsl.lk/english/?page_id=39>.

Huntingdon, Samuel P. (1993) "The Clash of Civilizations?," *Foreign Affairs* 72.3: 22–49.

——— (1996) *The Clash of Civilizations and the Remaking of World Order*, New York: Simon and Schuster.

Huq, Samia (2012) "Secularism and the Freedom to Transform Lives," *The Immanent Frame: Secularism, Religion, and the Public Sphere*. Online. Available: <http://blogs.ssrc.org/tif/2012/05/03/secularism-and-the-freedom-to-transform-lives/>.

Ibarrola-Armendariz, Aitor (2000) "Boundary Erasing: Postnational Characterization in Michael Ondaatje's *The English Patient*," in Rocio G. Davis and Rosalia

Baena (eds) Tricks with a Glass: Writing Ethnicity in Canada, Amsterdam, Netherlands: Rodopi.

Isaacson, Walter (2003) *Benjamin Franklin: An American Life*, New York: Simon and Schuster.

Ismail, Qadri (1999) "Discipline and Colony: *The English Patient* and the Crow's Nest of Post-Coloniality," *Postcolonial Studies* 2.3: 403–436.

—— (2000a) "A Flippant Gesture towards Sri Lanka: A Review of Michael Ondaatje's *Anil's Ghost*," *Pravada* 6.9: 24–29.

—— (2000b) "Speaking to Sri Lanka," *Interventions* 3.2: 296–308.

—— (2005) *Abiding by Sri Lanka: On Peace, Place, and Postcoloniality*, Minneapolis: University of Minnesota Press.

Jaidka, Manju (1998) "Suspended in Time, Like the Seasons," *The Tribune* [Chandigarh] (Nov. 1) Online. Available: <http://tribuneindia.com/1998/98nov01/book.htm#4>.

Jameson, Fredric (1984) "Postmodernism, or the Cultural Logic of Late Capitalism," *New Left Review* 146: 53–92.

Jayatilleka, Dayan (2010) "Postwar Sri Lanka," *Nethra Review* 11.1: 51–54.

Jazeel, Tariq (2009) "Geography, Spatial Politics, and Productions of the National in Michael Ondaatje's *Anil's Ghost*," in Cathrine Brun and Tariq Jazeel (eds) *Spatialising Politics: Culture and Geography in Postcolonial Sri Lanka*, New Delhi, London: Sage.

Jeganathan, Pradeep (2000) "A Space for Violence: Anthropology, Politics, and the Location of a Sinhala Practice of Masculinity" in Pradeep Jeganathan and Partha Chatterjee (eds) *Subaltern Studies XI: Community, Gender and Violence*, London: Hurst.

John Paul II (2006) "Faith, Reason, and the University: Memories and Reflections," Lecture at the University of Regesnburg (Sept. 12) Online. Available: <http://www.vatican.va/holy_father/ /benedict_xvi/speeches/2006/september/ /documents/ hf_ben-xvi_spe_20060912_university-regensburg_en.html>.

Jussawalla, Feroza (1996) "Rushdie's *Dastan-e-Dilruba: The Satanic Verses* as Rushdie's Love Letter to Islam," *Diacritics* 26.1: 50–73.

Juvenile Justice (Care and Protection of Children) Amendment Act, 2006 (2006) *The Gazette of India* (Aug. 23) Extraordinary, Part II, Section 1: 1–7. Also online. Available: <http://wcd.nic.in/childprot/jjactamedment.pdf>.

Kanaganayakam, Chelva (1992) "A Trick with a Glass: Michael Ondaatje's South Asian Connection," *Canadian Literature* 132: 33–42.

Kanner, Ellen (2000) "New Discoveries from the Author of *The English Patient*," BookPage.com (May) Online. Available: <http://www.bookpage.com/interview/ new-discoveries-from-the-author-of-the-english-patient%0B%0B>.

Kapferer, Bruce (1988) *Legends of People, Myths of State: Violence, Intolerance, and Political Culture in Sri Lanka and Australia*, Washington, DC: Smithsonian Institution Press.

Keethaponcalan, S. I. (2011) "Ethno-Political Conflict and the Civil War: Domestic and International Impact," in V. R. Raghavan (ed.) *Conflict in Sri Lanka: Internal and External Consequences*, New Delhi: Vij Books India Pvt Ltd.

Kemper, Steven (1991) *The Presence of the Past: Chronicles, Politics, and Culture in Sinhala Life*, Ithaca: Cornell University Press.

Kempner, Brandon (2009) "'Blow the World Back Together': Literary Nostalgia, 9/11, and Terrorism in Seamus Heaney, Chris Cleave, and Martin Amis," in Cara Cilano (ed.) *From Solidarity to Schisms: 9/11 and after in Fiction and Film from Outside the US*, New York: Rodopi.

Kertzer, Jon (2003) "Justice and the Pathos of Understanding in Michael Ondaatje's *Anil's Ghost*," *ESC: English Studies in Canada* 29.3: 116–138.

Khanna, Stuti (2008) "A Tale of Two Cities," *Biblio* (May–June): 5.

Kishwar, Madhu (1990) "A Horror of 'Isms': Why I Do Not Call Myself a Feminist," *Manushi* 61: 2–8.

Knowles, Sam (2010) "Sri Lankan 'Gates of Fire': Michael Ondaatje's Transnational Literature, from *Running in the Family* to *Anil's Ghost*," *Journal of Commonwealth Literature* 45.3: 429–441.

Kristeva, Julia (1991) *Strangers to Ourselves*, trans. Leon Roudiez, New York: Columbia University Press.

Kumar, Priya (2008) *Limiting Secularism: The Ethics of Coexistence in Indian Literature and Film*, Minnesota: University of Minnesota Press.

Kumari, Ved (2010) *The Juvenile Justice System in India: From Welfare to Rights* (2nd edn), New Delhi: Oxford University Press.

Kuortti, Joel (2007) "*The Satanic Verses*: 'To Be Born again, First You Have to Die,'" in Abdulrazak Gurnah (ed.) *The Cambridge Companion to Salman Rushdie*, Cambridge: Cambridge University Press.

Lessons Learnt Reconciliation Commission (2012) "About Us," *Lessons Learnt Reconciliation Commission Website*. Online. Available: <http://www.llrc.lk/index. php?option=com_content& view=article&id=18&Itemid=2>.

Levinas, Emmanuel (1979) *Totality and Infinity*, trans. A. Lingis, The Hague: M Nijhoff.

Lewis, Bernard (1990) "The Roots of Muslim Rage," *Atlantic Monthly* 266.3. Online. Available: <http://www.theatlantic.com/magazine/archive/1990/09/the-roots-of-muslim-rage/4643/>.

Lloyd, David (2000) "Colonial Trauma/Postcolonial Recovery?," *Interventions* 2.2: 212–228.

Mahmood, Saba (2001) "Feminist Theory, Embodiment, and the Docile Agent: Some Reflections on the Egyptian Islamic Revival," *Cultural Anthropology* 16.2: 202–236.

—— (2005) *Politics of Piety: The Islamic Revival and the Feminist Subject*, Princeton: Princeton University Press.

Major, John (2010) *Air India Flight 182: A Canadian Tragedy*, Ottawa: Public Works and Government Services Canada. Also available online: <http://epe.lac-bac. gc.ca/100/206/301/pco-bcp/commissions/air_india/2010-07-23/www.major-comm.ca/en/reports/finalreport/volume1/vol1-chapt1.pdf>

Mallot, J. Edward (2006) "Body Politics and the Body Politic: Memory as Human Inscription in *What the Body Remembers*," *Interventions* 8.2: 165–177.

Mandair, Arvind-Pal (2009) *Religion and the Spectre of the West: Sikhism, India, Postcoloniality, and the Politics of Translation*, New York: Columbia University Press.

Marius, Richard (1999) *Martin Luther: The Christian between God and Death*, Cambridge, MA: Belknap Press.

Mbembe, Achille (1992a) "The Banality of Power and the Aesthetics of Vulgarity in the Postcolony," *Public Culture* 4.2: 1–30.

—— (1992b) "Prosaics of Servitude and Authoritarian Civilities," *Public Culture* 5.1: 123–145.

—— (2001) *On the Postcolony*, Berkeley: University of California Press.

Mendieta, Eduardo (2010) "A Postsecular World Society? On the Philosophical Significance of Postsecular Consciousness and the Multicultural World Society: An Interview with Jürgen Habermas," trans. Matthias Fritsch, *Social Science Research Council Website*. Online. Available: <http://blogs.ssrc. org/tif/wp-content/uploads/2010/02/A-Postsecular-World-Society-TIF.pdf>.

Menon, Nivedita (2000) "Embodying the Self: Feminism, Sexual Violence and the Law," in Partha Chatterjee and Pradeep Jeganathan (eds) *Subaltern Studies XI: Community, Gender and Violence*. New York: Columbia University Press.

Mishra, Vijay (2007) *Literature of the Indian Diaspora: Theorizing the Diasporic Imaginary*, London and New York: Routledge.

Morris, Rosalind C. (ed.) (2010) *Can the Subaltern Speak? Reflections on the History of an Idea*, New York: Columbia University Press.

Moslund, Sten Pultz (2010) *Migration Literature and Hybridity: The Different Speeds of Cultural Change*, London: Palgrave Macmillan.

Mufti, Aamir (1991) "Reading the Rushdie Affair: An Essay on Islam and Politics," *Social Text* 29: 95–116.

—— (1995) "Secularism and Minority: Elements of a Critique," *Social Text* 45: 75–96.

—— (1998) "Auerbach in Istanbul: Edward Said, Secular Criticism, and the Question of Minority Culture," *Critical Inquiry* 25: 95–125.

Mukherjee, Arun P. (1984) "The Sri Lankan Poets in Canada: An Alternative View," *Toronto South Asian Review* 3.2: 32–45.

—— (1985) "The Poetry of Michael Ondaatje and Cyril Dabydeen: Two Responses to Otherness," *Journal of Commonwealth Literature* 20.1: 49–67.

Mukta, Parita (2002) *Shards of Memories: Woven Lives in Four Generations*, London: Weidenfeld & Nicolson.

Nair, Rukmini Bhaya (2002) *Lying on the Postcolonial Couch: The Idea of Indifference*, Minneapolis: University of Minnesota Press.

Nancy, Jean-Luc (1991) *The Inoperative Community*, trans. Peter Connor, Minneapolis: University of Minnesota Press.

Nandy, Ashis (1983) *The Intimate Enemy: Loss and Recovery of Self under Colonialism*, New Delhi: Oxford University Press.

—— (1998) "The Politics of Secularism and the Recovery of Religious Tolerance," in Rajeev Bhargava (ed.) *Secularism and Its Critics*, Oxford: Oxford University Press.

—— (2002) "An Anti-Secularist Manifesto," in Ashis Nandy, *The Romance of the State: And the Fate of Dissent in the Tropics*, New Delhi: Oxford University Press.

—— (2004) "A Billion Gandhis," *Outlook Magazine* (June 21) Online. Available: <http://www.outlookmagazine.com/>.

Narain, Mona (2006) "Re-Imagined Histories: Rewriting the Early Modern in Rushdie's *The Moor's Last Sigh*," *The Journal for Early Modern Cultural Studies* 6.2: 55–68.

Nasreen, Taslima (1994) *Lajja*, trans. Tutul Gupta, New Delhi: Penguin.

Nayar, Pramod (2010) "The Postcolonial Uncanny: The Politics of Dispossession in Amitav Ghosh's *The Hungry Tide*," *College Literature* 37.4: 88–119.

Needham, Anuradha Dingwaney and Rajeswari Sunder Rajan (eds) (2007) *The Crisis of Secularism in India*, Durham, NC: Duke University Press.

Nietzsche, Friedrich (1998) *Beyond Good and Evil: Prelude to a Philosophy of the Future*, trans. Marion Faber, Oxford: Oxford World Classics.

Neuman, Justin (2008) "The Fictive Origins of Secular Humanism," *Criticism* 50.4: 675–682.

Ondaatje, Michael (1976) *Coming through Slaughter*, New York: Norton.

—— (1982) *Running in the Family*, Toronto: McClelland and Stewart.

—— (1989) *The Collected Works of Billy the Kid*, London: Picador.

—— (1992) *The English Patient*, London: Picador.

—— (1996) "Michael Ondaatje Responds," *The Globe and Mail* [Toronto] (Dec. 6): C5.

—— (1998) *Handwriting*, London: Bloomsbury.

—— (2000) *Anil's Ghost*, London: Picador.

—— (2008) "Pale Flags," in Chelva Kanaganayakam (ed.) *Arbiters of a National Imaginary: Essays on Sri Lanka: Festschrift for Professor Ashley Halpé*, Colombo: International Centre for Ethnic Studies.

Otto, Rudolf (1923) *The Idea of the Holy: An Inquiry into the Non-Rational Factor in the Idea of the Divine and Its Relation to the Rational*, trans. John W. Harvey, London: Oxford University Press.

Pandey, Gyan (1990) *The Construction of Communalism in Colonial North India*, Delhi: Oxford University Press.

——— (1994) "The Prose of Otherness," in David Arnold and David Hardiman (eds) *Subaltern Studies VIII: Essays in Honour of Ranajit Guha*, Delhi: Oxford University Press.

——— (2008) "Remembering Partition: Violence, Nationalism and History in India," in Gyan Pandey, *The Gyanendra Pandey Omnibus*, New Delhi: Oxford University Press.

Parmar, Prabhjot (2008) "'Moving forward Though Still Facing Back': Partition and the South Asian Diaspora in Canada," in Anjali Gera Roy and Nandi Bhatia (eds) *Partitioned Lives: Narratives of Home, Displacement, and Resettlement*, New Delhi: Pearson Longman.

Pathirana, Leel (2011) "Vacuum Left by Richard: An Elegy," *Asian Tribune* [Colombo] (Feb. 21) 11.258. Online. Available: <http://www.asiantribune.com/news/2011/02/21/vacuum-left-richard-elegy>.

Pecora, Vincent (2006) *Secularization and Cultural Criticism: Religion, Nation, and Modernity*, Chicago and London: University of Chicago Press.

Pollock, Sheldon (2006) *The Language of the Gods in the World of Men: Sanskrit Culture, and Power in Premodern India*, Berkeley, CA: University of California Press.

Prakash, Gyan (1990) "Writing Post-Orientalist Histories of the Third World: Perspectives from Indian Historiography," *Comparative Studies in Society and History* 32.2: 383–408.

Presson, Rebekah (1996) "Fiction as Opposed to Fact: An Interview with Michael Ondaatje," *New Letters* 62.3: 80–90.

"Prohibition of Forcible Conversion of Religion Bill" (2004) *Sri Lanka Department of Government Printing*. Online. Available: <http://documents.gov.lk/Bills/2004/ Prohibition of Forcible Conversion of Religion/H 20502 (E) Prohibition of Forcible 1–4.pdf>.

Radhakrishnan, R. (1993) "Postcoloniality and the Boundaries of Identity," *Callaloo* 16.4: 750–771.

Ramanujan, A. K. (trans.) (1973) *Speaking of Siva*, Harmondsworth: Penguin.

Ramaswamy, Vijaya (1997) *Walking Naked: Woman, Society, Spirituality in South India*, Shimla: Indian Institute of Advanced Study.

Ranasinha, Ruvani (2007) "The *Fatwa* and Its Aftermath," in Abdulrazak Gurnah (ed.) *The Cambridge Companion to Salman Rushdie*, Cambridge: Cambridge University Press.

Randall, Don (1998) "The Kipling Given, Ondaatje's Take: Reading *Kim* through *The English Patient*," *Journal of Commonwealth and Postcolonial Studies* 5.2: 131–144.

Ranjan, Anjana (2011) "Memory's harvest," *The Hindu* (May 11) Online. Available: <http://www.thehindu.com/todays-paper/tp-features/tp-metroplus/article2017464. ece>.

Rawls, John (1993) *Political Liberalism*, New York: Columbia University Press.

Ray, Sangeeta (2000) *En-Gendering India: Woman and Nation in Colonial and Postcolonial Narratives*, Durham and London: Duke University Press.

Renan, Ernest (1865) *Life of Jesus* (*La Vie de Jésus*), London, Paris: M. Lévy Frères.

Robbins, Bruce (1994) "Secularism, Elitism, Progress, and Other Transgressions: On Edward Said's 'Voyage In,'" *Social Text* 40: 25–37.

Roberts, Gillian (2007) "Ethics and Healing: Hospital/ity and *Anil's Ghost*," *University of Toronto Quarterly*, 76.3: 962–976.

Roy, Nalinjana (2006) "In His Own Element," *The Hindu* (April 2) Online. Available: <http://www.hindu.com/lr/2006/04/02/stories/2006040200601000.htm>.

Runte, Roseann (1996) "Reading Stones: Travels to and in Canada," *University of Toronto Quarterly* 65.3: 523–533.

Rushdie, Salman (1981) *Midnight's Children*, London: Vintage.

——— (1988) *The Satanic Verses*, London: Vintage.

——— (1990) *Haroun and the Sea of Stories*, London: Penguin.

——— (1991) *Imaginary Homelands: Essays and Criticism 1981–1991*, London: Granta Books.

——— (1995a) "At the Auction of the Ruby Slippers," in *East, West*, London: Vintage.

——— (1995b) *The Moor's Last Sigh*. London: Vintage.

——— (1996) "The Salon Interview: When Life Becomes a Bad Novel," *Salon Magazine*. Online. Originally available: <http://www.salon/com/06/features/interview.html>. Also available: <http://islam-watch.org/SalmanRushdie//SalonInterview.htm>.

——— (2003) *Step Across This Line: Collected Non-Fiction 1992–2002*, London: Vintage.

——— (2005) "The Trouble With Religion," *ExChristian.net* (March) Online. Available: <http://articles.exchristian.net/2005/03/trouble-with-religion.html>.

——— (2006) *Shalimar the Clown*, London: Vintage.

——— (2009) *The Enchantress of Florence*, Toronto: Random House.

——— (2010) "The Composite Artist," *Lapham's Quarterly* 1.50: 183–190.

——— (2010) *Luka and the Fire of Life*, Toronto: Alfred A. Knopf Canada.

——— and Gauri Viswanathan (2008) "Salman Rushdie: Religion and the Imagination," *Institute for Religion, Culture, and Public Life Website.* (Nov. 6) Online. Available: <http://ircpl.org/2008/rethinking-religion/events/transcripts/salman-rushdie-religion-and-the-imagination/>.

Said, Edward (1984) *The World, the Text, and the Critic*, London: Faber and Faber.

———. (1993) *Culture and Imperialism*, London: Vintage.

———. (1994) *Orientalism*, New York: Vintage.

Salett, Elizabeth Pathy (1996) "A Queasy Feeling about *The English Patient*," *The Washington Post* (Dec. 4): C6.

Salgado, Minoli (2007) *Writing Sri Lanka: Literature, Resistance, and the Politics of Space*, London, New York: Routledge.

Schimmel, Annemarie (1985) *And Muhammad Is His Messenger: The Veneration of the Prophet in Islamic Piety*, Chapel Hill and London: University of North Carolina Press.

Sealy, I. Allan (1988) *The Trotter-Nama: A Chronicle*, London: Viking.

——— (1991) *Hero: A Fable*, London: Secker and Warburg.

——— (1993) "Writing a Novel," *Indian Review of Books* 3.1: 29–30.

——— (1994) *From Yukon to Yukatan: A Western Journey*, London: Secker and Warburg.

——— (1999) *The Everest Hotel: A Calendar*, London: Anchor.

——— (2003) *The Brainfever Bird: An Illusion*, London: Picador.

——— (2006) *Red: An Alphabet*, London: Picador.

Sen, Amartya (2005) *The Argumentative Indian: Writings on Indian Culture, History and Identity*, London: Penguin Books.

Sengupta, Debjani (2011) "From Dandakaranya to Marichjhapi: Rehabilitation, Representation and the Partition of Bengal (1947)," *Social Semiotics* 21.1: 101–123.

Sharpe, Jenny (1993) *Allegories of Empire: The Figure of Woman in the Colonial Text*, Minneapolis: University of Minnesota Press.

Shin, Andrew (2007) "The English Patient's Desert Dream," *Lit: Literature, Interpretation, Theory* 18.3: 213–235.

Sidhwa, Bapsi (1991) *Cracking India: A Novel*, Minneapolis: Milkweed Editions.

Singh, Amardeep (2006) *Literary Secularism: Religion and Modernity in Twentieth Century Fiction*, Newcastle: Cambridge Scholars Press.

Singh, Khushwant (2008) *Train to Pakistan*, New Delhi: Ravi Dayal.

Slaughter, Joseph R. (2007) *Human Rights, Inc.: The World Novel, Narrative Form, and International Law*, New York: Fordham University Press, 2007.

Smith, Graeme (2008) *A Short History of Secularism*, London and New York: I. B. Tauris.

Solecki, Sam (2003) *Ragas of Longing: The Poetry of Michael Ondaatje*, Toronto: University of Toronto Press.

Spencer, Jonathan (1990) "Collective Violence and Everyday Practice in Sri Lanka," *Modern Asian Studies* 24.3: 603–623.

Spivak, Gayatri Chakravorty (1993) *Outside in the Teaching Machine*, London: Routledge.

—— (1999) *A Critique of Postcolonial Reason: Toward a History of the Vanishing Present*. Cambridge: Harvard University Press.

—— (2001) "Righting Wrongs," in Nicholas Owen (ed.) *Human Rights, Human Wrongs: The Oxford Amnesty Lectures 2001*, Oxford: Oxford University Press.

"Sri Lanka War Crimes Accountability: The Tamil Perspective" (2010) *WikiLeaks* (Dec. 2) Online. Available: <http://wikileaks.dd19.de/cable/2010/01/10COLOMBO32.html>.

Srivastava, Neelam (2008) *Secularism in the Postcolonial Indian Novel: National and Cosmopolitan Narratives in English*, London and New York: Routledge.

Staels, Hilde (2007) "A Poetic Encounter with Otherness: The Ethics of Affect in Michael Ondaatje's *Anil's Ghost*," *University of Toronto Quarterly* 76.3: 977–989.

"Statement Issued by the National Christian Evangelical Alliance of Sri Lanka on Proposed Anti-Conversion Laws" (2005) *National Christian Evangelical Alliance of Sri Lanka*. Online. Available: <http://www.nceasl.org/NCEASL/rlc/statements/proposed_anti_conversion_laws_2005.php>.

Steinfels, Peter (2002) "In This Postmodern World, What Religious Thinkers May Need Is a Scholarly New Postcolonial Posting," *The New York Times* (Aug. 3): Section A: 12. Online. Available: <http://www.nytimes.com>.

Strauss, David Friedrich (1972) *The Life of Jesus Critically Examined*, ed. Peter C. Hodgson, trans. George Eliot, Philadelphia: Fortress.

Sugunasiri, Suwananda, H. J. (1992) "'Sri Lankan' Canadian Poets: The Bourgeoisie That Fled the Revolution," *Canadian Literature* 132: 60–79.

Suleri, Sara (1992) *The Rhetoric of English India*, Chicago: University of Chicago Press.

Suleri Goodyear, Sara (2008) "Rushdie beyond the Veil," in Daniel Herwitz and Ashutosh Varshney (eds) *Midnight's Diaspora: Critical Encounters with Salman Rushdie*, Ann Arbor: University of Michigan Press.

Sunder Rajan, Rajeswari (1993) *Real and Imagined Women: Gender, Culture, and Postcolonialism*, London and New York: Routledge.

——. (2007) "Righting Wrongs, Rewriting History?," *Interventions* 2.2: 159–170.

——. (2010) "Death and the Subaltern," in Rosalind C. Morris (ed.) *Can the Subaltern Speak? Reflections on the History of an Idea*, New York: Columbia University Press.

Tambiah, Stanley (1992) *Buddhism Betrayed: Religion, Politics, and Violence in Sri Lanka*, Chicago: University of Chicago Press.

—— (1996) *Leveling Crowds: Ethnonationalist Conflicts and Collective Violence in South Asia*, Berkeley, London, Los Angeles: University of California Press.

—— (1998) "The Crisis of Secularism in India," in Rajeev Bhargava (ed.) *Secularism and Its Critics*, Oxford: Oxford University Press.

Taylor, Charles (1975) *Hegel*, Cambridge: Cambridge University Press.
—— (1989) "The Rushdie Controversy," *Public Culture* 2.1: 118–122.
—— (2007) *A Secular Age*, Cambridge, MA, and London: Belknap Press.
Tejani, Shabnum (2007) *Indian Secularism: A Social and Intellectual History 1890–1950*, New Delhi: Permanent Black.
Tötösy de Zepetnek, Steven (2005) "Ondaatje's *The English Patient* and Questions of History," in Steven Tötösy de Zepetnek (ed.) *Comparative Cultural Studies and Michael Ondaatje's Writing*, West Lafayette: Purdue University Press.
Trainor, Kevin (1997) *Relics, Ritual and Representation in Buddhism: Rematerializing the Sri Lankan Theravada Tradition*, Cambridge: Cambridge University Press.
Ty, Eleanor (2000) "The Other Questioned: Exoticism and Displacement in Michael Ondaatje's *The English Patient*," *International Fiction Review* 27.1&2: 10–19.
United Nations (1948) *Universal Declaration of Human Rights*. Online. Available: <http://www.un.org/Overview/rights.html>.
—— (2002) *Document CAT A/57/44*. Online. Available: <http://www.bayefsky.com/html/srilanka_cat_article20.php>.
Visvis, Vikki (2009) "Traumatic Representation: The Power and Limitations of Storytelling as 'Talking Cure' in Michael Ondaatje's *The Skin of a Lion* and *The English Patient*," *A Review of International English Literature (ARIEL)* 40.4: 89–108.
Viswanathan, Gauri (1998) *Outside the Fold: Conversion, Modernity and Belief*, Princeton: Princeton University Press.
Wachtel, Eleanor (1994) "An Interview with Michael Ondaatje," *Essays on Canadian Writing* 53: 250–261.
Walcott, Derek (1992) "The Antilles: Fragments of Epic Memory," *Nobelprize.org: The Official Website of the Nobel Prize*. (Dec. 7) Online. Available: <http://nobelprize.org/literature/laureates/1992/walcott-lecture.html>.
Welch, Dave (2000) "Michael Ondaatje's Cubist Civil War," *Powells.com* (May 23) Online. Available: <http:// www.powells.com/authors/ondaatje.html>.
Whetter, Darryl (1997) "Michael Ondaatje's 'International Bastards' and Their 'Best Selves': An Analysis of *The English Patient* as Travel Literature," *English Studies in Canada* 23.4: 443–458.
Williams, Douglas (1998) "The Politics of Cyborg Communications: Harold Innis, Marshall McLuhan, and *The English Patient*," *Canadian Literature* 156: 30–55.
Wyile, Herb (2007) "Making a Mess of Things: Postcolonialism, Canadian Literature, and the Ethical Turn," *University of Toronto Quarterly* 76.3: 821–837.
Young, Robert (1982) "Post-Structuralism: The End of Theory," *Oxford Literary Review* 5.1: 3–20.
—— (1995) *Colonial Desire: Hybridity in Theory, Culture, and Race*, London: Routledge.
——. (2001) *Postcolonialism: An Historical Introduction*, Oxford: Blackwell.
—— (2003) *Postcolonialism: A Very Short Introduction*, Oxford: Oxford University Press.
Younis, Raymond Aaron (1998) "Nationhood and Decolonization in *The English Patient*," *Literature/Film Quarterly* 26.1: 2–9.
Zbavitel, Dušan (1976) *Bengali Literature*, Wiesbaden: Otto Harrasowitz.
Zornado, Joseph (1992) "Negative Writings: Flannery O'Connor, Apophatic Thought, and Christian Criticism," *Christianity and Literature* 42.1: 117–140.

Index